CAR

W. W. Norton & Company

New York   London

CAR

***

A DRAMA OF THE
AMERICAN WORKPLACE

Mary Walton

For information about permission to reproduce selections from
this book, write to Permissions, W. W. Norton & Company, Inc.,
500 Fifth Avenue, New York, NY 10110.

The text of this book is composed in Bembo
with the display set in Bodoni.
Desktop composition by Chelsea Dippel
Manufacturing by The Haddon Craftsmen, Inc.
Book design by Judith Stagnitto Abbate

Library of Congress Cataloging-in-Publication Data

Walton, Mary, 1941–
Car : a drama of the American workplace / Mary Walton.
p.   cm.
Includes index.
ISBN 0-393-04080-1
1. Taurus automobile—Design and construction—History.   I. Title.
TL215.T243W35   1997
338.4'76292222—DC21
96-49953
CIP

W. W. Norton & Company, Inc.
500 Fifth Avenue, New York, NY 10110
http://www.wwnorton.com

W. W. Norton & Company Ltd.
10 Coptic Street, London WC1A 1PU

1 2 3 4 5 6 7 8 9 0

To my husband, Charles, and daughter, Sarah

Contents

Acknowledgments

ON JANUARY 7, 1993, IN
a letter to Harold A. Poling, the chairman and CEO of Ford Motor Company, I proposed to write a book that would "trace the production of a car, from the planning and design phase through engineering, manufacturing, and sales, into a dealer's showroom." I told him I saw such a book "as less a technical treatise than the story of the people who make and market the cars, touching on as many lives as possible."

Ford not only gave me the go-ahead, but chose America's best-selling car as the vehicle for the story. For the next three years I had a front-row seat—that is to say, a cubicle in the basement of Ford's Design Center—with the team of planners, analysts, and engineers who were redesigning Ford's fabled Taurus and its Mercury twin, the Sable. Midway through the redesign, Ford changed CEOs and undertook an ambitious reorganization. The experience of my companions in the basement as the giant corporation grappled with the future became an unexpected but fascinating element in the story of the 1996 Taurus. In return for this access, Ford asked only that I omit sensitive proprietary information related to costs and profits. I am exceedingly grateful to the company for the rare opportunity to write about an extraordinary event in such an unfettered way.

Sadly, after reading the completed manuscript, Ford management came to regret having allowed a journalist such a candid look at its operations. No writer had been given such access before, I was told, and it would likely be a long time before it happened again. Team members, who had spoken freely to me in the past, were instructed to refer my calls to public relations.

Notwithstanding this turn of events, I should like to thank some of the many people at Ford who made this book possible.

John Roberts retired as public affairs manager of North American Public Affairs before my research was done, but he ushered me in and I shall always think of him as my godfather at Ford.

My gratitude to Dick Landgraff, the man in charge of the 1996 Taurus/Sable program, knows no bounds. Not only did he give generously of his own time and ask members of the team to do so as well, he and his gracious wife, Connie, welcomed me into their home on several occasions. His secretary, Nancy Donaldson, made my life easier in many ways.

I would like to offer my appreciation to the hundreds of people who enlightened me about their work on the Taurus. Some of them spent many hours explaining technical issues to a journalist whose expertise was limited to high school physics, and then responded to calls of distress when I sat down to write. In that regard, I wish to thank especially George Bell, Andy Benedict, Tom Breault, Jerry Brohl, Bob Damron, Larry DeFever, George Evalt, Amir Fallahi, Len Flack, Tom Gallery, Angelo Guido, Mark Jarvis, Fred Jorgensen, Steve Kozak, Tom Kelley, Len Landis, Lindsey McMahon, Jim Mikola, Larry Moliassa, Tom Moran, Ed Opaleski, Kim Peterson, Rick Schifter, Bob Tremitiere, Mike Vecchio, Mary Anne Wheeler, Dennis Wingfield, and Brian Wolfe. When I arrived, much of the car had been designed. John Doughty, Doug Gaffka, and David Rees patiently helped me reconstruct that stage of events. My thanks to Kinder Essington for his invaluable journal on team activities. Rand Bitter, Wendy Dendel, Brent Egleston, Joe Ghedotte, Tom Gorman, Eric Koefoot, Kathy Matsos, Brad Nalon, and Richard Pettit shed light on the company and its processes. Sharon Pettit gave me a lesson on the founder, Henry Ford. Lichia Bucklin and Karin Dean offered friendship as well as information. The Morrissett clan—Heather, Dick, Judy, Richard Sr., Helen, and Mike and Michele Sowers—graciously shared their family history.

Bob Rossiter at Lear Seating and Dave Hall from United Technologies made it possible to explore relationships with suppliers and to visit their plants in Juárez. In Mexico, Ronald Phillips went out of his way to provide an extensive overview of Lear's operation.

In Atlanta, plant manager Wheeler Stanley allowed me to glimpse the enormous pressures of his job and to roam the lines at will. My thanks not only to him but to others there, including Chuck Ledford and his band of vehicle schedulers, and Anne Kilcrease, who provided statistics and encouragement. In the Atlanta office of Ford public affairs, Tom Boyle and Anne Booker were always helpful. Back in Dearborn, public affairs launch leader John Jelinek was kind enough to keep me informed and involved. I am also grateful to Judith Mühlberg, Ed Miller, Tom Rhoades, and David Scott.

Thanks to Ross Roberts at Ford Division, I was able to chronicle both the marketing and advertising campaigns. Gerry Donnelly, Beryl Stajich, and Ernie Beckman sat still for numerous interviews. Jim Bright, the division's public affairs man, could not have been more helpful. At Lincoln-Mercury Division, Keith Magee and Ben Lever were similarly obliging. For much of the history, lore, and inner workings of the Detroit Auto Show I am indebted to John Love, its public relations honcho. Everything I know about robots I learned from Bob Doornick.

The people at J. Walter Thompson graciously entertained me and my many questions. Thanks especially to Mike Priebe, Lauren Crane, and Matt Stoll.

For their recollections of Lew Veraldi and the development of the first Taurus, I am indebted to George Balos, Nick Baracos, David Breedlove, Christy Cane, Karen Gietzen-Stewart, Pete George, Kaywin Goodman, Jim Graham, Chuck Gumushian, Fred Simon, Terry Glowacki, Richard Marburger, Bob Puffer, John Risk, Fred Simon, Joe Veraldi, Irene Veraldi, Frank Veraldi, Dan Schneble, Mimi Vandermolen, Carla Veraldi Wilson, and Frank Zoline. Retired CEOs Harold A. Poling, Donald Petersen, and Philip Caldwell shared their memories. Nancy Badore enlightened me on Ford's cultural revolution during the 1980s.

Writer and automotive savant Jim McCraw seemed to know everything and then some about every car ever built, every car company that built them, and everybody who was anybody in the automotive press. He was incredibly generous with both expertise and introductions. He and Sandy Thomas enlivened my trips to Dearborn.

Among other automotive journalists, Patrick Bedard, Paul Eisenstein, Jim Healey, Michelle Krebs, Kathleen Kerwin, Chris Jensen, Al Haas, Tom Lankard, Micheline Maynard, Oscar Suris, Alex Taylor, Jim Treece, and Warren Brown shared insights and information. The *Detroit Free Press* is fortunate to have a reporter as hardworking and feisty as Alan Adler, and I am glad to have benefited from his knowledge and experiences. Jim Dunne introduced me to hidden corners of Detroit.

As the Taurus went on sale, I had the help of Ford's Philadelphia regional office. My thanks to Jim O'Sullivan and his staff, and to manager Ron Leicht.

Don Slipp, general manager of Winner Ford in Cherry Hill, New Jersey, whom I met at a Ford dealer meeting, agreed to let me be a fly on the wall in the car's first month on the market. Thanks to him, the chapter reflects the real world of car salesmen, not a sanitized version. Ford dealers Bob Tasca, Fred Beans, and Joe Holman broadened my knowledge of their business.

Starling Lawrence, editor-in-chief of W. W. Norton & Company, supplied not only enthusiasm but redirection at a critical point in the writing when I had gone astray in a thicket of words. Assistant editor Patricia Chui cheerfully brought order to the enterprise. I am grateful to them both. A whiz in the darkroom, Rebecca Layton coaxed images from my recalcitrant negatives. Don Drake lent his skills as a narrative writer to make suggestions. My dear friend Emma Edmunds provided shelter and succor in Atlanta. And every writer should have an agent like Alice Martell, who is funny and savvy and cares beyond words.

One person above all others performed heroic deeds on behalf of this literary venture. For three years, Charles Layton drove me to the airport before sunup for the first flight out to Detroit on Mondays, and met me on Friday nights when I returned exhausted, babbling about car parts and car people. A superb editor, he vetted each chapter, usually more than once, and we spent many hours discussing structure and themes. His support never flagged. What a guy! I did what any smitten female writer would do, given the opportunity. I married him.

Introduction

ON THE THIRD Monday in May, 1993, a shiny black Lincoln Town Car pulled up to a low metal shed at Ford Motor Company's Dearborn Proving Ground, where a knot of men waited in bright sunshine. A small, tanned, compact man with little button eyes, an outdated mod haircut, and a commanding nose climbed out of the back seat and began to complain. What a trying time this little man had had! His weekend had been exhausting, there had been a golf tournament with movie stars, followed by some of the worst weather known to man, bad even for the inhospitable British Isles, and on the way to this Ford gig he'd very nearly missed the Concorde. He was still tired, even after a night's sleep.

The people waiting for the little man ushered him into the shed, displaying the respect due a dignitary, especially one with so fatiguing a schedule. "Would you like something to eat, Jackie?" A cloth-covered table held plates of fruit and muffins, assorted sodas and bottled spring water. Jackie Stewart, one of the finest automobile drivers in the world, winner of three Formula One World Championships a couple of decades back, declined refreshments and took a seat for a briefing on the day's agenda.

He had been summoned by Ford to drive three prototypes of the 1996 Taurus, which would go into production in two years. The Taurus was the most important car in Ford's lineup. In 1992 it had been the best-selling car in America, and it appeared headed for first place again in 1993. For the four years before that, it had been in the number-two spot, just behind the Honda Accord. The Taurus had history, the Taurus had class, the Taurus had status. It was the flagship of the Ford fleet. America's car! Not only was it Ford's most successful car, but it was widely credited with rescuing the company from its downward slide in the 1980s. It was The Car That Saved Ford. Redesigning it was like reformulating Coca-Cola. Misreading the customer in some fundamental way would be a disaster.

A redesign of this magnitude was like a gigantic cinematic extravaganza, years in the making, with a mega-million-dollar budget, a staff of thousands, and no guarantees. For all its collective research and artistic convictions, neither Ford nor any other car company could predict with certainty the direction of public lust. The Taurus was the company's best, most educated guess in terms of style, content, performance, and price, but it was still a guess. It could be a smash hit, a must-have, or it could be merely okay, another capable car from Ford. But if it were neither, if in fact people did not like the 1996 Taurus when the curtain went up, if they did not buy it when the wraps came off, the flop would be spectacular.

Motor vehicles ruled America. The nation's paved landscape was tooled for cars and trucks, not the other away around. A stone's throw away from Ford's test track, in a replica of Independence Hall, was the Henry Ford Museum, which housed a representation of gasoline-powered vehicles since the dawn of the automobile age, just a century ago. In so brief a time the car had transformed the American landscape. One might speculate about how a map of the United States would look had the same amount of capital, labor, and ingenuity been poured into the housing industry, so that every year there was a new crop of houses with added features and a variety of price tags. Or one might consider whether, if the taxpayer were footing the bill for new cars, so many billions of dollars would be spent on retooling to give them a little less vibration and noise than last year's models, or a different palette of colors, or devices designed to pamper—heated seats, heated sideview mirrors, lumbar cushions, speed control, compass readouts, keyless entry, automatic temperature control, power door locks, power windows, power seats, power radio antennas. Not to mention micron air filters, storage consoles, lighted glove compartments, and cupholders in three different sizes. But the United States was car country.

People looked to their cars not only for transportation but for independence, identity, and escape. Amid the hurly-burly of work, friends, foes, and family, the car was a refuge, a man-made shell in the ocean of life. Your car stood for who you were or aspired to be. You were thrifty, bold, a sport, or a mom. To the extent you had a choice, you drove what drove you.

No consumer product was as complex as a car. In the final assembly plants in Atlanta and Chicago, 1,775 major parts would come together on the line to form the new Taurus, and most of those parts also had parts. The seats alone had 82 subcomponents. That didn't include the 12,000 or so nuts and bolts and screws and rings that held everything together, and had to be accounted for. There were 810 electrical circuits and 3,425 feet of wiring.

The two dozen or so Ford people hosting Jackie Stewart on this spring day were among the 6,742,808 Americans—over 7 percent of the work-force—who had jobs in automotive and related industries such as highways, transportation, petroleum. (And there were millions more who made auto-motive commercials, staged automotive trade shows, worked for scores of automotive publications, from *Road & Track* to *Car Wash News*, or had occu-pations several times removed from but nonetheless dependent on the industry—a count that by one oft-cited estimate constituted one of every seven Americans.) At any given moment, these Ford engineers and thou-sands of their colleagues at other car companies were performing minor or major surgery on some 140 models sold in North America, or they were cre-ating new models altogether.

And it was all for this, never more than this: to create a car that by its very nature would be, could be, only marginally different from any car on the road, and then to persuade buyers otherwise, that this was a car to dream for. "This is a business of smoke and mirrors," automotive writer Paul Eisen-stein would say, sitting behind the wheel of a Taurus prototype in the spring of 1995. "Above all, never forget that. Why do you need a Lincoln when a Hyundai will get you to your office? This is a business that appeals to us for emotion."

THE CODE NAME for the 1996 Taurus and its Mercury counterpart, the Sable, was DN101. The "D" stood for the D segment of the market, which were the mid-sized cars, the "N" for North America, and the number denoted its order in Ford's sequence of new models. In-house, "DN101" was used more often than "Taurus" or "Sable" as a designation, to distinguish it from the old Taurus, DN5. The DN101 team was sometimes called the Tau-rus team, but they were one and the same.

Although there had been two minor redesigns since the original 1986 Taurus, this new model would be the first in ten years with a markedly new look and feel. Ford would spend more than $2.7 billion on the car and its powertrain. Although it had some carryover parts, notably the underbody and the standard engine, everything else in the 1996 Taurus was new: the exterior pieces, the interior fittings, the steel cage that formed the passenger compartment, the engine computer and the wiring harnesses, the head-lamps and taillamps, the suspension system.

But the prototypes awaiting Jackie Stewart bore little resemblance to the ovoid confection of steel, plastic, and glass that would reach 4,300 dealer showrooms in September 1995. Across the street in the Ford Design Center, on life-sized models made of clay, engineers and designers were still arguing over corners, moldings, buttons, and other fine points. Today's prototypes, cobbled together from boxy chunks of sheet metal and bolted-on parts, looked as if they'd been salvaged from a junkyard. But beneath the makeshift exterior, much of the engine, transmission, suspension, brakes, and other systems were in the final stages of development. A knowledgeable observer would notice a pronounced rake to the windshield, signaling a more aero-dynamic car on the way.

The Ford people were eagerly awaiting the reactions of Stewart, who had logged more than a quarter of a century as a consultant for the company. They doubted that there was anything Jackie could tell them about the car that they didn't already know. Each of the three prototypes had a "car mother"—an engineer who knew it inside and out, plus other engineers who worked on subsystems. Still, you could get too close and overlook the obvious. And if Jackie Stewart did notice shortcomings, maybe the higher-ups would give them more support to make a better car. You could never have too much support.

But everyone was hoping Stewart would like the cars and by extension the job each one of them was doing. Stewart had the ear of Ford higher-ups. Specifically, he had the ear of CEO Harold A. "Red" Poling. It was widely believed that Jackie could walk into Red's office on the twelfth floor of World Headquarters whenever he wanted, sit down in one of Red's chairs, and talk to Red about whatever was on his mind. No one wanted Stewart to tell the chief executive officer of Ford Motor Company that he was disappointed in the new Taurus.

The car was shaped with a new buyer in mind. This was no time to play it safe. That was a lesson Henry Ford had learned the hard way by stubborn-ly clinging to his beloved Model T until people just quit buying it. Today's Taurus buyers were teetering on the threshold of old age. Their median age was fifty-one, whereas that of the Taurus's rival, the Honda Accord, was just forty-two, and even Honda was worried about the graying of its customer base. That being the case, Ford needed to worry even more.

Ford marketing had come up with a profile of the younger person they wanted to buy the new Taurus. He was "the Varsity Captain," a forty-two-year-old, $60,000-a-year middle manager with two kids and a wife who was a teacher. But lately there was real fear along corporate corridors that the

Varsity Captains and their bouncy cheerleader wives might be reluctant to part with the $19,000 or $20,000 that the Taurus would likely cost. Stewart had his own viewpoint on this subject. He didn't hesitate to tell Ford moguls to their faces that they were too interested in profits, thereby placing the company at a competitive disadvantage with the Japanese, who reinvested their earnings in the product. Stewart was like an advocate for cars, poor mute creatures who couldn't speak for themselves.

In redesigning the Taurus, Ford was taking on Japanese automakers more directly than ever before. The DN101 mission statement—a mission statement was *de rigueur* these days in corporate America, something else the Japanese had initiated—was "to deliver a Product Competitive with the Japanese in Quality and Function, and Better in Styling, Features and Value." In other words, the Taurus would perform as well as Japanese cars, but look better and offer superior indulgences, while costing less.

The mission statement talked about the Japanese in generic terms. But the Taurus team had specific competitors in mind. Until Toyota introduced its redesigned Camry in 1992, the Taurus target had, in fact, been the Accord. But the new Camry was in a class by itself. And so the mission statement had been boiled down to two words.

"Beat Camry."

Ford was even going so far as to challenge the Japanese on their own turf. It was planning to take a right-hand-drive Taurus into Japan, where the car had a following among maverick Japanese yuppies, such as they were. These hip yuppies had been buying Tauruses, mostly station wagons, that were taken off the line and modified to meet Japanese requirements. But they were still left-hand-drive vehicles. The DN101 team would engineer the right-hand-drive export model from scratch, a U.S. car designed by Americans for the Japanese market.

The Jackie Stewart drive was one review or test among the hundreds to which Ford exposed its vehicles in the four years or so that it took to bring a car to market. While no complaint was trivial, those emanating from one so eminent as Stewart had a particularly inspirational value.

Stewart customarily traveled with his personal, tartan-wrapped helmet and was therefore equipped at a moment's notice to transmogrify into an incarnation of his former racing self, wired for sound and hot-lapping round and round the high-speed course. The thing that amazed people was the way Stewart could drive and talk at the same time. Most racing-car drivers didn't have that kind of concentration. But today Jackie was supposed to comport himself like a regular person who might one day go down to the local Ford dealer and take a Taurus around the block and out on the highway for a demo drive.

Last week, while the cars were being readied, there had been trouble with the prototype that housed the new four-valve, three-liter modular engine. Truth to tell, the mod engine had been skittish from the beginning and last week it wouldn't even start. The mechanics promised to have it running by Monday. And here it was Monday, and of course the engine was running, but there had been some gallows humor earlier among the car mothers as they waited for Jackie. Someone noted that the modular-engine guys were out in full force in case the engine fell apart. "I don't see them carrying a basket," joked Mike Reed. "That's a good sign." Reed was shepherding the fuel system and the brakes through development. What did he care?

No SOONER HAD the car mothers and other engineers settled down at long tables in the shed for a pre-drive briefing than Stewart went into his attack mode, by now familiar to those who knew his routine. Stewart loved to rip into his hosts on occasions like these; it was part of his job. He lambasted Ford for using the phrase "semi-active suspension" to describe the system on the SHO prototype. The Taurus SHO, for "super high output," was a sports sedan priced in the mid-twenties, with a peppy 235-horsepower V-6 engine made by Yamaha and other performance-car attributes, one of which was the suspension system whose nomenclature so irritated Stewart. Active suspension, which was still in the experimental stage, employed little motors to adjust each corner of the car as it hit a bump. The Taurus SHO did not have little motors; it had four electronic sensors that could measure the car's response to a bump and quickly force the shock absorbers to stiffen the body. These were sometimes called "fast shocks" or "fast-reacting shocks." They were in no way, Stewart insisted, active suspension—semi or otherwise. "It's absolutely imperative that we as a company keep our integrity at the highest level," Stewart said. "Active suspension is not what we've got. What if Nissan is going to come out with real active suspension? Our bluff's going to be called."

Stewart said all this in a thin voice with roiling vowels that marked him as an outsider from some cold, wet isle. He didn't say car, he said *caaa*. Although he now lived in Switzerland, he was a Scotsman, and true to the national stereotype, he seldom smiled when he talked. When he did, it was often after a self-deprecating remark about his stature or lack thereof, and then the listener had to wait for the smile itself to well up from a nether region before daring to laugh. On the rare occasions when actual mirth got the better of him, the button eyes narrowed into buttonholes.

With his serious demeanor, his concern for the cars, and his proper

Gaelic accent, Stewart came across as, maybe, the Conscience of Ford. Yes, in fact, he was the Conscience of Ford, here to deliver the Calvinistic reminder to waivering workers that their mission was something more than money, more even than quality. Talk about a slippery, overused, much abused word. "Quality Is Job One"—Ford Motor Company's slogan for a decade—had about as much meaning as "Say No to Drugs." No, their mission was something called integrity.

Integrity, as Stewart employed the word, had a very special application in the car universe. "Integrity," the Conscience would later say as he talked and drove at the same time around the high-speed track at an even 80 miles per hour, "integrity" meant that nothing had been cheated "to get the right result." How do you cheat in making a car? Stewart explained: "Sometimes they will engineer around a problem. The problem won't be removed, only disguised. It's like I can't be accused of telling a lie, but I haven't told the truth." For example, if someone asks a problem drinker if he drank anything the night before at the party, he might truthfully answer "Not a drop," without mentioning the three drinks before the party and the ten afterward. All can agree that this answer, while not actually false, displays a certain lack of integrity.

By the same token, the engineer will pack a car with bushings, lots and lots of little rubber things shoved in every opening to cushion noise, friction, or movement. He will just hurl bushings at the problem to make it go away rather than, said the Conscience of Ford, fix it. This bushing business, to make the ride softer and quieter, gave the car something known as compliance. Compliance was another important word in car talk. A definition in a Ford glossary made compliance sound like a good thing: "A light resiliency or 'give,' designed to help absorb bumps." Indeed, the glossary went on to give an example of good compliance. "Good compliance allows the wheels to move rearward a bit as they hit bumps but doesn't allow them to move laterally during cornering," said the glossary, crediting *Car and Driver* magazine for this helpful illustration.

Stewart, however, did not use compliance in a positive way. A car that had compliance often lacked integrity. In the car world, as in the real world, integrity took courage. It could be tough to hold out against demands for a soft, cushioned feel, so often equated with luxury. "You're going to be asked to make this car less harsh as you go up the ladder," the Conscience warned, meaning the corporate ladder that led to his friend Red Poling. "The reason is, they're older." And there it was. The people who liked compliance were generally old and rich. Geriatric Ford executives who rode around in Lincoln Town Cars and the Lincoln Continentals ("the worst cars we have"), who liked, one might say, the soft feel of a featherbed on wheels, a "love-boat ride." And quiet. They liked quiet. They might say, "Let's hear the clock tick." And the obliging engineers would pick up handfuls of bushings and jam them in the car. "We've overbushed everything," said the Conscience. ("We" meaning Ford.) These same people claimed that customers wouldn't buy cars that offered a firmer ride (integrity). "But the customer is buying it. They're buying it in the competition." The Conscience of Ford thought a firm ride was good for you, and this idea too had standing in the market-place. After all, firm mattresses that gave good support cost more than the soft varieties.

The first car Stewart was scheduled to drive was a cranberry-colored prototype with the carryover V-6 three-liter engine, the one currently in use on the Taurus. But it seemed as if Stewart would never actually get into a car that morning. He stood by the door and wiggled the door handle from side to side. It wiggled too much. "That tells you a story right now. Unless we get on this right now, somebody'll tell you it's too late." He pushed the closed door. It gave a little. "You're still making seals with the old technolo-gy." He got in and snapped the brake release. "There's poor quality in all the handles we use." He turned the key in the ignition and found "a lot of winding before we actually kick in and start the car." He imitated the engine cranking. "*Dih-dih-dih-dih-dih.*" Five generations. Too many. He turned the key again, and again. Each time it sounded louder and longer. "You know, I've got this thing about doing things sixteen times," he said. His eyes disappeared into the buttonholes and his lips stretched in his sneaky smile. *The little guy was making a joke!* "Ten isn't enough. Twenty is too many." Finally he let the engine run. At last he found something positive to say. "The kick-in is very smooth. . . . After you've got it open, it modulates quite nicely." But the brake pedal had a little stop on the upstroke. And by the way, the brakes were too sharp. "The way it feels right now, it's the rear calipers." It was now an hour into the drive, and Jackie hadn't even left the parking lot.

In the end, he drove all three prototypes around both the high- and low-speed tracks. The 2.7-mile low-speed track was a particularly creative assemblage of every road surface known to man: a 1,320-foot-long brick road, a 600-foot-long stretch with 2-foot up-and-down sine waves and another 1,200 feet of 4-foot sine waves, an 1,850-foot undulating road, then 1,850 feet of random bumps that test drivers called "cow plops," followed by 1,950 feet of harshness, 1,850 feet of grooved boulevard, 400 feet of pitch and jounce that made the front end porpoise, 60 feet inlaid with bars and drop-offs that simulated potholes, a 310-foot water bath, a 200-foot mud bath, a 100-foot rumble road, 100 feet of Belgian block, 1,320 feet of cob-blestones, and 330 feet of something described as body twist.

As he drove, Stewart delivered critical comments to note-taking engineers. Later summarized, the comments numbered thirty-one, including the offensive handles and the noisy brake pedal. Stewart had not appeared to notice a low rumble emanating from the rear of the base Taurus with the V-6 engine. And in the other two, the one with the pesky modular engine and the SHO with the Yamaha motor, he didn't mention the floor shifters that some drivers thought rough.

The unspoken rule among the engineers was that if you knew something was wrong, but Jackie said nothing, it was okay. No need to bring it up. But then, after the drive, a supervisor asked Stewart straight out what he thought of the floor shifter that had been in two of the cars. And only then did Stewart pronounce it "junk." The floor shifter went on the list of problems.

The morning ended with an examination of the new snap-and-twist gas cap. The previous cap, which screwed on, had been rendered obsolete by federal regulations on gasoline vapors. To create a closed system, one, that is to say, that didn't give off vapors, it was important that the gas cap have a tight seal. In the event of leakage, a pressure sensor would pick up a vapor leak and a light on the instrument panel would flash on, warning drivers to "Service engine soon." Like the snap-and-turn cap itself, this message too was new, and changing it had caused a controversy. Previous Ford cars advised drivers to "Check engine" when one of any number of things went wrong. Seeing this message light up on the dash for the first time was enough to panic even an experienced driver. "Check engine." *Maybe the goddamn thing was going to blow any second. Better pull over fast, slam on the brakes, and get out of this death trap. Women and children first.*

"Service engine soon" was the alternative allowed under California regulations, which had become the industry standard. But to complicate matters, some said, those wily Camry people had sneaked in a graphic in place of words. Was a graphic better or worse? No one knew. And how did they get it past the California authorities? Was it even true or just another news flash of competitive activities that would now require a major investigation, the kind of thing that constantly kept them on edge?

Jackie and the guys approached the gas cap in good spirits. Here was an opportunity to end the morning with a positive spin. "Come look at our gas cap, Jackie." Like all Ford gas caps, the new one was anchored to the car by a thin plastic strap called a tether. Stewart unsnapped the cap and let go. It bounced off the side of the car with a metallic sound. Stewart bounced it again. And again. People watched as if hypnotized, all with the same thought. Imagine a brand-new Taurus with a glistening coat of Midnight Red, Willow Green, Iris Frost, or even standard old Performance White.

Now imagine this sharp-edged gas cap striking the surface. For God's sake, was he going to do it sixteen times? Someone opened the fuel door on the Toyota Camry that was standing by for reference. It had a neat little ledge on which to rest the cap. Finally Stewart pronounced his verdict. "I think it's a piece of crap." Gas cap maven Mike Reed, who earlier had cracked jokes about the modular engine, looked crestfallen.

What irritated the Conscience of Ford about the gas cap was the tether. "It's going to break anyway. I know you're going to tell me it's not going to break. You're the only place in the world that does this." And why was that? Well, of course, the tether was for those forgetful people who might drive away from a self-serve station leaving the cap on the bumper or the ground. Some said it dated to the terrible accident in the late 1970s when three girls died in a Pinto conflagration. The gas cap was missing, apparently having been lost or forgotten.

In any event, there was no point in telling Jackie Stewart that the tether was not an issue. When at last Stewart inspected the gas cap itself, however, it didn't make him any happier. He could have cared less about its extra-special vapor-sealing properties. The thing didn't twist right. There was too much free play before it engaged. This was one of his chronic complaints with pedals, wheels, and handles. "To have that amount of movement with no action is wrong." In short, it lacked integrity. Just in case someone had missed the point, he summed up his position. "You're not going to win my heart with this."

Crap! Junk! This was not a business for the faint of heart. In a battle for the dreams and dollars of the American consumer you had to have skin as thick as sheet metal and as resilient as plastic.

CAR

 O N E

A Declaration of War

T HE MAN WHOM Ford Motor
Company chose to head the redesign of the all-important Ford Taurus did
not come across as corporate. Tough, yes; flinty, direct, smart, and determined—but neither polished nor cautious. Dick Landgraff seemed to be a
man with a mission more than a career. On the management ladder he was
a rung or two below vice-president, but he had no illusions about rising
higher. He did not play golf, he did not politic, he was outspoken. And he
turned down most of the invitations that came his way as a high-ranking
Ford manager. He had little interest in socializing with all but a few colleagues. "These guys just talk about cars. I do that all day."

Landgraff had just turned fifty-one when he took over DN101—the
Taurus/Sable program—in 1991. Words for his physical appearance—thin,
medium height, dark brown hair combed lankly to one side—did not capture the intense quality of a man who was always listening and looking. His
mind did not wander. Nothing got by him. He listened and then he snapped
out questions. When he took off his glasses and rubbed his forehead, or
began to interrupt, it was a sign that his patience had run out and someone
was in trouble. He was most definitely not without humor, but it was so dry

as to escape the linear thinkers who designed and built cars.

Landgraff was not a military veteran, but he issued orders with the ease of someone who was used to giving commands. All in all, it was not too difficult to imagine him in officer's khakis atop a rise in some jungle scanning the terrain through a pair of binoculars, with a first lieutenant at his elbow. Colonel Landgraff, *sir!*

Landgraff had started out in the Ford finance division with an MBA from the University of Pennyslvania's Wharton School. But he had not become a permanent member of Ford's fabled tight-knit finance community. In his nearly thirty years with the company, he had amassed a bio that listed twenty-five diverse titles. High on his list of favorites was his very first assignment as an auditor for the Lincoln-Mercury sales division, investigating dealers whose reimbursement claims for warranty work were suspiciously high based on statistical averages.

He liked the freedom of being on the road, the drama of finding crooks. "Most of the people we audited were cheaters. . . . The only issue was could you catch them?" He'd get on the phone to a customer; in his hand would be the $400 claim the dealer had submitted to Lincoln-Mercury for repainting her car.

"Mrs. Smith," he'd say after introducing himself, "you've got this new Mercury. How do you like it?"

"Oh, great car, great car."

"Ever have any problems with it?"

"Well, I had a problem with the engine."

"Oh, really? Did you ever have your car repainted?"

"No, paint's great."

Bingo. They'd nail the dealer. Although termination was rare. Those were tough years for the division and Ford didn't want to put people out of business who were selling cars.

Landgraff, an intern on Ford's College Graduate Program, learned the job traveling with guys who'd done it for years, a colorful group. For some reason they all seemed to be hypochondriacs. "I learned not to ask these guys, 'Did you have a good night?' You'd get a long song and dance about their medical history. 'I was up half the night, coughing, sneezing,' whatever."

For the next twenty years, except for two years in Mexico, most of his subsequent jobs had been staff positions in either marketing or planning, working out of Ford World Headquarters in Dearborn. People who held such jobs were called "staffies." They had a lot of expertise but no authority over people or cars. He did not want to be a staffie the rest of his life. "Staff jobs are really good in learning the entire business, and how big a company Ford is, and all its worldwide and business issues. The problem with staff jobs of course is that . . . you're advising people and making plans and all that stuff, but eventually you get tired of that. You want to be in charge of something." In 1983 Landgraff moved to car product development, where cars were created. For a time he worked on the cycle plan, a ten-year schedule of introductory dates and costs for new and remodeled vehicles.

In 1987, he was put in charge of year-to-year changes in the Taurus/Sable program. When he was posted to DN101, he had just brought a comparatively minor 1992 facelift of the two cars in on time and under budget. The ambitious 1996 redesign was his reward for a job well done. But the stakes were bigger. Not only did the Taurus troops have to overhaul Ford's most successful car since the Model T, they had to do it faster than ever.

Ford was desperate to make cars in less time. Honda took thirty-seven months. Nissan took forty-two months. Toyota took forty-four months. And there was Ford, sucking its thumb as the months slipped by: fifty-one months . . . fifty-two months. There were cases of *six years*. In that length of time, some Japanese companies could turn out two new models. Lately Toyota was talking about a goal of twenty-four months. *Twenty-four months*. And Ford hadn't even cracked four years. During the 1980s, when other automakers were getting more efficient, Ford actually increased its development time by 25 percent.

The companies that redesigned cars faster also did so more cheaply. It stood to reason that the shorter the process, the less paid out in engineering salaries and benefits, the fewer resources consumed. Also, the longer the time from when work started to when the product went on sale, the greater the chances of misreading fickle buyers. Ford's solution was a new product-development schedule called World Class Timing, which would shrink product development by up to a year, depending on the model.

World Class Timing, or WCT—yet another acronym in a corporate lingo clogged with letters—essentially rearranged events that had always taken place. It eliminated some prototypes and made sequential events simultaneous. Where once the exterior designers started six months ahead of interior designers, in separate studios, both now began work together in the same studio. Physically working together was perhaps the biggest change of all. World Class Timing specified that car programs would be carried out by a "dedicated, collocated team"—one composed of employees assigned exclusively to the new car and all situated in one place. In the past everybody had remained in their home offices, whether body engineering or finance. The brake guys sat together in Building Five, and did brakes for all Ford vehicles. Financial analysts monitored the costs from their cubicles on the second floor of Building Three. These corporate fiefdoms—and hosts of others—jealously guarded their power and resources.

The theory was that grouping people together would be another time-saver. Engineers could more easily resolve differences when they were sitting next to each other rather than halfway across Dearborn, in some other building, or in some other town. Moreover, the theory went, as members of the team bonded, they would put the best interests of the car ahead of the parochial interests of the various departments from whence they came.

Japanese automakers had long used teams. In 1989, after studying Honda, Chrysler reorganized the entire company into platform teams. But Ford held back. Even though the first Taurus was created by an ad hoc team under an extraordinary vice-president named Lew Veraldi, the company continued making cars the old way for another decade. No one was against teamwork, it was as noble as motherhood and Old Glory, but teams—discrete agglomerations of bodies—were something else again. In the world of business during the 1970s and into the 1980s, teams were regarded as an import from Japan; they were peculiar to an alien culture that squashed individualism and discouraged enterprise. Unions suspected, sometimes rightly, that the work teams known as "quality circles," copied from Japan, were a management trick to undercut their authority. In certain far-flung corners of the empire, notably Hapeville, Georgia, home of the cotton-mouthed good ole boys and girls who built the Taurus, the mention of "teams" branded you as a left-wing agitator from up north. In Hapeville you had to use the euphemism "groups" or something else, because people wouldn't cooperate if they thought they were on a team. Even a United Automobile Workers proposal to modify the mind-numbing sequence of individual tasks on the assembly line by sharing tasks among work teams had gone over like sushi at a church barbecue.

Although Americans commonly teamed up to play sports, there was some feeling that a softball field was different from an office or a plant floor; people could not mesh their work activities in the same way because the virtue of individualism was so ingrained in the national psyche. Americans were inventors; Japanese were copycats. Before the old nature–nurture debate could really take root, however, corporations began to see that there just might be something to this team thing after all. It was hard to overlook the considerable innovation now present in Japanese products and the manner in which Japanese enterprise had reversed the balance of payments. So, beginning in 1991 with the Taurus and three other vehicle programs, Ford planned to produce cars with teams, more or less the way the Japanese did.

When Landgraff got the assignment in early 1991, DN101 was in a kind of embryonic, pre-development phase. The World Class Timing clock was to start ticking in August, at a budget approval point called Program Implementation. Forty-two months later, on February 6, 1995, the first official production car would roll off the line at the Atlanta assembly plant: Job One, it was called. In addition to the Taurus and Sable sedans, the DN101 worker bees had to design and engineer two station wagons, the SHO performance sedan, a Taurus that ran on alternative fuels, and a right-hand-drive model, for export to Australia and Japan. The sedans and wagons would come in both low-budget and more expensive high-series versions, featuring different engines and interior features. So complicated were engines, however, that they were on a separate sixty-month development schedule over in the powertrain division. The responsibility of the program manager was to shoehorn them into the car and oversee their interaction with other parts.

Landgraff saw this assignment as an opportunity to do more than stamp out another car, however stylish. This was his opportunity, perhaps the only one he would ever have, reached at the high-water mark of his Ford career, to impose his management philosophy on the country's most significant consumer product. For the last twenty years he had watched the American auto industry in general and Ford in particular do one stupid thing after another, despite warning signs from Japan. In 1973 or 1974, when he was on the marketing staff at World Headquarters, he foresaw that quality was Ford's Achilles' heel. He wrote a paper predicting growth in Japan's market share. But Ford, like GM and Chrysler, went on making turkeys for another decade. He found himself questioning whether he had made the right career choice. "Don't work for a big company," Landgraff cautioned his children— he had three and they were all headed for careers in business. In big companies, he told them, you were dependent on others to do their jobs, which was at best frustrating, at worst, a recipe for failure.

With the 1986 Taurus, Ford had produced a worthy car. Quality in the following decade improved dramatically. But as American cars got better, so did the Japanese. Detroit lost a generation of car buyers who couldn't visualize themselves ever again behind the wheel of anything but a Honda, Toyota, or Nissan. But Landgraff believed in America. He believed American engineers were as good as Japanese engineers, if given the chance. And he believed that American designers were better.

A lifelong reader, Landgraff's bookshelves were lined with books on Ford, the auto industry, and business, most of which he hadn't read. The last fiction he could remember was *The Andromeda Strain*, Michael Crichton's first hit. Military history was his passion. And he believed that certain military principles applied to business. Ford, for example, had been right to put him in charge of the car—not because of who he was, though possibly that too, but because under World Class Timing, power and authority were concentrated in one person in charge of a comprehensive team. In military terms, as he saw it, the job represented unity of command. Until now, no single person had authority other than suasion over design, body engineering, chassis, finance—the powerful fiefdoms that participated in the development process. Until now, the only guy who could be held truly accountable for getting out a car was whoever was running North American Automotive Operations. It didn't all come together until you got to the top.

Unity of command, that's what had just won the Gulf War, that and maybe smart weapons. Back before the conflict began, Landgraff was with some colleagues, some pretty big names in the company, on a company plane. These were people he thought would have some insight, but they were talking about how America was going to get its ass whipped in the Gulf. That was the conventional wisdom, that the country was headed into another Vietnam. The reason that didn't happen, in his mind, was that for the first time—with the exception of some small campaigns like Grenada—you had one guy, Norman Schwarzkopf, who had responsibility for the whole mission from start to finish. Schwarzkopf had the air war, the land war, the sea war . . . the British, the French, the Arabs, everybody. And we had won.

And Taurus now had unity of command, in the person of himself, Dick Landgraff, the maximum leader. For the first time, Landgraff would have the chance to run a car program the way he thought it should be run. If he failed, he would have no one but himself to blame.

Of course, Ford would blame him too if he didn't meet company objectives. Everyone knew what had happened to Tony Kuchta, the man in charge of the 1989 Thunderbird, when the program overran the cost and weight targets. Some seventy-five people from the program gathered for what they thought would be a pat on the back after the Thunderbird won *Motor Trend* Car of the Year. Instead they got a tongue-lashing from CEO Harold Poling. Kuchta, humiliated, was gone five months later.

And Landgraff's accountability did not extend to dealer showrooms when the car went on sale in four years. The sales strategy belonged to the guys at the top of the two sales divisions, Ford and Lincoln-Mercury. Even so, if the car that replaced America's number-one best-seller were a dud, the fingers would point in his direction.

But Landgraff believed his team could produce an irresistible new car. For that, he was relying on another military principle: never attack head-on. The idea of a direct assault had a certain appeal: sound the trumpets, fire off a zillion rounds of artillery, cross no-man's-land, and assault the enemy directly. But it was a prescription for mass slaughter. In World War I, the British and Germans just about destroyed each other in frontal clashes.

Many had read of T. E. Lawrence, or at least had seen the movie, but fewer knew of *Allenby of Arabia*. Landgraff not only knew who he was, but had taken his lessons to heart. Edmund Henry Hynman Allenby, a successful

British field marshal in the Middle East, hit the other guys where they least expected it, because they never anticipated that he would go to all the trouble. Always round about, even if they had to cross swamps, mountains, whatever the hell. Like Allenby, Landgraff would take the indirect approach.

In their assault on the American auto industry, the Japanese had found the weak point: quality. Now Landgraff would counterattack where the Japanese were vulnerable: on style. Japanese cars were boring; they looked as if they had been designed by engineers. It went without saying that the new Taurus would have to be well made—quality was no longer an option. But it would also be the best-looking damned car on the road.

This was World War II all over again.

ONLY THE CAMPAIGN wasn't getting off to such a great start as 1991 got under way. It was February, and on the thirty-six-inch chart for World Class Timing, the Taurus team was to begin the "functional analysis of alternatives," the "vehicle system assessment studies," the "workhorse build and testing," and some other kickoff events. And there was no team.

There was no team and there was nowhere to put the team. Dick Landgraff had just taken charge, he was the Maximum Leader, and he was sitting with an advance guard of seventy people in a converted warehouse called the Danou Technical Center in the town of Allen Park, a few miles south of the Ford complex in Dearborn. He was supposed to be notifying the various engineering divisions to cough up team members—he needed people from body engineering, from chassis, from powertrain, from the vehicle office, from electronics, from climate control, from all those divisions that were collectively known as Product Engineering Offices, or PEOs. Plus he needed other bodies from finance, planning, purchasing, customer service, and so forth, and there was no place to put them; for that matter, he didn't yet have anyone from personnel to help with the recruiting and paperwork. So in a very real sense DN101 was behind schedule on Day 1.

ON MATTERS HE KNEW something about, Dick Landgraff was seldom without an opinion. And he had decided that the introduction of World Class Timing had been well-intentioned but mishandled, another of the improbable episodes he had witnessed during three decades at Ford. The people who had produced World Class Timing were called the 411 Group because they met in Room 411 of an office building. Landgraff happened to know one of the people in the group. He had been plucked from his post in finance for the assignment. Having started out with Ford in finance, Landgraff knew the foolishness of having a finance guy, however bright, tell people how cars ought to be produced. Recounting the story, he marveled at the insanity of it. "A finance guy . . . he's never worked on a program. I found that astonishing. Now, the reason they did that, was they couldn't find any operating guys to go off and do it." The operating guys like himself didn't have time for this bullshit! They were too busy working on car programs. So the master plan to reshape car product development was drafted by people who hadn't worked on car programs. Landgraff thought this was hilarious. He had two laughs, a kind of raspy *heh-heh-heh* when confronted with incompetence of an outlandish sort such as typically surfaced in meetings, and a softer chuckle heard at moments like this, when he was more genuinely amused.

Armed with rolls of butcher block paper, Post-Its, pushpins, and yarn, the 411 Group had constructed a wall chart with the months and years across the top and the deadlines arranged vertically beneath them. This was titled the Total Program Work Plan and was reproduced in a three-foot-long version suitable for posting and distributed to the worker bees who would carry it out. Soon everybody called it the "Twip." A step-by-step written guide was in the works. But at the moment, the Twip was all they had. Landgraff wrote notes to some timing people asking them to explain in plain English how he was supposed to squeeze six months to a year out of the usual timetable. Their answers were no help. "So I concluded that we were on a hope and a prayer mission and we'd just go off and see what worked."

But first he had to find a place for the team. One location under discussion was some warehouse in deep, dark Detroit. Another was a big empty building in Dearborn itself, but they would have had to park across a busy street in a lot that belonged to a bowling alley. There was even talk of constructing a new building, but of course there wasn't time. Nothing annoyed Landgraff like this kind of wheelspinning. It would take all his control to say in a civilized voice, "If there isn't time, then why are we talking about it?" Meanwhile, two of Landgraff's stalwarts, chief engineer George Bell and Tom Breault, another top engineer, were having discussions with the Design Center about using space.

If the Ford Motor Company had a soul, it was its Design Center, built in the fifties. From its airy, high-ceilinged studios had come some great cars: Mustangs, Thunderbirds, and, of course, The Car That Saved Ford. And great trucks, too. From the outside it was an undistinguished low-slung redbrick building without windows. Within, it was larger than life, with dimensions sized to cars, not people. The corridors were fifteen feet wide so cars and trucks could drive through them. There was a huge domed showroom equipped with eight turntables and a sound-and-light system for mini auto shows; on the walls of the showroom lobby were full-length portraits of Edsel Ford and son William Clay Ford. Edsel had started a design department against his father's wishes in the early days of the company, when Henry I was content to turn out cookiecutter Model T's, then A's. The first Lincoln Continental was his creation; its successor, the Lincoln Mark II, was William's. Now in his sixties and seldom seen, William Clay was said to roam the studios late at night as if he were the ghost of Ford's past. In Detroit, he was best known as the owner of the Detroit Lions.

Veterans of past car programs, Bell and Breault knew how convenient it was for engineers to work near the clay models that designers used to rough out their ideas. But the Design Center chieftains wanted no part of the DN101 team. The building was filled with artists and artisans, people of taste and refinement who did not fancy an invasion of outsiders. The artists designed the cars, picked the colors, chose the seat fabrics and the materials. The males—almost all the car designers were males—wore pleated pants, dark shirts; they wore doubled-breasted suits. You were as likely to find a copy of *GQ* in their offices as *Car and Driver*. The artisans, many of them, were old-school craftsmen who made models of clay, wood, and fiberglass that were wonders of verisimilitude. To the Design Center community, cars were works of art. To the pragmatic engineers, planners, and analysts who would constitute the team, cars were infinitely malleable objects, subject to change for reasons of cost, function, or market research. The two camps—design and product development—might have to have a relationship, but that didn't mean they had to live together.

Sorry, no space, said the people from the Design Center. No sweat, said Bell and Breault; the Design Center had an interior paved courtyard that was ringed with studios where designers could work in natural light hidden from the spying eyes of the outside world. "We can just bring in some double-wide office trailers and park them in the courtyard." The Design Center could see where this was headed. The courtyard would look like some low-rent downriver mobile home park strewn with tires and fenders, and engineers coming and going in short-sleeved white shirts. It was already home to ducks, who nested in the shrubbery alongside the building and ate handouts from the clay modelers. Okay, okay, the DN101 team could have the basement.

This was not Tom Breault's first encounter with Design Center gentry, or the basement for that matter. He had been one of the engineers on the first Taurus, and they, too, had been housed belowdecks. Once he and a colleague had passed Gene Bordinat, then Ford's vice-president for design, in an upstairs hallway.

"Who are *they*?" Breault heard Bordinat ask a companion.

"They're the people in the basement," he was told.

"I hope they'll be gone soon," Bordinat said.

But some were there for three years. And for the entire time, the Taurus people had security passes with a "V" on them. It stood for visitor.

THE BASEMENT MIGHT not be primo real estate, but it had two things going for it: It was indeed close to the clays. Close! It was right under them. The studio where DN101 designers were starting to sketch and sculpt models was just up the stairs. And it was available. Landgraff loved the idea. To be sure, he had not actually seen the basement at that point. He knew it would have to be renovated, but so would every other place they were talking about, and, besides, Ford's own construction crews could do the work, rather than his having to hire and supervise a general contractor, as if he didn't have enough to do.

Most recently, the basement had been used for storage of clay models and supplies for the model-making shops, plus it housed a small computer-aided design group. David Vaseau, a Design Center facilities planner who got the assignment to make room for the DN101 team, was told that perhaps 350 or 370 people would be coming in for a year. The basement could accommodate half of them. In a few months, a studio on the first floor was scheduled to close; the rest could go there. If he had known plans would change and the team would occupy the basement for nearly five years, Vaseau said later, he wouldn't have dropped the big heating and air-conditioning units in the middle of the room. He did that so they could be moved easily and reused after the team left. But they blasted on every twenty minutes with a noise that ripped through the surrounding cubicles like the buzz of a chainsaw. And that went on for the whole five years.

Okay, so the basement wasn't ideal. It was dark and it was damp. Okay, so it was a dungeon. Dick Landgraff knew that going in, but he felt that he didn't have much choice. It wasn't as if anyone had a better idea. And why did people care so much? If you looked at *his* offices since taking over the Taurus program, you might conclude he was headed down the corporate ladder, not up. He had started out with a rug-and-jug in a decent office in Building Three, the power base of planning and finance. From there he went to an office in distant Danou, where it was always cold. And now this basement. But it didn't bother him. His secretary had arranged his photos and a little lineup of Brazilian carved animals on the credenza, along with some colored marble straightedge he couldn't remember acquiring. So much for decor.

And actually, the basement didn't look that bad, once the cubicles were in place and furnished with versatile Steelcase 9000 "systems" furniture, a variety of floor and pre-wired wall units assembled in different cubicle configurations. David Vaseau ordered dark blue carpet and gray metal furniture. As he heard it, someone in the Design Center had decided a long time ago that gray induced creativity. Peering into some of the front offices of ranking designers was like looking into caves, they were so dark. They had walls covered with gray fabric and chrome parabolas hanging from the ceilings; they had smoky Lucite room dividers and chrome-trimmed black furniture. Someone in Vaseau's position could choose any color, the joke went, so long as it was gray. This was reminiscent of Henry Ford the Founder's dictum that you could have any color car, so long as it was black.

Preparing to move the fledgling DN101 team from the Danou Tech Center, a fifteen-minute drive from Dearborn, the new personnel manager, Wendy Dendel, set up a diagram with cubicles represented by Post-Its. The one big team would be subdivided into smaller teams, mixing people from different organizations. But when she tried to reflect that arrangement on the diagram, people came by and moved the Post-Its. All the body engineers wanted to sit together. All of chassis. All of finance. Collocation frightened people. They didn't even know for sure how to pronounce it, until the company issued a clarification. Dendel understood what they were going through. Although she had volunteered for the team, she had put off the physical move, out of apprehension. She didn't know what her job would be and she didn't know the people she would be working with. She would be all by herself, without her colleagues, without even her boss. Meanwhile, there was plenty to do where she was in Building Three, wrapping up work on her old job. Not until she got a call saying Landgraff wanted her now did she drop everything and go to Danou.

In May, as team members began to move into the Design Center, they precipitated an immediate shortage of 300 parking spaces. For years the Design Center had more parking spaces than it needed: big glorious country club berths ten feet wide. The parking crisis raised the very emotional question of whether, in the new spirit of teamwork, to do away with reserved spaces, a treasured perk for people who reached grade nine on Ford's numbered job ladder, a level known as management roll. The general salary roll people, grades one to eight, quite naturally had no objection. And many of the management roll people were in favor of equal access. The Design Center thought it was worth trying. DN101 could be the pilot program to see how it worked. Unimpressed with the Design Center suggestion, Wendy Dendel, speaking for the team, said DN101 would give up reserved parking if Design Center employees would do likewise. The Design Center spurned that solution and another as well: to restripe the lot with spaces eight and a half feet wide, the Ford standard. For the next three years—until a new parking lot was added with narrower spaces—lower-ranking team members had to battle for openings, sometimes circling the lot until a car pulled out.

The team disturbed the tranquility of the Design Center in other ways. Even before everyone had moved in, Dendel got a call from Dave Vaseau. He was upset that team members were piling stuff on top of their overhead cabinets so that it stuck up above the cubicles. The desks of engineers were littered with car parts. An entire sheet-metal skeleton sat outside the team's basement headquarters. Nor was the Design Center used to the steady stream of visitors from suppliers and other Ford organizations that arrived for meetings with team members. Access to the building had always been limited. What went on in the studios was top secret, after all. And it had long been the custom to discourage any visitors at all on Mondays, the day employees had adopted for casual dress. The Taurus team entertained visitors, regardless of the day. Also, they wore casual clothes on Friday, like most of Ford. And they wore them on Monday, like the Design Center. And then, on their own, they added Wednesday. The Design Center made its unhappiness known in small ways. For the first six months, the Taurus team did not have a copier that could process large quantities. They were told that the one in the Design Center belonged to the Design Center, and so did its paper.

Despite the inconveniences, the DN101 secretaries were happy to be in Dearborn, where Ford was headquartered. A number of secretaries had grown up close by and had applied to work at Ford on graduation from high school. Dearborn was both a suburb of Detroit and a substantial city of 89,286, of whom just 494 in 1990 were black, thanks to years of highly effective racial discrimination. There were 14,114 residents of Arab extraction, who had blessed Dearborn with several excellent Lebanese restaurants.

The secretaries liked Dearborn because it had places to shop and places to eat, although—as a gross generalization—they preferred the $5.95 specials at the Salad Bowl on Michigan Avenue or one of the restaurants in the new Fairlane Town Center mall to more adventuresome Arab food. Such amenities were important to secretaries, because, unlike engineers and planners, who were always scurrying off to meetings, their lunch hour was the only time they could get away from their desks. Secretaries were wives, mothers, caretakers, friends. They had lives. They had people to see, errands to run, things to *buy*. They did not like to work in outlying areas such as Allen Park, where the Danou Technical Center was. Allen Park was the first in a chain of modest downriver communities, with little houses that looked as if they belonged on a Monopoly board. For shopping, you could choose between Sears and Arbor Drugs. Some of the DN101 sites that had been under discussion—that warehouse in some prostrate Detroit neighborhood—well, you had to wonder how Ford found these places. Kathy Matsos, the chief engineer's secretary, had a friend with the Ford value analysis group who ended up in Livonia, on Detroit's western border, in a building where the secretaries had to maintain the supply of toilet paper. Really. Kathy was embarrassed for her friend. At a Ford-owned building you could make a phone call and get whatever you needed.

For shopping, Dearborn offered Lord & Taylor, Hudson's, and Saks Fifth Avenue in the Fairlane Center, or Jacobson's right in town on Michigan Avenue, with its old-fashioned department store tearoom. Plus, Dearborn was the headquarters of the secretary mafia. Ford secretaries were plugged into an incredible underground, with people in every high place. Maybe the secretaries were weak on some of the details of technical intrigue, but they knew when bosses took freebies against company rules, had girlfriends, were the target of sexual harassment complaints, hid candy in their desks, or had body odor. They even knew their boss's performance ratings. The secretaries' main job was setting up meetings, so they were forever talking to one another. Many had made several moves in their careers, so they knew people in other buildings: Building Three (finance and planning), Building One (trucks), Building Five (chassis), the Triple E Building (powertrain), and World Headquarters. They knew the secrets, and they knew each other.

Moving into the birthplace of the original Taurus gave Tom Breault a case of déjà vu. In the early eighties, the furniture had been orange and tan, and half the space had been occupied by drafting boards. Now computer-aided design (CAD) operators did designs in much less space, and the colors were blue and gray, but otherwise it looked pretty much the same. But Breault, in charge of a department of forty people, did not have much time for nostalgia. Owing to wiring that was improperly installed, the computers were losing power and wiping out the work of the CAD guys in his section, who then had to work overtime to make it up, and there were other crises. But once in a while he would find himself thinking of the first Taurus, and the guy in charge, a brilliant, charismatic, controversial engineer named Lew Veraldi.

Veraldi's legacy to the DN101 team was not only a best-selling piece of hardware, but a willingness to experiment. Before there was World Class Timing, there was Lew Veraldi's "Recipe for a Perfect Launch," a checklist of pivotal events that had to take place before Job One. Before there was the job of program manager, Veraldi created the post for himself, then sought to formalize it on other car programs.

And before there was the DN101 dedicated, collocated team, there was

Lew Veraldi's Team Taurus. On his own, Veraldi recruited people from all corners of the company to work on what was then a top secret project. "If Lew Veraldi said you were on the team, you were on the team," said Neil Ressler, a Ford vice-president who in those days was chief engineer of the climate control division. At the time, Ressler was lobbying for radiators made of aluminum rather than steel. Veraldi called him up and said he wanted one for the Taurus, and by the way, he said, Ressler was on the team.

In choosing people, Veraldi set out to realign the hidebound sequence by which a car moved from planning to design to engineering to purchasing to manufacturing and thence to public relations and marketing. The closer the car got to market, the more difficult it was to reach back in the sequence to make changes. By bringing people from various departments together at the outset, he hoped to get everybody talking early in the process. Unlike its reincarnation in 1991, however, only a fraction of Veraldi's team had physically moved into the basement. The rest remained in their home offices.

At a time when "benchmarking" was a foreign word in corporate America, Veraldi ripped apart competitive cars and emulated their best elements. He sought suggestions from assembly-line workers as the Japanese did. When the designers came up with a sensational new aerodynamic shape, he was behind them all the way. The name Taurus sprang from the chance discovery that Veraldi and his chief planner, John Risk, had wives born under the astrological sign of the bull. Taurus was to be a code name, but it researched so well among potential buyers that Ford kept it.

Veraldi's temper was legendary. He was a name-caller, a table-pounder, and a book-thrower. As the engineer in charge of tracking weight, Tom Breault frequently ran afoul of Veraldi. Weight was the biggest determinant of fuel economy, which was of new and considerable importance in the wake of the energy crisis promulgated by the Arab world. And because cars rarely got lighter during development—engineers added more than they took away—Breault was seldom the bearer of good news.

Veraldi was impatient with lengthy, step-by-step explanations. He wanted the conclusions first, then he would ask questions. When the discussion got too complex, you could lose him. If he said "Am I the only person in this room who doesn't understand this?" you knew you were in trouble. Breault, as eager as anyone else to stay on his good side, came up with a system to guide him through dense material.

When Breault presented a report, he would highlight both his copy and Veraldi's, using different colors for different sections. Then he could proceed: "Lew, down in the blue section . . ." Eventually, Veraldi realized something was odd. "Am I the only one in the room with a highlighted copy?" he asked suspiciously. "Why? Am I the only one who can't follow this?" Breault thought quickly. "No, sir," he answered. "It's because you're the only vice-president in the room."

Veraldi's father, who was from Italy, had been lured to Detroit by Henry Ford's promise of a $5 day, although he ended up working elsewhere as a janitor. His mother, Carmela, had taught herself English at night after the children were asleep, and got four of her five sons into the Henry Ford Trade School, for worthy children of poor people. Veraldi's brother Frank, also an engineer, had preceded him to Ford. Lew Veraldi worked his way through Lawrence Tech, a popular college for working students because it had a night program. He was halfway up the corporate ladder by the time he graduated after sixteen years.

He borrowed his father's serge suit for his first Ford interview. Because the suit was so scratchy, he wore a pair of pajamas underneath, not knowing he would have to undress for a physical. It made a good story for the rest of his life. If anyone wondered why Veraldi always wore his belt buckle to one side, he explained that he had developed the habit as a draftsman, when the belt buckle tended to bump against the board. Perhaps it was also a reminder of his humble origins, before he rose to vice-president and became a member of Motor City's ruling caste, with a custom home in the lovely northern suburb of Birmingham.

Among the successes that propelled him upward was an elegant design for a section of steering linkage that impressed the bosses in chassis as he was starting out. His design was straight where it could be straight and thin where it could be thin, with a marked savings of weight and cost. In the mid-1970s, he presided over engineering for the Fiesta, a small, peppy, front-wheel-drive car for Europe that did very well.

But the Taurus was his triumph. A movie might open this way:

The year is 1979. Ford's car sales are in a nosedive. The following year Ford will lose $1.6 billion, its first loss since going public. Thank God trucks are making money, or it would have been much worse. There are discussions of getting out of the car business and getting into something safe, like banking.

The chairman of Ford summons Lew Veraldi to his spacious office on the twelfth floor of World Headquarters, overlooking Michigan Avenue and, beyond it, the lush greens of a private golf course. Philip Caldwell is looking out his window as Veraldi arrives. He half turns.

"Lew, I'm not going to beat around the bush. As you know, Ford Motor Company is in desperate financial shape. But we've decided to do one

more car. It has to look better than anything GM is doing, and it has to be as high in quality as the Japanese." The chairman pauses for a deep breath. "Lew, if this car doesn't sell, it could be the end of Ford Motor Company. We're betting every cent we can borrow. And we want you to be in charge."

The way Ford made decisions to do a new car was much less dramatic, of course. At any given moment, dozens of designs and engineering studies were incubating, nurtured by seed money. Some survived and grew into small advanced programs; of those, a few developed over time into full-fledged vehicles. By the time the Ford board of directors authorized the necessary millions, there was already a design and primitive prototypes.

But still, the bottom line was the same. During the Taurus years, Lew Veraldi would tell friends, "Phil Caldwell has trusted me with the last $3 billion Ford Motor Company has."

THE TAURUS WENT on sale on December 26, 1985, squeezing in under the end-of-the-year deadline for the *Motor Trend* Car of the Year award, a very big deal for carmakers, because of its promotional value. Part of the reason Taurus took six years to premier was a change in size. Because of the success of little Japanese imports during the energy crisis, Ford had set out to build a small car too. But then an amazing thing happened. The energy crisis went away! And gas flowed back into the nation's gas pumps like milk into a mother's breast. So Veraldi was ordered to start over with a longer Taurus. Another delay was a troubled startup in the Atlanta plant, where workers had to learn to assemble 3,000 or so new parts with untried high-strung automated tooling.

After a shaky start in showrooms, owing to the radical design and some quality problems—it was, for example, necessary to replace a few engines—the car became a huge success. Buyers were undeterred by the car's flaws. It was as if the Taurus wore a halo. In 1986, 263,450 Americans bought a Taurus. In 1987, 354,971. In 1988, 374,627. Thanks in large part to the infusion of Taurus/Sable sales, Ford's share of the car market grew from 19.2 percent in 1985 to 22.3 percent in 1989.

Taurus did, in fact, get *Motor Trend*'s Car of the Year award. And Lew Veraldi was praised for masterminding the most noteworthy Ford since the Mustang debuted in 1964, and the best American car since the energy crisis. The magazine *Automotive Industries* named him Man of the Year in 1987 and featured him on its cover. For a car guy, this was like receiving an Oscar. After the car's success was well established, two books appeared that glorified both Taurus and Veraldi: *Reinventing the Wheels: Ford's Spectacular Comeback* and *Taurus: The Making of the Car that Saved Ford.* Veraldi was in constant demand on college campuses and at industrial forums, where people wanted to know the inside story of the Taurus. He told them all about Team Taurus, the benchmarking, the suggestions. But he didn't tell them about his disappointments.

Fred Simon, the car's interior planner, was there when Veraldi returned from a conversation with "Red" Poling, the president of Ford. Poling was a finance guy, a man to whom the cost of a car was paramount. Ford measured cost in two ways: the total investment to design, engineer, test, and build the car, and the variable cost, or unit cost per car. The finance people kept a running tab on both. With an expenditure of $2.9 billion, Veraldi had brought the car in under the authorized investment of $3.1 billion, but he had exceeded the variable cost by $216 and he also had missed the Job One date by three months. Every lost day represented lost sales.

As Veraldi described the meeting with Poling, he couldn't contain his anger. According to Simon, "He said this was the first performance review he had ever gotten that wasn't an outstanding performance review. Red said he couldn't trust him because he'd overrun his budget." At that same meeting, Veraldi told Simon, Poling had accused him of being "too emotional."

"This is an emotional business," Veraldi said he replied. "If you're not emotional there's something wrong with you."

Reminiscing about Veraldi after his retirement in 1994, Poling said he could not recall such a meeting. As president of Ford at that time, he said, he was not Veraldi's immediate supervisor, and would not have given him his performance review; he would merely have signed off on it. "I thought very highly of Lew Veraldi," Poling said. "He was a very dedicated individual in terms of quality. He was not as concerned with cost as I felt he should be."

When Veraldi told some of the team executives that he hadn't gotten his bonus that year, they offered to share theirs. To his secretary Terri Glowacki, in whom he confided, he said, "It doesn't matter, Terri." He said it again when he was passed over for the position he wanted and that everyone thought he would get, vice-president for car product development, overseeing all of Ford's car programs. The job went instead to another vice-president, Max Jurosek, who had presided over powertrain.

One of Veraldi's last assignments was to kick off a minor remodeling, or "facelift," of the 1992 Taurus. Veraldi was very protective of the Taurus. To head the program, he chose Richard L. Landgraff, who had worked for him on the cycle plan. Having dealt with Ford products on paper for many years in one way or another, Landgraff was eager to plunge into the high-visibility, high-stakes, high-risk cosmos inhabited by designers, engineers, and planners. Like Veraldi, he had a reputation for being outspoken and tenacious.

Landgraff soon discovered he had little influence over the entrenched engineering fiefdoms that designed the body, chassis, powertrain, and other systems. Jurosek, occupying the job Veraldi had wanted as head of car product development, made it clear that he intended to leave his mark on the car. Though outranked, Veraldi refused to move out of Jurosek's way. Landgraff often found himself in the middle. "Max and Lew fought all the time. Lew would come up and say, 'I don't like this back end. It looks too Japanese.' Then Jurosek would come up and say, 'I know what Veraldi told you. Don't pay any attention.' " Every design review was like that. The job was impossible. Landgraff began to wonder why he'd accepted it.

In 1988, Veraldi moved into World Headquarters as vice-president for engineering and manufacturing. The title sounded impressive, but in reality it was a lateral move to a nebulous staff position. Ford had literally kicked him upstairs in his final years. He occupied an office on the twelfth floor of World Headquarters, where he had a great view and no clout.

Veraldi had long suffered from diabetes. Now his heart gave out. After the first heart attack, he came back to work. Landgraff puzzled over the man's loyalty to Ford. He was at a meeting where Lou Ross, an executive vice-president, singled out Veraldi in front of his colleagues for the same cost overruns that had led to the poor performance review. Certainly Veraldi didn't have to take this, Landgraff thought to himself. Ford vice-presidents were all millionaires. Why didn't he just quit?

After another heart attack, Lew Veraldi did retire on November 1, 1989, forty years and one month after he had come to Ford. He was fifty-nine. He died the following October. As the widow of a vice-president Irene Veraldi was entitled to a free Lincoln Continental. Openly bitter at her husband's treatment, she sold it and bought a Mercedes.

Veraldi might have had a terrible temper, but he had a soft heart. People loved him or hated him. No, said one engineer, "you loved him and you hated him." Said his older brother Frank, who rose to become an executive engineer in the powertrain division, "He was well-liked and well-disliked."

So it was kind of a coincidence that, thanks to Veraldi, Dick Landgraff would in a sense pick up where Veraldi had left off, with some of the same people, down in the basement of the Design Center, with the water, the bugs, the odd-looking flakes of dirt that dropped from the ceiling, the pungent smell of clay, and the heating/cooling hunks of metal that sounded like a team of lumberjacks clearcutting the forest.

———— ⭐ ————

Seeing the Light

DOUG GAFFKA, THE exterior designer for the 1996 Taurus, saw a car as having one of three primal faces: aggressive, friendly, or sad. To his way of thinking, a good front-end design could be aggressive or friendly, but not sad. Sad could be seen in the hangdog expression about the grilles of certain aging GM models—cars that had seen better days from a company that had seen better years. Sad was for losers.

What largely determined the expression on a car were its headlamps. Less had been demanded of them in the era when drivers could afford to drag around some heavy metal. But now, the bumper, that noble jowl of chrome that stretched from fender to fender, gone! And in its place, a prominent plastic chin called the fascia. The toothy grille, composed of chrome slats, globes, grids, bullets, nibs, twists and twirls, gone! The chrome factories, shuttered. Chrome workers, out of work.

Until the 1980s, there were just four garden-variety lamps: big round ones, little round ones, big rectangular ones, and little rectangular ones. These were known as sealed-beam headlamps. When the bulb burned out, you had to replace the whole thing. With the 1984 Lincoln Mark VII, Ford blazed a new frontier in car optics, producing a lamp whose shape was tailored to the car's aerodynamic front end. Because these lamps came with replaceable bulbs, they were supposed to be cheaper to maintain, although somehow that part of it didn't work out.

The new aero headlamps lit up the Taurus, and just about every Ford that followed. In addition, changes in bulb technology made it possible to shorten the lamps and still meet federal standards for road illumination. The headlamps in the original Taurus were 145 millimeters tall. Those going into the 1992 model were 92 millimeters. And when Gaffka took over the exterior design of the '96 Taurus, both designers and engineers were working on the supposition that the headlamps would shrink to a height of 75 or possibly even 55 millimeters. Fifty-five millimeters translated to approximately two inches.

These squinty headlamps explained in part the hostile expressions on the full-sized clay models that greeted Gaffka in the spring of 1991 when he reported to work in the DN101 studio. On one, a pair of narrow, elongated headlamps, graceful in their way but full of menace, glared out from beneath a hooded fold. The windshield slanted sharply backward, and the hood was short and low. This face seemed to wear the predatory expression of a snake or a shark. Imagine, if you will, a scene in a movie where the good guy is walking to his car in a dark parking garage. Suddenly a pair of beams stabs the darkness, and a car leaps into motion, its wheels squeeling and men firing guns out the side windows at the good guy. *Bam! Bam! Bam!* This could be that car.

Gaffka thought America's redesigned family car should look less like a barracuda and more like a pet you wanted to take home and put in your garage.

Not only did the designers have to do a sensational makeover—"makeover" was just one of the insider words for a model change, and it was not the only one that suggested cars were female; another was "facelift," and there were also "re-skin" and "freshening"—but like everyone else they had less time than usual under World Class Timing.

Sometime during the following spring of 1992, chairman and CEO "Red" Poling and three vice-presidents, collectively known as the design committee, were to assemble in the Design Center showroom for a rite known as "Theme Decision." They would approve a design for the new car that everybody wanted to be as phenomenally successful as the 1986 Taurus. That gave the designers a year.

What had set the first Taurus apart from the competition was not only an aerodynamic profile that gave it a low coefficient of drag and improved fuel economy, but its clean, rounded shape in a period when cars were boxy, with sharp, hard edges. Despite early references to jellybeans and hippos, praise poured in. In *Fortune*, Jack Telnack was "The Stylist Who Put Ford Out in Front." The "hottest car in years," said *Business Week*. After a long dry spell of being nothing but the "number-two carmaker," it was now Ford, the Styling Leader. The company that had launched the Mustang and the Thunderbird was back in the ring, a contender.

Years later, when other carmakers had rounded off their edges and there were jellybeans in every garage, it would be hard to remember just how revolutionary the Taurus had seemed. The first time Chuck Gumushian from Ford public affairs had seen a full-sized model in the studio, he thought it was a concept car—a futuristic prototype designed for auto show displays. "I said, 'I can't believe this. We're going to build this car?'"

The pressure on both DN101 designers and engineers to match the styling and improve the performance of that car, the flagship of the Ford fleet, was understood by everyone. No one described it more perfectly than Helen Bell, the wife of chief engineer George Bell. Redesigning the Taurus, she said in a remark Bell liked to quote, was "like repainting the *Mona Lisa*."

Jack Telnack, the man who designed The Car That Saved Ford, had done as much as anyone to advance today's automotive minimalism. Telnack had hired in at Ford in 1958, a time when "bigness was goodness," but he had hated the fins, the chrome, yes, all the slavering excess that dripped from the cars of that period. For a time, he moonlighted as a part-time designer of boats; he preferred their clean, purposeful lines. With the company desperate for a home run in the mid-1980s, Telnack had the freedom to express his taste. Moreover, it was critical to cut cost and weight to compete with small fuel-efficient Japanese cars. Chrome was expensive and it was heavy. Even so, eliminating the grille on the new Taurus had been a step so extreme, so daring, that the designers presented two front ends to the executive-level design committee, one with the traditional mouth of egg-crate chrome, and one without. The committee made the decision. Between the headlamps of the Taurus front end would be a body-color panel in which the blue Ford oval floated within an oval opening. "The Ford navel," autowriters later quipped.

In the years after Taurus, Telnack struggled to hold on to Ford's new reputation for styling leadership. He convened Ford's top designers for two years running, first in Europe and the following year in Dearborn, to discuss a "design breakthrough." There was general agreement that the next frontier in car design would incorporate "lumps and bumps," meaning ripples, swells, and bulges. Outside their inner circle, designers didn't talk so much about "lumps and bumps," a phrase that failed to communicate the majesty of a product whose cost was equal to a half year's pay to the average Joe. The formal term for a lumpy, bumpy car was "complex sculpture."

It was easier to understand what a complex sculpture was not than what it was. It wasn't an egg, which was a smoothly shaped three-dimensional oval. It was more like a potato, a tomato, or a green pepper, albeit one whose bumps were symmetrical. You could look at it like this: The simplest way to fashion the hood was to make it stretch smoothly from fender to fender, windshield to front bumper. Put a hump down the center, and you had a complex sculpture. The same with a bulge in the bodyside. There was general agreement as well on a new look the designers called "cab forward": cars with shorter, lower hoods, steeply raked windshields, and longer wheelbases. The interiors of these cars were much roomier.

But when the time came to freshen the Taurus for 1992, Ford had played it safe. The car was in the number-two position, just behind the conservative Honda Accord. No sense in jeopardizing a formula that had gotten them this far. But how to be new without seeming new? The company's answer had been dazzling in its simplicity. The new 1992 Taurus would look *almost exactly like the old one.* When the car came out, you could hardly tell the difference.

As a rule, redesigns kicked off four to five years before the new model was introduced. Even though it had not yet gone on sale, by the spring of 1991, the 1992 Taurus was history so far as the guys in the Design Center were concerned. And they knew they couldn't get away with another minor tinkering for the 1996 model.

T HE DESIGN OF A CAR was very much a collaborative effort. And the DN101 stylists had plenty of help from on high. Telnack, now vice-president for design, sat just a stone's throw away from the DN101 studio in the corridor of executive offices known as Mahogany Row. He often stopped into the DN101 studio on Saturdays around 11 A.M. for a look-see, casually dressed in blue jeans as if he was just one of the guys. So far as the headlamps went, Telnack agreed with Gaffka that the current crop lacked character. He was especially put off by a pair that resembled elongated peanuts. Gaffka remembered his simple yet eloquent observation: "I don't like peanut headlamps."

Nor was it unusual for top company executives to drop into the DN101 studio. David Rees, director of mid-sized car design, would not soon forget a Phil Benton visit. Trailing a retinue, the president and chief operating officer of Ford had scolded him because there weren't more clays available for inspection. Rees felt humiliated. Then Benton called a few days later as if nothing had happened to ask what kind of interior Rees thought would look good in the Lincoln Mark VIII he was about to order. Try to figure these guys out.

From time to time Alex Trotman, vice-president for North American Automotive Operations, came by unannounced on his way to his office. Doug Gaffka would look up around 7:30 A.M. and see him, a small dark-haired man with a mustache, his leather jacket slung over his shoulder, having been there for who knew how long without uttering a word.

Below Gaffka, in a literal sense, were the moles in the basement: Dick Landgraff and his DN101 team of engineers, analysts, and planners. They also had ideas about what this car should look like in order to engineer it properly. Gaffka was a member of the DN101 team too, along with Chris Clements, the head interior designer, and the seven designers who worked for them. And so was their boss, the design exec John Doughty, a peppery little Australian. No problem there. The designers were on the team. They all believed in the principles that the team represented: working together, compromise, accommodation, understanding, communication, and mutual respect, except of course on those occasions when the engineers were wrong and the designers were right.

And by the way, there was the question of what to call these people. They preferred "designers." But often they were called "stylists," a word they did not much care for. "We are not stylists," John Doughty might say to someone who made or could make such an egregious mistake. As he explained it, stylists were people who cut hair, period. Clearly they did not rank as high in status as car designers, at least not in his corner of the former British Empire. But the engineering community had co-opted the word "designer," using it to refer to people who performed computer-aided design. And, really, they were nothing but *draftsmen*, retrained to ply their trade on a screen rather than a table. Car designers, the ones like Doughty and Gaffka and Telnack, were losing ground in this struggle over nomenclature. Tubes were popping up in dark corners like mushrooms, and there were more and more CAD designers every day sitting in front of them. As a further complication, engineers who designed parts were called "design engineers." But there were instances when one of them too might be referred to as a "designer," as in the designer of a certain part.

Collectively you could allude to Gaffka and his colleagues as "the DN101 studio" and everyone would know whom you meant. That was quite acceptable. But individually, there was a bit of a problem. It wasn't so much the potential for confusion that bothered the people in the design studio, but rather that the preemption of their genus label suggested insufficient regard for their unique talents. Although not all of them were as sensitive as Doughty about "stylist." "I don't mind it," said Dave Turner, another executive designer. "It says we're in the fashion business, which we are."

THE DN101 STUDIO faced out through floor-to-ceiling glass panes onto the Design Center's paved courtyard, where cars were frequently parked for observation under natural light. It was equipped with big electric ovens for warming the gobs of brown clay the modelers slapped on wood and foam constructs, then whittled into recognizable forms. The clays took shape beneath metal frames known as bridges, which were calibrated to control the dimensions.

Sculpting the clays was the job of some thirty modelers, who had staked out one end of the studio and turned it into a steamy psychic swamp of frustration and resentment. Modelers felt abused by designers and engineers alike. People didn't realize that it was they who actually translated some designer's hapless sketch on an index card or scrap of paper into something that looked like a car or a part thereof. Once the modelers clayed it up, engineers merely took the dimensions.

In fact, you might say it was the modelers who really designed the car. That was how they saw it. They did all the work and designers got all the glory. Tony Paladino had clayed up the steering wheel in the original Taurus, artfully crafting each little ridge. "There are 600,000 people holding on to my work and nobody knows about it," he said. The number grew to millions and millions if you considered all his steering wheels over the last thirty years. It was as if he had a little grip on their lives, or they on his. Steering wheels were Paladino's specialty. His colleague Tom Mullee preferred the sweep of a body panel. Mullee avoided the steering wheel, with its "seventy little convolutions. You can work eight hours and not know what you've done."

Young modelers started at the bottom, lying or squatting on the studio floor, carving rocker panels and wheelhouses, then graduated to shaping parts of the car that required a more upright position. Most of them had been to college; some had degrees in fine arts. But the senior modelers like Paladino and Mullee were unschooled veterans of the early days following World War II, when Ford taught them their trade and they made their own tools from dowels and piano wire. In those days the master modelers were Germans, who had practiced their craft in wood and traced its origins back to shipbuilding. Mullee had worked on the Edsel. The Edsel! Ford's Famous Flop. He knew the inside story. "It was a beautiful little car when they began. But they kept adding on carryover parts because the economy was so bad."

Modelers didn't think of themselves as being on the team, or at least the old ones didn't. As far as they were concerned, the young ones were a different breed; they could do what they wanted. The two age cohorts had been at odds during a recent union organizing campaign that failed by a small margin. The older modelers had been in favor of joining the United Auto Workers, and they blamed the defeat on their younger colleagues. The old guys could see the future and they weren't in it. Already their ranks had been thinned by computerized milling machines like the one at the other end of the studio that could read the measurements of half a handmade clay model and carve out the other half. In darkened caves across the hall, there were computers that could render solid shapes, turn them to any angle, and cast highlights upon the surfaces.

The clays had an undeniable mystique, a cosmic force, a yin-and-yang pull for the car guys who ran the company. Buried within each massive earthen chunk was the soul of a new car. Ford management said they could never do without at least some clays to convey the look and feel of a car in progress, but in the next breath they touted advances in 3-D modeling, so the modelers had to wonder what lay ahead.

ONE DAY DOUG GAFFKA was in a meeting—later he would think it might even have been a meeting on headlamps—doodling little car faces on the back of a handout, when his boss, John Doughty, who was sitting next to him, glanced at his sketches. "I like that," he said. "That's good." Gaffka looked to see what he'd drawn. A car stared back at him with rounded eyes. It was different, it was friendly. It was also familiar. Why, it looked a lot like a Jaguar XKE from the early 1960s.

Gaffka's imagination took off. He could visualize this shape in an exciting new headlamp called a complex reflector that he had seen on some recent imports. At the moment, the Big Three Detroit automakers employed headlamps that used the front lens as an optic plate. Made of tough, bullet-proof plastic, the lens had a back surface patterned with ridges and grooves. As the light struck it from behind, the optic plate dispersed it in an acceptable pattern over a wide variety of road surfaces. Viewed from the front, the lens was opaque.

Complex reflectors were different. They bounced light from the bulb off a mirrored housing, then forward through a clear lens. They would give the Taurus a pair of eyes that sparkled like diamonds, Gaffka thought, clear and bright. By comparison, optic-plate lenses looked milky and dull, like a car with cataracts.

Some imports were also featuring yet another kind of lamp called a projector beam, which resembled those small spotlights buried in the ceilings of modern, white-walled art galleries. Their lenses, too, were clear. On a car, they gave the front end a high-tech industrial look. These cooler, more aloof projector beams would be so right for the Mercury Sable, the Taurus's problematic sibling. The Sable was like a staid older sister; the Taurus was not only younger, but prettier and more popular. Although Ford did not advertise the fact, beneath the sheet metal the Sable was exactly the same as the Taurus. There was just one important difference between the two cars: the Sable cost more. The same relationship was true of the Ford Escort and the Mercury Tracer; the Ford Tempo and the Mercury Topaz; the Ford Crown Victoria and the Mercury Grand Marquis. Ford had separate sales divisions for the two marques. Ford Division sold Fords; Lincoln-Mercury Division sold its namesake. In their more candid moments, the Lincoln-Mercury guys confessed to an image problem for Mercury. Older buyers thought of Mercurys as little more than "dressed-up Fords." Younger buyers had no image at all.

As a consequence, the parents (Ford Motor Company) were always looking for ways to make the Mercurys distinctive without spending much money, either that or just kill the whole damn Mercury badge, which was an occasional discussion, but no one was ready to go that far at the moment. So, for the price of developing a mere set of headlamps, the Sable could have a distinctive front end.

THEY CLAYED UP Gaffka's puppy-dog face in August—with bright oval eyes that were slightly more elongated than the ones he had first drawn, and a delicate oval mouth. John Doughty added little round parking lamps in the inside corners. The Gaffka front end joined the fleet of clay cars parked side by side in the studio. These clays sat naked and unadorned, like flesh-colored mannequins strewn in random poses about a department store window, waiting for someone to dress them. Some of the models were hybrids—half a car on one side, a different half on the other. The goal was to have as many ideas as possible rendered in clay. In addition to various headlamp and taillamp treatments, the studio was experimenting with flat bodysides, rounded bodysides, and bodysides with variations on an S-curve soon to be seen on the new Lincoln Mark VIII. One "S" was pear-shaped, with the bulge at the bottom. The other had a profile like an old-fashioned Coke bottle, and was more popular with engineers, who saw an immediate advantage to a substantial bulge at the top of the door. New federal regulations for protection against side impact crashes required a thick chunk of foam in the handle area, which was already crammed with hardware for opening and closing the doors, operating the power windows, and activating the power locks. The upper part of the S-curve swallowed the stack-up nicely. You had to be careful about the door hinge, though. The thicker the door, the longer the hinge had to be, but if it grew too much, the door would feel loose and it wouldn't shut right.

Several clays came in from Ford's California studio, which was sometimes a source of fresh ideas. But this time the designs seemed merely weird. The headlamps on one of these cars looked bolted on, like something from the thirties. There were unrefined tail sections that suggested the designer had walked out on the job to go surfing. The engineers called them the "California clays."

That summer and fall, as clays went up and came down rapidly, a poisonous atmosphere enveloped the studio. Manager David Rees sensed it on his periodic visits. He and John Doughty had chosen the most talented designers they could get for the Taurus, and the two men wanted each of them to see his or her best work in clay. But it took modelers as long as a week to throw up even a rough clay, which meant you couldn't render every drawing. As a consequence, what was intended to be a creative exercise had developed into a design competition. Somehow he and Doughty had ended up with a bunch of prima donnas. They complained when their sketches weren't chosen. They complained when their clays were torn down. Rees could sense the hostility emanating from the little knot of people who stared in his direction each time he entered the studio. They had turned on him! It was going to be necessary to take care of a few . . .

Compared to some of the underlings, Doug Gaffka was a model of modesty and professionalism. You could give him an impossible assignment and he wouldn't whine about not having enough modelers to help, or—and it amazed Rees when he became a manager just how many designers would stoop to this—ask for overtime pay. Gaffka's reputation as a team player as well as for talent had brought his name to the surface as the management talked over candidates for the plum Taurus assignment. It was typical of Gaffka that he felt unworthy. Maybe once in his career, if lucky, a designer got the chance to work on a program with such high visibility.

I N   T H E   M I D D L E of the studio sat a clay model that no one could love but an engineer. It was ugly as sin, but it was everything the engineers wanted in a car. It incorporated the fixed points in the car's architecture, which were mandatory in the design. Ford had decided early on, for example, to keep the same underbody as the outgoing Taurus, to save hundreds of millions on equipment in the two assembly plants that built the Taurus and Sable. The new design had to fit the old floorpan, so it could move down the same line of robots.

In a sense this clay was a composite of minimums: the overall minimum height, width, length, angle of the windshield, volume of the interior, location of the seats and the steering wheel, size of the engine compartment, all that and much more, determined by a welter of strategic manufacturing and regulatory considerations. Whatever the designers came up with in the way of an exterior skin, it would have to cover this construct, the car's architecture. The windows, collectively known as the greenhouse, were among the first targets. Until the glass planes were established relative to the underbody, you couldn't determine the shape and placement of the doors.

"Feasible" was the operative word. Would the metal "make," that is to say, would it bend into the shapes the designers wanted, rather than split or fall short? Metal stamping was a black art. It took years of experience to understand the mysteries of how metal flowed under pressure. Other questions: Would the engine fit under the hood? Were the doors thick enough to house the wiring and hardware for the power locks, power windows, and speakers, along with the new steel beam and foam padding required of all cars by 1997 for side impact protection? Could people get in and out without banging their heads? Would the body shape reduce wind noise, the number-one complaint about the outgoing Taurus?

The engineers spent hours on end playing with their homely clay, measuring it, debating it, stroking it—it was the one model they could freely touch. Designers and modelers hated it when engineers pawed their clays. A designer could do anything he wanted to a clay, but an engineer couldn't make so much as the tiniest mark with his fingernail without someone snarling at him. A modeler would as soon cut off that soft engineering hand. And heaven help him if he leaned against a clay or set his notebook down on the front end. The engineers loved this particular clay not only because it was their very own, but because it would also *be* a car one day very soon. A group of structural prototypes, called SPs, would be built to its dimensions and used for testing.

The gulf between designers and engineers was as old as the industry. Bill Mitchell, a legendary GM stylist, was once quoted as saying that body engineers looked like house detectives, "wearing their hats all the time, suspenders and belts, button shoes, with pencils in their pockets and their taste in their mouths." Now the shoes were wingtips. "Here come the wingtips," the grizzled old modelers would say, when smooth-cheeked baby engineers came over to tell them what to do. Mitchell's line to describe engineers was still in use: "Their taste is in their mouths."

David Rees often spoke about the difference between the two disciplines. With their poor little left-lobe-dominant brains, engineers were baffled, even annoyed, by designers' unpredictable bursts of creativity and their failure to produce on demand. Rees and other designers had been working for months on an interior design for the 1993 Lincoln Continental Mark VIII, when inspiration struck during a plane flight. Rees rapidly sketched the solution on a cocktail napkin. Doug Gaffka had come up with the Taurus headlamps in much the same way. Said Rees: "Engineers say, 'Why didn't you do this two years ago?' It's left brain/right brain. You can't schedule creativity. They don't understand that." No, they didn't understand it. And after the cocktail napkin story found its way into print, the left-brainers at Ford even made fun of it. One of them might say that if a designer had a problem, just give him a cocktail napkin. Or that a car took a lot of hard work, it didn't just happen on a cocktail napkin coming back from Europe.

"You must listen to engineers if they say it would not meet a certain safety aspect," said John Doughty. "It would be immoral to ignore it." But beyond that lay a big expanse of glass, metal, and plastic, where designers would push for what they wanted, engineers would say they couldn't make it, and the finance guys would say it cost too much.

Dick Landgraff, the designated mediator, wanted to head off as many confrontations as possible. He instructed the engineers, "You guys have got to do your best to deliver the design because the style of the car is going to play a gigantic role as to whether or not it's going to be really successful, as opposed to being ho-hum moderately successful." And he told the Design Center to compromise where it wasn't a big deal.

In the beginning the new Taurus was to have the same wheelbase as the old one, 106 inches between the centers of the front and rear wheels. But Ford was adding another new car to its lineup that also had a 106-inch wheelbase, the 1995 Ford Contour/Mercury Mystique. In so doing, Ford was eliminating its Tempo/Topaz line, so the Contour would be the next step up from the low-priced Escort. This happenstance provided designers, whose druthers always included a longer car rather than a short stubby car, the better for highlights and sleek graceful lines, with an argument for lengthening the Taurus that went like this: By late 1995, the Contour and the Taurus would be side by side in dealer showrooms. If the new Taurus weren't longer than the Contour, buyers might be reluctant to pay its higher sticker price. John Doughty and the design team could simply make the Taurus sheet metal longer. They could, for example, give the Taurus a longer rear overhang, no problem, but without also moving the wheels rearward, it would look unbalanced, like a bird with a long tail. By the engineers' calculations, the wheelbase could grow to 108.5 inches without jeopardizing the fit of the underbody on the automated fixtures in the assembly plants. The design community wanted that extra length. And Dick Landgraff did too. They could use the additional 2.5 inches to stretch the interior of the car; they could make the rear seat area big enough that tall people could experience some degree of comfort.

But the body engineers, who were in charge of the sheet metal and most of the other parts of the car that you could see, inside and out, were alarmed by the prospect of a bigger car. Additional material meant added weight and added cost, and they were responsible for holding down both. Their bonuses, reviews, and promotions were tied to meeting these targets. During one high-level meeting the vice-president responsible for body engineering called Landgraff "stupid" to his face.

Andy Benedict was the chief body engineer on the team. The other body engineers reported to him. But he reported to a boss back in the big body engineering mother ship, a building that adjoined the Design Center. He was torn between what Landgraff wanted and the direction he was getting from his management. He could see it both ways. Merely stretching the sheet metal without also moving the wheels would give the car a choppy ride. A longer wheelbase would smooth it out. And a larger rear seat with more knee room was an improvement. On the downside, the added weight would decrease fuel economy. Buyers didn't care anymore about mileage, gas was so cheap. But there were still government regulations that said the company's corporate average fuel economy (CAFE) had to be 27.5 miles per gallon. The company carefully monitored the balance in fuel economy between its low-mileage luxury cars that made tons of money and its high-mileage economy cars on which it barely broke even. The more cheap, fuel-efficient Escorts Ford sold, the more lucrative gas-swilling Lincoln Town Cars it could sell without jeopardizing CAFE. But an overweight Taurus would drag down the average. Furthermore, it was getting late in the old World Class Timing scheme of things to make a change in the architecture. It was time to build structural prototypes and test them. And, the deadline for final sheet-metal specifications was approaching. It took twenty-five months to design, order, manufacture, and fine-tune the dies.

Landgraff called a meeting of the key members of the DN101 team, which had grown to include not only designers, but planners, engineers, and financial analysts. Everyone had seen clay models of a longer Taurus. "The team is going to decide," he told them as they gathered around the massive polished wood table in the Design Center's subdued executive conference room. Most of their meetings were down in the basement around an expanse of Formica. This change in venue suggested the magnitude of the decision.

One of the first to speak was Tom Gorman, the head finance guy. He knew a lot of people in California who drove imports. Still in his mid-twenties, he was the youngest member of team management. Gorman said he believed the car was too long. "It's not your call," Gaffka snapped. Gorman was startled. It was the only time Gorman ever saw Doug Gaffka lose his temper. On the other side of the table, Ron Heiser, a planner just out of college, was also thinking of his friends, particularly one who lived in Chicago. Heiser imagined him trying to parallel-park the Taurus or Sable on a city street. "I have to agree with Tom," he announced. This time, as Heiser recalled it, Landgraff terminated the discussion.

At a sales meeting attended by vice-presidents, Landgraff heard nothing but objections when he said the team recommended an extended wheelbase and longer sheet metal. Ford marketing was convinced that women and import buyers wouldn't buy long cars. The best-selling car in America, the Honda Accord, was only 184 inches long, which was also the length of the original Taurus. And what about California, where imports held 40 percent of the market? So many Californians had been buying imports for so long that they now built their houses with little import-sized garages. Would a longer Taurus even fit? Marketing eventually caved in to the studio and the team, as long as the bumper-to-bumper length didn't exceed 200 inches. Ben Lever, who was Dick Landgraff's boss, had come from marketing and he helped argue its case. He was suspicious of the way the studio measured, always along one side of the car. It seemed to Lever that the tape never reached all the way from end to end.

The debate raged, and yet there was a way in which it didn't rage at all. It was an axiom among engineers that the design community always got what it wanted. An engineer could tell designers that something ought to be a certain way, and they would work up a clay following the engineer's mandate, and that clay would be so ugly the poor engineer could hardly believe it. *Their* way, the designers' way, would just be an absolute work of art. Unless something absolutely, positively had to be a certain shape or the car would fall apart, fail a safety test, or refuse to run, an engineer might as well give up and try to the utmost to make the designers' version as functional as possible.

Doughty got hold of some automotive intelligence suggesting that Honda was planning a longer Accord for the future. Chrysler's next generation of mid-sized sedans, code-named LH, promised to be relatively long. Doughty pledged that the designers would use all their cleverness to ensure that the 1996 Taurus would not *look* longer than the old one, except when it sat next to the Contour in a Ford showroom. The design hierarchy rallied behind Doughty. Jack Telnack complained that the shorter clays looked stubby.

To Landgraff, the significant part of the whole struggle over length was that nobody said "No." *No, you can't make it longer.* He wasn't surprised. After thirty years at Ford, he knew that people rarely told you that you couldn't do something. What they did was this: "They complain and expect people to follow their complaints." But unlike the Japanese, where an objection was really a veiled negative, at Ford you could disregard the complaints and, *mirabile dictu*, not only would no one stop you, there were no reproaches! "Nobody says 'I told you not to do that.' " Because of course they hadn't. People didn't like to take a stand. It was kind of wonderful in a way.

That being the case, said Landgraff, "We just went ahead and did it." They extended the Taurus to 197.4 inches, nearly six inches longer than the '92 model; the Sable sneaked in under 200 inches, at 199.7, thanks to a slightly flattened bumper.

B Y   T H A N K S G I V I N G   O F   1 9 9 1 , with Theme Decision scheduled for the following April, the studio was in trouble. In a market research clinic earlier that month, Chicago car owners had looked at photographic blow-ups of proposed themes. "Too futuristic" was one of the kinder opinions. When Tom Gorman walked through the studio these days, he saw the young designers churning out frenzied sketches. Maybe this was creativity, but maybe it was panic. Maybe not panic, take that back, maybe that was too strong a word. *Concern*. The studio felt it. The team felt it. The clays were changing so fast that Gorman told his half-dozen financial analysts to try to look them over at least once a day and preferably twice. The size and shape of a car had major implications for costs. Gorman was a member of the team, yes, but he also reported to the finance division.

The engineers did their best to make feasibility judgments as the clays changed. On trips to the studio Rick Schifter, the DN101 bodyside engineer, would bring an old hand named Chuck Witt from metal stamping operations. "Can you make that?" he would ask, pointing out a questionable curvature. This method—asking Witt—was faster and more accurate than trying to figure it out on a computer.

As a complication, the holidays were upon them, and it was extremely difficult to get anything done in Dearborn during December. Not only was there the usual round of departmental lunches and potluck open houses, plus big supplier bashes with free liquor and cocktail shrimp over at the stately Dearborn Inn, but offices emptied out as people took whatever remained of their yearly vacation allotment. Between Christmas and New Year's, Ford shut down completely, giving employees the week off.

As 1991 drew to a close, however, the pace in the DN101 studio quickened rather than slowed. People stayed on Friday nights. Friday nights! It was a long-standing Design Center tradition to bail out early on Fridays, even if it meant coming back on Saturday to finish your work. But they were staying Fridays and coming back on Saturdays as well.

Going into the Christmas shutdown, there was still nothing on the floor that anybody liked. Some pieces here and there showed promise. Gaffka's round-eyed front end was definitely a contender. But it had no flanks, no tail. Even the engineers—and everyone knew engineers had as much design flair as a Bic pen—made fun of some of the models. One in particular had a dippy front end that grubbed the ground like a vacuum cleaner. Andy Benedict, the head body engineer, called it the anteater.

Stylists and modelers worked through the holidays. Dave Rees dropped in several times. He knew that there were people out there, his so-called colleagues, who questioned his and Doughty's credentials to oversee the transformation of Ford's bread-and-butter flagship car. Both he and Doughty had spent large chunks of their careers working in car interiors, which was widely viewed as a backwater. Rees could recall the time when, if you were assigned to interiors past a certain age, you asked "What did I do wrong?" It was true that interior designers today commanded more respect than in the past. Highways were clogged with commuters who spent more time in their cars than in their living rooms, and who therefore cared a lot about seats, radios, vanity mirrors, and other creature comforts like coffee cup holders. Especially coffee cup holders. But a car was still first and foremost a flash of metal and glass on the highway. Exterior designers had more status. Not only did Rees believe some of his peers in the Design Center were bad-mouthing him, he knew they would have liked a piece of the Taurus themselves and it seemed to him that they were, as a consequence, rejoicing somewhat at the ripples of concern emanating from the DN101 studio.

Designers and modelers worked straight through the holidays. When the engineers returned in January, their first stop was the DN101 studio. A new crop of clay models commanded the studio floor. One in particular was a stunner. It was Miss America! The headlamps were ovals, with matching oval parking lamps. The rear window was an ellipse. The grille opening parted the fascia like a pair of luscious lips. The rear side panels curved inward, forming a tight little downward-sloping rear end. The designers called it the "no-corner" car. There wasn't a straight line on it. The body engineers looked at it, loved it, and saw trouble ahead.

Some of the heaves and swells in the sheet metal, those lumps and bumps, were not engineering-friendly. If you wanted to know how metal behaved on a curve or in a corner, you simply took a piece of paper and tried to duplicate the shape. If the paper wrinkled or tore, metal would do the same thing. The engineers were looking at the potential for a lot of crumpled paper.

Engineers and designers were judged by different standards. To the designers, appearance was everything. Their decisions were ratified initially in market research clinics and then, years later when the car was on sale, in customer acceptance. But engineers got bonuses and promotions based on numerical targets for cost, weight, and quality. For them, the simpler the car, the easier it was to build, the less time and expense were involved, and the more assured they were of reaching their targets. And what was wrong with a simple car? As Rick Schifter, the engineer for the bodyside sheet metal, pointed out, "Toyota and Honda seized a lot of market share selling boring cars, because they are well made, and they're all made the same."

Veteran engineers knew that three years from now, when the curvy, swervy, redesigned Taurus went into production, they would be at the Atlanta plant trying to even out the A-margins between the slabs of sheet metal that started narrow and grew wide and the V-margins that started wide and grew narrow, the joints between the front and rear doors that bowed out when you sighted down the side (known as tenting), the gaps where corners failed to meet (known as ratholes), and the trunk lids that were lower on one side than the other (the high part said to be proud to the bodyside). And the uneven highlights called kinks.

To summarize: The designers would be in their air-conditioned studios giving interviews to awed car writers about the beauty of their creation, and the engineers from Detroit would be in Atlanta assembly plant hell, in hundred-degree temperatures with cars rolling off the line that had A-margins, V-margins, tenting, ratholes, kinks, the whole sheet-metal schmeer, while grizzled tobacco-chewing, profanity-spewing plant bosses hounded them with a kind of good-ole-boy joy, as if the guys from Dearborn had purposefully designed parts that the diemakers couldn't make dies for, the stamping plants couldn't stamp, and the assembly plants couldn't assemble.

Was it any wonder that the body engineers regarded these lumpy, bumpy, complex sculptures on wheels with both admiration and dread?

"We wanted the cheap, easy ones," Schifter said. "We got the hard, expensive ones."

THREE

★

Dick Landgraff
Takes a Ride

ONE DAY IN early fall, 1991, while DN101 was still a sightless, tailless whelp in the Design Center studio, Dick Landgraff slid behind the wheel of a 1992 emerald green Toyota Camry with a V-6 engine and set out for his home in peaceful Bloomfield Hills, a northern suburb thick with auto company executives. To the east was the steamy urban blob called Detroit. He had met his wife, Connie, a nurse, in the city when he was a young Wharton School MBA, working at Ford as a financial analyst and living in a scantily furnished apartment with his underwear in a kitchen cabinet.

Landgraff drove fast. He did everything fast. He walked fast and he wrote fast. After three years as his secretary, Nancy Donaldson had learned to recognize words that in his haste he often failed to complete. She herself was a 10K runner; at least she could keep up with him. As he drove, Landgraff kept an eye out for police. His radar detector was in his Taurus back in Dearborn. He had so many tickets that his license was in jeopardy, and what good was a car guy who couldn't drive? He'd have to be careful the next morning, too. The local police liked to squat at the end of his street.

Landgraff had been waiting for this car. According to advance reports, the 1992 Camry was something special. The DN101 team had obtained a right-hand-drive version from Japan a while ago, but the American model had a waiting list at the local Toyota dealer. He hadn't seemed to think that Ford's order was all that urgent.

Landgraff was not a car guy the way some Ford guys were car guys; he had not spent his adolescence buried in bearings, although he did pump gas and do lube jobs after school in Falls Church, Virginia. His mother brought him dinner every night, wrapped in aluminum foil, while his co-workers, real car guys, grabbed burgers at a greasy spoon. He had, for a time, considered becoming an engineer, but not in the mechanical and electrical disciplines automakers hired. Thinking to work for an oil company in the great outdoors, to travel to exotic places, he started out in petroleum engineering. But after a semester of study at Penn State, Landgraff realized he could spend the rest of his life looking at rocks. "I began to question why." And there was this other thing: his classmates, the ones with pockets full of pencils and slide rules dangling from their belts, seemed so, how to put it? . . . narrow. He switched to business. A Ford recruiter nabbed him in graduate school at the University of Pennsylvania. He had spent more time in the company with his fingers on calculators than steering wheels. But during the last ten years in car product development, he had learned his way around under the hood. And this ride told him that Taurus was in for trouble.

The Camry purred along. This was some car. It was heavier, larger, more expensive than the old Camry, it was upscale in every way. It was quiet, smooth, and responsive. The gears seemed to glide into place. In fact, the powertrain was just amazing. He'd have to give it a 9.5 on a 10-point scale. If this test drive were any indication, Landgraff would bet that the Camry's quality ratings would make even the Accord look inferior.

The car was still a basic box, but it was one in which all the parts fit snugly, both inside and out, and they all matched in color. There were no exposed screws; the instrument panel and interior trim didn't have that tacky plastic finish found in comparable Ford cars. It had *craftsmanship*.

He wasn't quite sure how to define craftsmanship, nor was anyone else, but Landgraff knew he wanted it. Craftsmanship went beyond quality. It was nothing you could measure. It was more the look, the feel, the smell, and the sound of quality. It could be summed up as "well made," an attention to detail, a return to first principles, when skilled carpenters and metalworkers painstakingly turned out cars by hand, individually shaping and mating parts, so they fit together and matched in color and texture, turned smoothly, and wore evenly.

Not that anyone planned to increase the amount of manual labor on the assembly line. God forbid. Not with the direct labor amounting to a dollar a minute, with all the benefits factored in. And also, the truth was that, if you could do without those charming little irregularities that characterized handmade products, robots were far better craftsmen than people. A computerized weld tip could hit the same location time after time; a worker might be off a millimeter. Nor could a human lay down a bead of adhesive around a windshield at sixty-seven jobs an hour with the same uniformity as a machine. So, you might say it was more the *idea* of craftsmanship.

Landgraff didn't know it at the time, and he wouldn't have cared, but that little trip in the Camry was going to cost Ford a half billion dollars.

UNTIL THAT RIDE, the DN101 team had set its sights on the Honda Accord as the car to clobber. At that very moment, Landgraff was preparing a $1.6 billion budget for the bold new Taurus exterior, an all-new interior, and nifty features and structural upgrades that would make the Accord, by comparison, seem even more boring than it already was. The engineers were pretty cocky about it. They thought the Accord was good, but it wasn't *that* good. If the Accord was the target, said one, "I guess we can all go home right now."

The Accord was the biggest-selling import, and of course it was also the biggest-selling car in all America. In 1991, it had outrun the Taurus, 399,000 to 299,000. Also, some 60 percent of Taurus sales were to fleets, but just 40 percent of the Accord's. Fleet sales counted in the total roundup, but they were not as profitable as retail sales, and therefore they were less desirable and they also carried less status. Selling to a fleet was not as fulfilling as selling to a retail customer armed with *Consumer Reports*.

Cars were segregated according to size, ranging from the smallest subcompact "A" car up to the big-boat luxury "F"s like the Lincoln Town Car. Both the Taurus and the Accord were in the fiercely competitive "D" class of cars, along with the Sable, slugging it out with the Toyota Camry, the Chevrolet Lumina, the Nissan Maxima, and some twenty other models. The Chrysler Intrepid would likely join them once it went on sale. In 1991 one in four American car buyers chose a D-sized car.

Between 1980 and 1990, Ford's share of the segment had risen from 11 percent to 22 percent, largely on the strength of combined Taurus and Sable sales. But the Accord alone had a 22 percent share. And Japanese imports as a whole had risen from 17 percent to 30 percent. Chrysler's share had gone from 8 percent to 9 percent; the Europeans declined from 6 percent to 4 percent.

Ford's increase came largely at the expense of General Motors, whose D-class share declined from 57 percent to 35 percent. The market analysts believed Ford had just about exhausted the pool of disgruntled GM owners. The remainder were likely GM diehards or buyers who would switch directly to imports without stopping by their local Ford dealership. Only by going after import buyers could Ford increase its market share.

From a marketing standpoint, Accord buyers outclassed Taurus buyers by almost any measure. They were younger, with a median age of forty-two, compared to the Taurus median age of fifty-one. They were richer, with a median income of $52,000 a year, compared to the Taurus, $44,000. They were better educated, 60 percent having finished college against 50 percent for Taurus. Fifty-nine percent worked in managerial, professional, or technical occupations, compared to 44 percent for the Taurus. Not only were Accord owners younger, richer, and smarter, they were more loyal, returning again and again to buy Accords. Even though Tauruses cost less, Accord buyers seldom bothered to check them out. Or they did so only to review their shortcomings to confirm that they had made a wise decision.

Buyers' number-one reason for choosing the Accord was that it held its value; after four years, it retained 55 percent of its purchase price, compared to 42 percent for the Taurus. Next came its superior quality, its durability and reliability, and its quietness. Taurus buyers did not primarily equate their car with value, or with quality, or with reliability, or with quiet. Space, yes. Space was the Taurus's big selling point. Its buyers were almost equally attracted by its trunk volume and its seating capacity—it was one of the few cars where people could sit three abreast both fore and aft. Next came interior spaciousness. Fourth on the list was safety.

The sales data did not give the full picture. The Accord was a phenomenon: a yuppie cult car. Ford was no stranger to car cults. Even now, an embryonic group of fans was coalescing around the Taurus SHO, a high-performance sedan with a 24-valve, V-6 engine made by Yamaha. An SHO devotee in Atlanta had started a magazine and an annual convention. The Ford Mustang, of course, had a formidable following. The Mustang Club of America claimed 110 chapters. Five magazines were dedicated to Mustang. And some thirty businesses did nothing but supply parts to Mustang owners.

A sensible sedan did not normally inspire such passion. But the Accord was different. An Accord owner talked about his car as if it were a longtime family retainer. His mother had bought one, driven it for several years, given it to a daughter-in-law, it had 200,000 miles, had never been repaired, and it was still running great. A married couple had bought one when the husband got his promotion, they'd driven it to Alaska and back, now they owned two, and their teenager was on the threshold of inheriting the first. All they'd done was change the oil.

The Accord had barely altered its basic box shape for years, but buyers still said it was a styling leader. It was the car they recommended to their best friend or their kid's coach. Whereas owners of Tauruses, according to an internal marketing study, didn't have the confidence to suggest that others purchase one as well, no matter how satisfied they themselves were. You didn't want your best friend or kid's coach to blame you for some wretched squeak or leak.

Steve Kozak, the leader of the DN101 sheet-metal team, had a younger brother who was a Honda salesman for several years. "It was the easiest job he'd ever had. The people who bought Hondas came in . . . and bought Hondas.

" 'I want a Honda.'

" 'What color do you want?' And that's all he did. . . ."

Kozak's uncle had switched from Chevys to Hondas. Kozak was dumbfounded by the change in the man afterwards. He had abused his Chevys horribly. "He had a Chevy and he'd drive that thing into the ground. Then he'd buy another Chevy—he was a Chevy buyer, he'd drive them into the ground, he just pissed all over cars. . . . He'd never change the oil." Kozak mimicked his uncle's annoying voice: " 'You know when I'd change the oil? When I needed a quart, I'd put a quart in.' That's how he took care of his American cars. Okay? He bought a Honda. I was sitting there talking to him one day, he said, 'I took my car in, got the annual checkup, cost me 300 bucks.'

" 'Yeah, what did they do?'

" 'They looked it over from top to bottom.'

"I say, 'What are you talking about? You paid 300 bucks to have your car . . . ?'

" 'Oh, yeah,' he says, 'it's part of the service thing that they have, they schedule you for this thing, and then they go in and they just fix the car all up for you and make sure everything's right.'

"I said, 'Excuse me . . .'

"He said, 'Oh, yeah, and I been changing the oil every 4,000 miles.'

"He's owned three Hondas now. That's all he buys is Hondas. He won't buy anything but Hondas. . . . It's a different whole mindset these people have. . . . It's almost like a born-again Christian kind of thing."

Car thieves preferred the Accord. It was popular even among people who worked for the government, who might be expected to have a little more loyalty to the American economy than the average corporate supply-sider. But no. Some 53 percent of Washington-area drivers owned imports, according to a *Washington Post* survey. *Post* automotive writer Warren Brown saw so many Accords that he had a name for the craze: "the Crete, Nebraska, syndrome."

"You grow up in Crete, Nebraska, go to the local high school, the state college, you have an affection for school colors, but you also make the honor roll; you're president of the student government. You want to explore the world, you end up in Washington, on Capitol Hill. You've driven a Ford or a Chevy all your life. It's gotten you everywhere you want to go. But now your Chevy no longer suffices. You can't afford a BMW, but you want a car that is smart, that says you are smart. You look around the parking lot, all you see are Hondas, Toyotas." So you buy one.

The Accord owner, on the subject of buying imports, could be dangerous, sarcastic even, attacking American carmakers for the shabby workmanship which had forced him or her to purchase an import. Employing a twisted form of logic, the Accord owner might say that buying an Accord was patriotic, because the increased competition from Japan forced Detroit to improve its product. "I wanted to buy a domestic car but . . ."

But what to do when the Honda broke down? If you owned an Accord, if you were so smart and your car so good, what was it doing at the dealership with a crappy alternator? Everybody you knew was happy with their Accords. How could you have been so stupid as to buy the *one* bad Accord that Honda ever made? And by the way, those Honda repairs could be *very* expensive. So you didn't necessarily tell anyone if your Accord was giving you problems. Or else you shouldered the blame. There was only one reason that something could go wrong with an Accord, and that was neglect—the owner's failure, *your* failure as a mere mortal, to maintain it properly.

Sometimes Warren Brown got calls from worried Honda owners. They spoke in a confessional whisper. "Has anyone complained to you about a shimmy in the front end?"

"Yeah, I've had a couple calls."

And the caller would heave a sigh of relief. A sigh that said, "I am not alone." It was kind of like Accords Anonymous.

But weren't these people right, after all? Why should a smart person spend money on a car that did not hold its value, was not reliable, and did not last? Everybody knew the jokes. Ford: Fix Or Repair Daily. Ford: Found On the Road Dead. In 1991, owners of 1988 Tauruses and Sables reported 3,740 "things gone wrong"; 1988 Accord owners, only 2,433. Seventy-four percent of Taurus owners said they were satisfied; 93 percent of Accord owners.

You couldn't blow these people out of their Accords with an H-bomb, their hands were, like, riveted to the steering wheel. But forget the Accord, Dick Landgraff was thinking to himself as he drove the Camry. Now there was a Japanese car that was even better. Holy-moly! Was Ford in trouble, or what?

Just two weeks after Landgraff drove the Camry, the product planning committee, composed of the twenty top executives of the company, approved the $1.6 billion Accord-beater budget for the new Taurus. All the while he was making his presentation, Landgraff kept thinking about the Camry. They had targeted the *wrong car*. He considered that old business saying that you can go out of business two ways, by spending too much or too little. They were spending $1.6 billion. That was a lot of money, but it was not enough to be better than second best.

O T H E R   D N 1 0 1   M A N A G E R S impatiently waited their turn in Camry drive rotation. There was a delay of several days when George Evalt, the powertrain guy, drove the car home and a neighbor's kid ran into it on his bicycle. The kid was okay but his parents sued. However brief his stewardship of the Camry, it was enough to impress Evalt with its powertrain, especially the transmission. The shifts were so smooth they were barely perceptible. The V-6 engine was astonishingly quiet.

Because engines took even longer to develop than the car itself, what could be done to improve the DN101 powertrain was limited. The decision to use a carryover V-6 engine in the base model Taurus had been made long ago, largely for financial reasons; the two new engines—a three-liter, four-valve engine for the more expensive high-series car and a V-8 Yamaha engine for the SHO—were in the final stages of development. The DN101 base engine was a reliable, hard worker. The two new engines were extremely promising. The Camry engine didn't seem to pose a threat, if they could match its noise levels. It was a different story with the transmissions.

Engines, with their roughly 300 parts, were complicated, but the transmission, with 700, made them look simple. Evalt didn't really understand how transmissions worked, but neither did anyone else. There was a trans guy on the DN101 team, Tom Cranston, but even he didn't know everything. He was a gear train expert. "Don't ask me any specifics in the valve body." Shift quality was so sensitive that changing an orifice from the diameter of a toothpick to that of a coffee stirrer could make all the difference. "You don't want to know how sausages are made or transmissions work," said a sign above Cranston's desk.

As recently as twenty years earlier, transmissions were no better than the rest of the parts in the clunky little shoeboxes Japan shipped to America.

Ford had actually formed a joint partnership with Jatco, a Japanese firm, to teach them a few things. Now Japanese transmissions were the best in the business. Angelo Guido, who had worked on the first Taurus transmission and was a manager on the DN101 program, thought their elegant designs reflected a different thought process. He was struck by the language in Japanese technical publications. They used "pleasant," even "gentle," to characterize shifts, words that suggested they had a vision of a driver whom they wanted to please. Americans spoke of shifts as "smooth," which was cooler, more distant. Maybe he was reading too much into it, but he wondered if they had managed to translate this sensitivity to people into the performance of the whirring, turning disks that propelled the car forward.

The low-series Taurus was using the AX4S transmission that Guido had helped develop ten years ago. The "S" stood for synchronous shifting, which one transmission text explained with a comparison to a relay race using sacks of potatoes. The arriving runner handed the sack to the next runner, who had to adjust to its weight and take off. In a synchronous transmission, gear sets could engage only when one was moving and the other was not. The Camry transmission used nonsynchronous shifting, where both parts were in motion. The result was a faster, smoother shift. The crazy thing was that GM had the technique long before the Japanese and abandoned it.

Ford was now making a transmission that employed the technique in two downshifts and an upshift, the AX4N, which was teamed with the new modular four-valve engine going into the high-series Taurus and Sable. But it was not as good as Camry's. Altering a transmission-shift strategy was like a major revision to a crossword puzzle. Change one entry and everything around it would have to change. At this late date, the DN101 powertrain was locked in. It could be fine-tuned, but not modified.

Following Evalt's mishap, the Camry was down again, this time for a month, after some of the chassis engineers accidentally ripped out a wire buried deep within a harness while doing a test on the accelerator mechanism. They didn't know how to fix it because they didn't have a service manual, and the Toyota dealer wasn't very cooperative.

Nevertheless, as everyone eventually drove the car, they had similar reactions. The Camry was superb. It was almost frightening, Tom Moran said, "to think they could make a car that good." Moran was in charge of the development engineers, who were waiting for prototypes to drive and test.

Ben Lever, Landgraff's boss, glimpsed his first 1992 Camry on a lift at a Lincoln-Mercury dealership in Seekonk, Massachusetts, just outside of Providence. The dealer he was visiting, Bob Tasca, had borrowed it from a friend who sold Toyotas. Tasca occupied a position of rare influence at Ford. By virtue of his high sales volume and customer satisfaction ratings through the years, Tasca had become a company insider, a man whom Henry Ford II, every subsequent CEO, and many vice-presidents had consulted at one time or another. Tasca often visited Dearborn to see his pals in high places and drive the latest crop of prototypes. On one occasion when the original Taurus was under development, Tasca turned up with a crude sound meter and used its readings to critique the car's noise levels. Lew Veraldi banished Tasca from the program with a blast of his famous temper. After "Red" Poling asked what had happened, Tasca was reinstated.

Tasca still had a sound meter. He placed it in the back seat area as he and Lever set out for a ride in the Camry. They circled around a golf course, then headed out onto an interstate highway. Then they drove a Sable. The sound meter simply confirmed what their ears told them: the Camry was quieter in every way.

L ANDGRAFF HAD DECIDED that Ford had to either challenge Toyota or throw in the towel. How long could you go on being second best? At this very moment, the guys doing the new Lincoln Mark VIII, Ford's luxury coupe, planned to match Cadillac. Cadillac! It had about as much future in the market as a hearse. You could be sure the Japanese didn't get where they were by planning to be second best or by following General Motors. Toyota said it planned to be the dominant manufacturing company by the year 2000. Toyota planned to rule the world.

Sometimes he wondered how it happened. "Did Toyoda, the guy who runs the company's name is Toyoda, did he suddenly have the idea one day? Did it bubble up from the bottom? Bubble down from the top? Did it have—you know the Japanese—consensus? It's overblown, it isn't quite as consensus-oriented management as you might think—but did they consense on this over twenty years? I don't know how they did it. They somehow said, 'We're going to be the best.' And that's how they build cars like the Camry.

"It's very difficult in this business, and I suppose in a lot of businesses, to try to be the best. Because to be the best means you have to spend more, you have to work harder, and you have to have some vision. And those things are not in abundance in any company as far as I can see."

At Ford, Landgraff knew he was considered an outsider, a maverick. He tended to say what was on his mind and do as he saw fit. He believed that it was best not to ask permission for what you had in mind. That only led to questions and delays. Just do it, until someone told you not to. So after his drive in the Camry, he had quietly ordered the DN101 engineers to compare it to the Taurus, chunk by chunk. Who had what, and what it cost.

Where Taurus was as good or better; where the Camry had the edge. What it would take to match Toyota.

As soon as another Camry was available, the team dispatched it to the Teardown Center in the body engineering building, where cars were painstakingly disassembled and their parts, including the tiniest screws, bolts, and brackets, were mounted in grids on white 4-by-8-foot wooden panels suspended from an overhead track. You could slide them back and forth, as if you were standing inside a giant file drawer. DN101 engineers went over to examine the splayed-out Camry innards, which had been methodically labeled, weighed, and evaluated for cost. The boards told them several things. Camry engineers had gone to extraordinary pains in the design of every component. Moreover, some parts were identical to those in the Lexus, Toyota's luxury car off the same platform. That kind of quality didn't come cheap. Toyota had spent maybe $1,000 per car more than the amount budgeted for Taurus.

Word of the comparision got back to the finance management through its appointees to the team—finance people all talked to each other—and Landgraff heard *sotto voce* criticism that he had embarked on what appeared to be a risky course. But no one tried to stop him.

One night he sat down to write the DN101 mission statement. Yes, it was wrong, the mission statement was supposed to be a team effort; the boss was not supposed to sit down and write it all by himself. In fact, Landgraff had given the planners the assignment, but he didn't take the time to explain what it was he wanted, and they produced several pages of bullshit that didn't really say anything. One of the problems at Ford, one of the *many* problems at Ford, was that people were afraid to be specific, to make commitments, because they might get nailed if things went awry. So he sat down one night and wrote it himself.

The DN101 team, Landgraff wrote, would "Deliver a Product Competitive with the Japanese on Quality and Function and Better in Styling, Features and Value."

Then Landgraff added two words at the bottom: "Beat Camry."

I N M A Y, L A N D G R A F F was scheduled to go before the executive-level product planning committee to request the first chunk of funds to pay for DN101 tooling and plant renovation. The point in time when the top guys were asked to spend money was when they got really interested in what was happening in the program. And that was when Landgraff would tell them what Ford needed to do.

FOUR

Chrysler Steals
the Show

T HE STUDIO'S Christmas
breakthrough was somewhat tempered by the debut at the North American
International Auto Show—better known as the Detroit Auto Show—of the
1992 Intrepid, a member of Chrysler's new LH line. Chrysler hadn't had a
big hit since its minivan, and people joked that LH stood for "Last Hope."
Not to worry. The Intrepid was a winner. As expected, it was long, almost
202 inches. And it had the same low-slung profile as the Taurus clays. But
the Intrepid was glass and steel. The Intrepid was now, the next-generation
Taurus was three years away. And the expression Chrysler used to describe a
shape that featured a longer, more sharply angled windshield, a shorter
hood, and an expanded wheelbase? *Cab forward.*

How was it that designers at different companies so often had the same
ideas? The public thought it was industrial espionage. But there was so much
information around that nobody really needed cloak-and-dagger operatives.
The concept cars that car companies so proudly displayed at auto shows
offered credible clues to what was going on in their design studios. Japanese

automakers such as Toyota and Honda introduced new models first in Japan, giving U.S. companies a preview of what was headed their way. Spy photographers haunted test sites for shots of prototypes, which they peddled to automotive publications years in advance of a model introduction. Hundreds of suppliers got to see early designs, and some were not beyond sharing them with interested parties. Finally there were raids on each other's staffs. In the 1980s, in particular, a number of well-placed Ford executives and a host of lesser-knowns had trailed Lee Iacocca to Chrysler.

Moreover, designers read the same magazines, talked to the same people, and went to the same shows. They asked the same questions. And they were not difficult questions. What do we do after boxes? How can we go more aero? So, was it any surprise they came up with the same answers? Jack Telnack recounted the story told him by a designer who had traveled to some remote corner of Russia. The designer stepped off a train and made his way to a plant so primitive that it had dirt floors and lanterns, like something out of the pages of *Doctor Zhivago*. But on the walls were the flowing sketches typical of car stylists, as up-to-date as anything you could find anywhere. Telnack imagined that you could shut a designer up in a cave and he'd somehow find out what was going on. It was as if the stuff was in the ether.

That said, there were those who said Chrysler had swiped the design for the LH cars from Ford. The first time he saw an LH spy shot in a car magazine, Dennis Wingfield, a DN101 engineer who worked on the engine compartment, blew it up on a copier and measured some of the key dimensions—the angle of the windshield, the wheelbase, the height. Bingo. Not only had he seen a car like this before, he had worked on it at Ford until very recently.

Code named D-FC55, the car was to have been a family sedan for the nineties, marketed in Australia, Europe, and the United States. "D-F" meant it spanned the large "D"-, "E"-, and "F"-sized cars, from Taurus to the Lincoln Continental. The "C" in the D-FC55 code name stood for "Concept," and "55" denoted its place in a sequential order. Had it followed its initial schedule, D-FC55 would have been out before the Intrepid.

Wingfield had started on the top secret D-FC55 way back in 1985 when he was based in the Ford Scientific Laboratories. Ford had a number of what were called advanced engineering offices, but the Sci Lab was the most advanced of all. There were people there who wore white coats and drank coffee from beakers. It was nicknamed "Sky Lab."

Wingfield had already worked on several vehicles that Ford had shelved, including a little two-seater commuter car called the Optim. When the Honda CRX debuted, Wingfield couldn't believe it. His first thought was that somehow Honda had snuck into the Sci Lab and got photos of the

Optim styling clay. It was that close in looks, just a little bigger. The thought haunted him: *We could have had it first.*

When in 1987 D–FC55 acquired a program manager with a budget and a staff, Wingfield allowed himself to believe that Ford might actually build this car. The advanced design studio produced first clay and then fiberglass models with raked windshields and short hoods, plus some lumps and bumps, which did well in market research clinics. Wingfield spent most of his time trying to come up with an engine that would fit a drastically smaller engine compartment, while pleasing the three constituencies for whom the car was intended. Australians, a nation of boat and mobile home towers, liked big V-8s and rear-wheel drive. Europeans, who vastly preferred front-wheel drive, needed a narrow turning radius to negotiate their quaint but dinky streets and small engines that consumed minimal amounts of their expensive fuel and met quirky tax laws based on size. Americans, it was now clear from sales of the Taurus, also loved front-wheel drive, but they wanted a V-6 engine and plenty of interior space as well.

With all that was demanded, Wingfield and his colleagues at one point had thirty-seven different powertrain configurations. Not only standard four-, six-, and eight-cylinder engines, but 45-degree V-8s, V-10s, and V-12s. A 15-degree V-6. Four- and five-speed experimental transmissions. Wild and crazy stuff.

In 1989 the project moved to Advanced Vehicle Engineering Technology (AVET) in the Danou Center, a step closer to commercial production. But just a year later, Ford canceled the program for financial reasons. The company was already spending $6 billion on its first global car, the European Mondeo, which was coming to the States as the Contour/Mystique. So it was that D–FC55 died a fiberglass embryo, a crack-up on Ford's highway to the future. It never had a name, never had an engine, never knew the hard road beneath real wheels or the wind across its hood.

No one took the loss harder than Fred Simon, who had been the manager of the ill-fated D–FC55 program for three years, a job that Lew Veraldi had helped him get. Simon knew of course that people at Ford believed Chrysler had somehow learned of their plans, just as it was popularly believed that Lee Iacocca took Ford's minivan project with him when he went to Chrysler. To Simon, however, the essential fact was that Ford in both instances had lost its nerve at the critical go/no-go point.

Premiering at the Detroit Auto Show under the same Cobo Hall roof as the Intrepid was the prosaic 1992 Taurus. Most people didn't even notice the new sheet metal or narrower headlamps that were supposed to give it a slightly more nineties look. Ford's longtime ad agency, J. Walter Thompson, produced commercials showing the 1986 Taurus dissolving into the '92 model, a computerized filmic procedure known as "morphing," suggesting to people who wanted a change that one had taken place and to those who didn't that very little had happened. (When morphing got cheap, politicians used it to turn their opponents from a Dr. Jekyll into a Mr. Hyde.) The timid redesign was not overlooked by the media, however. Many car reviewers wrote of their disappointment, and *Fortune* magazine saluted the '92 makeover on a list of worst business decisions of the year.

Guess which car would get the kudos? Guess which company now would be acclaimed the styling leader? And *cab forward*. Wasn't that Ford's line? In just a few short years, judging by the 1992 Taurus, Ford seemed to have lost its way. If there were a bright side to this unhappy turn of events, it was this: praise for the Intrepid and scorn for the 1992 Taurus would surely soften up any opposition to a dramatic new design for DN101. The 1996 Taurus was fast becoming the company's next, best hope.

C H O O S I N G   T O   R E V E A L a model well in advance of its sale date, as Chrysler had done, was a calculated risk. There was no better venue for national publicity than the Detroit Auto Show, the country's biggest and best. But after the hordes of reporters and photographers had gotten their stories and left, a wave of engineers, planners, and analysts from Detroit's huge automotive infrastructure descended on the new models, to see what the competition was up to. They snapped photographs, poked around engine compartments, and measured parts. They ran magnets over car bodies to determine what was plastic or aluminum and what was steel.

Early one morning, Ed Opaleski headed for downtown Detroit with an assignment to investigate the layout of the Intrepid. He was a DN101 vehicle design supervisor, one of several people responsible for seeing that the 2,000 or so major parts of the car fit together without encroaching on each other's space or performance. In Cobo Hall, he threaded his way among the exhibits to the platform where the 1992 Intrepid was on display. It was surrounded by a Plexiglas barrier to keep people at a distance, particularly people such as himself, a Ford engineer. He took photos of the new Chrysler sedan with a colleague standing next to it; they would use his height as a reference point to calculate the overall dimensions. But the annoying Plexiglas barrier stood in the way of closer inspection.

Still, there was one mystery he might be able to solve—if he could just find the right position. While it was not uncommon to weigh down show cars so they looked sportier and more powerful, the Intrepid was mere inches above the pedestal. The engineers wanted to know its true stance. Back at the Design Center a team of modelers was standing by, waiting for

Intrepid dimensions. Ford wanted an LH to throw into a lineup with proposed Taurus/Sable exterior designs for market research.

Opaleski looked around. He had arrived early, before the crowds. There were no security guards in sight. He didn't want to call attention to what he was about to do, not that he knew of any rule against crawling around a show car on your hands and knees. But he'd rather be discreet. Satisfied the coast was clear, Opaleski climbed onto the pedestal with the Intrepid, then dropped down and began to circle the barrier. The few people present looked with curiosity at the dark-haired guy on his belly, peering up at the car's underside, but no one tried to stop him. Finally he found an angle where he could see into the chassis. It was as he had suspected. There were big metal clamps on the springs holding the car down.

THE STYLISTS HATED market research. Did the Vatican recruit Catholics to review Michelangelo's sketches for the Sistine Chapel? Did Frank Lloyd Wright run his architectural plans by a panel of home buyers? Dick Landgraff was in their court on this one. He thought the pendulum on market research had swung to an extreme. He was delighted to come across a newspaper article that attributed hard times in the fashion industry to overdependence on a handful of influential consultants, who had believed women when they said they wanted nothing but practical work clothes, which of course was not true. They wanted clothes with pizzazz, just as they always had. It would have been preferable, some said, to rely on the instincts of fashion designers. "That's what you've been saying all along," Landgraff told Jack Telnack when he ran into him and Fritz Mayhew, another high-ranking Ford designer. " 'To hell with all that market research.' " According to Landgraff, they said, "Yeah, that's fantastic."

But it didn't matter what Landgraff or even influential designers thought. Ford Motor Company wouldn't so much as mold a button if some focus group somewhere hadn't seen it or touched it. Or if not an official paid focus group, then at least an ad hoc group of Ford employees. Too much was at stake to trust a few individuals. The beauty of market research was that no one who worked for the company had to make a decision. The research could do it for them. In the case of disagreements, research could break the impasse with no bad blood. And if no one made a decision, no one was responsible. Blame it on the research.

The Christmas clays from the studio were good, but not good enough. In February, they flunked a round of market research, their second. If the designs Chicagoans had seen in November were judged too far out, these were too conservative. "The vehicles shown are unlikely to have the same styling impact achieved by the original Taurus and Sable," concluded the subsequent report.

The amazing truth was that Ford never quite understood precisely how or why it had scored with the original Taurus. Kaywin Goodman, a planner under Veraldi, worked afterward on two Taurus successors: the aborted D-FC55 world car and DN101, where he was program manager for a year before Dick Landgraff took over. In each case, Goodwin said, "We were trying to determine what we needed to do for the next-generation Taurus that would have as great an impact as the original Taurus, and the original Taurus was just dumb luck. . . . Excuse me, not dumb luck. It was a lot of hard work. But we happened to hit the marketplace just perfectly with it."

World Class Timing provided for only two market research clinics of the kind DN101 had just flunked. But there was no way the team could go to Theme Decision in April without some positive numbers. The market research department arranged a third clinic in March, composed fifty-fifty of Taurus owners and import owners. Although it would never say so publicly, Ford realized it was probably too late to pry most people out of their Hondas and Camrys. But every year a new crop of buyers went shopping, virgin buyers, their first time in a dealership; used-car buyers now able to afford a new car; buyers trading up; buyers sizing down. Young, rich, educated buyers, import *intenders* who might be persuaded to buy a Taurus or Sable, if they believed the car was good enough.

J. Walter Thompson, Ford's advertising agency, had produced a profile of this target buyer. He was the Varsity Captain and his cheerleader wife. Their names were Dick and Jane.

> The 1995 Taurus buyer and his wife are the heart & soul of middle class America. They live a family-oriented lifestyle and, while not exactly affluent, have an income that can afford a limited set of luxuries. They are people like Dick and Jane, neo-traditionalists who are a little more progressive than most people give them credit for.
>
> Dick's a middle manager who recently got that long-overdue promotion and Jane teaches in a suburban school district. Unlike many of their friends who have given up on marriage, Dick and Jane find themselves increasingly devoted to each other. In a world where people seem confused about the direction they should go, they draw strength from each other, their faith and their kids.
>
> They are the kind of people the neighborhood kids like to talk to about the things they can't seem to talk about with their own parents. There's always a couple of extra kids in the yard who prac-

tically live there. He likes to joke about claiming one of them as a dependent on their income tax form . . . does that kid *even have* a home besides this one?

Sure they considered a mini-van, but they just don't like them. They like cars. They remember the first Taurus and they've seen the new one. And now this is one of the few times he's seen where Detroit actually *improved* on a good idea. . . .

Functional . . . but hip. A family car that's modern and with it. A car they *like* to drive. Hey! Even the kids like it! Win this guy, and the rest will follow.

The Varsity Captain owned a Toyota Corolla. But, the profile said, he and Jane had heard about improved quality among domestic brands. "And, with all the important things being equal, they'd feel better supporting our economy."

It would be easy to make fun of goody-goodies like Dick and Jane. And maybe they were a myth. But they were not just Ford's myth. They were our myth: the typical American family, living the American Dream. We saw them all the time in commercials.

W ITH MARKET RESEARCH, Ford would tailor a car to the Varsity Captains of this world. Ford considered them "progressives." You could almost substitute Californians for progressives: younger, better-educated import buyers with enlightened tastes. People who drank sparkling water and had e-mail addresses. There was another class of buyer known as "conformists." If conformists liked the car now, some three years before introduction, it was the kiss of death. By the time the car came out, it would be sour milk. The trick was to turn on progressives; if conformists were turned off, no big deal. They'd eventually come around.

Ford's conventional market research went like this: You asked people for the reasons why they bought a given car—please check the box marked price, engine size, the number of doors, the dealer's presentation, and so forth. You also asked people what they wanted in their next car. (Check the box marked price, engine size, the number of doors. . . .) You showed them models. You like this grille or that grille? This fabric or that fabric? You added up the yeses, the nos, the maybes, and then you did what the numbers dictated. After the car was for sale, you checked the number of sales to see if you had been right.

But market research was tricky. Beyond the multiple-choice possibilities, the going got rougher. If you weren't careful how you phrased questions, people lied to you. One time Lincoln-Mercury had asked owners of luxury Continentals and Marks if they objected to having them serviced by the same mechanics who worked on humdrum little Mercury Tracers. Oh, no, they said piously, not so long as they were treated fairly when their turn came up. You could almost hear the national anthem in the background. That was the right answer, the democratic answer, but it was bullshit and everybody knew it.

Fred Simon, the program manager for the D-FC55 car program, did not believe that Ford's approach always gave the right answers. In search of a different technique, he had once hired a firm from California, Edwards Associates. Mention the name of Darrel Edwards to the guys in Ford marketing, and eyes would roll.

Edwards had an extensive background in clinical psychology, philosophy, and psycholinguistics. Of mixed Mormon and American Indian parentage, his degrees were from Brigham Young University, a Mormon institution. His Ph.D. research into the methods that smart people used to make decisions had attracted the support of NASA. He had done postdoctoral work at Penn State and the National Naval Medical Center. His bio was strange, but not enough to disqualify him with the Ford MBAs. Then he turned up in person, in rumpled clothes with ties that always seemed too short. The corporate guys wore neatly pressed suits and dress shirts. A chubby, cheery man, Edwards talked about feelings. The analytically trained Ford guys talked about perceptions. He talked about values; they talked about qualitative and quantitative findings. Edwards's woo-woo stuff made them crazy.

Simon was particularly impressed by the work the Edwards firm had done for a bank whose customers said they hated the long lines at tellers' windows. The commonsense solution was to speed up transactions or open more windows. But Edwards discovered that customers wouldn't mind waiting nearly as much if they had a place to sit down, maybe a cup of coffee and a friendly hello from a bank person.

The Edwards interviews for Ford, preserved on videotape, were like nothing the company had done. Long after the D-FC55 had faded from the computer screens at the Danou Technical Center, an unfulfilled blip on the cycle plan, people would remember a 1986 Sable owner from Boston, who wore a black jacket and a white dress shirt without a tie. The camera captured him with one arm thrown across the back of his chair as if he were in someone's living room.

"I get inside," he said in a flat Boston accent, "and I grab the wheel and I look at the cockpit and I think flight and I think pilot—not that women can't be pilots—I guess I think . . . I think this is *grrrrrrrr*—a manly thing to do." The man pawed at the air as if reaching for his steering wheel. "I do grab it kind of like this." To be sure, he confided in a more sober moment, he had bought the Sable only after *Consumer Reports* said it was an okay car, because this was a lot of money to him; he had never before paid five figures.

What the tape didn't reveal was that the man from Boston, who sounded like a car-crazed adolescent, was in fact a rabbi. The questions of his artful interrogator had triggered a riptide of emotion, tugging him back through oceans of time, swamping whatever rabbinical decorum he might have had. He said he was getting older but feeling younger. That he thought of the family Sable as his own private sports car. The car gave him a feeling of "pep and liveliness." It "wakes me up when I get in it." And also, he said, "there's a lot of things to do in there." The radio? The air conditioner? The power windows? What *was* the rabbi talking about?

A beefy Taurus owner in a shiny orange jacket reported that "everything on the road out there looks like a damn shoebox that somebody stepped on the front edge of." That is, until "Ford came along with a brand new look that looked like it was going 40 miles per hour when it was standing still." Relaxed, picking at his nails, the man confided that buying the car gave him "the feeling of winning . . . I won this one round with the car people."

Said another Taurus owner, "They thought enough of me, they thought enough of the customer to put in things they didn't have to put in, to help make the sale of the car."

It was clear: People were crazy about cars that made them feel sexy or loved. They loved the Taurus's sleek, head-turning looks. They also praised the friendly little features that Veraldi & Company had installed. The trunk had a cargo net to hold grocery bags in place. The sunvisor consisted of two parts that separated, so the top one could be pulled to the side window to block sun coming in; an adjustment bar under each front seat replaced a hard-to-find handle. It was kind of amazing that a woman would spend $12,000, the price back then, because the car had a cargo net that cost a few bucks that kept bags from toppling over so that oranges didn't roll all over the trunk, or that the seat bar and dual sunvisor drew more buyers than the quadra-link suspension, but it appeared that just might be true. After all, every car had a suspension. Through some crazy kind of karma—or was it Lew Veraldi himself?—Taurus had found the G-spot in the car market.

Except for some incidental work on electric cars, Ford never used Darrel Edwards again. The marketing division failed to see how this kind of research was relevant. But Fred Simon sometimes thought that if Edwards had been 100 pounds lighter, wore a pinstriped suit, and used more jargon, he might have found a niche at Ford.

ON MARCH 14 AND 15, the DN101 clan gathered in the Design Center showroom for what everyone hoped would be the penultimate round of market research. Doug Gaffka was exhausted. He felt like designing the car was secondary to inventing new clays to show focus groups. This time they had three new clays with a mixture of front ends and body sides. Each was designated by a letter between "L" and "S."

They also wanted reaction to the Chrysler Intrepid, which was not yet on sale. Within weeks after engineers produced dimensions from the auto show, the modelers had clayed up a car, coated it with plastic wrap, and painted it. These guys were good. If you didn't get close enough to see that the interior was only roughed out, it looked like the real thing. The model had cost $200,000, ten times what the car itself would sell for, but they didn't have time to wait. The stakes were too high.

All the models on display had received the same treatment as the LH. Called "glamour clays," they looked real. The 1992 Taurus and Camry were also on hand for reference.

Over two days, 173 owners of D-class cars filed into the Design Center to look at models and fill out questionnaires. Fifty-four percent drove either Accords or Camrys; the rest were Taurus owners, divided into over-fifty and under-fifty groups.

The two-day session concluded with three focus groups. These were people who might never again have the opportunity to tell Detroit what to do. They took their assignment very seriously. Hanging on their every observation were three dozen engineers, planners, and executives, arrayed at three long tables behind them. Alex Trotman did not often attend market research clinics, but he stopped at this one with his wife, en route to another function; the Taurus was that important to North American Automotive Operations. Sitting next to Dick Landgraff, Trotman sipped a Diet Coke and took copious notes.

A woman who tended "to back into things" worried about a rear bumper that protruded like the lip of a pouting child. A man wondered if so much glass would heat up the car like a greenhouse. A woman whose family owned three Accords and a Civic thought there was just *too* much window glass and maybe they could lop off the little one in the rear of one of the models. To one, the trunk looked too small, like some kind of add-on, some kind of *fake trunk*. To another, there was something "squishy" about the front and rear ends.

No single model had won their hearts. The final report read like a Chinese menu. People liked the front end from model "S," the rear end of "R," the bodyside of "L." But in what they liked, there was a future Taurus, one with limpid, oval eyes, a perky tail end, and a sporty S-shaped shoulder, with enough positive attributes left over to craft a Sable. The team was happy at last.

Another good sign was that fans of the Intrepid turned out to be Taurus owners who were even older, less educated, and farther down the economic scale than the average Taurus owner. On the spectrum, these were conformists. Soon, Ford believed, their opinions would be dated. It was okay if they preferred today's Chrysler to tomorrow's Taurus.

FIVE

The Bosses Say Yes

T HE NIGHT BEFORE Theme Decision, David Rees stayed up making notes, his head full of designer talk. The models the studio would present the next day in the Design Center showroom were so stunning. The new Taurus, with its *sporty, youthful design . . . how they had really stretched in an effort to re-create what we did with the original Taurus . . . looks like it is moving even when standing still . . . sculpted surfaces . . . elliptical shapes . . . no hard edges . . . tautness in design.*

And the Sable they had developed: *aimed at a different buyer . . . more dramatic . . . opulent . . . teardrop rear end . . . amazingly, they share the same door panels, while still achieving maximum definition.*

Unable to contain himself when he greeted Harold A. Poling, Rees told the chairman that he had been up all night and why, and then he immediately regretted it. Rees was the ranking designer on the Taurus program and its spokesman here. Couldn't he have thought of anything more dignified to tell the boss of bosses? And what did the chairman care anyway how he had spent the night? "Well, good for you," Poling said, or words to that effect.

The four top executives of Ford Motor Company, reconstituted as the design committee, took their seats on a platform. In addition to Poling and

Telnack, there were Philip E. Benton, Jr., president and chief operating officer, and executive vice-president Allan D. Gilmour. Alex Trotman was not an official member, but he was there as well to represent North American Automotive Operations, along with Ken Kohrs, vice-president for car product development.

The executives pretty much knew what they were going to see. The last thing you did to Ford management was surprise them. Ford management did not like surprises. Last month, this very group had reviewed the models that were used in the market research. They knew the studio planned to pull the Coke bottle bodyside from one model and mate it to the front end of another. Theme Decision would merely ratify this and other changes.

There was also a spiffy new station wagon in the lineup, thanks to Alex Trotman. To save money, Ford originally had planned to combine a redesigned front end with the boxy back end that was on the outgoing wagon. It wasn't the greatest-looking shape, but the stylists said they could make it presentable. Then Trotman had reviewed the station wagon model. He thought the back end looked like a refrigerator. "Why are you doing *that*?" he asked Landgraff.

Landgraff took in the wagon as if seeing it with new eyes. Damn, it *did* look like a refrigerator. He was suddenly slightly embarrassed, not a feeling he was used to. How could they have been so dumb? He explained about the financial constraints. He was grateful when Ken Kohrs, the vice-president in charge of car product development, backed him up.

"Change it," Trotman said.

Trotman's edict had produced one of those synergistic creative moments that designers found so exhilarating. David Rees, John Doughty, Doug Gaffka, and Fritz Mayhew all pitched in, swapping ideas and taping new lines on the old clay to rough out a design. In a matter of hours, they had a rounded rear end and an oval rear window that echoed the elliptical theme of the sedan. True to form, the engineers wished the stylists had been more creative a little sooner. The station wagon was going to throw a wrench in World Class Timing, not to mention require an enormous additional investment.

Every care had been taken to anticipate problems at Theme Decision. Landgraff had already briefed Poling on the trunk. Taurus buyers loved the 18-cubic-foot trunk, one of the biggest in the industry and bigger than the Accord by 3.6 cubic feet. And so did Poling, an avid golfer, who thought a car that held four people should also hold four golf bags. If you asked DN101 team members what the chairman cared about, they would first answer costs, and then golf. He was widely believed to have said he would veto any Taurus design that had a smaller trunk.

But the old Taurus had a big, squared-off rear end, and the new Taurus design that had scored so well in market research had one that tucked in, with a downward sloping trunk lid and rear quarter panels that swooped inward. Bottom line: its trunk was only 16 cubic feet.

Landgraff had broken the news to Poling at a previous meeting. "Red will never buy a smaller trunk," the senior guys told him as they gathered nervously for a review. Landgraff ran down the dimensions for the CEO. When he came to the trunk, Landgraff noted that they had lowered the rear opening to make it easier to lift things over and in. They were strongly considering rear seats that would fold down, so that long objects like skis or planks could extend into the interior. Poling didn't utter a peep. Ben Lever, Landgraff's boss, was impressed. He and Landgraff were not especially close, but this time Landgraff had earned his respect. "You could sell refrigerators to Eskimos," Lever told him. Or maybe he said ice. It was one of those expressions.

FRITZ MAYHEW, WHO ranked just under Jack Telnack in the Design Center hierarchy, offered a greeting to the executives. Flashing a nervous smile, he asked for their indulgence. Rees knew that Mayhew had confidence in the designs. It was the show ahead that had him on edge. Usually at Theme Decision the big shots walked in, sat down, listened to some remarks, and looked at spinning cars. Then they would offer their comments. This time, Rees and Doughty had decided to offer a presentation with something more, something worthy, something with smoke and mirrors.

The lights dimmed. Pulsating, New Agey music filled the showroom. The curtains parted to reveal a Taurus model, a Sable model, and a station wagon. Smoke engulfed their bodies and colored laser beams swept across the shiny surfaces. It was the kind of spectacle you might expect Ford sales to throw for a bunch of dealers, but it was a radical departure for the dignified Design Center.

Dick Landgraff, who was there to describe business implications of the design, shot a glance at Poling. The chairman and chief executive officer of Ford Motor Company was a finance guy with a calculator for a brain. If Landgraff was any judge of body language, Poling's stiff posture and frozen features suggested he was toting up the cost of this razzamatazz. Landgraff himself would have preferred the usual straightforward presentation. After all, it wasn't like they had to snow anybody. They were all Ford people, and this was internal business. But, hey, they were a team. This was how he saw it: if it made the designers feel good, why not?

Other than that, things went well. The executives made a few remarks. Landgraff took notes. "Rear bumper 'sags' on wagon." "Widen Taurus rear lamps to avoid 'pinched' look, i.e., carry lamps more into quarters." "HAP continues to be concerned about trunk volume." Nothing major. They were home free.

Now Landgraff could concentrate on his campaign to storm next month's meeting of the product planning committee, which was composed of most of the same executives who had been at Theme Decision and then some. If Theme Decision was a studio event, this meeting for long lead funding was the program manager's showcase.

The DN101 engineers were completing their analysis of the Camry and what it would take to match it. It would take, among other things, a split fold-down rear seat with rear folding armrest that would cost an additional $72, better seat fabric and construction ($33), stronger door hinges ($8), a new turbine fuel pump ($6). In all, it would take $255 in upgrades. By the time Landgraff tacked on other odds and ends, the variable cost of each car had risen to $790 over the old Taurus, twice as much as planned. And the investment kept on climbing.

For each car, the price would have to go up and the profit would have to shrink. This was not something Red Poling wanted to hear. People told Landgraff he was nuts. He would never be able to sell management on the higher prices and lower profits. Landgraff knew that, but he also knew that Poling would give him a fair hearing. And he had a plan that he thought would win over the CEO. Landgraff was, after all, a finance guy.

The program manager concocted a formula to save money by extending the shelf life of the Taurus from four years to more than five. Development costs were thus spread out over a longer period. Then he reduced what were called marketing costs—the rebates and dealer incentives Ford had to pile on its cars to keep them moving. The Japanese didn't spend as much as U.S. companies because they could sell their cars without them. Landgraff would argue that with the upgrades the new Taurus, too, would require fewer discounts. By the time Landgraff economized on a couple of teeny-weeny environmental programs that no one would ever notice, and were voluntary anyway, and threw in some other savings, he came up with a $75 million profit increase over the most recent budget projection in October. This was great, this was magic! They would spend more and make more.

Yes, but everything hinged on building a car as good as he said. What if Ford couldn't do it? He knew there were people in the company who believed Ford engineers were hopeless laggards compared to their Japanese counterparts. He believed Ford's people were every bit as good. The team already had crude prototypes that reflected major improvements in wind noise, handling, and vibration. As part of his lobbying campaign Landgraff set up a day at the track for the product planning committee; if they drove the prototypes, they could not help but see how much better they were than the old Taurus. He also arranged a show-and-tell in the teardown room, where engineers would explain what they would do to match Camry. There was nothing like being able to see the physical contrast between a cheap Ford part and an expensive Camry part. On the day the committee visited, the teardown room looked especially nice, having been repainted top to bottom by body engineering in preparation for the dignitaries. Alex Trotman made some joke to Landgraff about whether that was what they paid people to do. Had Poling known, he might have been annoyed at the unnecessary expense.

THE PRODUCT PLANNING COMMITTEE customarily met in the paneled boardroom on the twelfth floor of World Headquarters around a huge, handsome expanse of wood. It was the same room where the Ford family, the founder's descendants, gathered for their annual briefings by the CEO after a day at the track. Having been to a lot of these high-level sessions, what Landgraff hoped would follow his presentation was a moment of total quiet. Poling would say, "Any objections?" And then . . . total quiet. When you got questions, you got problems. Silence was the mark of a successful meeting. To that end, he had to reassure several dozen departments in advance that their concerns about upgrading the Taurus would be addressed. Public Affairs was worried that not enough attention was being paid to the Chrysler LH cars. The corporate quality office wanted Things Gone Wrong targets for cars in service three years extended to four years, a stronger standard. As Landgraff circulated his proposal for comments, he knew his campaign was becoming the talk of the powerful twelfth floor.

By the day of the meeting, Landgraff had a go-ahead from North American Automotive Operations, Alex Trotman's operation, which had responsibility for domestic vehicles. All the corporate staff offices supported the plan, including marketing, the one that mattered most. Bottom line: They didn't want to sell an inferior car any more than they wanted to produce one.

Landgraff began with slides of the new designs approved by some of these same executives at Theme Decision the month before. He used some of the designer language: The Taurus, *very distinctive, sporty, aerodynamic, and well proportioned.* The Sable, *will be perceived as stylish and advanced.*

He pointed out the sharp decline since 1980 in GM's mid-sized car sales, from 57 percent to 29 percent. "The lesson is that old loyalties are dying and significant share gains will accrue to those having a competitive advantage." He mentioned a recent survey of import owners who said they believed the Taurus should be priced as much as $2,000 less than the Camry because of its lesser quality and lower resale value. $2,000! It was an astonishing figure. It meant that a customer wouldn't buy a Taurus unless it cost $2,000 less than a comparable Camry. Looking at it the other way, Toyota could net $2,000 more per car than Ford. The only way to compete in the long term was with a Taurus so good that people would pay as much as a Camry cost. Ford wouldn't need discounts or rebates. And then Landgraff reviewed his proposition for matching Camry features and craftsmanship by spending nearly $800 more per car than the old Taurus and investing an additional $700 million. He concluded with the $75 million bonanza in profits.

As he spoke, Landgraff kept glancing at Poling. This was going better than he had dared to hope. Along the way there were scattered comments, but no protests. Nobody said "What a dumb idea." But of course nobody said "What a great idea" either. These people didn't go out of their way to pat anybody on the back.

At the very end, after formal approval, Poling added, "Now you'll have no excuses." This was a typical closing statement, like a coach saying, "Go get 'em." Only not quite as upbeat. Poling's voice was pleasant enough, but still it sounded threatening.

The remark didn't bother Landgraff. He didn't plan to make excuses. As he left the meeting with George Bell and two other DN101 managers, he silently congratulated himself. "My God, you sold it."

For the team, the Camry upgrades were a good news/bad news development. The good news was that they were getting more money and the chance to create a truly superior car. The bad news was that it meant more work, and no additional time to do it. Because of changes to the station wagon, they already had been forced to seek a two-month delay in the Job One date, now scheduled for April 1995. The World Class Timing clock was ticking.

That May marked the first anniversary of the team. People were beginning to form friendships and alliances that cut across department lines: engineers and planners, planners and finance guys. Personnel manager Wendy Dendel was pleased to see that rank seemed to matter less and less. In the beginning, when they all landed together in the basement and the converted studio overhead, no one knew anybody's grade. So people were cautious and respectful of each other. You didn't want to offend somebody higher up in the organization. Then, as they got to know each other, the sixes, sevens, and eights bonded with each other, likewise the nines and tens. In the past it would have been unheard of for a seven to tell a ten he ought to do something. But she had seen it happen here. She thought it was because of the signals Landgraff sent. All that mattered to him was what you knew and what you produced. Casual days didn't hurt either; they made it more difficult to tell who the bosses were. And they saved on dry cleaning.

As they got to know the boss, people had mixed feelings. In an era of empowerment, Dick Landgraff was an unreconstructed micro-manager. He relied heavily on his chief engineer, George Bell, for technical decisions, but he made the final calls. In Bell's last position, the program manager hadn't bothered with changes to the car under 25 cents in variable cost or over $50,000 in investment. But Landgraff insisted on approving them all, every penny. When the chief engineer ran things in his absence, Landgraff redid his paperwork. When the planners wrote papers, Landgraff rewrote them.

The Camry commitment was evidence that he would do what was right for the car. "I would do anything for Dick," said Steve Kozak, the head of the sheet-metal team. Finance manager Tom Gorman called his leadership "heroic." But many were less convinced of his commitment to the team itself. Suffice it to say that Landgraff did not have a reputation as a "people person." As the troops saw it, he might fight for the car, but not necessarily for promotions or justice or a better environment for the people who worked on it. The common wisdom among team members was that Landgraff had gone about as far as he would go at Ford. The same outspokenness and refusal to play politics they so admired had likely cost him further advancement. He was known to make intemperate remarks about this boss and that one. At a meeting where Kozak heard Landgraff challenge Alex Trotman, "I thought he was committing political suicide."

Some team members who had been on road trips with Landgraff reported that at the end of the day, over dinner and a couple of beers, he turned into a regular guy, full of funny stories from his years at Ford. But most people never glimpsed that side of the boss. To them, he was a mystery man—all business, the car his only priority. They wondered what made him tick. He seldom indulged in small talk. He had no interest in their private lives, nor did he talk about his. Once another secretary said something to Nancy Donaldson about her boss's personal phone calls. "He doesn't make personal phone calls," she said.

One night Hank Buick, the marketing guy, stuck his head into Landgraff's office to report that one of the team members had become a father.

"Oh, is that right?" Landgraff said.

"After they . . ."

"They lost a child. . . ."

"Yeah," Buick said. "They lost a child five hours after the child was born."

"They got back in the picture pretty quick," Landgraff said.

"Yeah, this is wonderful," Buick said.

"Yeah, right," Landgraff said.

He shook his head after Buick left. "I don't really like to know all this stuff," he said. "But, you know." Even for Landgraff, it would have been bad form to say so. A secretary once heard him say of a deceased colleague during a meeting, "Would have been nice if _____ could have been here to give us some help." When his secretary, a runner, slipped on a patch of ice and broke her ankle, Landgraff announced it to his staff in a way that suggested she should have known better. "She was jogging at night in the wintertime."

Sometimes it was hard to tell if he was aloof or merely shy. Heading to the Romeo proving ground for a team drive, he never rode the van; he never hitched a ride with others to a meeting. He preferred, he said, to drive himself.

Mary Anne Wheeler, the head climate control delegate to the team, had once spotted him across a crowded restaurant sitting with his family. She was having dinner with her husband and son. Landgraff passed her table on the way to the men's room, his eyes glued to the floor. On his return, she hailed him. "Hi, Dick," she said as he walked by. "Hi, Mary Anne," he said without breaking stride. It reminded her of how kids want to run the other way when they see a teacher outside the classroom.

The few people who had met Landgraff's wife, Connie, a slim woman with cropped black hair and striking good looks, were surprised to find her as friendly and outgoing in social situations as her husband was ill at ease. Nancy Donaldson always looked forward to seeing Connie at Christmas when the Landgraffs took her to lunch at the Dearborn Inn and presented her with a generous gift certificate.

If the troops knew anything about Landgraff's private life it was, perhaps, that he liked to hunt. In fact, he was crazy about it. He loved his guns, his decoys, and Star, his boisterous yellow Labrador. He liked duck hunting best and all that went with it: the pristine marshes in early morning and late afternoon, the challenge of felling small, swift targets, Star's expert retrievals. But he also liked to bag deer and elk and wild turkeys, provided he spotted them in open terrain. He did not much care for stalking game through dense woods. And he preferred hunting alone, or with one other person—his son Peter or neighbor Conrad Clippert—to group gang-banging. He cherished the right to keep and bear arms. He was a letter-writing member of the National Rifle Association.

His other political positions were equally conservative. He thought *Leadership Secrets of Attila the Hun* made some good points. When the liberals on National Public Radio got too heavy-handed with their opinions, he switched to Rush Limbaugh. He preferred market forces to government intervention and he believed the auto industry made too little use of cost-benefit ratios. He had formed his opinion of the government as a college student during a summer job at the Federal Housing Administration. Assigned to process fire insurance on foreclosed homes, Landgraff got his work done by noon. The rest of the day he read newspapers and wandered around. His desk was in a bullpen filled with other students and none of them had enough to do. "I mean it was just unbelievable. There were guys there shooting spitballs at one another." One of the head honchos stopped by one day and acknowledged the lack of work but instructed them to at least look busy. Nothing Landgraff had learned since then about the federal government made him think that it had grown any more efficient.

Rick and Jane Maibaurer, the couple to whom the Landgraffs were closest, thought Landgraff was very different from most auto company exec-utives. Not only did he seldom discuss business, he displayed none of the desperate yearning to be a vice-president that they saw in a friend of theirs at General Motors.

In coping with the world outside of Ford—a world that often struck him as dim-witted and irrational—Landgraff had a comic side that would have astonished the troops. The Maibaurers occasionally went skiing with the Landgraffs. They remembered when he decided to learn. "I think I'll go buy some skis," he announced. They suggested he might want to try the demanding sport with rented equipment. Landgraff thought that made no sense. "You wouldn't rent a bathing suit," he told them. "You wouldn't rent a gun."

Landgraff was not a natural athlete. He played tennis badly, and he once fell off a horse. But that didn't stop him from skiing anything, anywhere. He was fearless. He was also, said Rick Maibaurer, "the world's weirdest skier." Not bad, "just weird." He skied standing upright, with his arms pressed to his sides. For Maibaurer, the choice was either to be amused or to panic at the sight of his friend cruising down a steep slope, holding himself erect like a figure in a child's stick drawing. Maibaurer was an orthopedic surgeon who set a lot of broken bones.

Looking out the window at his neighbor's home after a snowy night, Conrad Clippert would see a scene that looked like a clown act, with Con-nie in her bathrobe lugging sand and ashes, and Dick cursing the snow and yelling at his three kids to shovel harder. He seemed always to have a little car with a big motor and no traction.

Landgraff could tell stories on himself, like the time he killed a goose on a hunting trip in northern Michigan and threw it in the car. He checked into the lodge, leaving his dog overnight in the car with the dead goose. Only the goose wasn't dead. The next morning, the car was smeared with goose excrement. And the goose was still flapping its wings as the dog watched.

When Landgraff chaperoned his daughter Gretchen and ten of her sorority sisters on a ski vacation at the family's second home in Snowmass Village, Colorado, the boss man turned into a doting dad. He rousted the girls out of bed in the morning, sectioned grapefruits and cooked waffles, and organized their days. His daughter's friends thought he was cool. By the end of the trip a chorus of girlish voices was constantly calling "Mr. Landgraff," "Mr. Landgraff." He even presented one of the sisters with a birthday card. It was that more than anything else that impressed Gretchen. This was a man who remembered at 8 P.M. on his wife's birthday, while he was still at work, that he had to buy a gift before the dinner celebration for which he was already late. His daughter had never seen him in such rare form.

———— ✦ ————

SIX

The Rise
of the Engineers

ON APRIL 16, Andy Benedict,
the head body engineer on the Taurus team, sent a memo to his bosses: "The
DN101 final clays were presented to Mssrs. Benton, Gilmore, Poling and Telnack on 4/15/92 at 8:00 A.M. The design committee enthusiastically approved
all three vehicles as shown with no 'mix and match' direction." Benedict
invited them to look over the clays at their earliest convenience. "The team
feels as though we have three outstanding vehicles to now execute."

The engineers were taking over.

AT THEME DECISION, the engineers had certified the car as 80
percent feasible. But some of that was "engineering judgment," a collective,
educated guess. Now they had to make good on their promises, plus they
had to complete the last and most troublesome 20 percent of their feasibility studies—*feasibilize* the car, if you will. It was like running a marathon
where the final five miles were up a mountain.

Week by week, section by section, DN101 was mutating from a clay model into a mathematical model. Back in 1966 when chief engineer George Bell had started with Ford, modelers took the x, y, z coordinates by hand from calibrated bridges that arched over the studio clays. Draftsmen connected the three-dimensional points, then adjusted them with cubic equations to make a smooth or "fair" curve. Now a computer probe scanned the clays for the coordinates. Surfacing software took the mathematical data and evened out the lines between the points, yielding a smooth skin with no ripples, unplanned highlights, or any of the other strange phenomena that could appear in uneven metal or plastic. Engineering drawings incorporated these math data; the drawings provide the information that the tooling companies used to make fixtures and dies.

The process took place on every styled or sculpted surface in the car—from the big plastic fascias, as bumpers now were called, to the door of the glove compartment. In March 1992 came the first of a series of sequential clay freezes, when certain areas of the car could no longer be changed. And owing to a particularly ill-advised sequence in World Class Timing, during those same spring months the engineers had to finish their drawings for the structural prototype build starting in January 1993. Their final target sat in the middle of the Twip with a bold star around it: "Final Sheet Metal Math Surface Data available 5-06-93," at twenty-five months before Job One. The dual deadlines were hard on everybody.

THE ENGINEERS WERE taking over the car. But they were also taking over more than that, judging by the way they were gobbling up power and promotions at Ford. It was payback time. For what had seemed like forever, at least since the end of World War II, engineers had been overruled by the finance guys and planners, and outdistanced by both on the career track. In Japan, automotive CEOs had technical pedigrees. But at Ford, as at other U.S. car companies, the top guys were usually from either product planning or finance. Lee Iaccoca was an anomaly: an industrial engineer who forged his career in marketing. Indeed, the only engineer ever to head the company, one might say, was Henry the Founder.

That one of their own, Lew Veraldi, had developed The Car That Saved Ford was a source of great pride to engineers. The Taurus had boosted Ford out of its doldrums. And Veraldi had changed forever the way cars were made. But to his superiors his image as an engineer prevailed. Former chairman Donald Petersen, a product planner, explaining years later why Veraldi wasn't better rewarded, said that he was a "remarkably good engineer" but a "little short" as a manager. And Henry Ford II mustered only the faintest of praise in an interview with Michigan historian David L. Lewis that didn't become public until after Ford's death. In 1985, with the fabulous new Taurus waiting in the wings, Ford dismissed Veraldi as "an engineer," albeit one who had "done a very fine job."

Product planners, not engineers, had long been the people with clout in car product development. They authored the program "assumptions": a working list of everything in the car. They assembled the recipe; engineers merely followed it. The problem was, complained body engineer Rick Schifter, speaking for himself and his brethren, that planners didn't budget enough for the ingredients. "They always gave us more content than they gave us money to do." Then, when things went wrong, planners blamed the engineers. "'The company gave you a good program and you screwed it up.'" In sum, he said, cars were under the control of people "who never designed or released a part and wouldn't know a piece of tooling—or what it takes to launch a car—if you dropped a press on them."

Planners wrote the cycle plan, Ford's ten-year projection of new models and model changes. In the heyday of planning, the cycle plans were forever changing. When these car programs were revised, engineers had to drop what they were doing and do something else. "There was a new ten-year cycle plan every three months," said Tom Kelley, a longtime body engineer. "People made whole careers doing cycle plans." Body engineering was in constant flux, trying to keep up.

In engineering, data were black and white. The planners fielded soft numbers. They projected sales volumes, reported market research, discussed pricing. But volumes changed, buyers' attitudes changed, market conditions changed. Veraldi was typical of engineers in his mistrust of planners. Because he was inexperienced in the business aspects of developing a car, Veraldi had to rely on planners but he suspected them of mauling the data. He seldom forgot a number. "You said it was $102. Now it's $148. Tell me what happened."

As a vice-president, Veraldi could put up an argument. Most engineers had no such leverage. Only the planners had the big picture. They wrote the big papers and gave the big presentations to upper management on the phases of a program. As a group, they were ambitious. Image was important, and they used presentations to show off. Some kept the written material to a minimum, and answered questions from memory, turning to assistants for additional information. Others, like Kaywin Goodman, Landgraff's predecessor on DN101, handled the whole show themselves, with backup material in black binders. Speed was at a premium. It did not do to keep a vice-president waiting as you flipped pages, searching for the answer. Goodman amazed the junior planners with his preparation for a major meeting.

The margins of his papers were filled with notes, the text was highlighted and crisscrossed by arrows, and attached to some pages would be smaller pages with reduced type, folded so they opened out like an accordian. Before the day of the meeting, Goodman might call the offices of the vice-presidents who would be there to find out their concerns and prepare for them.

The DN101 engineers had liked Goodman, who may have been a planner but who also had an engineering degree. He respected their work and left them alone. Their principal objection was to his hours—planners' hours. He often came to work late—late at Ford was 8:30 or 9 A.M.—and stayed late. Kaywin might decide to call a meeting for 6 P.M., way past the time an engineer who'd been there since 7 A.M. wanted to head home. Even the planners, who traditionally kept later hours than engineers, would panic on finding themselves in Kaywin's office around 8 P.M., when he was just getting revved up. They knew he could stay there talking about customers' wants and needs the whole damn night. They'd be stealing looks at their watches when Kaywin would boom out "Pizza! Who's going for pizza?" Their hearts would sink.

Since the 1970s, product planning had welcomed people like Goodman who had dual degrees. The promotions were popping, and a number of engineers switched over. But by the 1990s, thanks to changes sweeping car product development, engineers no longer had to become planners to get ahead. Those with business degrees could not only rule on technical issues but also on matters of cost and quality, as Japanese engineers were said to do. As DN101 business planner Brent Egleston put it, the company now wanted people who could "read a balance sheet and an electrical circuit diagram." In the expanding global economy, such people could speak the language that was universal: engineering.

No one had officially announced the rise of the engineers, but it was visible in small ways. As chief engineer on a prior car program, George Bell had ranked number three behind the business planner. Now Bell was the number-two man, with his own secretary. And the business planner, who shared a secretary with his staff, was a geographically distant three, in an office on the other side of the room. George Bell's cubicle, while dark and clammy, was no worse than Dick Landgraff's, and it was right next to it.

The new generation of engineering princes and princesses with night-school MBAs was well represented on the Taurus team. They controlled parts worth millions of dollars. Jim Mikola, who was in charge of headlamps, taillamps, and bumpers, was responsible for ordering $170 million worth of tooling for his parts and $826 of parts on each Taurus. Multiply that by 600,000 cars a year, he said, and it was "so many zeros I have to write it down." Some mid-level planners with engineering degrees were trying to switch back, only to find that engineers who had never left the fold had a lock on all the good jobs.

If these indicators were any evidence, Ford Motor Company had made a gigantic tactical decision. The engineers were going to have to save the company from the Japanese. The planners and bean counters had done all they could. . . .

. . . And still the Japanese kept coming. Wave after wave of Toyotas, Nissans, Hondas, Mitsubishis, and Subarus flooding the highways. What had thus far insulated the Big Three automakers to some degree was not so much their own gains in quality—the Japanese got better too—but Japan's failure to foresee seismic shifts in American taste, perhaps because they made so little sense on the surface. Who could predict that a suburbanized nation with shrinking families and dirty air would go nuts over big people-haulers and rough terrain vehicles that soaked up gas? Certainly not the sensible Japanese, who first missed out on the U.S. market for minivans and then on sport utilities. Nor were they prepared for the popularity of light trucks. And they moved into the luxury car market as wealthy Americans were moving out. But it would be foolish to think the Japanese couldn't catch up. Their cars kept getting better and arriving faster. And nine million to ten million Americans still bought new cars rather than trucks every year.

The car had come to represent more than mere transportation or status. While always a symbol of independence, now it was a source of comfort—both physical and mental—in a world destabilized by drugs, crime, violence, sex, governmental corruption, racism, downsizing, spouse abuse, child abuse, political upheaval, terrorism, famine, exotic plagues, environmental scourges, climatic devastation, ethnic warfare, overpopulation, grievous poverty, fractured families, mutations in health care, and a nervous economy. Their mood anxious, their spirits riven, Americans needed to trust someone or something. These days people looked to their cars for qualities missing in humans: reliability and integrity.

And only engineers could help. The marketing guys could divert traffic to Ford showrooms with advertising, promotion, and attractive prices. But only engineers could throw up a permanent roadblock. Only engineers could match Japan's technical accomplishments. And only engineers could push cars into the expanding computer universe. Ford vehicles hadn't had engine computers until 1978. Now they were in their fifth generation. The electronic engine computer or EEC (pronounced "eeek!") continuously adjusted the fuel mixture, told the gears when to shift, lit up lights in the dash, and diagnosed engine problems. Electronics also maintained an interior temperature, activated anti-lock brakes, fired off airbags, and modulated power steering. There was more wiring in the door of the Taurus than in the whole body of a 1950 Ford.

Like the materials they dealt with, engineers had strengths and weaknesses. There were the computationists, who were experts at manipulating mathematical calculations and could generate reams of data at a moment's notice, and there were hardware guys, who could take things apart and put them back together. And then there were the real thinkers. Engineering by itself wasn't fun, said Jim Mikola, the fun part was solving problems. Engineering was so *hard*, you had to love it to be any good, said Tom Gallery, a technical specialist, which was as high as an engineer could go without becoming a manager. Getting a patent was the ultimate kick. "It makes you feel good as an engineer," said Angelo Guido, who shared a patent on a transmission torque converter with two other people. Like, "I've done something for mankind."

Ford cubicles were still full of guys and gals turning out floorpans, transmissions, windshields, and struts. But the engineers with status were a new breed who placed the overall performance of the entire car above its components. *Holistic engineering.*

Chief engineer George Bell remembered his obsession with suspension arms when he was designing them as a young chassis engineer. "When I saw a car driving down the road, all the rest disappeared. All I could see were the suspension arms going up and down." And you had to believe that Bell, a gifted engineer, had come up with some pretty terrific suspension arms, in the same way that many engineers at Ford had turned out some excellent parts over the years. The poor workmanship in American cars did not necessarily stem from bad parts, but from ones that didn't work together smoothly. At this point in his career, Bell presided over the entire car. Where once he sat in meetings waiting for his part to come up, now all the parts were his. "One day," said Bell, "you've got to wake up and realize that you're not selling pieces."

Selling pieces, that was no exaggeration. In the old days, Ford had this attitude, Dick Landgraff said: "You want a car, we'll give you these pieces. You don't like it? Tough shit, that's what we've got today." Okay, maybe that was a little bit of an exaggeration, maybe it wasn't that bad, but it was pretty bad.

The emphasis on car pieces was reflected in the organization of the company around product engineering offices, or PEOs, with a vice-president at the helm. There was body engineering, whose people were in charge of the big visible chunks of the car: the body shell, the lights and bumpers, the front end, the seats, interior trim and restraints, the instrument panels, the doors, trunk lids, and hoods. On the DN101 team, each of those chunks was represented by a team of engineers and a leader. Other PEOs were chassis, powertrain, electronics, climate control, plastics, and glass—big, top-down bureaucracies that management consultants liked to call "chimneys" because they did not relate to each other. In the past, product planners assigned to a car program brokered arrangements among these engineering fiefdoms. Hence the planners' power and visibility.

To staff Ford's new collocated teams, engineers were plucked from their PEOs and thrown together in a situation where they were to collaborate rather than promote the narrow interests of their home organization. The whole car came first, not its brakes or its taillamps. Over in the body engineering mother ship or in Building Five, home of the chassis division, managers worried about what they saw as the downside of teams, that their collocated people were "going native" and forgetting who the real bosses were. (The real bosses still had the employee history sheets known as Form 60s. It was said at Ford that whoever had your Form 60 owned you. Whoever had the Form 60 did your performance reviews and recommended promotions.) Not only the engineering offices, but the management of divisions which were represented on the team, like body and assembly, finance, and product planning, felt threatened by the move to teams.

THE ENGINEERS WERE taking over, but sometimes it seemed as if it was only Steve Kozak, head of the sheet-metal or "body-shell" chunk team.

A rising prince among the DN101 princelings, Kozak had pocketed his MBA, and he was pushing the envelope on computer-aided engineering. CAE, as it was known, was being used extensively to predict a car's response to various crash scenarios as well as to reduce noise and vibration and undesirable motion. The computer could calculate stresses and strain in response to forces. If you did A, then B and C would occur. If you push up on this spring, this section will move.

Every time you turned around, there Kozak was . . . out there, up front, making one presentation after another: the case for inset doors, for triple door seals, for the one-piece body side, for a door-mounted mirror. He talked long and he talked loud. He didn't mind admitting it. "I talk very loud." Kozak had grown up with four siblings, and yelling was what they did. "Everybody in my family yells." His father was a beer supplier, whose southern Michigan territory was dotted with auto plants. "He was a major supplier to the auto industry." A joke! Kozak talked loud and he cracked jokes. He would have stood out in any group of people, but on the DN101 team he had a reputation as something of a wild man, among all those other engineers. By Theme Decision he was someone to reckon with. He had won three major victories for engineers, two of them in the early days before Landgraff's arrival.

Steve Kozak hadn't even known what an engineer was till late in high school. He was good in math, and he had done well at science fairs. He hung with the geeks. "I guess I want to be a scientist," he told the school counselor. "You could be an engineer," she said. Was she nuts? "I don't want to drive trains," he said.

He enrolled at the Dearborn branch of the University of Michigan because it had a co-op program, where students spent time in paid jobs, only later to learn that it lacked the status of the main campus at Ann Arbor. But that was okay. His co-op assignment was at Ford's transmission plant in nearby Livonia, where he earned enough seniority to escape the layoffs that occurred shortly after he hired on permanently in 1980. For years, until body engineering got some more people, he was the youngest guy there. They called him "the Kid."

He owed his visibility not only to his personality but also to his assignment. As leader of the sheet-metal chunk team, Kozak had responsibility in areas that customers cared deeply about. Safety was one: Over 100 prototypes would be crashed and smashed multiple times from the front, side, and rear to see if they met eight federal crash standards. Two dozen more would undergo other creative forms of abuse. They would be mashed in a roof crush test, their locks would be twisted, their seat belts would be subjected to the tugging force of a small team of wrestlers. In nearly all these tests, the response of the sheet metal was fundamental. Another critical area was noise, vibration, and harshness, commonly abbreviated as NVH. The car could not shake, rattle, and roll or squeak, twist, or bend. Nor could it leak. And all the pieces had to fit together so they looked right. A stiff, solid body would also improve the ride and the handling.

In the beginning, Kozak's most pressing assignment was to fix the number-one complaint on the outgoing Taurus. Customer complaints were known as Things Gone Wrong or TGWs. They were carefully counted and categorized, then expressed as the number of Things Gone Wrong per thousand vehicles. The categories covered all sorts of mechanical difficulties, from engine malfunctions to lights that didn't work, brakes that were too sensitive or noisy, rough gear shifts and oil leaks. Annoying squeaks and rattles translated into TGWs, as did flaws in the appearance, such as wrinkled seat fabric and chipped or scratched paint. But what really drove Taurus owners crazy was something that they could neither see nor feel. Nor did it require a bothersome repair, because it could not be fixed. That made it doubly annoying. It was wind noise.

More than 10 percent of Taurus TGWs were from people who felt as if they were trapped in a cyclone every time the speedometer went over 50 miles per hour. Drivers had trouble hearing cassette tapes. People in the front seat trying to converse with people in back might as well be in separate states. If nothing else, this sensitivity suggested the extent to which people looked to their cars for a little peace, quiet, and comfort in a high-decibel world. For there had been a period in our nation's history, children, when wind noise went with the open road. You just talked above it. But no more did people roll down their windows as a matter of course. Out there were loud trucks and unpleasant smells and free-floating danger. Inside were music and temperature-controlled air.

Wind tunnel data showed that the old Taurus's limousine-style doors, where the wide metal door frame rolled into the roof, wreaked havoc with the air flow. They would have to go. That was okay with the design studio. A decade ago the limo doors were stylish, but now they looked dated. The stylists, however, wanted to replace them with hard-top doors like those going into the new Mustang. The window glass formed the top edge of the door; there was no frame. But hard-top doors required a time-consuming adjustment on the assembly line, which was possible with the Mustang's lower volumes but not so easy at the car-a-minute rate at which the Taurus popped off the line. And there were other problems with hard-top doors.

The studio finally agreed to what were called inset doors, surrounded by a thin molding that fit snugly into the bodyside, which was welded, in turn, to the roof. Kozak had lobbied for these doors all along because they caused less wind noise. Now he wanted three rubber door seals—two around the doors and one around the bodyside opening—to block noise and moisture. At a cost of $59 per car more than the two-seal system on the outgoing Taurus, triple seals represented $35 million a year, an absolutely huge expenditure. And the customers would scarcely notice. No one was going to stand there and count the seals. This was the kind of thing that in the old days the little engineers would beg the finance guys for: "Please, sir, can we have better seals?" And the finance guys would say, "No."

Just before members of the executive committee met to review the budget in October 1991, the DN101 engineers had staged a show-and-tell of various upgrades. Murray Reichenstein, vice-president and comptroller, came over to Kozak's triple-seal display, which featured an illustration, hardware, and chart of data. Reichenstein barely glanced at them. Nor did he pick up the earphones and listen to the audiotape of sound levels on cars with and without triple seals. "Just answer me one question," Reichenstein said. "Does Camry have triple seals?"

"No, sir," Kozak replied.

"Is it quieter than our car?"

"We'll be just as quiet," Kozak assured him. But of course the import of Reichenstein's query was clear. If Toyota could produce a quiet car with two seals, why did Ford need three? Kozak had answers. The shape of the Camry was more square, and its powertrain was quieter, meaning that less noise reached the occupants. But Reichenstein walked away before he could explain.

Nevertheless, the executive committee approved the expenditure. Kozak saw it as a sign of changing times. "Here was a vice-president of finance who couldn't turn down a $59 decision that engineering said it needed for the functionality of the car."

H AVING WON INSET DOORS and triple seals, Kozak was two for two in the battle against wind noise. But it did not look as if he would be so successful in the campaign for a press that could stamp out a one-piece bodyside, which had a price tag estimated at $100 million. At present, the Taurus bodyside arrived at the Atlanta and Chicago assembly plants in front and rear sections, each containing a door opening. Two welded pieces were preferable to the seven or eight found in rattletraps like the earlier Fairmont and LTD, where no door opening was ever quite the same, but introducing a stem-to-stern stamping would diminish even more the potential for misalignment. The door openings would not vary beyond the normal tolerance in the stamped part. However slight the mismatch, lopsided doors not only looked bad but increased leaks and, yes, wind noise, plus the doors were harder to open and close. After wind noise, the sheet metal constituted the second highest TGW category, with multiple complaints about its blemishes, the way it fit, and the difficulty in opening and closing the doors, hood, and trunk lid. Kozak estimated that a one-piece bodyside would trim the TGW count by 25 to 30. The engineers wanted it bad.

The Accord had a one-piece bodyside. And more to the point, two forthcoming Ford vehicles would have it too: a minivan called the Windstar, and the Contour/Mystique car line. But Ford was in another recession— 1991 would bring a record loss of $2.3 billion—and the top guys were talking about taking money out of the Taurus program, not putting more in. Dick Landgraff was not yet on the scene.

More than being expensive, it was just too late for the one-piece bodyside. The window of opportunity had slammed shut. This is what the ranking engineer from manufacturing kept telling his DN101 teammates. To design and build a bodyside press took up to sixty months and there was less time than that till Job One. There was no love lost between the old-time manufacturing guys, who represented the stamping and assembly plants, and the body engineers. It seemed to Steve Kozak that this guy took pleasure in turning them down. Nevertheless, the one-piece bodyside seemed doomed until Landgraff arrived and lent his backing. The new program manager professed bewilderment at having to compromise on quality.

After a while the manufacturing guy left the team. Kozak was glad to see him go. "He was a worthless piece of shit." And the bosses in metal stamping operations began to think about how it might not be such a bad idea to have a second press for backup, in case the Contour press went down. And then, amazingly enough, the window of opportunity opened up. Half the lead time on the new press was for its design. Just tell the company that was building the press for the Contour/Mystique to build a second. Everywhere the order blank said one, just write two. Two $100 million presses. It was so easy it was ridiculous. In the Chicago stamping plant, where they were digging one pit, just dig two. The opposition seemed to melt away. At last NAAO vice-president Alex Trotman said they could have the new press.

Ford ordered it right away from the German manufacturer, a company called Schuler, with a plant in São Paulo, Brazil. It would be a magnificent three-story-high machine with windows through which one could watch as a smooth sheet of pressed steel proceeded through six automated die stations that bent, pierced, flanged, and trimmed it. Just 10 seconds later, it shot out the other end, a sleek, undulant piece of steel 140 inches long. The whole operation was so quiet workers didn't even need earplugs. Try doing without earplugs around the other big sheet-metal presses, those clanging monoliths built in the 1950s, and you'd be deaf in half an hour.

Getting the Schuler press was a great victory for the team, but Dick Landgraff told people that he didn't see why it had to come out of his budget. Why wasn't there a separate program to phase out old tools and replace them with new ones? Why should DN101 have to pay to retool the stamping plant? He raised the same argument when he had to shell out $40 million for new robots in Atlanta and Chicago. But that wasn't how budgets worked. Trotman told Landgraff to find a way to save $100 million, an "offset." "We'll look for it," Landgraff told him, "but I doubt we'll find it."

T HE DN101 ENGINEERS were under a lot of pressure. Not only did they have to produce a superior car in less time—stretched above every desk were copies of the Twip, the World Class Timing Chart, packed with deadlines—but they had to do so in their new communal environment. Many team members had been wrenched from home offices where they had worked for years; they were among strangers in an unfamiliar place. And under the new scheme of things, they were expected to make business decisions or, if not decisions, at least recommendations. All this held the promise of advancement, sure, but it was so hard for people who just wanted to be left alone.

And this was the great paradox about the rise of the engineers. In its quest for excellence, the company had turned to a subculture that found it difficult to negotiate or compromise, or even chatter idly about something as simple as the weather. (Of course, down in the basement they did not know what the weather was, unless they called Debby at the security desk or consulted a handmade weather board at one entrance. The board had a movable sun, clouds, and other icons, plus a thermometer, which people adjusted as they came in from the outside.)

In the general population, extroverts—or extraverts depending on your preference—were said to outnumber introverts, three to one. At Ford, the ratio was approximately reversed. And since many extroverts worked in the marketing and public relations divisions, in the engineering strongholds of the company the concentration of introverts reached very high levels indeed.

The book *Please Understand Me*, by David Keirsey and Marilyn Bates, which Ford used extensively in the 1980s during a period of corporate introspection, described the introvert thusly:

> While the extravert [sic] is sociable the introvert is territorial. That is, he desires space: private places in the mind and private environmental places. Introverts seem to draw their energies from a different source than do extraverts. Pursuing solitary activities, working quietly alone, reading, meditating, participating in activities which involve few or no other people—these seem to charge the batteries of the introvert.

Engineers were the most impenetrable kind of introvert. On those occasions when they did speak out, only other engineers could understand them. Not even their wives knew what went on in their minds.

When Ann Landers announced the subject of engineer spouses, letters of complaint poured in. Said A Wife in Houston, "My engineer husband makes a fine living, but when it comes to expressing emotions, on a scale of 10, he's about a 4." From Tucson, "A crooked window shade must be adjusted at once. If, however, I am crawling around the house with a killer migraine, he doesn't notice." From Santa Barbara, "He feels no joy, but he is never depressed either. Everything must be in perfect order, or there is hell to pay." From No City, Please, "He would have been a better father if our children had been robots he could program." And this from a man married to a female engineer: "She's as cold as ice and so sure of herself she makes me sick."

In some respects, though, engineers made great spouses. At heart they were tinkerers and fixers; there was nothing they wouldn't tackle. On the eve of his sister's wedding, when his wife was frantically stitching brides-maids' dresses for his daughters, George Bell sat down at the sewing machine. No big deal. "I'm an engineer. I could figure it out." When Andy Benedict's wife, Margaret, opened up a gymnastics school that required special flooring, he obtained the specs, laid down a four-inch layer of foam, then drilled 1,800 holes for 600 brackets in 50 four-by-eight sheets of structural wood, and that was that.

Tom Breault, a top engineer on the team, might spend his Wednesday nights with a buddy restoring a 1968 Austin Healy, but he also built his daughter a computer out of stray parts and he once fixed the VCR. Lichia Bucklin, who worked for Breault, not only sewed clothes for her three daughters, but she was taking a course in home construction.

CONCERNED THAT ENGINEERS were too isolated, from time to time Ford sent them out to market research clinics to talk to customers. They were coached to "be *friendly*." They were to smile, sound genuinely interested, and use nontechnical language. They were not to be defensive.

In one Florida clinic attended by DN101 team members, a little old lady who lived in an apartment complex told interviewers how fearful she was of disturbing her neighbors when the brakes of her Taurus squeaked loudly as she drove off in the morning. Others complained about the difficulty in talking over the noise of the heating/cooling fan and how dismayed they were when the rearview mirror repeatedly fell off. "I'm afraid to adjust the mirror now," said one.

The hope was that these real-life encounters would sensitize engineers to how people used their cars. But sometimes what the engineers saw and heard had a demoralizing effect. There were engineers who invested whole careers in finding and eliminating squeaks and rattles. Then customers draped their rearview mirrors with tinkling rosaries; they threw coins in the glove compartment. Mimi Reyes, a body engineer who worked on sunvi-sors, displayed photos she had snapped during an inspection of cars whose owners were in a market research clinic. She took sunvisors very seriously, as did the federal government. Not many people realized that the sunvisor was a federally mandated part with tightly controlled specifications as to size and composition. It could not obstruct a critical viewing area of the windshield, nor could it be of a material so hard it could cause injuries during a collision. But people treated sunvisors like trash.

Reyes's snapshots showed sunvisors loaded down with glasses, maps, and tapes. Pity the head that collided with one of those babies. As for aesthetics, there were sunvisors covered with fake woodgrain. One Escort visor had been unaccountably mangled, as if a dog had chewed it to bits. Another bedraggled visor had been pressed into service as a rain shield by a smoker who kept his window cracked during storms.

And then there were the obscene things people did with substances to add sheen to car interiors. When they coated the dash, they had, with a single swoosh, undone the labor of Dan Jack, a research engineer whose mission was to minimize "veiling glare."

Veiling glare took place when outside light bounced off the instrument panel back onto the windshield. When the windshield looked like a mirror, that was veiling glare. The sharply raked windshields in the current generation of aerodynamic cars had intensified the phenomenon, and DN101 would do so even more, as the windshield went from a 59.5-degree angle to 64 degrees measured from the vertical. To calculate glare from various surfaces, at various angles, Ford had spent an enormous amount of time and money to equip a studio in the Design Center with simulated sunlight and sophisticated measuring devices. The easiest way to reduce veiling glare was to grain or stipple the section of the instrument panel in front of the driver. Of DN101's four interior colors, the tan shade, "Saddle," posed the most severe problem. The engineers eventually were forced to add a darker-colored oval to the dash to hold the glare to an acceptable level.

But Jack was under no illusions about what would happen when owners used glossy sprays. A fresh application could double or triple the reflectivity. "Customers," Jack said, "think shiny is very, very good. But when they turn the corner and the sun shines in the wrong way, they won't be able to see."

How little regard the world had for engineers and the good they did. An AT&T engineer named Len Winn had once written a page-long ode to his profession.

> They give birth to new tractors, reapers and materials that in turn provide the amber waves of grain.
>
> They provide water where there is only desert and warmth where there is only cold.
>
> Their monuments are everywhere—the highways, factories, telephones, computers, clean water—everywhere.

. . . And so forth.

E NGINEERS KNEW what the world thought of them. The world thought they were nerds, geeks, dweebs, dorks, and squares. The sad thing was when they apologized for being so uninteresting. It was endearing, really. And so, an especially outgoing engineer might say something along the lines of, "I guess it must be hard for you, being around all these engineers."

Yes, it was hard. They talked in a patois composed of technical terms and acronyms mixed with corporate jargon coined by planners that had spread through the company like an evil computer virus, attacking nouns and twisting them into verbs. People at Ford didn't agree, they *consensed*. They didn't decide, they *decisioned*. Why go through a transition if you could simply *transition*? And some manager was forever *cascading* information. Then there were the acronyms. *"Here is a case where CDW CR is PCI."* Once upon a time, *"We made a consensus decision to get all the CRs PCI'd by a certain date to make CPC."* Introduce some tech talk about the diameter of the tubular stabars, or the VAPS curve of the steering gear, or the valving of the struts, and all was lost.

Engineers: you might imagine them in colorful environments. Possibly—this being Ford—they were around cars, with grease on their hands and speed on their minds, in machine shops or laboratories full of intriguing test equipment, or out in manufacturing plants doing something with parts or machinery. And for some that was the case, for example, across the street at the test track where development engineers evaluated prototypes. But these basement engineers and their upstairs colleagues conducted business in windowless meeting rooms illuminated from above by humming fluorescent lights, where they spoke in a monotone without emotion or humor, unless they felt deeply about something, in which case they employed tightly controlled voices that gave nothing away. And if an Indian engineer were speaking, forget it. Ford had a number of very smart Indian engineers, two of whom, Suresh Gupta and Shabbir Kathiria, headed DN101 chunk teams. Like many if not most, Gupta had come to the United States to study, and stayed on. And why not? "It's such a fabulous country, who wants to go back?" But Indian engineers could be difficult to understand. They tended to speak rapidly in clipped accents, hooking words together as if they were rail cars. Out of their mouths came a version of engineering monotone that sounded like a train clattering down a track. As visual aids, the engineers unfurled fine-line layouts of cross sections turned this way and that, which could be as long as thirty feet. Ford wallpaper.

So you had the merciless hum of bright fluorescent lights, the drone of the ventilation system, the ubiquitous blue-and-gray motif, the long drawings filled with tiny numbers, and the Ford patois rendered in an engineering monotone. It was awful.

AND NOW THESE LONERS—these much-maligned nerds, geeks, dweebs, dorks, and squares—were the very people who had to play ball together. They found it painful to talk, and yet they were to communicate, to relate. By nature perfectionists, they now were expected to solve problems together, to give and take, advise and consent, listen and learn, in a word, compromise. The most *incommunicado* people in the world, and they were supposed to bond.

Was it even possible? *"The introvert can remain only so long in interaction with people before he depletes his reserves,"* said the book by Keirsey and Bates. And that period of time was approximately one half hour. *"If an extreme introvert goes to a party, after a 'reasonable' period of time—say, half an hour—he is ready to go home. For him, the party is over. He is no party pooper; rather, he was pooped by the party."*

To be fair, engineers could hang in there much longer in a meeting than at a party. Conversation in meetings was almost always of a technical nature; it drew on knowledge and expertise, not one's ability to be interesting or amusing or empathetic. In meetings, there were questions and answers, quids and quos, causes and effects. And often an engineer could get by without saying anything at all. Sometimes Dick Landgraff would find himself at a conference table where he didn't know who half the people were or why they were there. But they were engineers who would rather be in a meeting than in their cubicles, where someone might call or stop by. A meeting was a great place to hide. Also, it was important not to spend too much time at your desk. Someone might think that you didn't have enough meetings to attend. And, of course, you needed to stay informed.

It was amazing a non-engineer like Landgraff could get through much of what went on in these conference rooms. He didn't try to understand all the technical nuances, just the bottom line: how much time and/or money was involved. He trusted chief engineer George Bell to make the right technical decisions. His job, he said, was "to make sure no one does anything stupid." An example of something stupid would be a decision that cost too much money or upset the DN101 timetable and brought down ruination upon World Class Timing.

———— ✪ ————

SEVEN

Winners and Losers

O N AUGUST 5, 1992, a stranger appeared in the Design Center basement where the DN101 team was housed. He wandered up and down the aisles of numbered cubicles until he found the one assigned to him. A big molded plastic bumper sat on the desk. There was no chair. He set the bumper on another empty desk and claimed an extra chair from a nearby conference table; he hoped it didn't belong to someone else. He wiped away a layer of dust—didn't anyone clean down here?—and checked out the coffee station. Good news. A cup of coffee was only 20 cents and it tasted better than the stuff back at J. Walter Thompson, Ford's longtime advertising agency, where he was the manager of a research group.

Later that day Kinder Essington began the diary he would keep off and on for the next six months he was with the team. It had been Dick Landgraff's idea to involve advertising agencies early in the program. It had been Essington's idea to volunteer.

In the beginning he was much impressed with collocation—"a wonderful way to coordinate between the various speciality departments that create the components of a car." But after another month he could see that the team was not always a harmonious unit. Either he had missed the friction in the beginning, or it was growing more intense. In October, he wrote that there was "a little less cooperation. A little more insisting.

"A little less 'We're all on a marvelous journey together.' A little more, 'you guys aren't doing your jobs.'

"A little less 'That's great.' A little more 'That's unacceptable.'

"A long, long list of hard decisions is facing the group. If the group decides on one feature (additional use of solar glass for example), the group will have to find a financial offset somewhere else. In other words, for every dollar that's added to the cost, a dollar is going to have to be taken out. The same for weight. A pound in. A pound out."

He continued, "It's also a time when individuals within the group 'win' or 'lose.' So there's a lot of prestige and ego at stake."

E SSINGTON DESCENDED INTO the subterranean world of DN101 at a particularly fractious period in the life of the car. The decisions were getting smaller, but the arguments were getting bigger. Steve Kozak had scored victories on the big hunks of metal—the position of the doors and the seals that surrounded them, the one-piece bodyside—but now he was toe-to-toe with the studio over the placement of the outside mirrors.

Interior stylist Mike Webb was going back and forth with engineers and sales over the shape of the inside door handles: a paddle or a loop, a loop or a paddle?

The body and assembly guys on the team, who spoke for the manufacturing plants, were spotting all kinds of problems. The space between the doors and the body wasn't big enough in certain areas to install the seals. Where the bumper and fenders met, they needed a curve with a 5-millimeter rather than a 2-millimeter radius. There was no way they could paint the door sills black to match the moldings for better craftsmanship. The black paint would drip. Then you'd have worse craftsmanship. That's why door sills were always left in body color.

Also in the name of craftsmanship, an intern from the Ford College Graduate Program was assembling a list of every label in the car. The goal was to reduce visual clutter by standardizing and eliminating as many labels as possible. The surprise was just how many there were; he eventually counted thirty-four, and simplifying them wasn't so simple. Some were there for legal reasons, and company lawyers had dictated the wording. Now the team was going to have to argue with the lawyers.

The future of Doug Gaffka's bright-eyed, new-tech headlamps was looking dim. The designers, the team, a supplier, and two engineering units had turned the front end into a battleground. If you talked to them on a good day, a new optics group in the plastics division thought they might be able to make one of the lamps; a supplier had promised the other. But Body Engineering, the traditional source of lighting expertise, had turned thumbs down on both.

There had been less face-to-face fighting when cars were designed by people in different organizations who seldom talked to one another and much of the communication was in writing. In those days before company e-mail, it could take a week or two to get a response. In retrospect, said chief engineer George Bell, he wondered "how things ever got resolved . . . and sometimes they weren't. People just went ahead and delivered the part they said they were going to."

Often disagreements were kicked upstairs. Said Landgraff, "The Design Center would say to the engineers, 'This is a great design if you assholes would just figure out a way to make it.' The engineers would say, 'You design guys are just crazy. This is too far out. We can't manufacture it, we can't engineer it.' The Design Center would dig in their heels." Both designers and engineers would shove the disagreement up their respective chains of command. Only the calendars of the big guys in the chain would be full. Corporate gridlock. "You can't go up the ladder because you can't get on their calendars." And really, the big guys didn't want to hear about it. They didn't like trouble. "They would say, 'Why don't you work on it?'"

The problem that now arose with bringing everybody together on an equal footing, and giving them a voice in decisions, was that they all spoke out at once. And they often disagreed. Moreover, said George Bell, on a program like DN101, where you were pushing the envelope, mistakes were inevitable, delays were inevitable, conflict was inevitable. "Any set of objectives that can be immediately met is probably not aggressive enough." It was all very well to make "team decisions," but how did you do that in a timely fashion? World Class Timing was silent on the subject.

FORD MANAGEMENT HAD long viewed conflict as a healthy force that sharpened issues. Different divisions were set up as profit centers in competition with each other. Each of the components groups—glass, plastics, electronics—had to show a profit and vie for resources. "It was civil war at the top," one manager told Richard Tanner Pascale, author of *Managing on the Edge*, which devoted several chapters to Ford. "The question was never, 'Are we winning against the Japanese?' But rather, 'Are we winning against each other?'"

The fighting went on everywhere at all levels. In one Canadian assembly plant, the manager constantly badgered the day shift to be as productive as the night shift. In response, workers on the day shift began to hide tools from workers on the night shift. The night shift retaliated by storing the tools in padlocked boxes. The day shift took possession of the bolt cutters. By the time the manager got wind of the fracas, the plant was losing twenty minutes of production at the beginning of each shift.

"Management by conflict" was taught by Ford alumni in some of the nation's business schools in the 1950s and 1960s. When the inevitable disagreements arose, the theory went, proponents would fight it out with skilled referees brokering a solution. In this fashion, you didn't end up with something casually decided by someone in a back room. Get it on the table and hammer it out. "Sometimes it's a little hard on the constitution to be constantly battling," observed Bell, who was the designated referee much of the time in technical squabbles. "On the other hand it's exciting. Nobody complains that their day drags."

In the past, however, skilled referees were few and far between. The guys who won tended to be the yellers, or the ones with the highest grade level. At the top, where there was no one to referee, formal meetings were models of harmony. The real executive debates took place before and afterward.

Historically Ford was as hierarchical, authoritarian, rule bound, and status conscious as the military. In a sense it *was* the military. Following World War II, returning veterans were hired in large numbers to fill a management vacuum. The typical Ford manager was expected to give orders, punish malingerers, and ferret out wrongdoing. They were self-appointed dispensers of blame and punishment. After each new war, Korea then Vietnam, more veterans arrived to carry on in the traditional management style.

Brad Nalon, a DN101 planner, had worked early in his career for a Marine Corps Vietnam vet who had liked his first tour of duty so much he had volunteered for a second. This trained killer would come to work, flip the trash can over, sit on it, take a roll of tape, and chew on it. When there wasn't enough excitement, he'd throw the phone or create some other disturbance. Nalon had a friend, an MBA from the University of Michigan, who gave up a promotion and went back to his old job after working briefly for this maniacal supervisor. Years later, Nalon found he couldn't look his old boss in the eyes, he still hated him so much.

Fear ruled the company, from Henry Ford II on down. Executives knew to stay clear of Ford, especially if he'd been drinking. He might decide he didn't like the color of your tie and fire you. The higher you went up the executive ladder, the less people spoke out. Dick Landgraff was frustrated by how hard it was to find out what colleagues really thought. When he had the opportunity, he enjoyed talking to academics. They seemed so much freer.

In the early 1980s, multimillion-dollar losses prompted Ford to seek outside help for its management problems. Consultant after consultant told the company it was all screwed up. Internal battles were draining energy needed to fight the Japanese. The in-fighting had to stop; the organizational chimneys had to go. The "my-way-or-the-highway" style of management was passé. Rather than management-by-conflict, Ford needed conflict management—coaching in how to peacefully resolve differences. People had to learn to trust.

The consultants had a field day. Executive training that mimicked Outward Bound exercises was imported from California. Suddenly Ford executives could be seen walking planks that stretched from one tree to another in nearby Hines Park, as they prayed their colleagues were holding tight to the tethers that would catch them if they fell.

Thousands of Ford managers, salaried employees, and hourly workers listened to octogenarian W. Edwards Deming, peacetime adviser to Japan's corporations, preach the importance of cooperation, teamwork, continual improvement, and a workplace free of fear. "Export anything to a friendly country," Deming was fond of saying, "except American management."

Between 1981 and 1987, body engineering put 2,500 managers through a course in behavioral change run by Teleometrics International, a Texas-based organization founded by a psychologist. Based on a 1 to 10 rating on two scales, people discovered whether they were authoritarian 9,1 "taskmasters" or people-pleasing 1,9 "comforters," rule-following 1,1 "regulators," who just wanted to stay out of trouble, or 9,9 "team managers," who drew subordinates into the planning process and gave them the resources to do their jobs. In the middle of the scales was a 5,5, a compromiser. The only good managers were the 9,9s.

Taskmasters were thought by many to dominate Ford. As Teleometrics spread throughout Ford, the 9,1 rating entered the corporate vocabulary to describe an insensitive, order-barking boss. But Teleometrics data revealed that the majority of managers constantly switched styles, depending on the situation. While they considered themselves flexible, their subordinates thought they were confused. Gale Cook, of Ford's management and technical training department, labeled them "tapdancers."

An executive development center that brought the top 2,000 managers together in groups throughout the year became the scene of much soul-searching. Nancy Badore, a Ford psychologist who helped set up the center, employed a personality test called the Myers-Briggs Type Indicator, in the book by Keirsey and Bates, to help her charges see that conflict could result from innate personality differences. On the basis of a quiz, people could type themselves as introverts or extroverts, then further define their personality by letter in the following categories: sensation, intuition, thinking, feeling, perceiving, and judging. The book described each type.

By and large, Ford was dominated by "SJ" types: The "S" person preferred experience to hunches, the sensible to the imaginative, fact to fiction. "J" were judging people, who "tend to establish deadlines and to take them seriously." The opposite of an "S" was a "P," someone who acted on perceptions. A "P" liked to keep options open by avoiding decisions. "J's" thought "P's" were indecisive. "P's" thought "J's" were "rigid and inflexible." Let a "P" hesitate at a meeting of introverted, factual, decisive Ford "SJ's," and it was curtains. They'd rip the poor "P" apart.

Dick Landgraff avoided as much of this management stuff as he could. He said he believed that you should simply "find people you can trust and then empower them to do things. If they screw up, get rid of them." It was difficult, however, to fire someone at Ford. But Landgraff did succeed in moving a couple of people off the team. He also thought confrontation had a role to play in getting the job done. In Landgraff's experience there were few people who did not require "constant follow-up, exhortation, pressure, and even from time to time confrontation—you know, a really angry kind of session.

"Confrontation seems to do very well, if you don't go overboard . . . don't kill somebody. You can't always expect to get the job done without some pressure. You can't do that in such a way that you upset people all the time, but a little upset is not bad."

Landgraff knew he was bucking a trend. "It's become sort of conventional wisdom around the company: 'well, we want team players.' Team players became kind of a euphemism for somebody who could excel at human relations, who knew how to get the most out of people without being confrontational, without ever being in-your-face kind of thing, and that, I don't think, is realistic.

"You can't be this thousand points of light, all love, gracious and kind, all the time. It doesn't work."

Landgraff once told planners Brad Nalon and Ron Heiser, "I'm going to give you a piece of advice from thirty years at Ford, guys, never trust anyone in this company." Heiser had been at Ford for only a short time, and Landgraff's assessment made a deep impression. "In his view of the world, people are lazy, you can't trust them. The worse part is, he seems to be right."

Nalon agreed. "He wants you to go check on them, then you go check and they're sucking their thumbs."

In sharing his wisdom, Landgraff made one exception.

"You can trust me."

Despite his Hobbesian view of the workplace, it was Landgraff who came up with a way to resolve conflict and make decisions fast. In 1991 he had started a weekly review of design issues involving stylists and engineers; it was held in the studio around the clays. Soon the issues were so numerous that once a week wasn't enough; twice a week wasn't enough. By the time Kinder Essington began his journal, there were daily reviews that began at 4 P.M., when the modelers were done scraping, and often went as late as 7 or 8 P.M.

They were brutal. People who had started work at 7 A.M. were weary when they started, and only got wearier. George Bell's hands seemed always to be at the small of his back. He lost thirty pounds in six months. Andy Benedict twisted his ankle on one of the metal tracks on which clay models moved. For several weeks he rolled around in a little chair with wheels, the only person allowed to sit. But Landgraff never tired. He reminded Essington of a World War II general named Joseph Stilwell. Tactless and acerbic, Stilwell was recalled from his last assignment because of friction with Chiang Kai-shek. His nickname was "Vinegar Joe."

Some decisions were made on the spot. Landgraff didn't want to hear about body-color door sills. He sent the body and assembly guys back to work out a solution, pronto. "One way or another the door sills will be black, goddammit."

Other questions, such as the shape of the door handles—a loop or a paddle—appeared on the agenda week after week. Stylist Mike Webb had always thought there was a single way to open the driver's side door. You lifted up on the handle from underneath with your left hand and applied pressure to the door with your left elbow. But when he watched people try out handles, they grabbed from on top, they grabbed from below, and some even reached over with their right hands for leverage. He called on the women's marketing committee, an organization of Ford females who were often invited to put buttons, handles, and steering wheels to the small-hand, long-fingernail test. A loop or a paddle? The committee split fifty-fifty. He met with suppliers, he met with engineers. Landgraff and Bell tried to be helpful, but they didn't agree. In the end, the loop won. It was easy to grab, the Japanese had them, and the studio wanted it all along. They made it oval like the rest of the car.

Some issues, despite Landgraff's efforts to resolve them at his level, went all the way to the top just as in the old days. Such was the case with the location of the outside rearview mirrors.

Early on, the stylists expressed a preference for the triangular area bounded by the door frame and the window, known as the sail. In cars of a previous generation, a little vent window had occupied this spot. The DN101's raked windshield had forced the sail to be especially large and, in the eyes of the designers, especially ugly. If they didn't put the mirror on that big patch, John Doughty was afraid people would say, "Why didn't you put the mirror where the big patch is?" One way out was to make the sail a fixed piece of glass separated from the window with a divider, but that would have cost $35 a car and added weight. Glass in that location was thicker and heavier than metal. And glass would thwart a proposal from the electronics guys in charge of the sound system to use the inside surface of the sail to mount a small optional speaker that would supplement a larger one lower on the door. Their speaker would lend *purpose* to the sail. Not so fast, said the guys from climate control. Nothing could go on the inside of the sail that would disrupt the air stream from the dash that cleared condensation off the door window. Electronics could have their speaker, but it could protrude only so far.

Steve Kozak and his wind noise engineer Gregory Ehlert did not want the mirror on the sail, period. The sail-mounted mirrors on the outgoing Taurus were a major offender in the wind noise categories. The air flowed off the windshield, swirled around the mirror, and pounded the side glass. At speeds of over 50 miles per hour or so, it sounded as if a band of screaming banshees had glommed onto the strip of metal between the front windshield and the side windows, a section known as the "A" pillar, and was trying to rip it out. The mirror itself, a big blob of metal and glass, was originally designed for a Thunderbird. It was used on the Taurus to save money.

In 1991, as soon as the basic dimensions of DN101 had been locked in, Kozak's chunk team built a wind noise prototype to try out improvements and dispatched it to Atlanta, where Ford rented Lockheed's wind tunnel for testing. Ehlert went down with thirteen mirrors taken from various production cars; seven were equipped with door mounts, six with sail mounts. When the mirror was placed on the door beneath the window rather than on the sail, the results were almost miraculous. It countered the air coming off the windshield with another vortex of air. There was even less wind noise than when there was no mirror there at all. In terms of Things Gone Wrong, the door location improved the count by eight over the sail location. That was not a huge difference on a base count of 120, and it was only a projection, but it was still an improvement. Not only that, it improved fuel efficiency. Kozak and Ehlert made a case for placing quality above looks. John Doughty always said designers had to choose their battles. He decided not to make a stand on this one.

Having proved the advantages of the door location, Ehlert turned to the shape of the mirror, employing a sophisticated method of testing called a design of experiments that was useful in situations with many variables. He and a colleague spent three twelve-hour days running wind tunnel tests on seventeen different mirror heads. With those results in hand, they worked with the studio to style a mirror that had the optimal characteristics. The mirror-to-mirror width of the car could not exceed eighty inches. Any wider and the new Taurus would run into shipping problems.

By Theme Decision, the team had spent a half million dollars on the wind noise prototype and wind tunnel experiments. Ehlert and a colleague had put in hours and hours of unpaid overtime. But at least they had the satisfaction of knowing their efforts had paid off with what could well be the quietest outside rearview mirror in the history of humankind.

Perhaps most gratifying, the negotiations with the studio had been a model of teamwork. Designers Doughty and Gaffka seemed to understand where the engineers were coming from. For their part, the body engineers worked hard to minimize the size of the sail. But they were limited by the position of the door hinges, which determined where the window glass could drop into the door, and thus the area a sail had to cover. And the hinge position was largely locked in by the decision to use the old Taurus underbody.

Going into Theme Decision, Kozak thought the issue was settled. The mirrors went on the doors of the glamour clays. Then NAAO chieftain Alex J. Trotman spoke up. "AJT . . . is concerned about appearance of mirrors on door," Landgraff wrote in his notes of the meeting. That was bad news for Kozak and Ehlert.

Suddenly, there were high-level reviews with Ken Kohrs, vice-president for car product development. Would it be a big problem to move the mirror back to the sail? Ehlert got the feeling the higher-ups wanted the team to change its mind voluntarily, to make their life easier. But the wind noise engineers had hard facts on their side, and the whole team behind them. Well, almost the whole team.

George Bell didn't have strong feelings about it. But Landgraff had been following the issue closely. He thought the compromise on style was well worth making to dampen the noise. The electronics guys worried that the sail-mounted mirror would require hardware that would interfere with their speaker's location on the opposite side. They weren't going to lay down on the tracks on this one, but they were definitely on the side of their brethren from body engineering. The climate control team just wished they'd settle the issue. Their instrument panel de-mister had to clear condensation from the section of the door window through which the mirror was visible. Every time the mirror changed position, an engineer had to redo his calculations on the de-mister airstream. As far as the cost of the two proposals, it was almost a wash.

By August the decision could no longer be delayed. All the principals gathered in the studio. Alex Trotman was present, as well as Kohrs. The designers made their case, and the engineers made theirs. It was looks versus quality, pure and simple. Even though it was he who had raised the issue anew, Trotman had told Landgraff it was a team call. "The team recommends the mirror on the door," Landgraff announced firmly to the two bosses. It seemed to Kozak that Trotman appeared to be leaning toward the door location. Trotman and Kohrs huddled in a corner. Then they waved Landgraff over. They told him to put the mirror on the sail. You didn't argue with two vice-presidents in a matter of taste. "Okay, that's what we'll do," Landgraff said.

Trotman praised the work that had been done and he suggested that in the future Ford design less obtrusive sails. Ehlert appreciated his remarks, but he was devastated nevertheless. He had been so proud of their elegant engineering that he authored a paper published by the Society of Automotive Engineers. He thought about all the money they had spent and he also thought about all the unpaid overtime he had given the company. Now they were going to have to rush the part through design and development, just like the old days.

John Doughty was sorry about the way it happened. He thought a lot of Dick Landgraff; he appreciated all that Landgraff had done to support the studio in the past year. In his heart he believed the team consensus should prevail. If *only* they had decided to put the mirror on the sail. Trotman, too, wished it had been otherwise. He had done his best to stay out of the controversy. "I hoped the team would make the right decision." But the team in its wisdom had been wrong.

EIGHT

Left in the Dark

I N THE WORLD of automotive headlamps, you had your forces of light and your forces of darkness, that was how Kim Peterson saw it. And Peterson was a light force. He liked big bright headlamps, ones that illuminated a generous swath of highway with minimal glare. Truck headlamps were his idea of great lamps.

Peterson, a tall, sandy-haired engineer with wire-rimmed glasses, was Ford's resident authority on headlamps. His job was to design headlamps that met both federal regulations and company requirements that were often even more exacting. Federal law, for example, required illumination beginning at a point that worked out to be some fifty to sixty feet in front of the car. Ford believed that customers felt safer with additional fore-ground light.

Compared to taillamp development, what Peterson did required great precision. You could not, he explained with some pride, ask a taillamp guy to fill in on headlamps for a few weeks. "A taillamp is like a hand grenade; you throw a whole bunch of light out there, you don't have to aim. A headlamp is like a rifle bullet." His satisfaction, he said, was seeing his headlamps wherever he went, even overseas, in knowing that he was giving people "some way to see at night." He would not want to work on some invisible part under the hood.

It had come as news to Peterson that Dick Landgraff and the DN101 team had caved in to the demands of the stylists—he always called them "stylists" rather than "designers"—for new and different headlamps. Much as Doug Gaffka had envisioned, the DN101 strategy at Theme Decision was for a single sparkling complex reflector lamp in the Taurus, incorporating both high and low beams. The Sable would have two lamps on each side; the high beam would come from a complex reflector, and the low beam from a projector lamp. The marketing guys liked the headlamp strategy as much as the designers, because it gave the Sable a larger lens than the Taurus and thus a markedly different front end. The lamps cost more than those on the outgoing cars: $20 more in the case of the Taurus, $35 for the Sable. But the Design Committee was willing to see Ford foot the bill.

Although Honda had had complex reflectors on its Accord since 1988, and Toyota had stuck projector beams on the Lexus, Ford had never used either lamp. As far as Peterson was concerned, the illumination from both was inherently weak, it was sickly. Besides, it was simply too late for this stuff. According to World Class Timing, there was a deadline for incorporating inventions into a program. It was, as it happened, called the "Wall of Invention," and it had come and gone.

Peterson had voiced his objections. But the stylists were standing firm. And the team was on their side. In the summer of 1992, there was no bigger issue facing the program. In one sense, it was a classic struggle between the studio and engineering, a case of stylish, new-tech lamps versus the old standbys that offered tried-and-true quality and performance. But that was not the only question. The headlamps also touched off an emotional debate over whether Ford would surrender to the Japanese in yet another technology race, a particularly shameful proposition because Ford, until only recently, had claimed superiority in lighting.

And then it got personal. In the absence of the new technology, a rival group of engineers in Ford's plastics division saw an opportunity and grabbed it.

GROWING UP, one eye glued to a telescope trained on the heavens, Kim Peterson dreamed of becoming an astronomer. On the advice of a professor at the University of Michigan, who told Peterson there were approximately two job openings a year for astronomers, he got a degree in physics as well as astronomy, which opened up the field of optical engineering. On graduation he worked for a testing lab in Ann Arbor, then hired in at Ford to work on a new kind of headlamp.

For a lighting guy, there was no more exciting place to be in the 1980s than Dearborn. A revolution was sweeping the headlamp industry and Ford Motor Company was in the vanguard. First came halogen lamps, which gave brighter, whiter light at a lower wattage than incandescent bulbs. Ford rushed them into production ahead of other automakers. But halogen lamps, like their predecessors, confined stylists to a square frontal profile. They were actually just big bulbs that came in standard sizes. When one burned out, you went to K-Mart and bought another. Ford wanted a lamp whose lens and housing would stay with the car, and assume its profile, with only a small internal bulb to replace. Peterson played a pivotal role in the development of what came to be known as "aero lamps" because they could be tailored to an aerodynamic front end. In another advance, the lenses were made of light, shatterproof polycarbonate rather than glass, a plus for fuel economy and crash protection. It took a supplier many months to develop a coating that protected them against chipping and ultraviolet discoloration. Once these lamps had cleared difficult regulatory hurdles, Ford's plastic trim and parts division began to manufacture them. After they debuted on the 1984 Mark VII, every car program at Ford wanted its own set, including the 1986 Taurus.

In the early 1990s, as the Design Center experimented with the cab-forward profile, Peterson helped develop a powerful new bulb that made it possible to shrink the height of headlamps so they would fit the lower front ends. He knew by now that stylists never asked how big a lamp you could give them, rather how small. It had been Peterson's expectation that these narrow headlamps would go into DN101, until Gaffka decided he wanted a less menacing countenance on the best-selling car in America.

Gaffka, Doughty, and Rees—the studio triumvirate—were united. By comparison to the clear lamps in the competition, the current Ford lenses with opaque optic plates looked "dark, gray, and gloomy" even on a bright day, Rees said. If the headlamps were eyes, then Ford cars had monstrous hangovers, while the avant-garde competition appeared clear-headed and alert. And why *couldn't* the Taurus have them? "I know it may seem to the guys in lighting that I dream this stuff up," Gaffka said on one occasion. "But the Japanese have it now." Besides, absent chrome, the new Taurus had "nothing on it with any glitz except these headlamps," he said. "They just sparkle."

If they couldn't have new lamps, the designers said, they'd have to throw out the front end design and start over, they were that important.

We'll have to start over: this was the designer's ultimate threat. When an engineer named Conrad Kudelko wanted to finish off the DN101 plastic grille with a coat of glossy black paint, John Doughty got a stubborn look on his face. A glossy surface would call attention to the piece, Doughty said, which was only there to block the view of the engine compartment. People would suddenly notice it, and they would think it looked like a bunch of teeth. If Kudelko persisted, Doughty said, "we'll have to change the front of the car." Or, if engineers couldn't deliver the door handle the designers wanted, they'd get rid of it, and the whole door with it.

Peterson was unmoved by such threats. His job was to make a good lamp, not one that looked different. Turning down the studio went with the territory. "We have to say 'no' to these guys. That's our normal role."

Kim Peterson's cubicle was just a brief walk from the DN101 studio, over in the body engineering mother ship that adjoined the Design Center. But he could be found as often as not in the lighting lab down in the basement of the building, surrounded by headlamps undergoing various forms of torture. At any given moment, lamps were sitting in clear plastic chambers with devices that vibrated, baked, and blew cement dust on them. They spent two days in salt air and fog, five days in 90 percent humidity, and four days with the temperature cycling back and forth between 120 degrees and -40 degrees. Their lenses were rubbed with steel wool and wiped with gasoline. After such tests, they were examined for corrosion, discoloration, scratches, cracking, or leakage.

To test for light distribution, Peterson mounted the headlamp on a frame that attached magnetically to a goniometer, a computer-controlled aiming instrument. Located at one end of a 100-foot tunnel, the goniometer rotated the headlamps to preset positions; at the other end, a photoelectric cell took readings at 4,000 points. A computer plotted the data on an iso-candela graph that told Peterson how the light was distributed. A software program called I-view could interpret the pattern the way the human eye would see it. I-view made it possible to compare two lamps—the distance, for example, at which a road sign would become visible with one headlamp compared to another. But Peterson could tell simply by looking at the graph whether the illumination was overly concentrated in "hot spots" or otherwise unevenly distributed, and whether it could meet requirements. Federal regulations specified 36 points at which the headlamps had to meet a maximum or minimum amount of light. But on certain points Ford sometimes required two to three times the maximum to compensate for significant loss of night vision among older drivers. People were apt to complain about having too little light, but never in Peterson's experience about having too much.

Peterson was appalled by the Honda lamps he tested. They produced a scattered, blotchy pattern. As bad as projector beams were, he thought they showed more long-term promise than the complex reflectors. Although they did not do a good job of spreading light above the horizontal, they gave strong foreground illumination that might suffice for low beams, if they were large enough. But Peterson didn't think there was enough space to house them in the flattened Taurus prow. A supplier claimed to have a version on the way for DN101, but the Ford engineer had his doubts.

To settle the headlamp question, the team scheduled several nighttime drives that summer. Normally engineers liked to go on drives. But Detroit was on the far edge of the eastern time zone, and these rides didn't begin until 10 P.M. That was very late for people who rose at 5:30 A.M. or earlier. Kim Peterson didn't want to go under any circumstances. As far as he was concerned, the opinions of individuals were worthless. If the lamps didn't produce good results in the lab, they were no good. He called the rides "night follies," and managed to miss the first one.

And they *were* no good. Finally people could see for themselves that Peterson was right. A fleet composed of competitive vehicles with projector beams and a Taurus with mock-ups had traversed the curvy, unlighted two-lane roads in nearby Hines Park. No one except Doug Gaffka thought they produced sufficient light. Dick Landgraff was especially disappointed. He had pushed hard for projector beams. He liked their cool, high-tech look. The big surprise was just how bad some of the lamps were on the competition.

The group gathered on another night at the Dearborn Proving Ground to check out the complex reflectors on the Honda Accord. No one challenged Peterson's contention that the outgoing Taurus had better lamps, but that wasn't the question. The question, Landgraff said, was whether the Accord lamps were good enough. Landgraff had driven the Accord, at the moment the best-selling car in America, on numerous occasions. He thought they were fine. And so did the other drivers.

The team regrouped. The new plan was to use complex reflectors on both the Taurus and the Sable. The Sable would preserve its distinct appearance by continuing to use a lens large enough to cover two lamps, and sticking the parking lamp where the projector beam had been.

The supplier for the complex reflector was to be Ford's own plastics division, PTPD, which had heretofore only manufactured lamps, not designed them. But PTPD had a stake in mastering the new technology. Nothing prevented a car program from going outside the company for headlamps, as DN101 had been prepared to do with projector beams. PTPD could lose business and its unionized plants could suffer layoffs, a costly affair for the company. The designers had not been the only people at Ford intrigued by the Accord headlamps. To Amir Fallani, who had just come to PTPD from General Motors and was casting about for something to do, Honda's complex reflectors looked like an open invitation.

On the traditional optic plate lens, engineers laid out a configuration of tiny grooves, cylinders, wedges, and ridges that dispersed light in a calculated pattern when struck from behind. The complex reflector bounced light from the bulb off a metallized housing composed of scores of tiny faceted mirrors and forward through the clear lens. The pattern of illumination depended on the shapes and angles of the facets. The engineers could copy the Honda lamp through reverse engineering. But that would be like memorizing piano keys to a melody. Unless you could read music, you couldn't play anything else. Ford needed software to design lamps of different shapes and sizes. Unlike the Honda system, where there were two bulbs on each side, most Ford lamps had a single bulb with two filaments, one for high beams and one for low beams. The arrangement of mirrored facets on the housing had to reflect a pattern for each distinct filament.

Honda's experts had described their approach in a technical paper published in 1987 by the Society of Automotive Engineers. Fallani had tucked it away in his files with a bunch of other stuff he had collected on new technologies. Not until he began to pay attention to the Accord lamps did he remember the paper. Reading it, he could scarcely believe this piece of good fortune. While not comprehensive, it contained a bonanza of clues. That was just like a Japanese company. In his experience, they were more likely than Americans to boast about their achievements. Toyota was always publicizing its patents.

Fallani and two other engineers pored over the paper for six months. By 1992, the group was far enough along to promise a complex reflector as a running change on the 1994 Taurus LX, the high-series model. But the DN101 lamp was even more difficult. Not only was the entire lamp smaller, but the bulb lay at the end of a housing that was shaped like a tunnel.

IF KIM PETERSON represented the opposition to new headlamps, at the other extreme was Jim Mikola, the head of the DN101 chunk team for bumpers and lighting. Like Steve Kozak, Mikola was an engineering princeling with an MBA and a sense of adventure. The studio had persuaded him that they had to have this—how did they put it?—"rich, jewelry-like appearance." And if anyone needed a reminder that styling was critical, at that very moment critics were blasting Ford for having done so little to change the 1992 Taurus. As far as Mikola was concerned, the Wall of Invention didn't apply in this case because PTPD had been at work on complex reflectors before the deadline. To him, there was more at stake here than a pair of headlamps. Why hadn't Ford pressed ahead with a new generation of lamps, so the basic technology was on the shelf when DN101 needed it? The company didn't even have an advanced lighting lab. But that was history. Now the question was this: Did Ford have the courage, stamina, and smarts to master a new headlamp technology in time for the Taurus, and in so doing reclaim its former glory as a lighting leader?

Bouncing back and forth on the spectrum between Mikola and Peterson were the PTPD guys. The DN101 complex reflector lamps were really *hard*. And once they did come up with a computer design for the fifty or so little mirrors, there was no guarantee they could manufacture a housing that would do the job. If one facet were off 10 or 20 microns—a micron was 1,000th of a millimeter!—it could alter the beam pattern. The PTPD mood seemed to depend on whom they'd met with last. Mikola knew if they'd been talking to Peterson, they'd be down in the mouth and pessimistic about their chances of success. Mikola would have to rev them up and get them going again. At one meeting, Peterson and one of the PTPD guys got into a verbal battle. PTPD insisted they could deliver. Peterson said they couldn't. Both sides brandished computer charts to support their positions. The DN101 team scarcely knew what to think.

Peterson was growing increasingly isolated. At one point he had refused to accompany his boss at body engineering to meetings with PTPD. Big mistake. Now his boss had gone over to the other side. Undeterred, Peterson continued to speak up. Hearing him contradict his boss in public, DN101 planner Ron Heiser turned to Doug Gaffka, "If I did that I'd be out of a job." But Joe Hellmers, the DN101 chunk team headlamp specialist who had known Peterson for many years, could not help admiring him for saying what he believed.

Peterson not only objected to the quality of light, but to an internal aiming device as well. At present, workers adjusted the headlamps after they were installed on the car. To allow for the adjustment, a gap of several millimeters surrounded the lens. Customers who didn't understand its purpose complained when the adjustment produced uneven margins. The studio hated the gap. Landgraff hated the gap; it didn't represent craftsmanship. The new lamps contained a tiny bubble level for aiming, like those used in building construction, that would render the gap obsolete. Peterson knew the studio didn't like the gap, but he didn't care about that either. "Personally I don't think it's a problem." He thought the bubble level was less reliable.

The PTPD guys continued to plug away on their computers, but they were unable to guarantee success. As months went by, even the optimistic Mikola began to feel a "sense of uneasiness that we had the entire program styled to lighting devices that were still under much development." A sense of uneasiness that . . . *there were no headlamps* . . . conventional or otherwise. There were, in fact, just big gaping holes where headlamps ought to be.

There came a time when you had to protect yourself. The team would continue to press ahead on complex reflectors, but they would also design an optic plate lamp to fit the same oval opening, just in case. . . .

Two different headlamps: *a dual program.* Dual programs were a black mark against management. They were expensive, a waste of resources. And with a safety net in place, engineers might be less inclined to struggle with the more ambitious alternative. Nobody liked dual programs less than the engineers, because their workload doubled. Sometimes the proposal alone was sufficient to produce a solution. In this case, however, there would be two groups at work. Peterson would do the optic plate lens. PTPD under Fallani would continue its work with complex reflectors. Somehow—Landgraff said he didn't know quite how—the thing had turned into a design competition.

Peterson knew what they thought of him. He was a bad guy, a naysayer, a retro-technician, an arch-headlamp-conservative. But how could he be more correct? He was in favor of good lamps, lamps that were inexpensive, lamps that illuminated the road for people over forty (the night vision impaired), lamps that Ford just happened to know how to make. And the Wall of Invention! His opponents had climbed right over that little barricade as if it didn't exist. In the old days, the headlamp expert would have had the final word. But now he was in the grip of forces beyond his control. A basement away was this new entity, this dedicated, collocated team, cheerfully marching off in the wrong direction.

Still, the final chapter had not been written. Seldom did the media critique headlamps. But the 1993 Dodge Intrepid had come out with a set of complex reflectors that was so bad, the car writers had noticed. The lamps "look swell," said *Car and Driver,* "but throw a pitiful pattern." Said *Auto Week,* "We can't remember the last time someone complained about headlamps, but the Intrepid's are as dim as our hopes for a Pulitzer."

Peterson clipped the articles and stuck them in his files.

NINE

Pulling Together

ON MAY 19, 1993, an 18-by-24-inch sheetcake decorated with pale blue rosettes and the Ford oval appeared on a table outside the basement conference room to mark the DN101 team's second anniversary. There were no speeches or official acts. People just cut a piece of cake and stood around talking or went back to their desks. It was kind of grim, really. For a celebration.

But these were not party animals. During the first Christmas season, when the team numbered about 600, personnel director Wendy Dendel had lined up a hall and a deejay for holiday festivities. With food and an open bar, tickets were a steal at $14.50. But only twenty-five people signed up, too few. They preferred to bring food to an all-day buffet in the basement; those who wanted to talk could both eat and talk; those who didn't could merely eat. It worked out better for everybody. The folks who maintained the coffee station, principally CAD designers, who were rooted to their desks all day and had a stake in an endless supply of caffeine, contributed drinks and paper goods with the profit they had amassed on 20-cent cups of coffee and candy bars. Dick Landgraff had not been in favor of the basement Christmas spread. He told Dendel that he didn't like to see people standing around looking unproductive. Neither he nor his secretary Nancy Donaldson cared for the coming and going of people all day long just outside their offices, babbling and licking their fingers and leaning on the flimsy partitions. Landgraff was known to dislike lunch meetings, with people eating and talking and spitting out food. He also didn't like to see employees in the hallways, gazing up at the TV monitors which broadcast company news over the Ford Communications Network. Didn't they have anything better to do?

Still, Landgraff put in an appearance at the anniversary cake. Dendel was pleased about that. She considered morale one of her unofficial responsibilities. And Dick often didn't seem to realize how much influence he had. Dendel had her finger on the collective pulse. The door to her office was usually open, and there was usually someone in there deep in conversation. An ardent volleyball player, she looked healthy, sturdy, and wholesome; she radiated concern and competence.

The team had started small and, in Ford lingo, had ramped up to 700, about twice as many as the Design Center had room for. So half remained in their home offices, dedicated but not collocated, one might say. A recent defection by the chassis contingent had opened up several dozen cubes. Landgraff had been royally annoyed to find them gone. One day he had summoned someone from chassis, and no one was there. They had *uncollocated*, they had pulled out and gone back to Building Five without consulting him. They argued that they needed to be back in the home office because the same engineers were doing both the Taurus and the T-Bird, and it was better for testing. He could see their point, but he didn't like the way it had happened. Other people were down on chassis as well. They had not sent people to the team until the fall of 1991, their issues took longer to resolve, and now, after eighteen months, they were gone. They were not . . . team players. But they sure lined up with everybody else for their DN101 sweatshirts when Dendel got them in. She spent $14,000 and handed out 1,100 sweatshirts and still there weren't enough. People crawled out of the woodwork claiming to be team members.

As the team began its third year in the basement, both pressure and excitement were building. Having gone from a clay model to a math model, DN101 was being born again in three dimensions. In job shops around Detroit, tradesmen were bending sheet metal, molding plastic, shaping glass, and hammering out parts. Suppliers all over the country were filling orders for delivery in early fall to Ford's pilot plant down the road in Allen Park.

In November, workers at the pilot plant would begin to assemble these custom-made parts into what were called confirmation prototypes. And then would come the moment when gasoline would fill the lines and fire the motor of the first completed prototype, the staunch 145-horsepower organ would begin to throb, lights would blink in the instrument panel, and the gauges would spring to life as the electronic brain prepared for motion. For the first time, all the disparate pieces would be unified; they would become, in a manner of speaking, a living, breathing . . . car.

For each new car program, Ford handbuilt some 350 prototype units at an average cost of $250,000. Many were simple engine compartments or interior cabins that cost mere thousands. But these confirmation prototypes, which would look like Tauruses, run like Tauruses, and sound like Tauruses, constituted the bulk of the fleet and had price tags approaching half a million. Notwithstanding the cost, a lot of people couldn't wait to destroy them or push them to the limit in other ways.

A certain percentage would be crushed and crumpled in crash tests. Over at the Dearborn Proving Ground, the development engineers would drive others around the track and out onto the highways, suitably camouflaged front and rear with zip-on vinyl covers over chunks of Styrofoam, to check out big-ticket items such as the steering; suspension; noise, vibration, and harshness (NVH); and brakes. In the countryside north of Dearborn, near the town of Romeo, prototypes earmarked "durability cars" would begin a 51,500-mile journey round and round the roads of Ford's Michigan Proving Ground on a course intended to equate to 100,000 American driver miles, 4,000 of them logged on a punishing course of square-edged potholes, big lumpy cobblestones, a mud bath, a saltwater bath, and sudden stops, plus a test in which the car rammed into a curb at 50 miles per hour. The Romeo test track was the former estate of Edward F. Fisher, one of the first auto industry barons, who built his wife an elaborate Gothic-style stone mansion with 269 rooms. Unimpressed, she refused to move from the city to what then seemed like wilderness. Fisher had destroyed the uninhabited mansion and raised cattle on the land before selling it to Ford.

In the first week of January bands of engineers would drive more prototypes to the frozen wastes of northern Minnesota, and perhaps even farther north into the Canadian tundra, for subzero testing of engines and the heating system. One dreaded protocol called on participants to jump into ice-cold cars before dawn, and ride around with the heat on, gauging the time it took to reach comfort level. Some people never got warm after starting the day this way.

Job One was set in stone for June 19, 1995, having slipped four months since the program began, largely owing to changes in the station wagon. Normally the delay would be a black mark against the program manager, but in this case the changes had been set in motion by Alex Trotman, who had moved up to become the number-two guy in the company, so no one was making a federal case of it. Two years from now, when the assembly plants started production, many of the team members would have moved on to other programs. For them, the confirmation prototype was Job One. With the excitement came more work. Their parts were on the car; they were responsible for making sure they worked. The deadlines that had once seemed so distant on the Twip chart were now upon them. In the summer and fall months leading up to the build, they had to finish their designs and work with the suppliers to deliver prototype parts. Ford was spending real money, ordering parts and tooling. The heat was on.

T HE   WEEK   BEFORE the anniversary, Landgraff called a team meeting in the Design Center showroom to exhort the troops to make the confirmation prototype a "quality event." A few moments into the meeting, however, he dropped a bombshell. NAAO, he told the team, was billions over budget. The Taurus SHO was being canceled.

The SHO had limited market appeal. Buyers were middle-aged married men who yearned for a rugged macho machine, were willing to pay some $25,000, but needed a family car. A "hot-rod for the 40-something set," one car writer called it. A "stealth car," said DN101 planner Pete Sharpe. It looked like a Taurus but could outrun the cops. Landgraff drove a black SHO.

Everyone could understand the financial wisdom of canceling a model that sold only 10,000 to 12,000 units a year and lost money. But DN101 engineers, many of them car guys at heart, liked having a hand in the development of the SHO. It had a powerful Yamaha engine, which was to jump from six to eight cylinders in the 1996 model, a spoiler across the rear, leather seats, and other performance-car attributes. Not to do the SHO, George Bell said, would be "a signal to the outside world that we're pulling in our horns, that we've decided to do the bread-and-butter cars and not the excitement cars." Nevertheless, Bell was surprised that Landgraff had announced the cancellation so abruptly in so public a forum.

But Landgraff couldn't contain himself. He was damned mad. He had gotten the news the wrong way, through the grapevine. He tracked down his boss Ben Lever in Europe to confirm it. Killing the SHO was just a proposal at this point, Lever said. Landgraff fired off an angry note to vice-president Ken Kohrs, telling him they all looked stupid down here in the basement, what was going on? You couldn't take away the most fun part of the program without hurting it. The negative signals to dealers and the press would outweigh any savings. They'd been working on the SHO for two years. What was the big idea?

Immediately after telling the team the SHO was dead, Landgraff launched a crusade to save it. At 5:45 P.M. the night before he was to make the case for preservation to Kohrs, Landgraff gathered his finance manager Tom Gorman, business planner Rich Pettit, and SHO planner Pete Sharpe at a table outside the basement conference room to plot strategy.

He had a two-pronged plan for saving the SHO: he would trim costs and he would rally support of others in the company. Dick knew Lincoln-Mercury mogul Bob Tasca well enough to ask for help, and Tasca knew W. C. Ford well enough to pick up the phone and call him, or to call Red Poling for that matter. Wayne Booker, vice-president for Asia-Pacific Automotive Operations, would surely want to preserve the Yamaha relationship. Landgraff had once worked for Booker. The head of powertrain would make a good ally. Meanwhile there were ways to save as much as $25 million on engineering and additional hundreds of thousands on prototypes. He needed a written proposal by the next day.

"You want it stapled or not?" Sharpe asked. With Landgraff, you wanted to be sure.

"Handle it, Pete," Landgraff answered. "I'll delegate that to you."

They would include a propitious rave by the *New York Times*'s senior automotive writer, Marshall Schuon, published the preceding Sunday, describing the SHO as "something special."

"The V6 moves the 3,084-pound four-door as if it were a sporty coupe, with zero-to-60 acceleration in about 7.5 seconds, and the car rock solid at cruising speeds," Schuon wrote.

O N   T H E   O N E   H A N D, Landgraff was miffed by the move against the SHO. On the other, he knew that during the course of a car program, "there's always going to be a recession, a setback, something." And the guys at the top would come along and say, "Let's cancel part of it and save some money." At least things weren't as extreme as in the old days when they'd make a list of things to strip from the car and ninety days later it would all be gone—carpet, floor mats, whatever—they'd sell a car with a bare trunk, it didn't matter what you sold people. These measures were identified as a "profit improvement program." The acronym had become a verb: "Let's pip that." Get rid of it.

The team's campaign to save the SHO was successful, but just weeks later there was another anxious spell, triggered by an analysis of Toyota's probable future pricing. A Ford consultant, Hillburn & Associates, suggested that the Japanese company's "relentless pursuit of perfection"—the Lexus advertising tagline—had become a disease that made it "vulnerable to attack as an elitist premium-priced brand." The implication was that Toyota would decide its cars were too expensive and correct its course before a reaction set in, charting a path toward reduced costs and lowered prices. Just as the new Taurus shot up in price, the Camry's prices would plummet. Like ships passing in the night. Ed Hagenlocker, who had succeeded Alex Trotman as head of NAAO, wanted to reevaluate the cost that had been added to DN101 to match Camry. At the same time, there was talk of being more like Chrysler, which was announcing profit margins that put Ford and GM to shame. Landgraff, nose to the wind, said he was "beginning to sniff a less than total commitment to going after Toyota."

He reassured Hagenlocker that there was little evidence that Toyota planned to back off its quality commitment. If anything, its costs were increasing. According to Ford's trained cost estimators, the 1994 Camry just out contained $200 in upgrades. Toyota had installed passenger-side airbags two years before the legal requirement, and also converted to an aluminum block engine that alone must have added $50 to the cost. The weight save was thirty pounds, but they didn't especially need it. "I don't know why they did it," Landgraff said. "Maybe just to be the best."

T HE C AMRY WAS EVERYWHERE these days. Ford had to be one of Toyota's best customers in the Detroit area, with thirty Camrys and a dozen or so Lexuses scattered around company property. A Camry sedan was parked more or less permanently in the DN101 studio. In a debate on the width of the windshield molding, someone would say, "How does Camry do it?" And a clump of people would trudge over to the enemy vehicle for a look-see. "The Camry joints are almost invisible," Landgraff said in a discussion over how to connect one molding to another. "The standard for the joint is Camry." For some reason, the word was pronounced one of two ways at Ford: "Camery" or "Camray."

Struggling to unlock the Camry's secrets, George Bell tapped a plastic panel with his pen at the regular weekly meeting called "styling issues." Was talc one of the ingredients that made their plastic parts look less plastic? They shared a supplier, but he wasn't being helpful. Was that because talc was harder on his tooling, and he didn't want to see Ford use it? Another thing, Camry's plastic parts felt better to the touch than Ford's. Said Landgraff, "They don't feel greasy. We always get criticized by market research, who says our parts feel slippery."

And the parking brake: "Are you going to design it like the Camry?" Landgraff asked the engineers. "That's all I want to know. If you do you can make the rubber boot a lot smaller. And it's going to make a lot less noise because Camry makes a lot less noise."

The craftsmanship campaign was in full swing as well. Planner Ron Heiser got the assignment to make sure all the black stuff on the outside of the car was the same shade. His first surprise was how much there was. Of 220 pieces, 82 were black, consisting mostly of moldings around the windshield, the windows, the fascia, the doors, the headlamps. Some were made of plastic and rubber, and some of metal. Some of the plastics were hard, some were soft, some were molded in color, others were molded and painted afterward, and some were extruded like frosting pushed through a decorator's tube. His second surprise was how different blacks could be. There were twenty-one suppliers, each of whom was given a sample color chip with the code YGYA. Heiser had no idea what the letters stood for; he knew only that it was the black chosen by the Design Center. The suppliers also had to match a single gloss level; one part couldn't be shinier than another. The whole thing was like a big black jigsaw puzzle. He could see the pieces when he closed his eyes.

E ACH DAY AT NOON, Landgraff and Bell presided over a meeting called "change control," where engineers streamed in with problems. They were not called "problems," however, a word thought to be too negative. Ford much preferred "concerns," "issues," or, best of all, "challenges." And "control," they decided, was not the right word for what they needed to do here. In the beginning when their goal was simply to hold down the sheer number of changes it had seemed appropriate, but now there was more to the process than controlling the numbers. Some changes were critical. Others were desirable, but could be delayed. They rechristened the meeting "change management," which seemed to suggest an approach with some brainpower behind it.

Requests to change parts in the car were pouring in from the engineers at the rate of ten to twelve a day. Parts could change for any number of reasons. Assembly plant workers made periodic trips to Dearborn for practice builds. If they spotted something they couldn't assemble at sixty-plus jobs an hour, it was a "no-build," an automatic prescription for a redesign. Discovering a time-saving measure could prompt a change. Engineers also might have made mistakes; parts failed tests or they interfered with each other's performance. Or maybe the engineer just wanted to make a component better in some way. Continual improvement was all very well—it was the Japanese mantra, *kaizen*—but it was an engineering disease. Sometimes you just had to take the engineer's little part away and put it in the car.

Engineering changes were a very big issue in car product development. Ford typically changed every part two or three times, on average. Each change required extensive analysis for its impact on the cost, weight, and investment targets. Americans popularly supposed that the Japanese did a better job on their initial design, thus saving huge amounts of time and money. And yet an influential study of the car industry in Japan, the United States, and Europe, published in 1991 by the Harvard Business School Press, had concluded that was not the case. "Our comparative study shows that the typical Japanese project has almost as many changes as its Western counterpart," wrote the authors of *Product Development Performance*, Kim B. Clark and Takahiro Fujimoto. "[But] . . . procedures are less bureaucratic and oriented more toward fast implementation than toward checks and balances. In effect, this approach emphasizes early versus late, meaningful versus unnecessary, and fast versus slow."

It was the same old frustrating story. Japan, good. United States, bad. The Japanese knew how to communicate. They were more flexible. They knew what was important.

Sometimes Landgraff wondered how it would all come out in the end. Would the Japanese just get so damned good that you could go in and order the car you wanted, and they would build it overnight, have it for you the next day?

DN101 WAS SO TIGHTLY packed with parts that when one changed, everything around it was likely to change as well. And so, there was a group of engineers whose chief assignment was to preside over space in the car. They worked for Tom Breault, the vehicle office design manager. Their job was called "packaging." And the space they allocated was "real estate." In effect they were brokers. But there were no buyers and sellers, just people who wanted more space.

Battles raged all over the car. The doors were jammed with stuff, especially in the area around the handle, where the controls for the power locks and power windows were jousting with each other. In the trunk, the wrench that was supposed to be lodged under the spare tire no longer fit after the body engineers added ribs to strengthen the floorpan, shrinking the tire well. They shortened the wrench handle, but there were lingering concerns that the average driver wouldn't get enough leverage to loosen the nuts.

Competition in the engine compartment was the most fierce. It had been decades since you could open the hood of a car and see a patch of ground, it was so full of stuff. Not only was the engine swollen with valves, but the battery, alternator, and other neighbors had gotten bigger. There was a big bulky air cleaner. And with the conversion to front-wheel drive, a transaxle was jammed in there too. Meanwhile, the compartment itself had grown smaller over the last decade as the windshield slid forward. The hood of this newest Taurus was shorter and lower than ever; it reduced space in the engine compartment by 20 percent. The engines themselves, though, could neither budge nor shrink. They were a given, exempt from the packaging wars.

Two years ago Ed Opaleski, the Taurus team's head package guy on the engine compartment, was mapping out large parts such as engine mounts and upper intake manifolds. Now he was down to tiny things, like the cable that ran from the column shifter to the transmission. Small and flexible, the cable was something you'd think could go anywhere, but the column shifter people arrived after the electrical components people had grabbed all the choice places in the instrument panel. The vehicle office chose the best alternative location, but when workers from Atlanta dismantled the shifter during a simulated build, they couldn't hook it back up to the cable. As a temporary measure for the confirmation prototype, the team could use the old Taurus routing, but no one wanted to do that. There would be no value in it for proving out the design.

And with just months to go to the prototype build, the airbag crash sensors were still migrating around the front end, looking for a home. The sensors were small boxes the size of an AC power adaptor, containing a marble-sized ball that closed a circuit and popped the airbags when the car crashed at speeds over 14 miles per hour. Early in the program, Paul Kula, the body engineer for the sensors, put in a bid for the grille opening with Lichia Bucklin, the engineer who was in charge of packaging the front sixteen inches of the car. It was not to be. The sensors were bumped from that location in a chain of circumstances linked to the failure of the projector low-beam lamp proposed for the Sable.

The revised Sable scheme called for placing a bulb that was both the parking lamp and a turn signal inboard from the headlamps behind a lens that would cover them both. That plan ran afoul of a requirement that the turn signal be either four inches away from the headlamp or two and a half times as bright, so that you could see the signal when the headlamp was on. In this case there wasn't room for such a big, bright bulb next to the headlamp and there wasn't space behind the lens to move it four inches away. The only solution was to separate the turn signal from the parking lamp, and move it somewhere else.

That somewhere else had turned out to be the corners of the grille, where the airbag sensor wanted to be. Sure the stylists could find a different location for the lamps, but not without redesigning the front end.

It had taken a while—partly because Kula was diverted by work on the

1994 Mustang—but by April 1992, as Bucklin was preparing for a maternity leave, they had found a compromise that satisfied everybody: They would put the sensors into little out-of-the-way pockets molded into each end of the upper radiator support, behind the fascia. But when the crash guys ran a car dead center into a pole, the airbags didn't deploy quickly enough. Moving the sensors closer together would not necessarily address the problem, because they also had to pass a "corner test," when the car slammed into a wall at a thirty-degree angle.

Automotive safety was a sensitive subject. The rear-end Pinto fires that killed dozens of people in the late 1970s had left a permanent scar on the corporate psyche. People joked that "fire" had become a dirty word. The firewall, the divider between the car's interior and the engine compartment, was now the "dash panel." The company definitely did not want headlines about a hazard in America's number-one-selling car. There were ten crash guys over in body engineering designing and testing front-end crumple zones, so sections of the underbody collapsed like an accordion, rear-end protection for fuel tanks, door beams and foam padding, and other creative forms of impact absorption. The threat of bad press aside, people were genuinely concerned about safety. They and their families and their friends drove Fords. Mike Vecchio, the side impact engineer, had been in the safety department only a few months when the wife of a good buddy was severely injured in a crash on Hines Drive, a twisting road through a public park. She was turning left when a big Monte Carlo slammed into the side of her Chevy Citation. "All she saw were headlights," he said. That was in 1984, and he'd been doing side impact work ever since. He mentally replayed the scene every time he saw a car smack another from the side.

More than some engineers, crash guys could argue that they were helping humankind. "To me the whole idea about safety is about forgiveness," said Vecchio. "If someone makes a mistake—if you want to call it a mistake, because the consequences are kind of gruesome in some cases—they shouldn't necessarily have to suffer for that. Everybody makes a mistake. You need to get to the point where you can minimize the amount of damage to other people and to themselves that that mistake makes. That's the essence of crash safety."

RETURNING FROM MATERNITY LEAVE in August to find the airbag sensors still without a home, Lichia Bucklin was momentarily stumped. Another promising location was currently occupied by the ambient air sensor, which flashed the outside temperature to the car's occupants and helped regulate an automatic temperature control system inside the car.

Alas, the need for a ground further complicated the search. The crash sensors had a grounding wire already, to complete a circuit for the warning light in the dash that went on if they weren't working. But the wire wasn't sufficiently strong to ground the sensor itself; it could snap in an accident. Body engineering demanded a sturdy metal strap. If the upper radiator support had been metal, as in the past, grounding would not have been an issue for sensors situated somewhere on its surface. But the support in DN101 was plastic. It was a great leap forward for plastics technology, but a setback for the sensor.

The next proposal was to place both the airbag sensor and the ambient air sensor on a twisted fifteen-inch metal grounding bracket attached to the front of the radiator support and the front rail behind the bumper. Now the climate control division worried that the crash sensors, though tiny, in combination with the bracket could reduce the air intake through the grille for the air conditioning system. Burned on past programs, Mary Ann Wheeler, who was the climate control doyenne on the DN101 team, had made Tom Breault promise to give them the volume of air they needed. Now she accused him of allowing his people to renege on the deal.

Resentment was building on the team against Kula, the airbag engineer, who seemed to display a certain arrogance. He knew, and so did everybody else, that people would have to bend over backward to assure that his little safety device worked. In Kula's view, however, others didn't appreciate the sensitivity of the crash sensor. They talked as if you could just throw it anywhere and it would be okay.

One day one of Wheeler's engineers, a beloved old-timer named Len Flack, left a meeting on the crash sensor talking to himself. How could he, a mere air conditioning guy, who wanted to cool people off, compete for space with an airbag device? "They're Jesus Christ. They save lives."

There was also the possibility that the Mercury logo, known as the "Flying M," which dipped into the Sable grille in a V-shape, would divert air from the ambient air sensor so it couldn't perform its little temperature-measuring job. The climate control team was not happy about that either, or about having to cough up 52 cents for additional wiring for the bracket location.

The deadline for prototype parts was closing in on everybody. Ford was paying the upper radiator support supplier, who was supposed to pay the bracket supplier. But the bracket supplier claimed not to have received a check for design work. He had ordered a halt to tooling. Defending himself, the radiator support supplier claimed not to have received an official quote from the bracket supplier. Bucklin thought they were both jeopardizing their future with Ford with this kind of childish behavior.

In the early days of DN101, when there was more time and space, agreements were made on handshakes. Now the process for approving changes had grown into the multi-stage procedural horror known as a change control—make that *management*—which took place daily at noon in the basement conference room with either Landgraff or Bell presiding, and usually both, seated side by side. For middle-aged white men, the pair were quite different in physical appearance. Bell was as padded as Landgraff was spare. He had a bushy mustache and wore tinted, rimless glasses to Landgraff's rounded, old-fashioned frames. Landgraff oiled down his short dark curly hair to form a thin corporate layer across his scalp. Bell's thick wavy gray hair, one of his best features, spilled across his forehead; he wore medium-gray suits that matched his hair, whereas Landgraff was usually in navy blue. Landgraff leaned forward, intense. Bell looked more relaxed, an illusion he cultivated.

After change management on the schedule came the "social mixers," a light name for the deadly business of negotiating the proposed changes between warring parties. Depending on which part, the mixer featured one of six packaging guys who had been appointed as "stickmen," whose role was to prod people into agreement. They didn't teach this kind of thing in engineering school. Said Lichia Bucklin, "When I came to the company, people were arguing about millimeters. I thought, 'How silly. What difference does a millimeter make?' Millimeters are a big deal around here."

Before the airbag sensors and the ambient air sensor landed in permanent locations, and everybody got paid, Bucklin found herself in either change management or a social mixer on four separate occasions. With each meeting, her respect grew for George Bell. He never made her feel apologetic for coming in with yet another sob story. But more than that, she was in awe of his engineering aptitude. He seemed to have a mental image of every single screw, weld, and bracket in the car. She thought his mind must work like a CAD screen. *Click* and up came the car, *click* and the computer summoned a single joint. *Click-click-click* and the joint exploded until it filled the screen. Steve Kozak called Bell "the Leonardo da Vinci of the Design Center. It's amazing how he can make decisions based on so little information." Some engineers were surprised when Bell seemed to know more about their part than they themselves.

When she presented the request for 52 cents to move the ambient air sensor, Bell calculated its impact and made a little joke. "That's $300,000 a year, $1.5 million over the life of the program. . . . That's a lot of money to take out of the merit pot. You guys'll never get a merit raise." He pondered the layout, looking for a way to save money, his CAD-like brain clicking silently. "You can keep it on a shorter wire on the other side of the grille if you use a ninety-degree take-out." He sent them back to try again.

One day in a station wagon walkaround, some engineers asked Bell's advice about the access holes on the inside rear panel for the removal of the rear bumper in the event a repair was necessary. Carpet covered them, but the holes made the carpet susceptible to damage. What if kids poked pens into the holes, through the carpet? Bell suggested filling the holes with serrated, pop-out pieces. The guys looked at him like the heavens had parted and a celestial beam of light had burst through the opening. "That would work," somebody said. Maybe it wasn't rocket science, but they hadn't thought of it. Bell was modest about his abilities. Sometimes, he said, the components guys just got overwhelmed by all the tests they had to pass, the requirements they had to meet. "They can't see their way out. Sometimes they just need someone to tell them what to do."

Dan Rivard, who had come out of retirement to supervise special vehicle operations, a performance-car division, had been his supervisor when Bell was a young chassis engineer. Not only did he consider Bell one of the ten most gifted engineers he'd ever known, but "he was always a nice guy. He didn't have a mean bone in his body." If he had a fault, it was that he was *too* brilliant. When Bell became a supervisor, Rivard would see him at work from early morning till late at night. Back off and let your people do the job, the older man counseled. Given the three or four people reporting to him, Rivard told Bell, he might be "twice as smart but not four times as smart."

Tom Breault admired Bell's tact in sensitive situations. "He will do anything to allow a person to save face. He will say 'I probably didn't explain this. . . .' He watches situations to get cues. . . . How long will it take before we can establish who's at fault and we can do what we need to do?"

Sometimes Bell wondered if he should be tougher, more like Landgraff perhaps. But every time he yelled at someone, he felt so bad it took him a day to recover. His heart went out to newcomers on the team. He could spot them by their body language, chairs pushed back from the table, arms crossed defensively, and he knew they were thinking fearfully, "What if I have to *say* something?" He liked to set an example, to show them that while the car business was serious, it was not life and death. He tried to defuse tense situations with humor.

Engineers as a breed were not funny guys; their work did not lend itself to wisecracks. When they tried to joke, you got some pathetic little exchange like these actual examples: One guy says, "Well, that's water under the bridge," and the other comes back with, "Well, at least it's not water in the engine." Or one guy says, "Did you twist his arm?" And his companion answers, "Yes, but every time I twist it, it comes off."

Bell's humor took the form of similes. Sinking three-quarters of a million dollars into a prototype tool that might not work was, Bell quipped, "like measuring the depth of the water after you've jumped off the board." On how suppliers would say anything to keep Ford's business, he observed: "Promises are like babies, fun to make and hard to deliver."

Given the competition, Bell was a comedy club headliner. His similes were the talk of the team. People called them "Georgisms," wrote them down, and traded them back and forth. Were you at the wiring review? Did you hear what George said when he looked at the engine compartment? "This looks like a dog's breakfast."

Sometimes he would think of a comparison in advance. He'd bide his time, waiting to plug it into a conversation. But premeditated observations never seemed to be quite right. More often, old saws sprang to mind, or he invented something on the spot. "Let's stop lashing ourselves with barbed wire." Or, "let's shift gears and move on to transmissions."

Karin Dean, who took minutes of certain meetings, liked to end her summary with an overheard "sound bite." Many were from Bell, but there were others as well:

"Sorry, we didn't bring any fenders to fondle."

"Sorry, I slipped a digit."

"These are not real numbers."

She labeled some of them "Famous Lasts," for last words, as in: "Right now we know what we're doing," and "We are going to come back and save you some money." Readers reproached her if she failed to conclude the minutes with a quote. There wasn't much else to laugh at.

OTHERS MIGHT BE in a panic mode—the climate control people couldn't seem to get enough air, their condensor was positively gasping, and Goodyear, the instrument panel supplier, was trying to back out of the contract and sell its plastics plant—but Steve Kozak and his sheet-metal guys were in good shape, their crises behind them, thanks to good planning and, of course, some groundbreaking computer-aided engineering that simulated cars in motion. They had used CAE to the max, to calculate how to reduce the bending and twisting in the old Taurus, to rid the car of the dreaded boom—that moment when the body resonated like a giant bass drum to inputs from the chassis and the road, a sound that front-end honcho Ed Kuczera described as something "like being inside a 55-gallon oil drum and someone slapping on the outside." Boom had made the outgoing Taurus the worst car in its class for rear-seat noise.

To make the body stiffer, they had thickened the cross-car beams and strengthened the joints. The results were double some of the targets. The car was *solid*. As a consequence, the structural prototypes built in January were getting rave reviews. For purposes of camouflage, they had been slapped together out of sheet metal that somewhat resembled clunky Volvos. But under the drab exteriors rippled the fortified new musculature. The development guys loved the way they handled. Dick Landgraff and George Bell loved the way they handled. "We got a big problem with this car," Bell said in May after checking the cars out prior to Jackie Stewart's drive. "It's better than the Continental. It's better than the Mark. The steering is unbelievable." The big problem, of course, was that buyers might not purchase a luxury Ford product when they could buy a lower-priced Taurus that was obviously superior.

Even Jackie Stewart had taken a few moments out from flipping gas caps to note that "your body unit stiffness is definitely in evidence," although he thought it might get them in trouble with geriatric higher-ups in the company who wanted compliance.

"Shape the car any way you want," Kozak had told the studio. With such sturdy beams and joints, they had nothing to worry about. He felt confident enough to change some of the joints to make them easier to manufacture, even though it diminished performance.

Neil Ressler, a high-ranking executive in charge of advance vehicle engineering technology, wasn't so sure. He warned Kozak that there could be a loss of strength as they moved from the boxy structural prototype to the confirmation prototype that incorporated the studio's ovoid shape.

"No way," Kozak said.

"Watch it," Ressler said.

In the spring of 1993 CAE guys began to model the confirmation prototype. They had planned to get to it sooner, but they were delayed by the redesign of the station wagon. Kozak, meanwhile, was caught up in manufacturing issues, like the fit of the sheet metal, the position of the glass runs in the door, how the headlamps would package, and some lingering design questions, such as whether to spend $10 on a molding that would divert rainwater when smokers opened the window during a storm.

Kozak was riding a wave. He and his guys were the recipients of a Ford quality award for the sophisticated way they had set DN101 targets for structure, letting the customer be their guide. To give the steering wheel a certain feel in a driver's hands, for example, they calculated that a part in the front end called the "wheelhouse inner" would have to be of a certain thickness to resist bending and twisting, and so on throughout the car. Jackie Stewart was the keynote speaker at the awards banquet. He said he used to think the engine was the heart of the car; now he thought it was structure. Kozak and his guys went *Yes!*

When the CAE model was completed—it took twelve guys three and a half months—they called Kozak to come look at something weird. What he saw on the computer screen shocked him. The Taurus was bending and twisting like a break dancer. "We could see things moving that weren't supposed to—the quarter panel wagging in and out like a dog tail, the lower back flapping in and out, fore and aft, pumping the deck lid in and out."

Maybe it was the spot welds! They had changed the way they modeled them in the computer. It took two weeks to check all the data. And when the results didn't change, they knew they were in big trouble. They restored the original joints. Still no change to speak of. Neil Ressler had been right. As now seemed all too clear, exterior shape did have a major impact on the structure of the car. Had they done a quick-and-dirty model early on, they could have picked it up. But they were so confident, they had done the analysis with all 60,000 finite elements plugged in. In retrospect, the mistake was so obvious, Kozak felt as if he had flunked Engineering 101.

Suddenly they were as much as 18 or 20 percent below all their stiffness targets. And there was only a month before the deadline for ordering prototype parts. Safety was not an issue, with the possible exception of a rear impact collision. But the customer would find the steering vague and the ride squishy, not to mention an echo of the dreaded boom. They could not *not* fix it.

The only solution was to add more steel, increasing both cost and weight. And could they even get more steel? Nineteen ninety-three was a bumper year for car production. It wasn't as if Bethlehem Steel had extra rolls of thicker steel sitting around in case DN101 got into trouble.

Kozak shouldered the blame. "We screwed up big time." But even though CAE had lured them into complacency, in another way it was helpful. In the old days they wouldn't have found out about the miscalculation until they had a prototype on the road. And now they could use the computer to figure out where to stiffen the car. Scrambling to make the delivery deadline for prototype parts, they worked so hard that they overloaded the mother of all computers, Ford's Cray supercomputer, to the point that it would only sputter out stubborn refusals to cooperate. They had to tap into an even mightier machine in Cray Research Inc. headquarters outside Minneapolis. They used a program called Nastran, developed by NASA, and now in its sixty-eighth iteration. Talk about rocket science, this was it.

Additional cost was bad enough, but the weight increase in this case was even worse. Weight largely determined fuel economy. Under no circumstances could the Taurus exceed 3,387 pounds without jeopardizing the CAFE equation that allowed Ford to make porky, highly profitable luxury cars. Cars were classed by weight in 125-pound increments, and the new

Taurus was already one weight class over the old one, thanks to all the stuff they had added to match Camry. One of Tom Breault's guys was assigned to keep a running tab on the poundage as parts were added, subtracted, and changed. Early in the program, when the weight margin looked safe, Landgraff had ruled out an aluminum hood and aluminum fenders, for reasons of cost and styling. Since then Taurus had been bulking up like a 4-H steer headed to the state fair. In April, there'd been a twenty-eight-pound weight reserve. In mid-August they were down to ten.

The debates over what to do came to be known as structural summits. They were up to number five by the time Landgraff made the call to increase the thickness of the bodyside from 0.8 to 0.9 millimeter, and add additional steel reinforcements. A full millimeter would have been better, but they then would have had to retool every automated fixture that handled the bodysides in both the metal stamping plant and the two assembly plants, plus add even more weight. As it was, the car would gain 17.5 pounds, and an additional $32 in variable cost.

W AS THERE NEVER any good news? Heading out to the parking lot during the midst of the structural crisis, Landgraff was exasperated. "What other things are out there? Every day there's a damn surprise. What's next?"

Cars were officially weighed with their bodily fluids. To slim down the Taurus, Landgraff had already whacked a gallon off the fuel tank, a seven-pound save, and shrunk the washer fluid bottle to save another two pounds. A few doomsday measures remained. He could cut eight pounds with an aluminum wheel assembly, but it would cost $30 a car. Or make the floor mats optional, a three-pound save, even though Ford would look cheap as a consequence.

Sometimes he thought about how quickly the nation had geared up for World War II after the Japanese attack on Pearl Harbor. It had taken Henry Ford and his son Edsel less than two years to build the sprawling Willow Run bomber plant, hire 100,000 workers, and begin cranking out B-24s. He wondered how they had done it. "If the Taurus were going to save Western democracy," Landgraff said during a reflective moment, "the war would have been over by the time we got it on the street."

T HE CRISES WERE getting to everybody. Though outwardly calm, chief engineer George Bell was suffering from terrible insomnia. His home in the Michigan woods, where he lived with his wife and grown stepson, was an oasis. But still when he closed his eyes, visions of car parts danced through his head. It would be 5:30 A.M. before he knew it, he'd have had maybe three hours of sleep, and the first crew of engineers would be waiting in the basement conference room at 7:30 A.M. with their problems. Make that "issues."

Tom Breault was worried about his packaging engineers. They were in meetings all day long, doing their best to negotiate agreements on space between people who were sniping at each other. There was no place in the building to eat, so they snacked at their desks in the basement. Everybody was too tired to get together after work and let off steam. They just wanted to go home. He decided to schedule a stress workshop for his people. DN101 was beginning to remind him of dealings he'd had with the Japanese at Mazda. He would realize someone was missing, and then he'd learn they'd quietly disappeared to have a nervous breakdown.

But Steve Kozak, he was the team's "What me, worry?" kid. He had drafted a little presentation about what went wrong, a *mea culpa*—call it the pitfalls of CAE—and hit the lecture circuit. Here he was talking to the DEW98 people, who were designing the next big front-wheel-drive car. And the truck guys. And the World Class Timing pundits. He had gambled and lost, he had saddled the program with a huge cost and weight increase which would make life more difficult for everybody, and then he had turned the entire episode into a morality play. How did Kozak do it?

TEN

The Engine Story

MORE THAN ANY other part of the car, engines had history, engines had character, engines had soul. They had known glory and they had known shame. In the 1950s, engines had been stars; in the 1970s, bit players. Now they were good performers. They had learned humility and discipline.

The Varsity Captains of the world were not much interested in engines, or very knowledgeable about their attributes. They believed generally that it was better to have six cylinders than four. "Double overhead cams" sounded good. But for the most part, your average Varsity Captain simply wanted his engine to start; he didn't want it to stall; he didn't want to hear strange noises or see stains on the driveway; and he wanted to be able to spring onto the interstate from the on-ramp with a reassuring surge of power.

The car 'zine writers were another story. The gas-fired scribes for *Car and Driver, Road & Track, Automobile,* and *Motor Trend* relished the opportunity to put a new engine through its paces, and then to write about its performance in a gush of adjectives and action verbs. Their creativity was unrestrained when it came to parts of speech: cars were *bloodthirsty . . . primordial . . . staggering . . . silken . . . undeniably potent . . . corner burners.* They displayed *face-smearing accelerative force* and a *thrilling rush of power.* Engines could spin like *wild, whirling dervishes.* The car companies catered to these writers with free trips and a neverending supply of cars and trucks for trial use, so that a writer who played it right need never buy a personal vehicle. This generosity was prompted not so much by the magazines' direct influence on the market, which was nearly nil. But they influenced people who influenced the market, such as the office car nut to whom people turned for advice, or the car columnist in the hometown gazette. Car 'zine raves could be plucked and bannered in TV commercials. Apart from that, perhaps the people who cared most about what they said were the engineers who worked for the car companies. The buff books were their most astute critics.

Ford hoped to impress both constituencies—buyers and writers—with the three engines destined for DN101. The carryover six-cylinder base model that would power three-quarters of the Tauruses, known in-house as the Vulcan, was extremely reliable. It had the most experience, but also the least status. George Bell described it as a "nine-to-five salary man, a solid citizen." More exciting and more expensive was the new six-cylinder engine for the high-series cars, which was one of a recently developed "modular" group of engines that shared basic architecture and components. It was, Bell said, "our sophisticated engine, our cosmopolitan engine, our technology engine . . . smooth and more powerful than the Vulcan . . . more parts, but not as large . . . more torque." In all, "a more modern engine." The third engine was the 3.4-liter, eight-cylinder Yamaha developed for the 1996 Taurus SHO: "a sports star, a Michael Jordan, maybe a Carl Lewis or a race horse. Exciting, capable, handsome. It has a huge intake manifold and head castings. It dominates the engine compartment." George Bell didn't do too badly on the adjectival front himself.

The big money decisions to deploy this trio of engines had taken place long ago, independent of Dick Landgraff or the DN101 team, and they were directly influenced by a chain of events that had begun with the Clean Air Act of 1970. Almost overnight, that piece of legislation had put an end to two decades of big cars and big engines. No more the fearsome Fords, hard-charging Chevys, baronial Buicks, and epic Chryslers.

In the years following the law's passage, the mighty eight-cylinder engines sputtered to a halt. The big pistons pumped their last. Goodbye to high-riser manifolds, solid-lifter cams, and open pipes. Hello to catalytic converters that glommed onto the exhaust system like leeches, sucking out power and wasting precious metals. With fuel economy mandates in place, the heroic cars of yesterday suddenly turned into outlaws, unpatriotic gas guzzlers, environmental villains. By 1980, its engine division was the Sahara Desert of the Ford continent. The division was housed in a historic building that the founder had commissioned as a laboratory for scientific advancement, which was now known as the Triple E Building, for Engine and Electrical Engineering. Since its owner's demise, Henry Ford the First's corner office had been occupied by a succession of engine chiefs, who filled it with drab furniture and permitted fluorescent tubes to replace the chandelier. The executive offices along the front of the building, a handsome mahogany row, were more or less intact, but the rest of the building had been turned into a dense warren of cubicles. Bright young engineers wandered into the Triple E Building and were never heard from again.

WHAT A SORRY STATE of affairs for the company that had spawned the wondrous Flathead V-8 in the 1932 Ford, kick-starting a long and illustrious line of great engines. Well into the forties, the Flathead was the engine of choice for drag racers. It lent itself to all sorts of mix-and-match hot-rodding, with over-the-counter Canada heads, multiple-carburetor manifolds, stroker crankshafts, and welded, tubular-steel exhaust headers.

Ford lost ground when Oldsmobile came out with the Rocket 88 in 1949, featuring overhead valves. The company didn't produce its own version until 1954. In 1955, Chevrolet (The Enemy) premiered what is still maybe the most famous engine in the world, the so-called Chevy small-block V-8, more powerful and lighter than anything that had gone before, an engine that catapulted Chevy onto Ford's performance turf. Chrysler jumped into the fray with "hemis," named for their hemispherical cylinder heads. Now hemis were the preference among fickle hot-rod drivers.

In 1957, a feverish year, Chevy had a 283-cubic-inch engine with fuel injection; Ford countered with a supercharger. Car writers talked about the blown Fords and injected Chevys. *Sex-crazed cars on drugs.* And the drag racers were, in fact, running their cars with stuff that sounded like dope—potent blends of alcohol, benzine, and nitromethane or "pop." Every issue of *Hot Rod* magazine came out with some bigger engine or camshaft kit or high-compression heads or manifold for two or three carburetors. It got crazy. Just go down to your local dealer, give him $89, and he would give you a manifold and two more carburetors.

Ford's first overhead-valve engine had the same conservative displacement as the Flathead at 239 cubic inches. But in the fifties, the engines swelled. Along came the 252, 272, 312, 332. . . . Finally Chevy pushed the small block up to what everybody thought was the limit, 350 cubic inches, but then came Ford with not one, not two, but *four 351s,* the 351 Cleveland, 351 Windsor, 351 "M," and the Boss 351, although if you measured closely you might just find they were 350 cubic inches after all. In 1956, Chrysler's

354-cubic-inch-hemi yielded an astonishing 355 horsepower, a horsepower per cubic inch!

No one knew how big these things would get so they made the blocks large enough to grow. The size, that is to say the displacement—the volume of air inside each cylinder, multiplied by the number of cylinders—hovered around 350 cubic inches at the end of the decade, but the blocks were big enough to go to 400—and they did.

Logically, these were called big-block engines. The Buick 455 Stage-1, the Chevrolet 454 LS-6, the Ford 428 Cobra Jet, followed by the 429 Super Cobra Jet. Cadillacs of the early 1970s had a 500-cubic-inch engine. It wasn't a high-performance engine, but it was very, very big.

You had to tune those high-strung Detroit babies three times a week, and you could forget about using them for transportation. They were made to run at very high RPMs, like 7,000, for the Daytona 500. On the street, the spark plugs clogged up with fuel, becoming wet and crusty as the drivers revved the engine. But no one thought anything of it, that was just the way it was. They only got six or eight miles per gallon. And things were always going wrong. The fuel would get hot and boil. The bubbles interrupted the fuel flow and the carburetor would more or less quit with a bad case of vapor lock. By then the car was too hot to start. You'd have to pull over to the side of the road, open the hood, and let it cool off. You couldn't really drive a highly tuned big block for any distance, especially in cold weather.

Racing fueled the engine wars. But the Detroit Big Three displayed the same ambivalence toward the sport as the founder. Henry Ford had competed to attract investment and promote his cars, although he didn't really approve. Racing was all about speed and power. It was not about a Sunday drive with the family. And the growing number of highway deaths was giving speed a bad name. So were the greased-up backstreet drag racers who blasted through town or drove laps around the drive-in. They were guys like Don Garlits from Tampa, who wrote in his autobiography, *Big Daddy,* "Cars were everything and I spent every dime on my car. I drifted from job to job, only concerned with picking up change to keep the Ford on the road—and to keep it competitive in the countless drag races I won. I was a bum, but I was learning about automobiles." Who could know that one day drag racing would be so respectable that Garlits's Swamp Rat XXX would be in the Smithsonian, that he himself would have a museum of drag racing near his home in Ocala, Florida, and that he would run for Congress? (He lost.)

Even as they manufactured parts that racers could buy and bolt on, the car companies pretended they were up to something else. "Export parts," they called them at first, and then "law enforcement parts development," or "police interceptor" engines. In 1957 the Automobile Manufacturers Association banned racing. Of the Big Three, only Ford observed the ban more or less to the letter, and then only for three years. In 1960, the company jumped back in under the influence of Ford Division head Lee Iacocca, who was tormented by the prospect of losing the growing youth market. The wars began anew.

Jim McCraw was a car magazine editor in the 1960s, when motor madness gripped the nation. "It was nuts, it was really nuts. I lived through it. . . . Every time a new one would come out, I'd get a letter, 'Come to Detroit. We have yet another trick car to show you.' It was never ending . . . one after another. We had the small blocks for Trans Am, big blocks for drag racing and NASCAR racing. It was just everywhere you looked. Everything was horsepower and speed, tires burning. You started to feel it in the commercials and certainly in the print ads. They had special advertising just for these kinds of cars, in addition to regular Ford sedans, Caprice convertibles."

Over in the jungles of Vietnam, car guys were going crazy, wondering what was happening on the engine front. In a little-known episode of that horrid war, Don Garlits made his way with some other drag car racers to Saigon on a morale-boosting mission. Garlits wrote that he wondered why they were there as soon as they arrived. Kids were fighting over food scraps in the streets as officials drove around in big Cadillacs.

In those glory days, engines had character. Maybe the country was in trouble, but you wouldn't know it to listen to the healthy, full-throated roar of a wall-to-wall big-block thumper, announcing that Detroit was still in command. *DiDUHduhdiDUHduhdiDUHduh.*

In 1969 you could get a Mustang with one of ten engines, from a basic 200-cubic-inch straight six-cylinder engine to a 250-cubic-inch six, a 302 V-8, two 351s, a 390 FE V-8, a non-RAM Air 428 and a RAM Air 428, and the Boss 302 and the Boss 429. And speaking of the Boss 302, it was the personal favorite of many a drag racer. But the Boss 429 . . . the Boss 429, car fans, was a racing engine that needed a home, and that home was the aforementioned 1969 Mustang. The Big Boss was way too big for the engine compartment, so Ford took it over to a custom car shop named Kar Kraft, which spread apart some parts and shoehorned the engine into 860 Mustang SportsRoofs.

To be sure, though the average male driver might yearn for one of the big-bore Ford engines that breathed life into performance cars, he was much more likely to find himself behind the wheel of the family Ford, powered by a more prosaic six- or eight-cylinder hunk of iron that might or might not last the car's lifetime, or even till the warranty ran out.

Meanwhile, some long-haired, half-naked people on drugs were driving a little German aberration called a Volkswagen. A beetle, a humpbacked bug.

As a *car*, it wasn't a contender, but for an engine, it did have a sturdy air-cooled horizontally opposed four. A car guy could rip off the fenders, take the seats out, throw away the engine cover, and install snow tires, then take it out in the California desert, assuming he lived in California, as so many bugsters did. A dune buggy was respectable, but in the end it was still an import from a country that lost the war.

After the Clean Air Act put an end to these engine wars, Detroit was stumped. If engines couldn't get bigger and badder, what else was there? In the seventies, Ford was developing one humdrum new engine every three or four years. Powertrain engineers spent their days rearranging the basic engine architecture. The last big change in engine design had been overhead valves. From 1965 to 1985, such innovation as there was took place outside of the engine: fuel injection, the electronic engine computer. Hang-on technology, some called it. In desperation, the marketing people resorted to ridiculous tack-on exterior trim—psychedelic graphics, spoilers, scoops—things to make cars *look* fast.

Tom Howard, who would eventually rise to a management post in powertrain, joined with other young Ford engineers more than once in the mid-seventies in proposing to develop a high-performance four-valve engine. "We were always shot down." It felt like that, a body blow. "Customers aren't interested," they were told. Young engineers . . . well, soon there were no young engineers. The company wasn't hiring. Engine research was on hold. Even into the eighties, when Ford had made a fetish out of quality, crafting new and better engines was a low priority. It was one thing to hire some quality consultants and put the people on the assembly line through some problem-solving training—which held the potential to save money, by the way—and it was quite another to commit $1 billion to $1.5 billion to building an engine plant.

When the Taurus debuted in 1986, it had a puny 2.5-liter, four-cylinder base engine. Lew Veraldi had not wanted such a small power plant; it really wasn't big enough for the car, which had grown larger and heavier during the development cycle. But he bowed to pressure from the fleets for a model with a small, cheap engine. The four-cylinder was never popular. In 1990, Ford got rid of it. The standard engine became the one that had previously been optional: a new 3.0-liter V-6, the "Vulcan." Some people thought the engine was named for the old Vulcan Forge plant, which made connecting rods. In truth, marketing had dreamed it up as a name, then never used it, perhaps because Vulcan was the Roman god of fire and metalworking, and "fire" was such a disagreeable word, especially in the vicinity of engines. The high-series car received a veteran 3.8-liter V-6 that had been rejuvenated.

The Vulcan was a wonderful hardworking engine, but no one considered it new tech. Its most notable feature was multi-port fuel injection, which dispatched the same amount of fuel to each cylinder. Other than that, it represented mid-sixties engine architecture. Beginning with the Taurus, the Vulcan enjoyed a long and happy life. It went into the Aerostar, the Probe, the Ranger, and the Tempo/Topaz. In the words of Jim Mayo, one of its designers, "It gets you from here to there and it does it very efficiently. It does everything well, but nothing outstanding."

In time, the Vulcan's reliability was Ford's best; its levels came close to the Japanese. But many Americans refused to believe that Ford or any other U.S. car company could produce a car that would start on command and dutifully perform. They had nightmarish memories of being marooned in hostile, inbred rural towns waiting for parts, or being broke and late in the breakdown lane of a major highway, or stalling out in the left turn lane at rush hour, as horns blasted and people yelled obscenities. That kind of betrayal was like adultery. You could never quite trust your vehicle again. Even after carburetors and distributors had been replaced by electronic controls and it was barely possible to flood an engine with gasoline, the sound was indelibly imprinted in the memory cells of drivers of a certain vintage. *Rerrr-errr-errr-errr-errr.* Fear of flooding.

And if perchance you were lost in some crime-infested city neighborhood, and the engine in your American middle-class car gave out, what then would happen to both car *and* driver? That question mark was reason enough to buy a Japanese car.

Supposing you could convince Americans that home-grown engines were reliable, that was no longer good enough. Today's buyers not only expected the engine to crank over day in and day out for the entire life of the car, which could be eight to ten years, they wanted cars without noise, vibration, and harshness, known as NVH in car talk. Where once a deep low rumble had signified power, now it meant something was wrong. This was a sea change in engineology. Nobody wanted to *hear* engines anymore.

In a calamity that neither Ford, Chrysler, nor GM had anticipated, the automakers who were giving people the engines they wanted were Japanese. Since the 1970s Japan had been powering their small trusty cars with small trusty engines. In the mid-eighties they began to export cars with small but powerful, sophisticated engines and velvet-smooth transmissions. Thanks to the fundamental changes in engine design, their cars were quieter and smoother than Detroit's. And they offered more horsepower and torque as well. Taking advantage of their alliance with motorcycle companies—Yamaha was making engines for Toyota, and Honda owned Honda—the Japanese had learned to reduce engine size and weight without sacrificing power. Their engines had lightweight aluminum blocks and other aluminum components, four valves per cylinder for better performance and fuel efficiency, and overhead cams, heretofore available primarily in pricey limited-edition European cars. Overhead cams acted directly on the valves, eliminating pushrods. This was a big advantage, since pushrods could bend, or get out of place, and pretty soon the valves might not open and close as they were supposed to, and the engines would start to sound like a smoker with an all-day cough. The words "valve job" from your mechanic meant you might as well forget about a vacation. The introduction of Japanese engines with overhead cams really wounded the engine guys at Ford. They had developed a big-block overhead-cam engine as early as 1965 for drag racing. The company balked at the high price tag, and never put it into production. For a time Ford had an edge with its electronic engine control module, which had computerized many heretofore mechanical functions. But then the Japanese caught up.

Tom Howard couldn't get over the finish on Japanese engines. Even on the internal parts, he saw none of the nicks and internal scratches found on Ford engines after a trip down the line. A Japanese engine looked as if it had been hand-assembled by workers wearing gloves, and then painstakingly polished to give it the sheen of a fine Swiss watch. A guy who loved engines couldn't help but appreciate that kind of craftsmanship. Car guys to the core, half the powertrain engineers at Ford tinkered with engines in their spare time. And so, when there was so little inspiration at work, they went home at night to their suburban bungalows in Southfield and Northville and Farmington Hills, home to the wife and kids, and to their fabulous Fords from the fifties and sixties, where they could listen to the fabulous sounds of their youth, the comforting snort of a 427, a 428, a 429, *diDUHduhdiDUH-duhdiDUHduh.*

DONALD PETERSEN, FORD'S CEO in the mid-1980s, felt sorry for the guys in the Triple E Building. He made a point of telling them they were doing a good job, because they felt so bad about themselves. But it wasn't until he began talking big bucks that they realized they had a real friend in the Glass House, the nickname for World Headquarters.

The man Petersen sought out for guidance was a small, precise chemical engineer named Jim Clarke, who had achieved a measure of fame for nurturing a new, robust 1982 Mustang engine. That engine, wrote Mustang historian Bob McClurg in *Mustang: The Next Generation,* was a "hot-rodder's dream." It seemed to signal Ford was back in the game after a decade of Mustang II weaklings. It was a "new 4 bbl. 5.0L hydraulic roller cam H.O.V-8 engine package sporting 210 hp and 265 ft-lbs torque! The latest five liter

V-8 sported an 8.4:1 compression ratio, aluminum alloy pistons with a 4.00 inch bore and 3.00 inch stroke, forged steel connecting rods and a nodular iron crankshaft. Its aluminum four-barrel intake featured either a 600 cfm Motorcraft or Holley #4180 four-barrel carburetor and dual exhaust." True car fans loved this kind of information.

In addition to championing the Mustang five-liter, Clarke had also rescued a 3.8-liter engine that was scheduled for extinction, and turned it into a competent transverse engine for the high-series Taurus, updated with fuel injection. Although he had seen several tours of duty in the advanced engine unit, Clarke wasn't content with an improvement unless it was replicated hundreds of thousands of times on the production line.

From time to time Petersen would call up Clarke and suggest they go for a ride. The Ford CEO would be waiting in the executive garage as Clarke pulled up. On their way to the track, Petersen would ask questions about whatever vehicle they were in, gradually working around to the question of how Ford engines could be improved. Styling could lure people into cars, he would tell Clarke, but only engines could inspire love. Well, Clarke couldn't agree more. And Petersen would ask, what would Clarke do if he had a blank sheet of paper?

From these conversations grew a plan for a mix-and-match line of engines which not only would embrace the new technology but also would have common parts. Ford called them modular engines. The name "modular" was in a certain way unfortunate. It suggested modular housing—cheap, boxy prefab units. These engines were anything but cheap, or simple. But the idea was similar. As long as you built engines on a common block with interchangeable parts, you wouldn't have to build or redesign a new one from the block up. Engines of different sizes and configurations could move down the same production line, just as cars with the same platform could be built in the same factory.

One day in 1986, Jim Clarke slipped into a back room for coffee. He returned to his office trailed by a young job seeker named Brian Wolfe, who had heard about the new engines and wanted to work on them. Born in 1960, Brian Wolfe had grown up in Warren, Michigan, a General Motors enclave. Brian's father was a tool-and-die maker at Johnson Tool & Die, and his two brothers were draftsmen there. One brother raced Fords.

Wolfe was the last of a generation of car-country kids raised on the rhythmic beat of heavy metal, the *diDUHduhdiDUHduhdiDUHduh* of a full-throated big-block Motown thumper, choking on its own power, bucking to blast off on a track or a backstreet, where the raspy chant could power up to a defiant war whoop. And when they grew up, these car lads asked nothing more than to share their air, tuning them, timing them, training them, trying them, tailoring them, teasing them, tempting them into more horse-power, more torque, more speed.

At age fourteen, Wolfe was scooping ice cream at Baskin-Robbins for $1 an hour with just one thought in mind. Scoop-*car*. Scoop-*car*. At fifteen, before he could legally drive, he paid $375 in ice cream scoops for a 1969 Fairlane powered by a historic 428 Cobra Jet engine. At sixteen he took it apart and restored it. He wanted more than anything to work on Ford engines for the rest of his life. But when he knocked on Ford's door in 1982 with an engineering degree from the University of Michigan, the engine division wasn't hiring. So rooted was Wolfe in the past, he had not noticed the darkness that had descended on Detroit.

He took the only job at Ford he could get, in truck development. After two years a job opened up at Engine, in the fuel delivery unit. It had been so long since the division had hired anyone that Wolfe was the youngest engineer in the Triple E Building by about eight years. He was there when word spread of the new modular engines.

Clarke saw in Wolfe the talent and enthusiasm he wanted in the core group who would be permanently assigned to modular engines, taking their expertise from one engine to the next. Modular people, you could say. Yes, hard to believe that Ford's MBA management hadn't thought of this before, but it was true. Till then, each engine was born anew with a fresh group of recruits.

Wolfe went to work on the first of the modular engines, an eight-cylin-der 4.6-liter hunk destined for the 1990 Lincoln Town Car. He was so happy he could hardly believe it. This was why he had come to Ford. Some days he didn't know where he'd rather be, over at the dynamometer on Vil-lage Road, putting engines through their paces in a test cell filled with exhaust fumes, or at home working on the Mustang he had bought when he got his master's degree in 1986.

In 1991, Wolfe was drafted to work on Ford's other line of modular engines, the 2.5-liter for the Contour/Mystique program and the 3-liter for the new Taurus/Sable. By 1993 Wolfe was collaborating with the DN101 team to resolve issues related to packaging and NVH. Ford's engine renais-sance was in full bloom. The company had gutted and rebuilt engine plants in Romeo and Cleveland. Over at the dynamometer labs, the huge engines were lined up on pallets in the hallways, like patients on gurneys, awaiting their turn in the test cells.

Wolfe also had been recruited by Ford's racing unit—special vehicle operations—to test prototype parts on the 1986 Mustang he owned. When he got the car, it would do a quarter mile in 15.2 seconds at 91 miles per hour. Over the years, with continual modifications, it would do the distance at 154 miles per hour in 9 seconds flat! On the racing scene, Wolfe gained a national reputation in what were called match races, one Mustang against another. But to Wolfe, and to the other young engineers like him, the hero was Jim Clarke.

B Y 1993, EVERYBODY agreed that the need to give the modular engines a sexy surname had grown fairly urgent. People were forced to refer to the new Taurus engine as the modular 6-cylinder 3-liter 4-valve to distinguish it from the 6-cylinder 3-liter Vulcan or the 2.5-liter modular going into the Contour. Without a name, "we'll be at press gatherings calling it ten different things, and it'll get all muddy," said George Bell, when the subject came up during a Landgraff staff meeting. Dealers would end up using whatever came to mind, probably "modular," with its unfortunate connotations. Given that this new engine was going into the Taurus LX, or high-series car, and was the chief justification for charging $2,000 more for it than the Vulcan-equipped Taurus GL, the ideal name should suggest a certain grandeur. Bell was toying with "Force," until he remembered that was the name of a line of outboard motors once owned by Chrysler. They were cheap motors at that.

Ford's competitor, General Motors, was doing a pretty good job on engines, and maybe even better than Ford when it came to transmissions, but where the big old lumbering giant had really triumphed was in naming their primo system "Northstar." It blew the Ford marketing people away, how they had managed to come up with such an inspired label. Beryl Stajich, a DN101 marketing guy, had been to a luxury car clinic where people were asked about Northstar. "It was unbelievable. Those people talked about it, they remembered lines from the ads. 'You can take all the fluids out of it and it'll still run through the desert.' "

By fall 1993, Dick Landgraff was on the case. "The sales guys have offered to name it," he told the DN101 staff that December. He had heard possibilities like "V-Tech" and "Dynatech."

"It shouldn't have a fluff name," Bell said. Not just letters and numbers. "Z-28 would be a fluff name."

"Pegasus . . . Gemini . . . ," mused Landgraff. He had also suggested "Orion" to sales.

In the end, the team had no say. Alex Trotman announced the new name at the Chicago Auto Show. And Landgraff announced it at his staff meeting.

"Duratec." A combination of "durability" and "technology."

"It sounds like a contact lens," Dawn Denton from purchasing said under her breath.

Landgraff, in his disappointment, imagined a quite different but equally unrelated object. "It sounds like a pair of pliers to me," he said, mulling it over one evening. "Sometimes I wonder how we get into these boxes. 'Northstar' sounds fantastic. . . . Northstar. . . . Follow the Northstar.

"And we've got something called 'Duratec.' "

ELEVEN

Supply-Side
Economics

THE JOB OF A program man-
ager was to deliver a car on time that met its cost, quality, and weight targets.
To Dick Landgraff, that meant holding the 235 suppliers who had DN101
contracts to their promises every step of the way.

Landgraff's general attitude toward suppliers—and he was not alone in
this—could be summed up this way: you could not trust them. Suppliers
saw any change to a part as an opportunity to raise prices. They *knew* Ford
would change the part, so they lowballed their bid to get the job, then hid
markups behind the changes. Not *all* suppliers, of course. But you had to
watch them all with equal care.

They saw it differently of course. Ford insisted on 3–5 percent "productivity" savings—mandatory price reductions—during each year of a five-
year contract. Suppliers could end up going broke if they didn't start out
with a high enough figure.

As a corporation, Ford worried that its employees could become too
friendly with their brethren at other companies. They could stray over some

fuzzy line of righteousness, corrupted by supplier blandishments. The next thing you knew your own guys would be arguing the supplier's case, or worse. As a precaution, Ford had developed a policy on "gifts and social contacts." Employees were allowed to accept one meal per quarter per supplier, with a total of one meal per week from all suppliers; two entertainment events per year, per supplier (wives included), such as dinners or shows; one recreational outing (golf, hunting, fishing), with notification to a supervisor if there were an overnight stay. If there were *two* overnight stays, a supervisor had to give written approval. Ford employees were allowed to accept T-shirts, caps, and other small items with the supplier company logo. Wendy Dendel wondered why Ford didn't simply ban all freebies, for honesty and clarity. In practice, an engineer or a buyer had enough to remember without keeping track of who was paying for the pizza how often, and whether they were into a new calendar quarter by now.

Landgraff wasn't afraid to go on a supplier-sponsored hunting trip. No way was a supplier going to corrupt him. But he wasn't so sure the troops had his same stiff backbone. It wasn't that he thought they were dishonest so much as that they were soft. Some of the engineers spent a lot of time with suppliers. They could become sympathetic to their never-ending complaints about too little money and too little time for too much work. One day Landgraff had an inspiration. He invited the number-two guy in purchasing, Rich Honecker, to talk to his staff about how suppliers were raking it in. On average, their profit margins were three times bigger than Ford's. Honecker told the team leaders that no one should feel bad about forcing these guys to meet their objectives. Since 1983, when Ford had 1,800 suppliers, a campaign to reduce the number had cut it in half and the total was scheduled to shrink even more. Those who were left were doing $23 billion worth of business. "They're in pretty good financial condition and they're going to get a lot better," Honecker said.

From time to time, when a supplier's costs got out of line, Landgraff would personally take charge. "Let's bring these guys in and smash them," he would say. The finance guys loved this war talk. They could really get behind a remark like that. Taking a tough line was necessary, Landgraff explained. Otherwise, "Suppliers play dumb, they sit there and stare at you . . . and hope it goes away."

After an initial costing a year ago that showed DN101 over budget by $500 per car, DN101 finance manager Tom Gorman had paired up with Landgraff to go after the major offenders. One by one, the supplier's representatives would enter the conference room, Landgraff would close the door, and he and Gorman would yell at them. "You said $10, not $10.50!" Yelling did not come naturally to Gorman, who was young—the only

DN101 manager "with tight skin," he joked—with a genteel education and a background in banking. A Harvard MBA, he had received pay offers twice as high as Ford's, but he thought the car business would be exciting. And so it was. Here he was with Dick Landgraff, the Maximum Leader, yelling at suppliers, baiting traps. Like the time when one company wanted $20 more for a larger gasket. "Did we give you a drawing in the beginning?" Gorman asked innocently. "No," said the supplier. "Then how do you know the gasket size changed?" Bingo. Down went the price. Gorman might have started out as a Boston beanie, but he seemed to have adjusted to Detroit's hard-line, bottom-line economics.

Ford had two categories of suppliers: outside companies, and its internal divisions. Ford Electronics turned out sound systems, engine computers, and speed control mechanisms, and many other devices. From the climate control division came heating and air conditioning systems; from plastic trim and parts came lamps, bumpers, interior trim, and moldings. Much of the sheet metal as well as the engines and the transmissions were internally sourced. Although internal suppliers were more open with cost figures than outsiders, they were expected to show a profit as well. And even though they were all part of mother Ford, a program manager had to keep his eye on them. Lew Veraldi's cost overrun on the original Taurus apparently had been his undoing. And failing to watch costs was what got the T-Bird program in such hot water and cost the head guy, Tony Kuchta, his job. Landgraff spoke to Kuchta after both he and the program ended up in disgrace. "He said he assumed the PEOs [project engineering offices] would deliver the costs. He wasn't watching it. That was his great mistake—naïveté. It doesn't work. If body engineering doesn't deliver, what are they going to do? Fire all the engineers?"

Once, when he was running the 1992 Taurus program, Landgraff came into a meeting with Ford's plastics division holding an odd-looking red object. It was a taillamp from the outgoing car with a mockup of the new one taped over it. There was a $7 price differential. How could a few square inches of plastic cost so much, Landgraff wanted to know. The price dropped $5.

Landgraff didn't care if he wasn't Mr. Nice Guy. "The only thing that really counts is 'Did I make the objectives?' I'm not being graded on, 'Did I make everybody go away feeling good?' "

It was the talk of the company when Landgraff whacked the fold-down armrest in the rear seat of the '92 Taurus to save ten bucks. Dealers complained and auto writers noticed. The decision angered the sales division, which hated to lose any feature, let alone one so visible. Even Alex Trotman nailed Landgraff at a big NAAO meeting. Why had he taken out the arm-

rest? By then, Landgraff had had it with the armrest. If Trotman had objected previously, it would have been one thing. But Landgraff had pledged to
meet his cost objectives, it was on the order of a moral commitment, and the
armrest had helped him do it. As Landgraff told it later, he made a nervy little speech to Trotman, who was not just a vice-president, but one of three
executive vice-presidents, in charge of all of North America, to the effect that,
"If you're running the program, you can tell me what to do. I'm running the
program, then I decide. Who's running the program?"

"You are," said Trotman.

"Then it's coming out."

And no one could say Landgraff had been wrong, because of the really
wonderful thing that had happened since. The much maligned, press-panned
1992 Taurus, the also-ran at the Detroit Auto Show, had just become the
very-best-selling car in America for the first time! Beginning in May of '92,
Ford Division vice-president Ross Roberts had launched a personal crusade
to bump the Honda Accord out of first place with an avalanche of rebates,
incentives, advertising, and lease sales. A Texan, Roberts hated the Accord—
"the stinking thing"—and the hypocrites who bought them. "If it was no
good, they wouldn't tell anyone. They didn't want to be embarrassed."

Roberts set up a war room in sales headquarters on the thirty-seventh
floor of the Renaissance Center in downtown Detroit, installed a red telephone hot line, posted slogans and American flags, played military music, and
gave everybody camouflage caps and helmets. With a phone tree technique
he used as a fundraiser for the Boy Scouts, Roberts and others in headquarters called five people daily—three dealers and two Ford employees in the
regional sales offices—to pump them up. They posted dealer success stories
on a big board as they came in on the hot line. Every time a name went up,
the wife got a dozen roses. The whole company cheered him on. Roberts's
boss, Bob Rewey, manned the war room, as did Alex Trotman. The Lincoln-
Mercury Division sacrificed Sable production so there would be sufficient
Tauruses to sell.

Honda upped its incentives as well. But its dealers, outnumbered four to
one, were no match for the Ford juggernaut. Taurus won, 409,751 to
399,297, kicked over the top in part by $249-a-month two-year leases.

To Roberts, who seldom missed an opportunity to invoke his red-
blooded Texas origins, the Taurus victory was patriotism at its finest. "Finally an American car is the best-selling car." It also made the company over
$100 million that year. It wasn't a huge amount of money, but it wasn't
peanuts.

To Landgraff the victory was evidence that the absence of a rear-seat
armrest wasn't such a big deal after all.

O<small>N</small> A<small>UGUST</small> 10, 1993, a group of planners and engineers from the Ford electronics division filed into the DN101 basement conference room. The temperamental cooling system had plunged to an icy low, but this was not going to be the kind of session where people took off their jackets and relaxed.

The agenda consisted of a single item. There wasn't even an agenda, really, just a list of cost increases on the futuristic radio/climate control unit that electronics was building for DN101. The guys from electronics had put off this confrontation as long as they could, desperately trying to get back on budget. Engineers always believed they could fix things, given time. But time was running out. Electrical components were due at the pilot plant in little more than two months, on October 21. Mark Jarvis, a soft-spoken Minnesotan who represented electronics on the DN101 team, had politely nagged his compadres back in the home office to come clean. The unit was $12.10 over the cost target. It was bad enough to know that electronics was letting the team down, worse that they weren't telling anyone about it. As the room filled, the visitors were outnumbered two to one by DN101 team members. But it was the man at the head of the table who made them apprehensive. They did not want to be in this room with Dick Landgraff, no way.

Electronics had brought with them models of the new unit, a one-of-a-kind replacement for the usual two boxes, lodged atop one another in the instrument panel, that controlled the sound and the heating/air conditioning systems. As people slid into the front seat of the new Taurus, they would see a foot-wide black plastic oval slashed by large, ascending buttons, with a shiny, tear-shaped display for the clock and radio stations curving around the upper edge. But the appearance was only part of its novelty. For there was no actual radio behind the faceplate, just a glob of wires. You punched a button, imagining that some tiny element back there sprang into action, but no. The impulses flew through the wiring harness to the trunk of the car, where the tuner and amplifier were mounted to the wheelwell on the driver's side. It was spooky in a way. But the arrangement freed up space behind the instrument panel urgently needed for other things.

The plastic oval was initially called the Integrated User Interface, or IUI, a designation that seemed to lack inspiration. Mark Jarvis ran a little contest for a new working name. Among the suggestions were UCC, for Unity Control Center or Unity Command Center; ECS for Ergo Command System or Ergo Control System; AEC, Audio and Environment Controls; and IPP, Instrument Panel Pod. And also Jarvis's personal favorite: Control-O-Matic (COM). But the winner was ICP, for Integrated Control Panel. That

Lew Veraldi, the "Father of the Taurus," with the original 1986 model. *Lawrence Technological University*

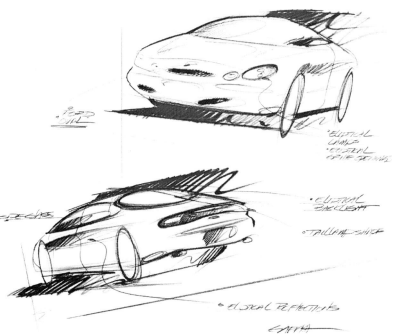

Exterior designer Doug Gaffka's sketches for the 1996 Taurus, code-named DN101. *Ford Motor Company*

Among designs that were vetoed—a front end with narrow, aggressive headlamps and a rear end with a tail-lamp cluster. Shown here in life size clay models. *Ford Motor Company*

Oval headlamps and an oval grille were thought to give the front end a friendly expression befitting the country's favorite car. *Ford Motor Company*

The 1992 Toyota Camry set new standards for excellence, which the DN101 team set out to emulate. *Toyota Motor Sales, U.S.A., Inc.*

Dick Landgraff (center), program manager of the 1996 Taurus/Sable redesign, in a discussion at Ford's test track in Naples, Florida, with Peter Creutz (left), the supervisor in charge of the new Duratec engine prove-out.

Exterior designer Doug Gaffka (left) and chief engineer George Bell at the pilot plant in Dearborn. *Ford Motor Company*

The basement of the Ford Design Center in Dearborn, the home of the DN101 team for nearly five years.

Ford consultant and champion race car driver Jackie Stewart, who frequently drove and critiqued Taurus prototypes. A Scot, he poses here with a helmet that bears his tartan. *Campbell & Co.*

Vehicle design manager Tom Breault gives a farewell speech for Wendy Dendel (see below), the team's well-liked delegate from employee relations, who was leaving for another post.

Wendy Dendel.

The official photo of the DN101 team. *Ford Motor Company*

A Taurus prototype in full camouflage during a 1994 Death Valley summer test trip.

Lighting engineer Kim Peterson on vacation on the island of St. Kitts.

Len Flack, a Ford climate control division engineer, in the breakfast room of the Xanadu Condo Resort on a 1994 test trip to Lake Havasu, Arizona. Walls are decorated with Ford memorabilia.

Heather Morrissett visits a temple during a trip to Japan with Nissan, her employer after leaving Ford.

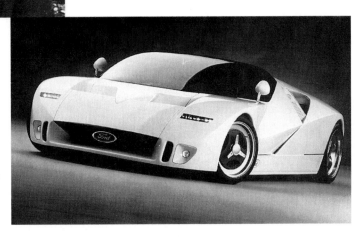

The GT90 concept car, used to lure press to Dearborn on December 6 and 7, 1995, for a surprise unveiling of the 1996 Taurus. *Ford Motor Company*

Official Ford "beauty shots" of the 1996 Taurus–released to the press January 3, 1995. *Ford Motor Company*

Dick Landgraff, pointing to the Taurus on display at the 1995 Detroit auto show, with body engineers Steve Kozak (left) and Andy Benedict (center).

Sarcos, Ford's $600,000 anthropomorphic robot, and friend. *International Robotics, Inc.*

Electronics division supervisor Mark Jarvis and components designer Nevenka Schumaker with the controversial Integrated Control Panel.

Reporter Alan Adler, who covered Ford for the *Detroit Free Press.*

Judith Mühlberg (left), director of Ford North American Communications, with Tom Rhoades of her staff and automotive writer Michelle Krebs.

A 1996 Taurus after a reporter lost control at the Charlotte Motor Speedway and crashed into a protective barrier. No one was injured.

Wheeler Stanley (left), manager of the Atlanta assembly plant, in a discussion over the rear end of a 1996 Taurus at his morning "tire kick."

Ford CEO Alex Trotman (left) and Chicago assembly plant manager Ran Griffin add their palm prints and signa tures to a Taurus decorated with those of workers at a Job One ceremony on July 17, 1995. Watching are Jim Traine of Ford public affairs and vehicle cent vice-president Jim Donaldson.

Gregory Henderson installs window glass on the line at the Atlanta plant, a job that pays $18 an hour.

Dora Ramirez Alarcon sews Tauru seats at a plant in Ciudad Juárez and earns $6.30 for a ten-hour day

Don Slipp, general manager of Winner Ford in Cherry Hill, New Jersey.

was what you got when you let engineers name something. And maybe it *was* better than Integrated User Interface, although parents of second-graders would note its potential for bathroom humor. Later there was a Detroit band called ICP, for Insane Clown Posse.

By whatever name, most people conceded that the ICP was a stunning decorative element and a brave departure for Ford. But it had been nothing but headaches for the engineers who took it over. And now its runaway costs had provoked this confrontation with program management.

As the meeting got under way, Landgraff took off his glasses and peered nearsightedly at a list of cost figures. "This is absolutely an unmitigated disaster," he said without looking up. "We're going to have to go over every item, line by line." Just for openers, the faceplate, which was called a bezel, with its buttons and knobs, was $6.27 over budget. "Why does a bezel cost so much?" he wanted to know. Landgraff sounded like a father going shopping for the first time for kids' shoes: *"Fifty bucks for a pair of sneakers?"*

"What does this stuff cost per pound? How thick is it?"

George Bell chimed in. "No way we can put $6 in a bezel, for Chrissake."

"It's just a hunk of plastic," Landgraff said.

A hunk of plastic . . . this was not quite how the guys from the electronics division regarded their masterpiece. One of them said something about higher-grade polycarbonate and thicker ink. "I never voted on thinner ink/thicker ink," Tom Gorman said peevishly. "And I never saw any of you guys before." Translation: Why haven't you guys come in earlier to tell us about these cost issues?

Landgraff seemed to be growing calmer. "We start out by saying it's too goddamn much. Now let's go forward from here." The electronics contingent breathed a little easier. That sounded good. *You've veered off course, but let's put that behind us and look to the future, marching toward a brighter tomorrow.* Only what was Landgraff doing? He was continuing down the list and getting steamed all over again. "How could we have dumped another four and a half bucks in the connectors . . . ?"

Because, explained one of the visitors, the compact disc player in the trunk forced them to go from two boards to three boards to accommodate all the new chips and whatnot, and that particular connector had added $1.70.

"Sounds like there's a bunch of money here in going from two boards to three boards?"

Heads nodded. No question about that.

Computers, as it happened, were kind of a mystery to Landgraff. His refusal to use the company e-mail system, PROFS, was the despair of his colleagues. You had to e-mail his secretary, Nancy Donaldson, who typed out the message, gave it to Landgraff, who scrawled a reply, and gave it back to Nancy to type and fax—a day or two later. "You've got to get him on PROFS," Landgraff's boss Ben Lever had told Wendy Dendel. As if she could get Landgraff to do anything he didn't want to do. He didn't even like to leave a message on an answering machine.

But even a computer dummy could see the potential for a cost save here. Two boards were cheaper than three boards. So maybe they could move some of the stuff and get back down to two boards, Landgraff suggested. That was a possibility, said one of the engineers, clutching the three boards and looking from one to another, as if that wasn't the stupidest thing he had ever heard of. You never told a boss no. You said, "We'll look into it," and hoped he forgot. Or you said, "That's a possibility," and hoped he forgot. And you looked back and forth at the boards with a studious expression, as if considering a few strategic Lego-like moves for your chips.

Now Landgraff wanted to know about the knobs that controlled the climate controls. "How much did the knobs go up by? What's the absolute cost of those little teeny knobs? How much of the $6.27 is the knobs?"

The knobs, he was told, accounted for $3. They were high-quality polycarbonate. "Who says we have to have polycarbonate?" he demanded. "How much warranty costs are we saving with polycarbonate?" He looked up at the visitors, blinking rapidly. Of course they didn't know. Landgraff knew they wouldn't know.

"Well, you *should* know."

That Landgraff. You had to feel sorry for these amateurs from electronics. All they did was set themselves up for another slamdunk. They were up against a pro.

J AY W O O D A R D, W H O W A S the point man from electronics on the ICP, was beginning to find the whole situation very painful. The ICP had started out as an exciting collaboration between the Design Center, the Electronics Division, and Human Factors, the ergonomics department, whose mission was to tailor machinery to humankind. But the others were largely out of the picture now. And he seemed to be taking all the heat. For Woodard, a thin blond and—these days—tense engineer, what had started out as a synergistic collaboration seldom found in a company as large as Ford seemed to be ending in a nightmare of blame and retribution.

In the early stages he had moved temporarily to the Design Center to work closely with Nevenka Schumaker, a designer in Ford's components studio. For her, the assignment to create a unique sculpted oval decorated with illuminated knobs and buttons for America's most popular car was a product designer's dream. Over time Schumaker became something of an expert on knobs, amassing a collection from flea markets and appliance stores that she tried out periodically on Design Center secretaries and shop workers. She wanted to know what was easy to turn, what felt good in their hands. Stove knobs turned out to be the most popular. Her overall plan, to design a set of controls that were convenient and responsive, represented a sharp break with the past. "The Japanese made us think that something was high tech if it was smaller and had lots of buttons," she said. But now there were so many diminutive switches and buttons that drivers almost had to pull over and stop the car to change radio stations or turn on the heat.

Dave Hoffmeister from Human Factors, a department staffed almost equally with engineers and psychologists, was her adviser on how people interacted with buttons and knobs. Generally speaking, they preferred knobs for continuous functions, such as volume and heat. But they liked buttons to select an option—whether, for example, to listen to the radio or the tape player. They read the faceplate as if it were a sign, moving their eyes from left to right, from top to bottom. But the egg-shaped ICP had no corners, so how would a driver know where to begin? Schumaker anchored the faceplate with a big volume knob on the upper left.

In Human Factors, Hoffmeister recruited people to spend time in a booth that simulated a driver's seat and steering wheel, with the road stretching ahead on a TV monitor, not unlike a video game. After a practice session, the subjects were given eighteen assignments on the ICP. Human Factors recorded the length of time they took to carry them out, the number of times they took their eyes off the road to look at the unit, and the number of errors. Schumaker designed the ICP with the more frequently used radio controls placed above the climate controls, and a center spine separating the two.

Meanwhile, the engineer Jay Woodard struggled to find three-dimensional computer software that could model the wavy surface of the bezel and make the rounded buttons. When finally successful, he ran into opposition from the computer honchos in electronics who advocated a different program. A sympathetic manager leaned on Alpha, an advanced engineering unit, to order Woodard's choice of software and the computer on which it ran for "research"; as soon as it arrived, Woodard commandeered it. Next, he had to find a supplier. Electronics merely assembled the unit at its plant in Chihuahua, Mexico, the way Ford assembled the car in Atlanta and Chicago. The parts were made by other companies. And none of the five on Ford's approved supplier list believed they could make the complicated bezel and buttons for the ICP. Woodard had been delighted to discover a small California company called Southern Plastics Mold, or SPM, not only because they thought they could do it with a process called in-mold decorating, but also for the can-do attitude the principals displayed. The founders were two brothers, who were eager to break into the automotive industry after several years of doing work for computer companies.

Although it presented a matte black finish, with a seemingly transparent display area for time and temperature readouts, the ICP faceplate, or bezel, was made entirely of clear plastic. It derived its color and graphics from a layer of foil incorporated during the molding stage. The bezel contours had to be such that the foil could take their shape without thinning to the degree that light would show through. The only source for the foil was a single remote, expensive Japanese supplier. In general, Ford tried to avoid doing business with Japanese firms. Although it wasn't widely known outside the company, Harold Poling had instituted a ban on Japanese suppliers, following his disastrous 1992 trip to Tokyo with President Bush and the heads of Chrysler and GM to press for more trade with the United States, the one where Bush upchucked in the lap of the Japanese prime minister. That incident and the multimillion-dollar salaries of Bush's CEO companions had received more attention on that trip than their appeals to buy more U.S. products. Poling's ban did not apply to contracts already in effect; nor did it prevent Ford contractors from subcontracting to the Japanese, as in this case.

In making buttons with numbers, letters, and icons, SPM proposed to use a process called cap-insert that was similar to in-mold decorating. It was more costly than the laser etching used on the outgoing Taurus, owing in part to 9 cents' worth of foil required for each button, but it was more precise to address complaints Ford had received about fuzzy images. SPM bid on the job after looking at a clay model of the ICP. But the new process had not worked as planned, because the buttons in real life were thicker than either SPM or Ford had realized. The revised process was even more expensive, adding to the cost overrun.

And now, Landgraff announced to the delegation from electronics, he had decided to bring in SPM and have them explain themselves down to the last button. When they finished with SPM, they would summon suppliers with overruns on other ICP parts. He had done this sort of thing before. For the 1992 Taurus, he said, "We spent ten hours on knobs."

Ten hours on knobs. You might imagine what the electronics guys were thinking on hearing this. Ten trips over from home base in Regent Court, down the cement steps, and into this ice-cold conference room for a session with Landgraff. SPM was just one of their suppliers. There were others for other parts: the clock display, the flex circuit, all those connectors and harnesses, and a whole bunch of other stuff that was costing too much. It would have been so much simpler to have made the same old pair of boxes.

THE DAY BEFORE the SPM meeting, Landgraff convened a dress rehearsal with two women from Ford purchasing and the usual cast of characters from electronics. Use "soft gloves," one of the buyers pleaded with Landgraff. The people from SPM weren't used to the rough-and-tumble world of car manufacturing. They wanted so badly to please that they might be frightened into making reckless promises.

Well, *of course.* Landgraff understood completely. To be sure, it would be necessary to inform SPM that the increases were unacceptable. But, he said, the thing was to "do it in such a way as not to scare them off." Tom Gorman was inclined to be less sympathetic. Given that SPM had bid a certain price, the finance manager thought he might say something like this: "What the hell happened? Why did you guys sign up to this?"

The buyer was quick to point out that Ford had made changes in the part. Yeah, that was how suppliers made their money, Gorman shot back.

As with all ICP meetings, the electronics guys had brought in show-and-tell models. During a discussion of turning efforts and button response, all the guys started turning and pressing the switches and buttons, like kids with Fisher-Price toys. Only Landgraff seemed to see the humor in the scene. "That's what we like," he said. "Get these little parts in here and play with them."

The next day the ICP clan gathered as scheduled with three guys from SPM, whose somber business suits were set off by bright ties and tans. The head of the delegation was brother/founder Larry Noggle. The Ford guys took off their jackets. The California guys left theirs on.

"This is the biggest car program that North American has got at present," Landgraff told the supplier. "We're spending almost three billion dollars. We have very stringent cost targets. All of us in this room signed up to objectives. If we don't make them, we don't have a job. This program is over objective twelve to thirteen dollars. That's a big chunk of money. We didn't price for it. We have to eat it." He paused for a moment. "Now, we get to where we are and what we're going to do to get out of this situation."

Jay Woodard explained how the new process for printing words on buttons had driven up the cost. "You guys gave us a quotation on something you didn't know how to do?" Landgraff asked the supplier with wonder.

They *knew* how to do it, said Larry Noggle. They just underestimated the depth of the button.

What could Ford get, Landgraff asked, for the original price? SPM said Ford could get a crummy button made in two stages that left an edge, or "witness line," where light from behind would leak through.

"Maybe you could raise the edge and make a styling feature out of it?" Landgraff suggested. He was joking, but the number-two guy from SPM thought he was serious.

"Not for now. . . ."

". . . down the road," Landgraff said.

Now the suggestions were rolling in. They could reduce the manufacturing time from sixty seconds to forty-five seconds, and save 2 to 3 cents a button and 20 to 30 cents a knob. "Write that down," Landgraff said. "When are we going to know about it?"

"It's hard to know until we get into full production," said the number-two guy.

"When will we get into full production?"

"July '94."

"July '94, write that down."

SPM had projected a 15 percent scrap rate. Landgraff asked why that was. "We tried to present the worst-case scenario," said Noggle.

"I'm used to the worst-case scenario," Landgraff said. "We get that all the time. That's why our costs are so high."

They could save perhaps 25 cents by eliminating the Ford logo on the cassette door. "That sounds like a good one to me," Landgraff said. "What else have we got here?"

"There's a possibility," Woodard said tentatively, "to go back to the laser-etched button." The outgoing Taurus had them.

Landgraff looked interested. "Where's the laser-etched button?" he asked. No one had thought to bring one. The Maximum Leader was frustrated. "It's hard to make a decision without anything to look at."

But Woodard said he didn't mean the laser-etched buttons that Ford had used on the old Taurus. He was talking about Japanese laser-etched buttons, which were far superior to American laser-etched buttons. Larry Noggle explained that his brother was in Japan at this very moment trying to set up a joint laser-etching venture with the Japanese.

Landgraff was wary. "Is that what we get or would we get our shitty old American laser etching?" he asked. And anyway, why were the Japanese better? With a sudden, almost alarming display of animation, Noggle threw up his hands palms out in a blocking gesture. "I know nothing about the process." Woodard said something about the Japanese having more Ph.D. chemists on their payrolls who spent a lot of time looking at inks. Landgraff could see possibilities here. If nothing else, perhaps there was a way to use the potential of Japanese laser etching to pressure the Japanese foil supplier to charge less than 9 cents per button. "This could force the foil supplier into competition."

A FEW DAYS AFTER that meeting, Jay Woodard sat in the Regent Court cafeteria, which looked out over a flat expanse of land once farmed by Henry the Founder. Now it was filled with office buildings, hotels, and strip malls. One view framed Ford World Headquarters. He felt, he said, as if he were being held responsible for everything that had gone wrong with the ICP—how much over cost it was, and how late. It was not that he sought glory. He wasn't looking for a patent. It would be enough simply not to get blamed. He thought back on his days at the Design Center with Nevenka Schumaker. "We tried so hard to give them what they wanted. . . . I could have told Nevenka, 'There's no way we can do this,' and my management would have supported me." Ford, he maintained, did not reward innovation.

And now there were rumors that Ford would never do another ICP. It had been the most exciting assignment in his career. To work on a lesser product would be a letdown. And so, he had made the decision to leave Ford. He had another job with another company in another state. His boxes were packed.

The meetings would just have to go on without him.

TWELVE

Meeting People

A̲RMED WITH A notebook, Hiroki Hirati stood by a Sable station wagon parked, liftgate raised, in the big, circular Design Center showroom. Newly hired, Hirati was an FCGP, a member of the Ford College Graduate Program, although the joke was that the letters really signified "Fetch Coffee, Get Parts." FCGPs typically spent two years rotating through three- to six-month assignments. At the moment Hirati belonged to the DN101 planners.

This particular afternoon his supervisor, Brad Nalon, had given Hirati a special task. He was supposed to enlist Design Center employees in a survey of the handle used to close the station wagon liftgate. Having moved the handle, located on the inside of the liftgate, to a position thought to be more convenient for passengers, the studio now questioned whether it might not have become more difficult for people standing outside the car to grab when the liftgate was raised. Both designers and engineers suspected that very few people actually used the handle, however. Hirati's assignment was to stop people as they cut through the showroom on their way to the opposite wing of the Design Center, and ask them to close the liftgate.

Stop people? It was like trying to turn back the Colorado River. "I'd just like to take a few minutes of your time," he'd say, stepping in front of someone. People looked at their watches and looked back at Hirati in dismay. They all said the same thing: "I'm on my way to a meeting." You would think Ford was in the meeting business, not the car business, and that people's jobs were to attend meetings. Screw the Sable, screw its liftgate handle, who cares if we sell any cars. Just let me get to my meeting.

As suspected, just two of forty people he managed to detain did in fact use the handle. It was faster simply to push the liftgate closed.

Ford *Meeting* Company, went a standard quip. Dick Landgraff's schedule, as well as the schedules of team members, and most everyone else at Ford, was jammed with powwows from morning to night. Landgraff *liked* meetings. If he didn't have one to go to, he wandered back and forth outside the cubicle of his secretary, Nancy Donaldson, rattling her nerves. He did his paperwork—reports, memos, letters—after everybody else was gone. He couldn't understand how people could work eight hours, go home, and expect Ford to have a future when the Japanese were working ten to twelve hours. "Goddamned guys who go home at five o'clock," he swore one night, dialing an extension and getting no answer. "It's beyond me."

A few years back, Max Jurosek, the vice-president for car product development, decided to ban all meetings on Wednesdays so engineers would have more disposable time. Jurosek summoned Steve Kozak, his aide at the time, and told him about the plan. "I've got this book here," Jurosek said, as Kozak told the story. "It's a book on Honda. Honda doesn't have meetings on Wednesday."

Jurosek ordered Kozak to read the book and prepare a blue letter on the subject. Letters from vice-presidents were called "blue letters" because they were typed on blue stationery. Only, Jurosek didn't want to part with the book. Vice-presidents could be funny that way. Kozak couldn't find a copy anywhere. He finally had to beg Jurosek for the book, then he stayed up all night reading it. For the next two weeks he met with his boss almost daily to draft instructions.

Managers who worked for Jurosek were told to submit copies of their current schedules with an explanation of how they would eliminate Wednesday meetings. Jurosek also wanted them to police conference rooms within their jurisdiction for unauthorized Wednesday use. Once the ban was in place, Kozak thought it worked great. Meetings were automatically reduced by 20 percent . . . although there were some suspicious-looking gatherings around people's desks. But after a few months Jurosek moved on, and people went back to their old ways.

Recognizing the importance of meetings in a team environment, where so many people needed to keep abreast of developments, Ford had employed a meetings consultant in the fall of 1991 to advise DN101. Before reaching any conclusions, he went to seven meetings, which totaled twelve hours in length. He counted 155 people and one decision. "This means 155 people spent 11 hours 'sharing information,'" he wrote. He calculated the cost of the seven meetings at $25,000. The consultant was especially distressed by the clay walkarounds in the studio. There were too many people, you couldn't hear half the time, and standing for two hours was "backbreaking."

Similarly concerned, the DN101 planners had initially tried with a microphone and a flip chart to bring order to these marathons. As the walkaround started, there would be maybe fifty people standing three deep around a clay model. The agenda was written on the flip chart, with time allotments for each item. Planner Ron Heiser would say something like, "Hello, this is how the meeting will run tonight." Then he would hand the mike to Landgraff. Only . . . Landgraff wouldn't take the mike, or he'd take it and forget he had it. Heiser would announce that the allotted fifteen minutes were up for that particular discussion, and people would simply go right on talking. By the third agenda item there'd be three groups of people having separate meetings around the clay and another clump of folks in the corner. Or Bell and Landgraff would duck into a car to discuss the interior and no one would hear a thing they said to each other. Decisions were made, but no single person took notes. To make matters worse, the ventilation system emitted a constant low-level hum and, for a time, the studio was under construction. The planners finally washed their hands of the whole thing. They would attend, but they would not officiate.

On the positive side, people didn't hesitate to speak out, the consultant took note of that. "Management has clearly sent the message that it wants to hear from all of the team members." They spoke out, but Dick Landgraff made the decisions. The consultant noted that too.

THE PROLIFERATION OF MEETINGS was by no means confined to Ford, or to the automobile industry. Across America, voice mail was answering the phones of people clumped together around long tables in little rooms. Sometimes there weren't enough people to go to all the meetings. And certainly there was little time left over for what used to be considered work. If employees were asked, they could tell you that 90 percent of the time they spent in meetings was a waste. But since no one asked them, the get-togethers continued unabated. As corporations began to downsize in the 1990s, the pressure mounted on people to be more productive with what little time they had. Adversity for some is opportunity for others—in this case, time management gurus.

Ford flirted with several systems before hooking up with Franklin

Quest, a Utah-based company named for Benjamin Franklin that publicized 20–30 percent gains in productivity among those who took its course. Founded in 1984 by a former insurance salesman, Hyrum W. Smith, Franklin Quest had elevated time management to a faith, and the to-do list to a daily expression of deeply held personal values. Smith promised adherents nothing less than "inner peace." The bible was the Franklin planner, where each day had two pages for lists and notes. Franklin followers assigned each item on their daily list of obligations an A,B, or C, according to its priority. Then they numbered the letters, placing the A's in a sequence, and so on. Each list was always headed by "P&S," an A-rated, prayerful fifteen-minute session for planning and solitude.

As you carried out your "prioritized daily task list" you marked each item with a check, an arrow, an "X," a dot, or a check in a circle with an initial, to show its status: completed, forwarded, deleted, delegated, or in process. There were sections in the planner for addresses, expenses, and mini-files. And the extraordinary part of it all was that you could not do any of this properly—the value defining, goal setting, daily planning, recordkeeping—without the all-day Franklin time management course that came with a sixty-minute motivational tape by Smith and the official Franklin planner starter kit. The most popular planner size was the 5 1/2-by-8 1/2-inch classic, but there were four other sizes. And you would almost certainly want to trade in the shiny vinyl planner that came with the course for one in high-quality leather. You could choose from an assortment of five different leathers and a half-dozen colors. The binder came with your choice of straps or handles, snaps or zippers; the calendar pages came standard or lightly printed like bank checks with decorative motifs—the seasons, where images changed four times a year, the blue-bordered Monticello, and a golf filler with pictures of famous courses. Every year you needed a refill. In addition, there were stickers, books, pens, hole punches, and an assortment of pouches for holding disks, credit cards, receipts, and photos. Plus books by Hyrum Smith and Benjamin Franklin, and more. And you could not buy any of this striking epochal array, not one page or one binder, anywhere but in a Franklin Quest Company store or by mail order. Oh, it was brilliant. And it would not, could not end, because approximately six times each year, according to a company survey, the average Franklin planner toter entered a store and asked, "What's new?" They were hooked on planning. Hyrum Smith once told the *Wall Street Transcript*, "If you're over twelve years old, you're a candidate for the Franklin day planner."

Michigan was a Franklin stronghold, thanks to the company's popularity with the automotive industry. Not only Ford, but Chrysler and General Motors were advocates. Smith estimated that more than 3 percent of the Michigan population carried Franklin day planners. At Ford, executives with secretaries had no need for the course, but engineers, analysts, and planners flocked to the seminars in search of inner peace.

It was only natural that a professional planner like Brad Nalon would find his way to a seminar sooner or later. Engineers might be in the ascendancy at Ford, but that didn't mean planners had less work. In the old days, before teams, Nalon had one boss giving him orders. Now he had Landgraff, Bell, the business planner, the chunk team leaders. Part of his problem was that he was so obliging, he would drop everything to help. He found himself caught up in "hot" assignments, while the long-term things didn't get done. Some days it felt as if people were coming at him from all directions.

At first some of what Nalon had heard about Franklin time management made him apprehensive. He had held back, resisting the first course offerings. What if he got so involved in planning he got nothing else done? "I could see me spending all day planning my day." On the other hand, what if others who took the course were suddenly so productive that they had the competitive advantage? And all you had were a bunch of notes to yourself that you could never find? *No more floating paper.* That was one of Franklin's mottos.

So Nalon eventually took the Franklin seminar and crammed his vital information into a jumbo-sized Monarch planner, which he used religiously. And then one day he drove away with it on top of his car. This was the very worst thing that could happen to a Franklin follower, and it frequently happened just as it had to Nalon. People set the planner on top of the roof to open the car door, then drove off. Some Franklin trainers suggested customers back up vital information in their computers, even though it constituted duplication of the sort Franklin Quest discouraged.

One of Wendy Dendel's friends had been a casualty. Said Dendel without much sympathy, "There went her friends, her plans, and her notes on important meetings. . . . Talk about get a life!" Dendel had once taken a course in a different time management system that advised people to organize their activities by dividing work into "A," "B," and "C" drawers. " 'A' was for things to do that day, 'B' was for that week, and 'C' was for never-until-you-were-asked." She never really tried to follow the system. First of all she didn't have three drawers. Second, the arrangement assumed all assignments were to be done, when some were a waste of time.

Worried that someone from Chrysler might find his lost planner, which contained confidential information, Brad Nalon scoured the side of the road for a week with no luck. He gave up and bought another big Monarch. On reflection, he decided it was prudent to carry around less material. He sold the Monarch and bought a Compact planner. Even that felt too big, so he got the smallest version of all, the Pocket. He also bought one for his wife, a hospital administrator.

Like most bosses, Landgraff carried his schedule around in his shirt pocket on an index card that Nancy Donaldson typed up daily. He had his own system of time management. He skipped those events he thought were pointless. One time he failed to turn up to "one-on-one" with his boss Will Boddie, the former head of the Mustang program who had replaced Ben Lever. Boddie's secretary called Landgraff's secretary, asking her where Landgraff was. Nancy Donaldson didn't know. Boddie's secretary acted like it was *her* fault, but Donaldson was used to her boss's unpredictable behavior. His failure to turn up for a Ken Kohrs's review produced another flurry of "Where's Dick?" calls. His name tag was waiting. So was Kohrs. And so was the audience. He was supposed to give a presentation on the new Taurus.

He hadn't gone to the victory party when his 1992 Taurus beat the Accord. He didn't even make it to the 1992 Taurus official team picture. And he never went to the monthly confabs at the Dearborn Inn, when program managers were supposed to trade information on World Class Timing and other topics of common interest. When Wendy Dendel told him he had to give a presentation on diversity, he threw the written notice down. "Why?" he asked. "Do you think I have a problem in my department?" Then he picked apart the numbers. So Ford didn't have as many blacks as the general population, but how many were graduating from engineering schools? He did go, read a script that had been prepared for him, and left early. He passed up the opportunity to be a "mentor" to younger Ford employees seeking career guidance.

"Brainstorm this . . . butcher-block approach," he carried on one day. Ford offered "too many distractions . . . going to meetings like that, being mentors to people. . . . It's more important to pay attention to the car. Every time you don't, something goes wrong. People get caught up with all of this other, what I call frivolous stuff. Like, going to seminars to hear about what's going on with the 1998 new steering column, and going to luncheon meetings to find out what truck operations is doing on some other thing. People lose their focus, they lose their ability to remember what it is they're supposed to go do, so they dissipate their efforts in a lot of interesting and perhaps even valuable sorts of things, but they're not critical to what they're really trying to accomplish."

No process involved more meetings than color selection. During the peak of the 1993 color season, in May, John Aiken, the head of color and trim, had gone to a Ford-sponsored seminar on "fast cycle time," with coaching on how to speed up product development. On his return, he counted the number of meetings since January—forty-plus and growing. By August his count was up to fifty-two. Everyone from the top down wanted to have a say in the selection of exterior colors, which were chosen three years in advance.

Aiken did not consider himself a snob. Car design, he said, was more technique than talent. Designers were merely people trained in "wrist skills" who loved cars. But he objected strenuously to the way color selection had become a free-for-all. If anything, the introduction of program teams had increased the number of people who thought they were empowered to render verdicts on color. "Everyone is willing to give you an opinion and think their opinion is value added. It's not. It's just an opinion. I don't need everybody from DN101 who's a fuel injection guy or a metal stamping guy or a cost guy who's a beanie advising me on what color we should have."

The process to select eighteen exterior colors and decide which ones would adorn which vehicles began anew each January as paint suppliers arrived at the Design Center to display their latest hues on platter-sized chips. Afterward the experts in the color and trim department fanned out across the country, dropping in on conferences of color professionals, hot rod and boat shows, anywhere they could get sneak previews of color trends. New colors popped up first in clothing, then spread to home furnishings and then to office and hotel interiors before ending up on cars. In fashion, actionwear peddled by mass marketers like The Gap was a more reliable indicator than quirky Paris offerings. The color people made a point of going to spring break in Daytona Beach, to see what college kids were wearing. The current generation of young people was not into wild colors. They wanted to appear mature and reliable.

By May, color and trim had narrowed the choices and painted them on cars for color reviews. Staged at the Dearborn Proving Ground, these were elaborate affairs. Vehicles in various hues paraded by seated invitees like fashion models on a stage. By July everyone would have seen the alternatives: program managers, segment managers, marketing managers, dealers, and vice-presidents. Despite the limited list of invitees, Aiken never knew who would talk their way into a color review. At the last one, three interlopers had snuck through security in a Mark VIII. Apparently the guard didn't question them closely because they were driving the car of choice for executives.

The whole thing made him nostalgic for the days when Don Petersen was chairman of Ford. The color reviews were held in Palm Springs, where more or less permanent sunshine ensured suitable weather. Petersen would look over the cars lined up like bright, new crayons in a box, and then make the choice. He also picked wheel covers. But even with so much input, the truth was that nothing had really changed. "In the old days everything was autocratic," Aiken said. "Now it *looks* different. You follow the group process and in the end one person still makes the decision."

When they offered a reddish-brown cordovan color, the Ford Division grabbed it for their truck lines. Then Lincoln-Mercury dealers said that they wanted cordovan, too, but they didn't want some truck color on their luxury cars. (The Design Center always found it painful when car dealers, questionable arbiters of taste, called the shots.) Vice-president Ross Roberts wouldn't give up Ford Division's cordovan. So the color and trim people had to find another cordovan in a slightly different shade for Lincoln-Mercury.

And there was at this very moment another case closer to home for the DN101 team. The color and trim department had recommended four colors for the interior: blue, gray, green, and a new mauve shade called "Nightmist." The absence of a saddle shade alarmed Ben Lever, Landgraff's former boss, who had left car product development and was now second-in-command at the Lincoln-Mercury sales division. Saddle had been in Fords since time immemorial.

The color experts opposed saddle on two counts: It would not look good, they said, in the seat fabric they had chosen for DN101, and it would require an unsightly dark insert on the top of the instrument panel to reduce glare from the steeply raked windshield. Lever was not persuaded. And in the end, he saved the day for saddle. The stylists weren't about to give up Nightmist. Blue was eliminated.

So enamored was marketing of green, the color of choice on 24 percent of 1993 Tauruses, that they wanted not one but two greens for the 1996 Taurus and Sable. Medium Willow was a shoe-in because it matched the green interior. Color and trim strongly suggested that the second green be the paler Light Evergreen Frost, but the dealers had flipped out over a shade similar to Willow called Pacific Green. To the untrained eye, they looked almost exactly alike. Planner Brad Nalon, to whom Landgraff had delegated color selection, was with the Design Center on this one. But they were no match for marketing. The car line ended up with the two look-alike greens.

Landgraff's vigilance over every aspect of DN101 made it all the more surprising that he did not exercise the program manager's prerogative to advise on colors. He did not even render an opinion. There had been a time when he was as involved as anyone else in his position, but he had lost all faith in his own judgment. It happened during the Great Green Debate of 1988, back when David Rees headed the Design Center's color and trim department. Rees was convinced that green was the color for the nineties. Landgraff was equally convinced that green had faded into the past. Ross Roberts agreed. Rees got word that Roberts had told his marketing people, in so many words, "The first man who suggests green, I'll fire him."

Landgraff staked out a position: He would use green on the Taurus if market research supported it. "I can tell you what the customer will say," Rees told Landgraff. "They will say, 'I don't want green.'" Customers, Rees said, did not know what they would like so far in the future.

Landgraff considered it hypocritical to use research for exterior styling, as Ford did extensively, but not color. "We show people shapes and say, 'What do you like?' and we believe them. We show them colors and say, 'What do you like?' and we don't believe them." It was another example of Design Center hubris. "Designers believe they are more sensitive, more intelligent, and certainly have better taste than the customer."

At Landgraff's prodding, Rees said, "We did $600,000 worth of research. The Design Center paid for it. We had a review in Palm Springs. Guess what? People hated green." Landgraff, Rees said, couldn't contain his satisfaction. He smiled as he told Rees, "The research proves it. People hate green." But Rees refused to give up. He lined up the Design Center high command, Jack Telnack and Fritz Mayhew. And then he persuaded Bob Tasca, the company's influential Lincoln-Mercury dealer, that green was the happening color, and asked him to lobby vice-presidents Max Jurosek and Ross Roberts. At a watershed meeting with Roberts, Rees made his pitch. "I'll be up-front. I've been told never to approach you and talk about green." Then he talked about the color trends; he talked about ecology and the green movement. As Rees later told the story, Roberts asked his people, "'What do you think?' They started to shake their heads no. But then Roberts said, 'I hate green, but if it's what the customer wants, I'm for it. If it'll sell more cars, do it.'"

Suddenly Ford couldn't make enough green cars. It was the smash hit of 1992, the customer choice on more than a quarter of all Escorts and 18 percent of Tauruses, trailed by white at 15.5 percent. Black Tauruses were the least popular, at 2.5 percent.

In time, Rees and Landgraff would laugh together over what had happened. "I was dead wrong," Landgraff said. Now he had sympathy for color people. "It's a tough job. People who wouldn't dream of criticizing your appearance will look at your life's work, a wonderful new color, and say, 'Where did this shit come from?'" But he never warmed up to green. Over at the test track one day to try out some new seats, he found himself confronted with a 100 percent green Taurus. "God, I hate this green interior," he said as he climbed in. "I feel like Robin Hood. I feel like I'm in goddamn Sherwood Forest. Do we sell any of these?"

THIRTEEN

A Car Is Born

FROM THE DESIGN Center, the Ford pilot plant was a right turn onto four-lane Oakwood Boulevard and a mile down, through a modest, settled neighborhood of brick homes, on a stretch of road between two expressways. A small plant with no automation and no moving line, it was the cocoon for the next stage in the life of the emerging Taurus, the build of the confirmation prototype. The first of a fleet of proto-Tauruses was due in vehicle development on December 9, 1993, where manager Tom Moran's guys would spend the better part of 1994 testing, tuning, and otherwise turning the car into "something that someone would enjoy driving," as Moran put it. A delay in this build could jeopardize the tight testing schedule, and torpedo Job One.

Dick Landgraff had made the delivery of prototype parts his personal crusade. Suppliers were notorious for missing delivery dates. Years ago some *never* arrived. Or when they did, they didn't match. Guys at the pilot plant just cobbled together cars with what was available, and vehicle development finished the job. "There've been times when they delivered the car to vehicle development on a forklift on a skid with no tires," said Roger Ferns, the DN101 timing guy. "Development would say: 'I can't drive it.' Car product development would say, 'That's your problem.'"

Dan Rivard, George Bell's old supervisor, once had a job like Tom Moran's. "When I was in vehicle development, they'd wait till we all went home, then they'd tow it to the garage. Half the parts would be in the trunk . . . but they made the delivery date. Sometimes it would take six weeks to get it together."

A few months before the DN101 build was to begin, Dick Landgraff had his people bring in every major supplier, one by one, to extract their personal commitment to the deadlines. Bodysides, hoods, and other pieces of sheet metal for the DN101 prototypes were due September 24. The last deadline was October 28 for seats, the instrument panel, and the rest of the interior parts designated "trim."

Suppliers who didn't think they could make the dates were supposed to send Ford "red border alerts," named for a form used by purchasing. But suppliers just hated to tell Ford they were in trouble. As electronics had done with the integrated control panel, they always tried to recover. Sometimes it was not they but their subcontractors who were running late. So just in case some suppliers were being overly optimistic, in early October Landgraff dispatched a crew of DN101 troubleshooters to drop in on manufacturers of difficult, critical components. He and George Bell warned people not to accept promises. "I want to see a box of parts that they're going to ship," Landgraff said.

"If anybody goes to a place and all you see are tools, we got problems," Bell said. He was talking about machine tools, not hammers and screwdrivers.

Said Landgraff, "Swing around to the docks." He wanted to see the boxes stacked and ready to load.

Said Bell: "Don't be fooled by a tool that's pushed out on the middle of the floor but not blocked in. If they show you boxes, look inside. I'm not kidding."

"We're out of the trust mode," Landgraff said. "We're into verification."

Some suppliers seemed unable to believe that Ford was serious about dates; the company had been so casual in prior years. On the eve of the sheet-metal deadline, Tom Kelley, a body engineering troubleshooter, tracked down Landgraff and Bell at the Goodyear plant in Logan, Ohio, with the news that a sheet-metal supplier in the Detroit suburb of Livonia was in big, big trouble. When Landgraff and Bell landed at the Detroit airport, they headed straight to the job shop. A gaggle of team members was huddled around a car part called a cowl top assembly, which ran from side to side in the engine compartment behind the dash. If its dimensions weren't accurate, it could throw off the fenders, the hood—in short, the whole front end. The more they measured the piece, the worse it looked.

"When did you set up?" Landgraff asked the man who had identified himself—somewhat reluctantly, Landgraff thought—as being in charge.

"Yesterday."

"Yesterday!" Landgraff almost yelled. This was unbelievable. He asked to see the fixture they were using for the assembly. It looked to him like a couple of sawhorses and some clamps.

"Here's the drill," Landgraff said. It was now Friday. "You guys are gonna deliver these parts on Monday. You got Friday night, all day Saturday, and all day Sunday." He gave the man his home number. "You call me at home and tell me you're going to make this date." He got his call on Sunday. The parts would be there.

Ninety-three percent of the sheet-metal parts arrived on time. Landgraff congratulated the team for improving on the previous best record of 83 percent, or whatever it was. He thought 83 percent sounded about right. Going into the October 28 due date, the situation looked even more promising. There were only eight red border alerts. As it turned out, however, eighty parts were late. Landgraff sent the offenders written reprimands with copies to the purchasing division for their files. "People need to learn to live up to their promises."

As components came in to the warehouse, they were divided into a half-dozen kits per car, to be trucked to the plant as needed. But first, two DN101 guys weighed them. Weight figures to this point had been an estimate. The news was good. The sedan was twenty-five pounds under target. Landgraff could restore the fuel tank to its original size.

When the ICP was among the parts that arrived on time—a true piece of serendipity given all that had gone wrong to this point—electronics supervisor Mark Jarvis was so happy that he offered to meet Landgraff at the pilot plant for a look. Almost immediately, Jarvis realized he had made a dreadful mistake. No one expected perfection in a prototype part, but this was awful. Switches wobbled; knobs were stiff. You pressed one button, and the one next to it moved. "This is a thing of beauty until you touch it," Landgraff said. Some of the electronics engineers got defensive. They tried to say it wasn't *that* bad, but Landgraff was already writing himself a little note. The next day he fired off a withering letter to the two top guys in electronics—the division vice-president and the general manager—with copies to his own bosses. The ICP was in such bad shape, he wrote, that it threatened to delay the entire car program. He recapped the previous day's review. "Frankly I was astonished and appalled and have lost confidence in the present Team's ability to design an ICP that works." Landgraff demanded the electronics division put a manager on the job with clout, who truly understood electro-mechanical devices and the importance of timing, maybe someone from a *Japanese* supplier.

The letter got the intended result. Within days, a senior engineering manager from electronics was assigned full time to the ICP, overseeing the efforts of the Regent Court engineers. Thanks to the miracle of fax, the letter also got widespread if unauthorized circulation. Back in the basement, Jarvis received messages from all over the company. People offered condolences for his troubles with the ICP; some thanked him for taking the heat off them and their problems with Landgraff.

As PARTS ARRIVED, newly annointed members of the DN101 launch team began to converge on the pilot plant for what promised to be a grand adventure, birthing the first Taurus. Landgraff, Bell, and the other team managers had chosen 140 engineers to spend the next two years more or less welded to the car, beginning with this prototype build of the sedan, and then the station wagon and all the other models, followed by more advanced prototype builds both here and in the assembly plants, culminating with the start of the production in June 1995. Atlanta was the lead plant for the changeover; Chicago would follow by several weeks.

Although product launch teams had been going to assembly plants for years, this was the first to move en masse to the pilot plant, yet another breakthrough for teamwork. In theory, when the DN101 launch team left for the Atlanta assembly plant after working together for a year or so in Dearborn, they would be a seasoned, compatible, competent crew. The launch team was to resolve the inevitable build issues—the parts that didn't fit or didn't work, that failed quality standards, or that could not be installed at the breakneck pace of sixty-seven jobs an hour. In Atlanta they would be expected to make on-the-spot judgment calls.

Old-timers with families were less eager for this assignment than young engineers for whom a new model launch was a notch in the belt and a stepping stone in a career, something like combat duty for a soldier. "Going on launch" was a tour of duty on the front lines, where the process of turning a virtual car into a driving machine required generous chunks of not only metal but mettle.

Along with the launch team, workers fresh off the line in Atlanta and Chicago were invading the pilot plant to help with assembly and to learn their way around the new model. On their return, they would train others. To dragoon honest-to-god workers—men with Georgia drawls and nicknames like "Crazy Horse" and "Junior"—would have been unheard of a decade ago. Now the company gave them a fancy name—"product specialists"—and put them up in suites at the Marriott Residence Inn in Dearborn.

His buddies called him "Crazy," and they called him "Hoss," but he was

Paul Harris from the chassis line, a twenty-eight-year veteran of Atlanta Assembly with a big tattooed eagle alighting on his upper arm, and he was telling engineers what to do. They didn't act pleased. "They didn't want to work with us, till they found out we wasn't gonna budge," he said later. When he saw how a tension strut bushing could work better divided into two pieces, "I took a pocketknife and cut it up like I wanted it and they bought it. . . . Ain't much you can't do with a pocketknife and a screwdriver." Nights, you might see Crazy Horse in one of the country-music halls on Telegraph Road, out there on the dance floor all by his lonesome, just a country boy in the big city, tapping, stomping, sliding, toe-heeling, hitching, and swiveling, vining left, vining right, to "Boot Skootin' Boogie," to "Elvira," to "Achy Breaky."

IN NUMBERS, THE DN101 team had peaked. Over the next few months, many of the engineers not assigned to the pilot plant would be recalled to their home offices, or dispatched perhaps to another vehicle team. Landgraff sometimes didn't find out they were gone until afterward. "Some people have the courtesy to come talk to me, other people just don't bother." The DN101 studio, the scene of such furious activity two years ago, had all but emptied out. Modelers were scraping away on other clays for other programs. John Doughty was in Europe, as head of interior design. And Doug Gaffka had taken his place as design executive, rising in a mighty leap from a grade ten to a thirteen. There wasn't a sweeter, more modest guy than Gaffka at Ford Motor Company, but news of his advance was hard on those who were less upwardly mobile, such as junior planners, now in disfavor and stuck at sixes and sevens, with slim prospects. Tom Gorman was also getting a promotion and a new job as comptroller in the Dearborn stamping plant, punching his ticket with some experience in manufacturing as he moved up the ladder in the finance division. Everyone knew that Gorman was one of the division's golden boys, whose career was being shaped from on high. Another up-and-comer with MIT credentials, Eric Koefoot, would take his place as the team's finance manager. Business planner Rich Pettit had been transferred to Japan with Ford's Mazda operations; Brent Egleston had replaced him. In the saddest development, the team's popular marketing guy, Hank Buick, had been diagnosed with cancer. He wasn't expected to live past Christmas.

In the Glass House, there was change as well. Harold A. Poling was retiring as CEO; his successor was Alex Trotman. Landgraff thought highly of Trotman, a product planner who had headed North American Automotive Operations when the new Taurus was in the styling phase. "A stand-up guy,"

Landgraff called him. Way back in the seventies, Trotman had supported him during a pricing dispute when he was catching a lot of flak. Trotman, sixty, the son of a carpet layer, was born in England—he had memories of hiding under the dining room table during the Blitz—but was educated in Scotland, and he had started at Ford as a trainee in purchasing. Though he did not have an undergraduate degree, having bypassed college and joined the Royal Air Force, Trotman had somehow landed in an MBA program at Michigan State University and secured his master's. His ascent to the top of Ford was a victory for product planning over finance, whose candidate was vice-chairman Allan Gilmour. Engineers who hoped one day to see one of their own at the top now looked to Ed Hagenlocker, executive vice-president of NAAO, who had a Ph.D. in nuclear physics. On taking charge, Trotman told the press he planned to cut costs, but that was nothing new, and no one knew what form it would take. One thing, anyway, Trotman had no known misgivings about DN101 storage capacity. "I hope Red won't be around to see the trunk," Landgraff had remarked at a review back in the spring. He no longer had to worry.

In Atlanta and Chicago, where the body shops were highly automated with scores of robots and few humans, and the line once started rarely stopped, it took ten man-hours to build a car. Turn away for a moment, and it was gone. A car begun on the first shift was completed on the second. At the pilot plant, though, men loaded and fused parts by hand. Build time there was four weeks, and longer for the first few cars.

As the first sheet-metal embryo crawled through a jungle of stout orange machinery and airborne wire vines, growing larger and more developed with each new day, engineers came to see it, touch it, measure it, and try out parts. Here at last was the fruit of so much inspiration, calculation, dedication, collocation, and altercation. Of hundreds, no, *thousands* of meetings. Two years of early mornings and late nights, snack bar lunches, and missed dinners. This was the engineers' Job One, everybody said. If ever there were a moment for emotion, surely this was that time.

"It just looks like a car body to me," said George Bell, standing with Tom Breault beside a sheet-metal skeleton in the body shop. "It doesn't look like something we've spent the last two years hammering out."

"It doesn't seem like that long ago we were massaging all these lines in the car," Breault said.

"Nobody realizes how you argue."

"Remember all that grief on that A pillar?" chimed in Rand Bitter, a finance guy.

Spotting Bell from afar, Steve Kozak came loping over. "The doors are sweet," he told the chief engineer. "Feel how strong the door frame is." He gripped the bodyside.

Bell lifted the front door up and down, not pleased to see that it moved. "The bodyside stampings don't look real good," he said. "There's some ripples and waves."

On the final line a couple of weeks later, a tall blond engineer crawled into the rear seat, and slapped a piece of material, the package tray sound absorber, on the sheet metal below the rearview window opening. "It's all screwed up," he said. Jim Mikola, whose chunk of the car included the glass pieces, pushed the button for the front door window and watched it go up and down, pleased as a kid that "it worked the first time." Dave Wilemott, a wiring guy, saw harnesses the length of the car slip into place more quickly and easily than he had dared hope. But "some 6-millimeter holes turned out to be 2.5." Lichia Bucklin peered at the front sixteen inches of the car, her turf in the real estate wars. Seeing the front-end moldings known as "gimp" brought back painful memories of standing for hours in reviews during the waning days of her pregnancy, when she was carrying fifty extra pounds. "That gimp shows up more than I thought it would," she said.

Landgraff, on one of his visits, overheard two workers talking about the ICP, now lodged in the instrument panel. "Look at that radio," one said to the other.

"You really like it?" Landgraff asked, buoyed.

"Goddamn, man," the guy answered. "I'm gonna buy one of these cars."

I T W A S I N E V I T A B L E , however, that what commanded the most attention were the problems. The outer edge of the instrument panel scraped against the door; no one was sure why. Maybe the A pillar that ran alongside the windshield was warped. The hood bent; it was probably going to need a reinforcement. Some of the radiator supports were cracked; possibly the hood was at fault.

And the seat fabric. Good God! There was something horribly wrong with the seat fabric. The pattern, called "Orient," was a paisley-like swirl of reddish-brown on a tan background. Bold patterns were the wave of the future, John Doughty had said as he made the selection, before he left for Europe. His first choice had been just a little *too* bold for Landgraff, who labeled it "flower power" and nixed it. The DN101 design executive had next latched on to this motif, which he discovered amid some swatches that had just come in to the color and trim department. In market research, people preferred it to the Camry's dull, nubby pattern.

But it was provoking such violent reactions. One development guy said it reminded him of the time his two-year-old grandson had pigged out on Thanksgiving turkey, drunk a lot of Hawaiian Punch, and then thrown up. The assembly workers seemed to be of a similar opinion. They stuck their fingers down their throats and made gagging sounds. Someone said it looked like a deer hunter had tossed a bloody carcass on the back seat. Neither Len Landis, head of the seating chunk team, nor his guys liked it. But being engineers, they knew they had no taste. . . . *"Their taste is in their mouths."* So they kept their mouths shut. Will Boddie, Landgraff's new boss, on seeing the fabric for the first time, wanted to know how this could have happened. Doughty wasn't there to explain. "I have to defend this," Landgraff complained. Brad Nalon tried to reassure everybody that the final version would be more subdued. The fabric supplier planned to adjust the balance between the red accent color and the tan background. No subjects had complained during market research on the interiors. And most people believed Orient was more attractive in the other interior colors.

ON NOVEMBER 16, Doug Gaffka pulled up to the pilot plant in his smoky purple Mark VIII and made his way to a section where people were swarming all over a car body, like ants on a chicken bone. Somewhere under there was the first prototype, sitting on an elevated track a couple of feet off the ground.

The hood and trunk lid were raised, and the doors were open wide, exposing the interior. The red car stared blindly ahead; the headlamp openings were still two empty holes. Gaffka hadn't seen the prototype before. And he couldn't quite see it now. He squeezed in for a glimpse. "Nice and short," he said. He looked inside. "It's amazing all the parts that go on this." In the rear, a guy was kneeling in the trunk, examining the seal that encircled him. The car's badge, "Taurus GL," was in Gaffka's handwriting, writ large in silver. He had scrawled it one day, and his version stuck. There had been some debate over whether the metal was shiny enough. But that was not what had caught the designer's eye. "The backup lamp is a mess," he said. It looked asymmetrical.

George Bell came over. "It's a nice car to wash," he said, standing next to Gaffka. "When I look at a car, I think, 'Am I going to want to wash it when I get it home?' "

"Every time you wash it, you scratch it," Gaffka said. He had a vintage Porsche at home. "I only wash it three times a year." He looked at the Taurus. "They'll have to get new car wash brushes for it just to get at all the neat shapes."

Bell and Gaffka chatted for a few moments. "Let's just hope it sells," Gaffka said.

"It will," Bell said. "It'll be a great car."

For a moment the two looked at it in silence, Bell with a beatific expression, his hands clasped in front of him, Gaffka with his hands thrust in his pockets. Then Gaffka asked people to clear away for a minute. "I just want to get a look," he said. "I just want to see what it looks like." Now the entire car was visible. "Thanks," he said softly. The word hung in the air, prayerful, as if he were thanking everyone for what they had done.

"There wasn't anything we backed off on," Bell said. "We didn't back away from anything if we thought it looked good." He grinned. "We're not going to be accused of a lukewarm makeover on this one."

"I wish John Doughty could have been here," Gaffka said. "I'll have to give him a call."

It PAID TO KEEP your eyes and ears open around the plant. When Rand Bitter, the finance guy on duty, heard Kozak talking about a hood reinforcement, he made a mental note to come up with the smallest possible steel blank. He saw a possibility to save money on the plastic radiator support, which was molded in gray fiberglass, then painted black by the supplier. In the plant, it was painted again in body color. So maybe they could eliminate the supplier's black paint and a couple of bucks.

Walking by a row of Mustangs in the plant, he noticed their cargo nets were about the same size as the ones on the outgoing Taurus, and came from the same supplier. Investigating, Bitter discovered the Mustang net cost $1.68 more. When the Mustang people tried the cheaper Taurus net at Bitter's suggestion, it worked fine. Ford decided to use it in both cars. The supplier had a fit, but Bitter had no sympathy for suppliers. He had been told by more than one underling that their job was to wring all the money they could out of Ford. By all rights, the cargo net supplier should rebate the additional savings gained by eliminating the Mustang production line and buying material in larger quantities.

"If the company was really serious about trying to be competitive," Bitter said one day, back in his cubicle in the basement, "they'd triple the number of finance guys on a program." Surrounded by files that were annotated in his small, extremely neat handwriting, Bitter opened one labeled "floor mats" that contained some recent entries. As the principal analyst on the car's interior parts, he was intimately familiar with the floor mats, whose cost had already been the subject of some controversy. In August the supplier, Masland Industries, had been turned down for a price increase. When he saw the mats for the first time in cars at the pilot plant, Bitter noticed right away that something was wrong. Without informing Ford, Masland appeared to have made an adjustment of its own. The ones in front had shrunk; they were scarcely larger than those in the rear. Checking the design, he saw that eight inches had been lopped off the one on the driver's side.

Now the front mats were different from each other in size and bordered with irregular scallops. "It looks like they tried to fit Maine where Idaho's supposed to go," George Bell would later say. It was not Bitter's place to have an opinion on the optimum size or shape, although he felt certain that if Masland squared them off, they would fit more economically onto a roll of fabric. What bothered him was that a design change had slipped through without anybody having notified finance. If the mats had grown smaller, then by all rights they should cost less. Bitter wanted to see the cost save on material returned to Ford. After Bitter briefed purchasing on the floor mat situation, the Ford buyer wrote Masland Industries, asking for a $2 decrease in the total price.

Bitter, a Mormon, grew up in Wyoming. On his two-year mission for the church, he was sent to São Paulo, Brazil, an industrial sector with U.S. auto plants, and he got to know some of the Americans who worked there. After attending Brigham Young University, he got an MBA from the University of Utah with the intention of working for General Motors, his father's vehicle of choice, but Ford found him first. In line with his faith, Bitter had formulated a personal philosophy: "To pay my way. To work hard and see a project through and do the job right." "Rand pays for his salary every week," said Eric Koefoot, his supervisor.

Bitter did not lust after a grade-fifteen management job earning $150,000 a year. That was okay for some guys, but not for him. His shaggy brown hair was not management hair. His clothes did not have management creases. But he had carved out his own route to riches. He was making a killing off Ford's suggestion system, which awarded points based on savings to the company. The points could be cashed in on merchandise. Bitter did not devote time devising ways to cut bureaucracy or produce other efficiencies. "I go straight for the cars." One 10-cent save on a program as large as the Taurus could add up to $60,000 a year. "For someone who's observant about the hardware, somebody who's curious enough to investigate the costs, you can go a long ways with that thing. It's a gold mine."

Bitter hoped to acquire enough points for a 1994 Windstar minivan before the year was out. He and four other finance guys had joined forces to design a new DN101 station wagon cargo net that saved $6 and 1.1 pounds. The award for saving money on the Mustang cargo net was all his. And he had dozens of other suggestions in various stages of approval. But he had learned along the way to steer clear of labels, at all costs. "Never recommend a label change," he now warned others. "It's a lot of grief." He had suggested replacing the two for the Windstar cooling fans with just one. "I had to get a label designed, had to take it to the label committee, had to take it to the safety office . . . talk about a nightmare."

Bitter's passion for thrift carried over to his personal life. One of the planners now balked at eating lunch with him because of the time they went to Pizza Hut for the $4.15 all-you-can-eat Wednesday special. Everybody slapped down $5, for the meal and the tip. Everybody but Rand. He put down a bill and then he did something weird, like took change back and left a dime. "Cheap, cheap, cheap," said the planner.

DICK LANDGRAFF WASN'T among the group of people who gathered on November 23 to witness the moment when the first prototype sprang to life, the trusty Vulcan engine obediently turning over in response to a key's thrust. This was taken as a good sign; prototypes didn't necessarily start the first time. But when Landgraff inspected the car later that day, he came up with three pages of items to correct before they delivered it to Tom Moran's people. It was a good prototype, but he could still see a million things wrong, from loose carpet around the console to the hood release, which was anchored by a bracket that felt like it was going to break off. "What's wrong with it is obvious," he grumped. "The guy didn't spend ten minutes designing it."

On Monday, November 29, ten days ahead of schedule, Bob Taylor, a snowy-haired vehicle development factotum, and Heather Morrissett, a slender, long-haired young engineer assigned to seats, climbed into the red Taurus prototype for its maiden voyage. For its debut on a public road, the prototype was decked out in full tailor-made camouflage. Covering its snout was a black vinyl cover commonly referred to as the "bra." The rear end was bulked up with Styrofoam and also covered with black vinyl to obscure the shape. Sections of glass were painted black so they would photograph opaque, as if they were sheet metal. And a wide white stripe ran down each side, to disguise the Coke bottle curve by eliminating the highlight. There were no telltale badges or logos in view. The camouflage was meant to strike a balance: It was not to be so pronounced as to cause gawkers to lose sight of the road and crash; but it was to be sufficient to foil spy photographers.

The most notorious of these was Jim Dunne, the Detroit editor of *Popular Mechanics,* who had already bagged a DN101 structural prototype in September, with a shot that revealed the distinctive curvature of the hood. *USA Today* and many automotive publications bought his shots. Dunne regularly prowled the test tracks and other known prototype haunts around Ford, Chrysler, and GM. He could turn up anywhere. He followed prototypes as they migrated north in the winter and southwest in the summer to areas of the country where test teams could expose their heating and cooling systems to extreme temperatures. In addition to Dunne, there were savvy amateurs who grabbed and peddled photos. Any tourist with a camera was suspect. Nor was the camouflage fail-safe. People had been known to peel it off parked cars and shoot.

As he set out for Dearborn, Bob Taylor wondered about the steering wheel. "Doesn't this wheel feel too thick?" he asked Morrissett. He considered the outside mirrors. "I don't like these small mirrors." But he liked the driver's seat. "You know, Heather, this seat bottom feels really good. I have a pretty big butt. I weigh 200 pounds."

"I like the seat level," Morrisset said. Seats were her baby.

"This is perfect," Taylor said.

When the pair pulled into the Experimental or "X" Garage, the home of vehicle development, Dick Landgraff was waiting with Tom Moran. They got in with two development engineering supervisors, Jerry Brohl and Peter Creutz, for a drive around the low-speed track.

"This is a great, great car," Landgraff said on his return. "The back end is still pretty harsh, but it's not metal on metal. For the first shot out of the barrel, it's pretty damned impressive."

"It's hard to believe this is a prototype," said Creutz, the development engineer overseeing powertrain NVH. "Twenty years ago this would have been a production car."

TWO WEEKS LATER, under a gray December afternoon sky, a black Lincoln Town Car pulled up to the small building at the track, the scene of the Jackie Stewart drive the previous May. Landgraff and several other men were waiting for the occupant. And so were a couple of prototypes. But this time there were no drinks, no muffins, no prepared statements. And no Jackie Stewart. This was a session for the legendary Lincoln-Mercury dealer, Bob Tasca. He was here to drive a Mercury Mystique, the counterpart to the Ford Contour, slated for introduction in the fall of 1994, and a DN101, hot off the line at the pilot plant.

Escorted by Tom Cavanaugh from Lincoln-Mercury sales, Tasca climbed out. He had shed weight since suffering a heart attack not long ago, but he was still a substantial man. He wore black tasseled shoes, chocolate brown pants, and a medium blue plaid jacket with a matching handkerchief and tie. Once he started talking, he kept going. He wanted to know about the Mystique, the first car he would drive today. "Did you take the harshness out? Did you take the noise out? Let me ask you a leading question: Is it as quiet as a Corolla? Because Corolla sells for $2,000 less." And by the way he hated four-cylinder engines. "That's why Honda's slipping. They don't have a six."

Tasca came to Dearborn maybe twelve or fifteen times a year, on visits such as this one, to drive prototypes and bend the ear of executives. He occupied a unique position of influence, owing to his historical association with Henry Ford II, his devotion to the company and his amazing ability to sell thousands of Lincolns and Mercurys each year from a tiny dealership on the outskirts of Providence. Thus far on this trip, he had met with the sales division vice-presidents Ross Roberts of Ford and Lee Miskowski of Lincoln-Mercury. Tonight he was having dinner with Ken Dabrowski, executive director of body engineering. Tomorrow he had meetings with vice-presidents Bob Rewey and Ken Kohrs and the general manager of Body and Assembly, Dale McKeehan; before leaving the next day he would see NAAO executive vice-president Ed Hagenlocker.

"He gets all the confidential information, including the cycle plan," said Landgraff, while Tasca was driving the Mystique. The cycle plan was Ford's top-secret ten-year projection of model changes and introductions. "There's nothing that Bob doesn't know. He doesn't bullshit. He's very sincere in his conviction that we've got to make Ford Motor Company the best in the world. If we don't give him a good product, he gets very mad, unhappy, and frustrated." Tasca, Landgraff said, was "ten times more influential than Jackie Stewart. When he calls, we send guys there. When he says there's a problem, he's more often right than wrong." And Tasca was also free. Stewart charged thousands a day.

Tasca frequently dropped in at assembly plants as well, to look over cars coming off the line. Those that met his standards received his personal award for quality, a plaque he had designed himself. No one dared ignore Tasca, however hokey his award. Even the manager of a high-volume plant like Atlanta set aside a day when Tasca came for a tour. A planner who had worked at the Wixom plant, which turned out large luxury Continentals and Marks, described preparations. "We'd jump through hoops. We'd clean, paint. . . . even more than if the chairman was coming through." When Tasca requested a part for his dealership, people dropped everything to accommodate him. "If Tasca wanted a Lincoln hood, we'd box one up and send it off." The crate would sit on the loading dock, marked simply "Tasca."

Tasca dated his association with Ford to 1930, when he was a four-year-old, hanging out in the backyard with an uncle who repaired Fords. The uncle went to MIT and became an architect. Tasca skipped college and became a car salesman. In 1953 Ford took a chance on his weak finances and granted him a dealership; he had been a company loyalist ever since. Tasca had been close to Henry Ford II. He knew family secrets, how Ford had written a tell-all book that the family squelched, how Ford spotted Cristina Austin, the fetching Italian who would become his second wife, at a state dinner with the king of Spain and told someone, "Get her for me." Tasca also bonded with Lee Iacocca, who persuaded him to switch from Ford to a Lincoln-Mercury dealership in 1971. But he turned down Iacocca's request to follow him to Chrysler. Other car companies had wooed him as well, and he happened to know precisely how many. Tasca liked numbers—dates, sales figures, percentages, he had a zillion at his fingertips. He had rebuffed precisely sixty-five offers to sell other makes, including the Lexus.

Visitors to his dealership on an out-of-the-way road in Seekonk, Massachusetts, were usually surprised at its modest size. The showroom held just six cars, too small even to display the full Lincoln-Mercury line. There were only thirteen service bays. A dealer like Tasca who sold more than 3,000 cars in good years might well have 50. "I don't like bricks and mortar," Tasca told other dealers. "A building never sold a car. People sell cars."

Every year but this one he had made more money than the one before. As 1993 drew to a close, Tasca's total sales weren't going to go much over 2,000. He told Landgraff later that he had made just $3 million, compared to his usual take of $5 million. He and his three grown sons, whom he had taken into the business, lived in separate homes in a fifteen-acre family compound. On this trip, Tasca was negotiating to buy a Ford dealership for his grandson. Just before arriving at the track, Tasca had dropped his wife off at the Fairlane Town Center, where there was a Saks Fifth Avenue and a Lord & Taylor. "Don't spend over $10,000," he cautioned. It was entirely possible that he was serious.

Tasca greeted Landgraff with enthusiasm. From a dealer's point of view, the program manager had done a great job on the 1992 model. "I can put you in a Sable today—the same car for less payment than I did five years ago," Tasca told the group gathered for his arrival, "And he's the reason."

Tasca and Landgraff shared a vision of product quality. Earlier this year Tasca had been invited to a two-hour review with vice-presidents Allan Gilmour and Bob Rewey at body enginering. He wanted to know what they were doing to be competitive with Camry. Said Landgraff, "Tasca says over and over, 'Just make the car as good as Toyota.'"

TASCA RETURNED FROM the Mystique drive complaining that every Ford car "makes the same goddamn mistake. Every Ford engineer makes you put the weatherstripping on the car. It should be on the door."

Also, "the ass end of the car is noisy," he said. "It's because of those frigging struts." His final verdict: "With the V-6 . . . make the back quieter, you got a good car. The four-cylinder is a disaster."

"We've got triple seals," Landgraff reassured him, as Tasca climbed behind the wheel of the DN101 prototype, and Landgraff slipped into the passenger's seat. "There's not going to be any problem with our seals."

They circled the track three, four, five times, as the others waited in the chill December air. When they returned, Tasca rated the steering a "seven." "I see no reason it can't get better." He thought the Vulcan engine was noisy. And they ought to let him design the car seats. He didn't like the length of the rear seat cushion. "I can make the car much more commodious inside if you let me do the seats over." Landgraff was reassured by the lack of more substantial criticism. But Tasca said his biggest worry was nothing he had seen. It was the price. He warned Landgraff not to go over $20,000.

"The word 'Sable' is twenty grand or under. . . . I got 5,300 Sable owners on the two-year plan, $1,000 down, $260 a month. The new car, if it's $1,000 down and $299 a month, will be duck soup. But at $350 or $360 a month I'm in trouble. 'Cause now I'm in Grand Marquis territory." The Grand Marquis was the top of the Mercury line.

FOURTEEN

Real Men Build Cars

NOT ONLY DID the pilot plant build prototypes, it also housed the general offices of powerful, insular body and assembly operations, which presided over Ford's forty-nine assembly plants around the world. Fortress B&A, the division was called by outsiders, or even more darkly, "the Kremlin." For the team, the shift in action to the pilot plant had been more than just a geographical move. It meant that the 1996 Taurus was no longer the sole property of Dick Landgraff and car product development. There was a new cast of characters, with a new agenda.

No more the days when George Bell and his engineers pondered the most elegant solution to a technical problem in the basement conference room. The new location for change management was a room off the floor of the pilot plant. A wall of windows faced out into the body shop, where orange sparks rose like clouds of fireflies from welding stations, carts zipped back and forth, and metal crashed against metal. Inside the meeting room, the sparks, the noise, and the movement were all human. The big blue-eyed middle-aged linebacker at the head of the table was Tom Green, the B&A launch manager, whose job was to make sure the heap of interlocking parts called DN101 was something workers and machinery could put together expeditiously. These were known as "pink meetings," for the color of the cover sheet on the printout of changes, and the total of changes in the works was the "pink count." To the degree that "pink" suggested anything lighthearted, however, it was a misnomer.

To Green's way of thinking, a change or "concern" was an "issue you don't have a fix for." It was a problem waiting to happen. The longer it took to approve a change, the later the part arrived. It was that simple. Green was not an engineer. His sole mission was to determine how soon a proposed change could be closed out. Engineers who wanted more time to meet cost, weight, and quality standards could find themselves on the defensive. Green was not a yeller or a screamer, like some B&A guys. He preferred humiliation. The worst thing you could tell Green was "I don't know." He would reply, "Let's get someone in here who does know." Better to lie.

Dick Landgraff understood where Green was coming from. The job of the B&A launch manager was to put pressure on engineers, who were chronically late with their design changes. The people who did that well were tough guys like Green, and so they were the ones who got these positions. If engineers did what they were supposed to, it wouldn't happen this way. "In the business we're in," Landgraff said, "you can't let people off the hook." He had had his ass chewed out any number of times by B&A, and he had survived, maybe even learned a thing or two.

But the DN101 princesses and princelings were in a state of . . . shock. They weren't used to this kind of treatment. For many, the pilot plant was their first exposure to the gritty world of Ford's manufacturing division. Although a new wing was under construction, for the time being they were housed in a crummy second-floor bullpen nicknamed "the fishbowl." The room overlooked the plant floor, the walls were dirty, and rows of decrepit metal desks faced forward like a classroom. The phones and computers were unreliable. When Jerry Behm, one of the packaging guys, called to get first aid for his phone, the woman he talked to said she couldn't take care of it, they were out of sync in the pecking order, his supervisor would have to call her supervisor.

After two years of team-like knitting and bonding, the DN101 engineers abruptly found themselves amid a crew of macho, status-conscious, secretive strangers, who appeared to regard them as a sorry collection of cerebral, self-indulgent, brainwashed engineering weaklings, with nothing but excuses when things weren't right. These tough guys were acting as if the Taurus were *theirs*, when really they'd had hardly anything to do with it so far. Even the engineers' good friend Fred Jorgensen, the chief B&A presence on the DN101 team for two years, now that he was back with his B&A buddies, had taken to crowing, "This is *our* time." Jorgensen had perfect deadpan delivery. It wasn't clear that good old Freddie was kidding.

Jorgensen had been delighted to learn that Green would be his boss, in charge of launch. Green was "a mover and a shaker." He was "connected"—to people high up in body and assembly operations. "I got a gift," Jorgensen said. "When Tom calls they listen." Like it or not, the launch team would be seeing a lot of Green. He was with them for the duration, here and in Atlanta.

A B&A archetype, Green was strong-willed, conservative, patriotic, and a sports fan. He had grown up on a 360-acre farm in mitt-shaped Michigan's eastern prong, known as its "thumb." In addition to raising beef cattle, his father had been a teacher who rose to the post of superintendent and was active in Republican state politics. A knee injury cut short Green's promising scholastic future in basketball and football.

After Green was married with children, he won election to his local school board. Not long afterward, he found himself at a high school game where the tape broke for "The Star-Spangled Banner." When the pledge of allegiance was substituted, Green was shocked that students didn't know the words. The pledge, it seemed, had been dropped years ago from the school regimen. His school board colleagues thought maybe it was illegal. In touring classrooms, Green was pained to see that houseplants hung from flagholders. He campaigned successfully to reinstate the pledge of allegiance after a legal investigation suggested that it was okay so long as no one was forced to say it. At a game a year later, kids sang "The Star-Spangled Banner," then recited the pledge. It was perhaps the accomplishment of which he was most proud during his eight years on the school board.

Misty-eyed patriotism was not uncommon among these men of iron and steel. Like Landgraff, Green saw the new Taurus as a military campaign. But where Landgraff plotted strategy, Green was leading a charge. "The Pentagon plans everything for you," he said, "but it's a whole lot different if you're the field commander and you're out there and those rifle bullets are being shot at you and the enemy's not really where you thought they were going to be, they circled behind you. . . ."

IN THE FALL, when the pink count stood at 300, Green had announced a goal of 50 by Christmas. By mid-December, Green was on the warpath. The count was nowhere close; it hovered around 180. Green enlisted Dick Landgraff's and George Bell's support in stepping up the pressure. Landgraff was as unhappy as Green about all the changes, but for a different reason. "It means we didn't do a better job than anybody else in doing the right up-front design. If we had, there wouldn't be so many changes."

When the DN101 team members filed into the meeting room on December 15, Green, Landgraff, and Bell were sitting side by side at the head table. Green opened the meeting with the announcement that pink meetings would now take place five days a week instead of three. "Is that a direct order or do we get to talk about it?" asked chunk team leader Jim Mikola. Covering five meetings a week, especially during the year-end holiday season, was going to be taxing. Green was not sympathetic. "It's kind of like running the plant with a lot of absenteeism," he said. "You've still got to run the plant. Got to bandage it up." In his last post, he had been assistant manager of a plant that assembled seventy-two Escorts an hour.

As was the custom, Green read off each proposed change for a status report from an engineer. When Green got to the heat shield, a powertrain item, George Evalt promised an update on Friday. Evalt was one of Green's frequent targets. "This is bullshit," Green said. "You just keep screwing around. . . . When am I going to have this taken care of? This thing has been open since July 8." Monday, Evalt said, on Monday it would be resolved. His powertrain colleague, Jim Mayo, who was in charge of the Vulcan engine, chimed in. "Let me explain. These are related to the fuel tank and the pressure sensor. We want to make sure there's no issue."

"After you've said all that what does it mean?" Green asked, although he didn't seem to care about the answer. He issued a deadline for closure. "I'm looking for the 22nd, maybe by January 5."

The room was thick with tension. It was okay if team members joked about Evalt now and then. Evalt had once banged up an Intrepid prototype that Tom Breault had swapped with Chrysler for a Mark VIII and promised to return in mint condition. He had also somehow done in the Camry back in late 1991 (the legal department wouldn't let him talk about it). And his basement cubicle was stacked so high with paper—every surface was two to three feet deep—that it was declared a health and fire hazard at the instigation of a janitor. Landgraff had to order him to clean up. "I feel like I'm running a kindergarten," he had complained as he wrote Evalt a note. But to the team, Green's attacks on Evalt were not good-natured. They were old-style 9,1 management, and they made people uncomfortable. Evalt might be a character, but he was *their* character.

Green turned next to Steve Kozak, who had come in late, and inquired about a sheet-metal issue. "Are you working the holes?" Green asked.

"We're working *between* the holes," Kozak quipped. Green was not amused.

"So this is going to stay open till testing is complete?" Green asked. *Till testing is complete.* It sounded like "till hell freezes over."

"If this bracket fails," Kozak snapped, "the engine falls out of the car."

Landgraff, silent to this point, spoke up. "Let's save this discussion."

Green greeted Ron Andrade, the head of chassis, in a voice dripping with sarcasm. Chassis was notorious for missing these meetings. "You showed up today. This has been an absolutely top-notch performance by chassis. How many people would say today was the best chassis performance in two months?" Some B&A underlings raised their hands.

Green threatened to hold the team hostage over the holidays if more wasn't accomplished. Then his voice became friendly. Green sometimes played good cop, bad cop all by himself. "You've done a good job as a team getting parts in—best program ever. But you're weak in supplier quality. Do all this hard work now and believe me, when we go to Atlanta, it'll be a cakewalk."

When we go to Atlanta. . . .

At a different meeting, in the middle of one of Green's analogies that had something to do with boyhood fights, Mark Jarvis turned to Mary Anne Wheeler from climate control, a small woman with delicate features and smooth skin, the highest ranking female on the DN101 team. "Does this have any relevance to you?" he joked. "Did you used to get into fights?"

As it happened, Mary Anne Wheeler had had about all of this B&A stuff that she could take. Recently Fred Jorgensen had come down on her hard for having five concerns. She had always liked Fred. But B&A seemed to have co-opted him. It seemed to her that people were forever picking on climate control. As far as she was concerned, her team was doing a bang-up job. Her parts were so big, they got so hot, and everybody was after her space, her water, and her air. A few months ago, she found herself in change management, loaded down with concerns and under pressure to resolve them more quickly. They felt like the weight of the world. One of her engineers alone had twenty-five. "They can't all be top priority," she said. "Just tell me what you want me to do." Rich Pettit, the business planner, asked if she needed engineering help. Before she could answer, George Bell said he didn't think it was necessary. She rose to her feet—she was not very tall—and gathered up her papers, starting out of the room, her face frozen in an angry expression. "Don't forget your purse, Mary Anne," called Kurt Boginski, the meeting facilitator. She grabbed it and left. The guys snickered. Wheeler had long preferred her home office to the Design Center, and she preferred them both to the pilot plant. Maybe she just wouldn't go to these meetings. . . .

Wheeler wasn't the only woman put off by B&A bluster. Joan Mansueti, a team member from purchasing, had emerged out of sorts from a particularly cantankerous shortages meeting, held at the plant at 7:30 A.M. daily to assess the availability of parts. People spent the hour grandstanding about a shortage of bodysides and who was at fault. "It's all show and now we have to go to Green," she muttered to herself. "Women would never do it this way." Concluding her minutes of one pink meeting, Karin Dean felt the urge to fabricate a sound bite for the first time ever: "Floggings will continue until morale improves."

The DN101 launch team members had signed up for a birth, not a battle. And their initial enthusiasm for automotive midwifery was flagging rapidly at the sight of blood. They would come back from the pilot plant and take turns in Wendy Dendel's office, describing the latest Tom Green attack. And Landgraff, what had happened to the Maximum Leader? He appeared to be taking orders from body and assembly.

THE HEAD OF THE pilot plant was Ken Reuther, no relation to Walter, the late UAW organizer and president. Reuther's first assignment on hiring into Ford had been a time-and-motion study on the 1954 Ford. The boss gave him a stopwatch, a group of mechanics, and orders to take the car apart and put it together again, timing each operation. The assignment took four and a half months and by the end of that time Reuther knew how a car was made. He'd been working with prototypes ever since.

Body and Assembly lifers like Reuther and Green were a band apart. They were blood brothers, their priorities as straight and narrow as the assembly line that Henry Ford had set in motion back in 1913 ten miles north in Highland Park. Many had earned their hash marks on the factory floor, beneath the smokestacks of a vanishing America. Their ears were tuned to the pounding and crashing of metal on metal, the high-pitched wail of air guns, and the slapping and crunching of nesting parts. This was a sweet symphony indeed; it was the sound not only of cars but also of money being made for Ford Motor Company. In Atlanta, they called the last 800 feet of production, where the wheels went on, the gas went in, and the protective scratch guards came off the fenders, "the final line," but they also sometimes called it "the money line." At the end, a worker was poised to crank each virgin V-6 and take the car on a brief maiden drive to a testing booth. It was at that point, said Jim Anderson, an assistant manager in trim, that "on a quiet day, you can hear the cash register ring." People in body and assembly took pride in their mission: "We make the money for Ford Motor Company."

When the line stopped, so did the cash, but not the costs. The cost of labor, the cost of running the plant, the cost of materials—all continued to mount. And it was the pressure to keep the line moving and the money pouring in, whatever it took, even if they had to chopper in a day's supply of alternators, that infused B&A dealings with a dark and somewhat lunatic edge, as if the slightest relaxation of control could rebound through the system and shut down every last assembly plant.

Body and assembly was serious about quality. More than any other single division, it had paid the price when the bottom dropped out of the market for U.S. cars in the 1980s. Plants closed; thousands of workers lost jobs. B&A lived and died by the Things Gone Wrong numbers. "Very frankly," Dick Landgraff said sympathetically, "manufacturing has had to bear the burden of poorly running cars for a long time."

Quality was the second most important element in performance reviews. But the first was daily production. In a showdown, quotas beat quality. That was true even in this prototype phase. Said Landgraff, "B&A in the pilot plant is not judged by how well the CPs [confirmation prototypes] are put together, but by how fast they get them together: ninety-nine cars in three months. . . . 'Get them out.' Otherwise the guy with the bullwhip comes down on them."

The new Taurus/Sable had followed the 1995 Lincoln Continental into the pilot plant. Hard on its heels was Ford's redesigned F-series truck. Anything that derailed timing was a crisis. One night Steve Kozak's phone rang at home. The plant had stopped building Sables, the caller said, because Kozak had rejected the right-hand bodysides for quality reasons. And Tom Green was plenty mad. "What?" screeched Kozak. Earlier that day he had rejected a single right-hand Sable bodyside because it didn't fit a gauge; it was warped or something. "Word went out that I had rejected all the Sable panels." It took him all the next day to sort the situation out. As a result, "they didn't build for two days." This incident spawned an unhealthy rumor "that the reason we weren't building Sables was that they had failed rear crash test." The truth was that they were building an early unit specifically *for* rear crash, to make sure that the structural changes hadn't affected safety in that area.

To the engineers, B&A seemed always to be a hair-trigger away from World War III. Confronted with a problem, an engineer's training was to step back, analyze what went wrong, figure out how to fix it, and test the recommendation. At Ford, this process was formalized in an eight-step problem-solving procedure called an "eight-D." The "D" stood for "disciplines." But at the pilot plant, when a piece of sheet metal was a little off, workers didn't put down their welding guns and call on Steve Kozak for a root-cause analysis. No, said Kozak. "Workers say, 'It doesn't fit. Grind it out of the way. Shim it out of the way.'"

In assembly plants like Atlanta and Chicago, it was the same story. On the final line, workers were poised with screwdrivers, hammers, mallets, and chisels, a whole arsenal of hand tools to square up the trunks, the doors, and the hoods—eliminating imprecisions that customers could spot immediately, and that managers, on daily visits to the final line, detected as they ran their hands over the margins to check flushness. No matter that a seal could be damaged, increasing wind noise, as workers adjusted strikers and hinges to make a door close smoothly. At least the boss, walking down the line slamming doors, wouldn't go nuts and start yelling.

Ken Reuther did not disagree that B&A had a crisis mentality. He argued that it was justified. "The manufacturing versus the engineering discipline is like day and night," he said. "When you're an organization like us that has a charter to build 20,000 cars and trucks a day, you're gonna do things in a disciplined manner. Every time you take a breath and you don't do it right, you lose *x* number of units a day, and that's at the cash register. That same pressure and discipline does not exist in the engineering community."

To him a pilot plant snafu was akin to a delay at, say, the Windstar minivan plant, where "the bottom line is $12 million a day. . . . My guys talk to me all night long, and I will talk to my vice-president at night. Would you talk to your vice-president, you think your vice-president would talk to you everyday if you were losing $12 million a day?"

In psychology, a leap from a small problem to the worst-case scenario is called "catastrophizing." Seriously depressed people do it all the time. But in body and assembly, it was the way normal people viewed life. Maybe the slip-up affected no more than a handful of Sable prototypes, but if that kind of thing were allowed to repeat itself, it could jeopardize the redesign of Ford's best-selling car and bring Ford Motor Company to its knees. "Engineers can't conceive that loss," Reuther said. "Their attitude is 'take your time.' "

Engineers. . . . When a B&A warhorse like Reuther referred to "engineers," he was not being respectful. There was an age-old conflict between the people who designed cars—the body *engineers*, the chassis *engineers*, the powertrain *engineers*—and the people who built them. Body and assembly had plenty of people with engineering degrees, including Reuther, but their first allegiance was to the plants. They were "factory rats."

So the engineers might be forgiven a certain satisfaction when what started out as another B&A rampage backfired in a most delicious way. One Monday when Landgraff got to work, Nancy Donaldson presented him with a message from Reuther's office that B&A was going to shut down the build. Landgraff got hold of Jorgensen, who filled him in. The sheet metal did not fit the tooling, Jorgensen said. The whole thing went back to Kozak's structural upgrade. The changes had made it into the sheet metal but not into the fixtures that held it. This was a showstopper all right. Landgraff raced off to meet with Reuther at the pilot plant, who told him the same thing. Kozak, meanwhile, was comparing the parts to their design to see if they were off. Then B&A discovered that the person at fault was not Kozak, or any of his people. The mistake was made by the guy responsible for updating the tooling, who worked for them. He had not put the changes through. *He was a B&A guy.* Reports of what had happened swept through the basement faster than a forest fire. *B&A screwed up.* People started referring to the guilty party as "the black hole." Kozak generously defended him. In all fairness, he said, the guy was overloaded with work. Metal Stamping Operations had dispatched several people to the team, who were able to keep up with changes in the sheet metal. But B&A had only one guy assigned to the tooling. The real culprit was B&A management.

The plant was able to modify the fixture within two days and get the metal moving again. In the end, said Landgraff, "it was a giant mountain that evaporated into a molehill."

THE NEW DEDICATED, collocated teams did not have many fans in Ford's manufacturing division, where people had been heard to call them "misguided, dislocated teams." Reuther, an influential B&A manager, thought Ford was making a gigantic mistake in breaking up its core engineering departments. Where once all the brake guys or seat belt guys sat together and traded information, now they were dispersed, one or two on a team, with no synergy. "We need old engineers and young engineers together," he argued. "Old engineers telling young engineers, 'No, you don't do this, it doesn't work that way.' You put the young guy on a dedicated, collocated team and he talks to himself."

Reuther claimed to see the same problems over and over again as a result. "Repetitive problems. That's my biggest problem. I'm absolutely fed up with taillamps and heater systems, okay? I get *tired* of hearing about them." Another hazard was team peer pressure or "euphoria," as Reuther put it. Members of a team, he said, "tend to work and reinforce and support each other's decisions, when in fact maybe they're impossible.

"For example, the T-Bird wanted a certain type of console because it looked nice. The general manager from the plastics division was very concerned. An engineer from plastics manufacturing said it couldn't be made. . . . But over time, the team kept showing how nice it looked. . . . The car really needed it. . . . He wasn't a team player if he kept saying 'no.' Ultimately, he said 'yes.' But he was right; they couldn't make it. It was one hell of a mess. . . . That's the danger of a team. . . . There's so much peer pressure: 'You can do it. Try harder.' So he rolled over. He would not have been a popular team member if he said 'no.' "

Back in body engineering, down in the basement lighting lab, there was a guy named Kim Peterson who couldn't agree more with Reuther's opinion.

Setting aside his misgivings about teams, however, Reuther had scored $3.2 million from Alex Trotman for a building to accommodate up to 450 visiting engineers. "The company believes in teams," Reuther said. "If the company believes in teams, we'll work with teams." And as teams went, Reuther said, DN101 was the strongest one out there, thanks to Landgraff. The respect was mutual. "Most of the time I agree with what the guy says," Landgraff said. "He has thirty-five years of building cars."

FIFTEEN

Len Flack's Last Car

"**W**E'RE LOOKING FOR A good number," Len Flack told the five men and two women, who had reported at 5 A.M. to the lobby of the Holiday Inn in Bemidji, Minnesota. Given the hour, they looked none too happy or wide awake.

Flack was a big gentle climate control division engineer, so full of jokes and stories it was hard to believe he was as serious as he sounded. When younger he had been a Scoutmaster. He was using his Scoutmaster's voice now: "We need you to give us a good honest evaluation number. We didn't come all this way to be tourists. We're not horsing around. It's time to go to work. The party's over."

Right, the party's over. The fun-filled two-day slog up the center of Michigan, four cars and a van in a radio-linked convoy, starting out from Dearborn at 7:30 A.M. on January 3 on clogged freeways, sunny weather giving way after a few hours to clouds, north over the graceful green and cream Mackinac Bridge, a sight worth seeing in clear weather, but on this trip almost entirely shrouded by snow, Lake Huron to the east, Lake Michigan to the west, and Mackinac Island, a car-free summer paradise, down there somewhere in the murk. Heading west on U.S. 2 across Michigan's upper peninsula, a winter wonderland of pines and birches, crisscrossed by snowmobile tracks, then across Wisconsin into northern Minnesota. Jumping out of toasty cars in swirling snow and minus-something temperatures every hour and a half for a driver switch, so everybody got a chance to ride and drive all the cars. Pit stops at gas stations and fast food restaurants. Engineer banter over palm-sized Motorola radios. "The floor discharge in the Lexus is 155, 160 degrees, but the most I can get on the Camry is 130 degrees. I think maybe the blend door isn't working right." The Camry was along for purposes of comparison. Bad news if it was a lemon.

Toward the end of the second day, rustic wooden Indian casinos and motels advertising "warm rooms" appeared by the wayside, hallmarks of the north country. Finally, Bemidji heaved into view, a town of 11,000 in north-central Minnesota—on the headwaters of the Mississippi River, just a trickle here.

And now the hour had arrived to begin the sole mission for the two-day journey: to jump into ice-cold cars and ride around for half an hour, jotting down numbers to indicate how fast the heating system was kicking in. Performed daily for the next ten days, this test would yield a single grand-slam "time to comfort" average that would amount to a judgment on the heater in the new Taurus. Scoutmaster Len Flack wanted people to know he meant business. One negligent number could screw up the average. "I don't want to scare people but that number is so important to me. I hate coming up here in zero-degree weather. This is not my idea of a good time."

As predictable as the temperatures that drew them here, development engineers swept into Bemidji in January of each year with the latest flock of prototypes. DN101 deadlines stretched ahead in 1994 as fixed as stations on a railroad. They had less than a year left to find out everything that was wrong or wanting in the new Taurus and fix it. In May, there was a structural sign-off, signifying a halt to all sheet-metal changes; and in August, a preliminary engineering sign-off, when the lion's share of the testing and development was to be completed. In October came the management review, when top guys in the company would drive prototypes in some sweet location, most likely California, an event hosted by vehicle development with plenty of good food and bonhomie. Following the drive, the executives would nitpick the car for a while and then give the go-ahead to build it; everybody knew it was far too late for big changes that would hold up a $2.7 billion program. The train stopped in November, the final sign-off, when the engineering offices certified that they were done: the sedans were ready to launch. After that, engineers would work only on those issues that surfaced in Atlanta, as they began to build prototypes on the line.

The climate control crew had arrived in Bemidji with two Taurus confirmation prototypes, hot off the line at the pilot plant, hastily wired with twenty or so collection points for temperature, pressure, and air flow. Later models would have ninety. They found the engine guys already there, revving up their Highland Silent Storm snowmakers and a 100-horsepower fan, to blow snow at the snout of a DN101 running on rollers at 40 miles per hour. This was a test called "snow packing" to determine whether snow was being sucked into vital parts, where it would melt and collect, then freeze as a car sat in cold weather, an event that generally occurred at night in cold climes. The driver in these situations discovered the condition the next morning when the car wouldn't start. Before they had snowmakers, Ford did this test with a Bronco towing a length of chain-link fence that dredged up a snowstorm. The guy following in the prototype couldn't see a thing. Once a Bronco ran off the road and into a ditch; the prototype followed it right on in. The Silent Storm machines posed a different visibility issue. Ford's test site was near the Bemidji airport. From time to time the Minneapolis airport picked up the man-made blizzards on its radar, and closed Bemidji to flights.

The powertrain guys, who were here for other tests as well, had four confirmation prototypes plus three structural prototypes with DN101 engines. As fast as the pilot plant could turn them out, other prototypes were heading for other destinations. In Naples, Florida, where Ford had a test track on the edge of the Everglades, engineers worked year-round on engines, tires, and chassis. Two sedans and two wagons were designated for durability testing at the proving grounds in Romeo, Michigan. Many other prototypes remained in Dearborn, among them scores to be crashed and crushed.

It was an awesome sight to see a shiny $400,000 prototype slam into a block wall, the front end crumple, the doors buckle, the dummies pitch forward against the windshield, shattering glass . . . there but for the grace of God. . . . Even engineers found it difficult to be blasé. Chassis manager Ron Andrade remembered when he was a young engineer, newly assigned to fuel systems in the wake of the Pinto fires. He had been working on a pretty candy-apple-red Mustang that was earmarked for testing. How he would have liked to take it home. Instead, he watched the Mustang crash into a barrier at 30 miles per hour. A little piece of his heart was destroyed with the car.

The various crash scenarios—from the front, side, and rear—and other highly instrumented safety tests on such components as headlamps and brakes left nothing to subjectivity. The data went into the files, in case federal authorities requested it. And how, one might wonder, had it been determined that in a 30-mile-per-hour encounter with a barrier the head could tolerate no more than 1,000 HICs—a "head injury criterion" being a measure of acceleration over time—without its owner almost certainly becoming a corpse or a carrot? It was a little-known but intriguing fact that federal crash regulations and other protective standards were developed using human cadavers. From time to time, the rediscovery of this procedure caused a minor scandal. "A German university has reportedly used more than 200 human corpses in automobile crash tests," said an Associated Press article datelined November 22, 1993, from Berlin. The AP article was based on two TV broadcasts, based in turn on an article in a German newspaper. Never mind that the tests had been going on since the 1970s. The corpses included eight children, and it was that, more than anything else, that provoked protests from both the Vatican and German car clubs. In a follow-up story, a Reuters dispatch from Detroit revealed that Wayne State University had been experimenting with cadavers for fifty years under contracts with automakers and the federal government. While crash dummies were fine in testing, they just didn't do the job for setting standards, authorities said. "At what point in a crash do ribs break?" Sherman Henson, manager of side-impact safety planning for Ford, told the Reuters reporter. "There is no way to know that except to test ribs." From a public relations standpoint, it was worse to use live animals. When airbags had been tested with chimpanzees as subjects, thousands of calls poured in from the animals rights activists.

The crash guys at Ford had heard stories from before their time, how they used to drop cadaver heads down elevator shafts at Wayne State to measure the injury. Sometimes cadavers were used that had not been embalmed, for an even more lifelike representation. Mike Vecchio, the side-impact crash specialist on the Taurus, had once had a conversation with someone who did these cadaver tests, who told him the work was bloody, with strict time constraints set by the health department on the use of corpses from the morgue. "Once they pull this guy out off the slab they've got to use him within twenty-four hours or they have to scrap the body," Vecchio said. It was amazing what you could pay people to do.

Many other tests had numerical outcomes as well. In the basement of Building Four—Len Flack called it Shake, Rattle, and Roll—radiators were hooked up to tubes, thermocycling from zero to 230 degrees; they were shaken 100,000 times; they were bathed in salt spray. Accelerator pedals attached to a motor pumped up and down, over and over, activating the throttle linkage; they looked as if they were operated by ghosts. One enormous machine jiggled entire vehicles, simulating the motion of a rail car. Transport was particularly hard on cars, especially engines, subjecting them to more stress than a driver ever did. Engine mounts were designed to cope with rail car coupling, an 8.5-mile-per-hour jolt. The Japanese preferred to ship by truck.

Fabric was tested for wear, tear, and fading; the results were up or down.

But color-coordinating car parts, a critical requirement, wasn't really a test at all. In a process called "mastering," incredibly color-sensitive human beings in the Design Center examined representative car parts in various colors under three kinds of light to determine whether they matched: Was a Willow Green plastic bumper the same shade as the Willow Green steel doors and the Willow Green vinyl on the interior?

Many tests were a blend of scientific analysis and human judgment. At the Dearborn test track, the NVH guys employed a head-and-torso mannequin they nicknamed "Elwood," who was equipped with very sensitive microphones in place of ears. They belted him into the passenger seat, and drove around the course making recordings of engine frequencies, road noise, whatever. Then they played the tapes for real people in a $250,000 sound studio to see what sounds were most pleasing.

Human drivers were still required for the bone-jarring, jaw-slamming, stomach-dropping durability tests over Romeo's course of roller-coaster hills, snake-track curves, and roads like washboards. Engineer Dennis Wingfield once had a job checking the front-end alignment on cars used in durability testing. They couldn't wash off the dirt because it was part of the test results. He'd be out there in the cold and mud, under the car with stuff dripping down. But people were hired for those jobs. They were paid for the misery. The cold-weather testing in Bemidji, carried out by employees for whom it was not part of their job description, was beyond the call of duty. Naturally the engineers from climate control had to participate, because if they didn't, who would? And without data, they couldn't do the analyses for which they were responsible. So they were there, along with any other lost souls they could press into service. It was widely known that no test was quite so awful as the so-called warm-ups that this group in the lobby of the Holiday Inn was about to perform, unless it was Lake Havasu in the summer without air conditioning, the so-called pull-downs. But that came later.

Clad in parkas, jeans, and athletic shoes—clothing any heavier violated the written protocol—the test subjects huddled near the fireplace, although there was no fire; nor, for that matter, was there coffee. In addition to Flack, the climate control division was also represented by the DN101 supervisor Mary Anne Wheeler and an intern, Jay Lorentz; from vehicle development, there were supervisor Dwight Smith, engineer Wayne Williams, and Gary Kraus, a mechanic, who had driven a van full of spare parts; from the DN101 basement team there was Mike Krupansky, a quality maven. And one stray writer.

In a few moments this group would adjourn unfortified to four cars that had been parked overnight in minus-six-degree weather. Two of the cars were Taurus confirmation prototypes. Another was a 1993 Lexus. The fourth, a 1994 Camry. This test was done before sunrise to forgo any warming rays.

For precisely five minutes the eight testers would stand outside the cars, approximating the time an especially diligent person might spend clearing away snow. By this time really, really cold, they would jump into two of the cars and take off, turning the heat on high and the blower on max. Every two minutes—fifteen times in the half-hour ride—one person in each car would call for a reading from one to five, and people would write down the number that best described their condition. The test measured how long it took to reach a comfort level. When they returned from this test, they would go inside, warm up for half an hour, then go out and do the same thing all over again in the other two cars. Only this time, they would feel even colder, their feet having warmed enough to sweat slightly, so that standing on snow they would feel like two bricks of ice. It was a test only a caribou could love.

Flack got to the heart of his briefing: the subjective evaluation numbers. " 'One' is totally cold/cold. 'Two,' you're cool/cold. Somewhere's cold and somewhere's starting to feel heat. 'Three' is cool/cool. Not hot, not cold. 'Four' is cool/comfort. It's hard to decide. Somewhere you feel pretty good. 'Five' is comfort. You could drive forever." He cautioned people not to put down a five just because everyone else had finished. He wanted honest numbers. "This is why we're here."

"It's the only reason we're here," his colleague Wayne Williams chimed in.

"Look within yourself," Flack said. Sometimes people just sat in the cars like zombies, too tired and numb to feel the subtle sensation of heat as it began to penetrate their bodies. "Concentrate on parts of your body. Try to feel your left foot and your right foot. Wiggle your toes." He issued a final warning before hustling everybody out the door. "I don't want anybody talking. I need you to concentrate on the test that the company has sent you here to do. If you talk I get irritated. I'm not nice when I'm irritated. That's why they call me the Bear."

BEMIDJI OWED ITS POPULARITY with test teams to its remarkably even temperatures. At this time of year, they hovered around zero at night and they did not increase much during the day, which made it ideal for the warm-up test, carried out at a temperature of zero degrees plus or minus five. There were colder places of course, and when Bemidji was too warm, as it had been increasingly of late, the engineers chased the weather . . . to Manitoba, or to Maine. The engine guys roamed far and wide as well. Their cold-start test required minus twenty degrees. The engine not only had to start, but to run without balking or excessive noise.

Ford was not the only company to have discovered Bemidji, home of a monstrous square-shouldered Paul Bunyan statue depicting the mythical lumberjack in a red plaid shirt and blue pants, and another of his sky blue ox Babe. Stationed beside a lake, the pair were known familiarly as "Paul and Babe." All manner of disguised prototypes—Chryslers, Mercedes, Volvos—turned up in the streets of the little town. Test teams from competing companies often found themselves eating together at Noel's, drawn by the $8.95 walleye special, $1 apiece for additional fillets.

The ninth guy hired when the climate control division was established, Len Flack had started coming here in the 1970s. One pre-dawn morning Flack's car full of testers stalled in minus-fourteen-degree weather with a storm on the way. The roads were empty. It was getting cold fast when Flack had a Boy Scout inspiration. Seeing cattails poking out of the snow, he lit them with a match. When the state police pulled up, he and his colleagues were warming themselves by a roaring fire. In those days Ford rented the garage where the airport stored its snowplow in warm weather. Now Ford had its own fourteen-bay garage and offices. Several years ago a test team had dated and signed a car part as a memento and hung it on a wall. Today there was quite a collection.

The 1996 Taurus was Flack's last car. In April 1996, he would have his thirty years in, and he could retire. He and his wife planned to sell their home in Garden City and take up residence in his Georgie Boy Cruise Air III, a thirty-four-foot white motor home with a purple designer stripe. "I'm going to take my home and go where I already been, only I'm gonna go where it's comfortable. Watch the weather. If it goes below seventy degrees, I move. If I don't like my neighbors, I move. Being in a motor home, you got a lot of flexibility. You can drive away from anything. The only tax I'll pay is gas tax."

In the right mood, Flack could spin story after story of his childhood. When he was a kid, growing up in a western Pennsylvania coal town where his father was a miner, he had sought to make small change selling scrap metal to an itinerant junk man. He discovered that copper fetched the highest price. Soon miners all over town were missing their copper washtubs. For fun, he and friends used to liberate a motorized rail repair cart and ride it up and down the tracks. One day they misjudged a train's speed, and it smashed the cart to smithereens as they dived for safety. Flack was being sent to a home for wayward boys, when the town priest stepped in to rescue his altar boy. Instead he found himself at a seminary school for Catholic priests in Dunkirk, New York. Flack swiped the headmaster's jug of pennies to buy a bus ticket home. He didn't want to be a priest and, more to the point, it was the first day of hunting season.

At Ford, Flack was the last of a vanishing breed: an engineer without a four-year college degree. His career had been capped at a grade eight. But he was the resident expert on heating and air conditioning hardware. Young

engineers came away from his discourses feeling as if they'd just met a professor. If those engineers happened to be working mothers, they also came
away with an earful of disapproving remarks. But it was hard to get angry at
Flack. He would say something incendiary such as "A woman's place is in the
home," and then he'd go out of his way to take a female to Bemidji's woolen
outlet to buy her kids mittens or a sweater. In one of life's little ironies, the
climate control division was represented by one of the few women, also a
mother, on the DN101 team: Mary Anne Wheeler. She had surprised Flack
with how hard she pushed for an electric blend door, a device that regulat-
ed the mixture of fresh and recirculated air, to replace one operated by cable,
something he had wanted for his last system. He gave her a lot of credit.

Automotive comfort and visibility were Flack's contribution to
humankind. One day he drove some people into Bemidji in an outgoing
Taurus. "See how nice these are," he said, pointing out how quickly the
front-door windows had cleared of condensation. "I did these in 1985." And
so, it was unfortunate that his last car, the 1996 Taurus, was not turning out
to be a totally happy experience. A power struggle was raging over who was
going to be in charge of DN101 climate control development, which
stemmed from having two sets of development guys with overlapping
responsibilities. One was the group at the climate control division for whom
Flack worked, and the other was lodged in vehicle development, represented on this trip by Dwight Smith and Wayne Williams. In the past, vehicle
development had merely set up the trips and signed off on climate control
products. Flack had supervised the testing. Now vehicle development was
trying to usurp the testing as well. Last summer vehicle development had
decided to take structural prototypes out west on a test trip, even though
Flack and his management maintained they weren't ready. He stayed back in
Dearborn, working on head pressure problems in the wind tunnel. The trip
proved unsatisfactory and Williams now deferred to Flack on testing procedures. But he remained in charge of cars and schedules, a position known as
"trip mother." No one, not even a supervisor, dared countermand the trip
mother. When the time came for a team picture in Bemidji, Flack was working on data back at the motel. Williams refused to reschedule another photo
to include him. Naturally, Flack said, he was hurt, but he would not abandon
his pursuit of quality. "I don't need a picture of my work," is what he said.
"The system has all the trademarks of Len Flack."

IN THE DAY THAT stretched ahead after the early-morning warm-ups,
members of the climate control team occupied themselves with other
chores. They rode around, for example, watching the defrosters clear con-

densation on the windshield. These patterns were as telltale as animal tracks in snow. They could see, for example, that too much air was directed toward the sides of the windshield, and that air coming out of the defroster grille hit the contoured windshield at too high a point. The Feds required that the section in front of the driver clear in no more than fifteen minutes, and the whole windshield in thirty.

The ICP buttons were turning out to be a real headache. The switch behind the heat control knob seemed to have rotated, and the settings weren't accurate. They had to epoxy two of the knobs. "This adds to my list of wondrous things about the ICP," said Dwight Smith. "They're worrying too much about the radio and ATC [automatic temperature control] buttons and not enough about knobs." They wrote up a concern for the electronics team.

They didn't need gauges to feel the cold air drafts. "The damn body leaks," Flack had said on the drive up, running a practiced hand over a door. "At this rate we'll have to warm up Bemidji before you get warm inside the car." Air leakage was measured in cubic feet per minute. The outgoing Taurus was on the high side, with up to 550 CFM. The DN101 goal was 200 CFM.

The amount of leakage was reflected in the time-to-comfort readings. In the front seat, the DN101 prototypes were averaging 15 to 18 minutes to reach a number-five level, which was much better than the Camry, at 21 minutes—although that particular car was suspect. But it was also better than the Lexus, at 16.5 to 19 minutes. The DN101 rear-seat levels, however, ranged all the way up to 27.5 minutes. That was a long time for someone to wait for warmth. They had work to do. The left rear duct was ten millimeters lower than the right side; when raised, it yielded more heat. And something was wrong with the door seals, all right. On one, snow collected between the inner and outer seals. Leaky doors didn't account for all the cold air in the rear, however. In one prototype where riders had complained about cold feet, they took out the duct and found the following items: a white nylon plug; a two-inch piece of plastic tubing as thick as a finger; a wad of tape; a little plug of dried goo, caulk maybe. This was terrible, of course. The gunk had clogged the duct badly enough to invalidate some of the back-seat data. Mary Anne Wheeler had to wonder how pilot plant workers had done it. Or was the question why? "It's too much to be a mistake," she said at one point, although it was hard to believe that the pilot plant would deliberately sabotage a climate control car. She wrapped the stuff up and stuck it in her briefcase, for the moment when she would show it to Fred Jorgensen, and suggest ever so professionally that the crack body and assembly operations had not been exercising due care.

Meanwhile, back in Dearborn, the DN101 team was scrutinizing the prototypes for visible imperfections, known as "fit-and-finish" issues. The first review, conducted by Landgraff in mid-December in a roped-off area at the pilot plant, was a four-hour affair that put people in mind of the marathon studio walkarounds. Instead of clays, they circled real cars. But some of the issues had the familiar ring of old arguments. Mike Hornai, an engineer who worked for the studio, objected to the way the windshield moldings cornered. "What you see is what you get," Kozak told him.

"We would never have approved that," Hornai said.

"Take a look at your clay," Kozak told him.

"This is unacceptable."

"I have the master drawings," Kozak said.

Landgraff jumped in. "You can't get any more molding on that class-one surface."

"That's not what you told us," Hornai said.

"That's what we told you, Mike," Kozak said.

Every review produced hand-wringing over the state of the black rubber moldings, which were known collectively as "gimps." They were loose, they were bad news. *"Gimp"*—people weren't sure of the word's origins, although it appeared to stem from the French *guimpe*. Some people thought it came from "gap improvement." Sometimes it was called a "gap hider." Whatever the origin, the word had come to have a negative connotation. By its very presence, a gimp was an admission of failure, and for that reason discussions about gimps often became emotional. In a perfect car, where parts were precisely aligned, you would not have gaps or mismatches and you would not need gimps along the hood or around the headlamps to mask them. Camry had gimps, but not as many. DN101 was especially gimp-laden because its rounded contours magnified the size of the gaps.

Zyg Gregory, who succeeded Jim Mikola as head of the lighting and closures chunk team, decided to replace the word "gimp" with the word "aeroshield." As it happened, "aeroshield" was also the name they had given the bellypan under the front end. So, here was another aggravation for Ford: there just weren't enough good euphemisms to go round. For example, it had been agreed that the workers who had come to Detroit from the assembly plants to work on the prototypes required some loftier designation than "operator," as they were known back home; heretofore they would be known as "product specialists." However, the Ford marketing people who were in charge of the auto show exhibits had also appropriated "product specialists" to refer to the good-looking young women and the handful of men who rode the turntables like Dinah Shore in days of yore. In the recent past they had been called "narrators," and they were commonly thought of as airheads who did nothing but read prepared scripts. To upgrade their status, they had been fortified with information to answer customers' questions; "narrator" no longer did justice to the scope of their knowledge. So you had this situation where "product specialist" could refer either to muscular tobacco-chewers with beer bellies and raw language or to gorgeous, well-dressed young people with a gift of gab. However unlikely, if their worlds met, if there were, say, an auto show at an assembly plant, it could be confusing.

Better just to say "gimp" and be done with it. By whatever name, the stuff around the headlamps was falling off, it wouldn't stay on for anything. The moldings looked as if they should be simple to fix. "What's wrong with glue?" Landgraff asked at one of maybe twenty gimp meetings he attended that spring and summer. Sometimes he had to pinch himself. "Thirteen months before Job One and we're all sitting around the table designing this gimp." He was told there was no known glue that would stick to the material they were using. Landgraff pressed further: "Can we change to something glue would stick to?"

A gimp engineer in the plastics division was working on a new process to mold gimps onto the headlamp, eliminating the need for adhesive or clips. The process had been used for taillamps, but the headlamps had a protective coating that made it more difficult. For sheer difficulty, the headlamp gimps rivaled the headlamps themselves, speaking of which, surely the complex reflectors would be along any minute now. Meanwhile, the prototypes had old-fashioned optic plate lenses, and the gimps were stuck on anyway they could do it.

With all that was wrong, Mark Jarvis experienced a sense of relief. His ICP was no longer the program's worst performer. The seats were the new disaster area, worthy of a chapter in themselves. The recliner handle wiggled; the sew lines didn't line up; the foam was showing on the headrest; the fabric was wrinkled. Not to mention the fabric design, that god-awful bloody swirl. And on top of that, Lear Seating Company was asking Ford for an extra $70 over their initial cost estimate. Along with an increase of $80 in the body and assembly labor estimate, it accounted for the bulk of a $200 upward creep in variable cost. "This is nothing new," Landgraff said. "This is an age-old problem. Every time we do a cost request, we get surprised. . . . I have never gotten a cost request back that wasn't higher than what we thought it should be. . . . It always goes up."

The body and assembly apologia, he said, generally went like this: "They thought they could do it this way, and on further investigation they can't do it that way, or they don't want to do it that way." Or they blamed design changes—"the way the parts are designed is different from parts they costed previously." For their part, suppliers pleaded amnesia to the agreements they had made less than two years ago, even when there were written signatures. Or they said the person who signed the original price agreement was no longer with the company. Or they, too, blamed design changes. It didn't matter to Landgraff. Costs that went up now had to come down. "We've got to go in there and smash them."

I T   W A S N ' T   E N O U G H that the team was doing twice-weekly fit-and-finish inspections, and that the development engineers tried, trued, and tested the hell out of the prototypes; body and assembly had instigated its own reviews as well. Theirs was called a "Nova C" audit, with criteria based on what a customer noticed in cars. Nova Cs were routinely held out in the plants to check manufacturing quality on cars coming off the line. But B&A also had scheduled three on the DN101 prototypes. In February, four auditors went over a prototype with a checklist. These auditors tried to see and experience the car as a customer would, although it wasn't always easy. "People comment on the strangest things," said auditor and engineer Gary Sopko. " 'Fuel sloshes in the fuel tank.' " Customers might not know that it was fuel, they might think it was brakes or the suspension, they might say it sounded like a bowling ball. But they knew they didn't like the sound. The Nova C team looked over the exterior and under the hood, operated the mirrors, windows, radios, and other equipment, then drove the car. Their review produced 276 DN101 "calls"—things they would like the engineers to fix. As always, the Camry was the benchmark. Sopko was especially impressed with Toyota's fit and finish. "Their paint is perfect; their doors are perfect. Everything fits real good."

As far as Landgraff was concerned, the Nova C audits might be worthwhile in the plants but they were a waste of time at this stage of product development. First of all, he didn't think they found anything that the team itself would not have caught: an unlabeled fuel door/trunk release; hoses visible in the fascia openings, unclear graduations on the dipstick. And much of what they turned up, the team already knew about. "Poor shift quality," for example. If it were within the power of the team to further improve the transmission, they'd have done so long ago. The auditors also singled out features that the team had previously debated and resolved; it was too late for change. For example, the auditors objected that the nifty new flip-fold center console, when flipped open to hold a coffee cup, blocked the ashtray "so you can't drink coffee and smoke at the same time." The team had decided to do it that way because there were so few smokers anymore. Chrysler was eliminating ashtrays altogether as a standard feature. What the B&A audits really signified, Landgraff thought, was a company weakness. "They occur where one organization does not trust the other."

Landgraff also objected to a final stage of market research, scheduled for later that year, for many of the same reasons. Potential customers were to drive prototypes. "The official story is, 'We'll do this market research and find out how to position the car in the marketplace.' The unofficial story is, 'We'll find out what people don't like and you fix it.'

"I love market research. People misinterpret what I say. People say, 'Well, you don't want to hear what's wrong.' Yes, I do want to hear about what's wrong, but I want to hear about it at the point in time when I can do something about it." Moreover, customers would be driving prototypes that were, as was now all too clear, far from perfect. He could imagine the sorts of things they'd notice. For example, he said, "People might ask, 'Why are these moldings falling off?' " It was a good question.

T HE FIRST PROTOTYPES were good, but not as good as predicated in the World Class Timing plan, which foresaw no others until a pre-production phase in the plants at six months before Job One. Landgraff and Bell decided to authorize a second-generation prototype build in Dearborn of three cars, to incorporate the changes to parts following the CP build. That was the only way to be sure the new parts worked. No one wanted to do it; it was more time and more money. And it also meant they had failed to engineer the car right the first time. On the first pass, they found 256 issues—256 things wrong!—many having to do with the seats and the front end.

One good thing, life at the pilot plant had taken a definite turn for the better. The launch team had moved into the second floor of the new addition, which was positively luxurious compared to the basement. It had bright new furniture—even if it was the same tiresome gray and blue motif—and lots of windows. Moreover, they were getting to know their body and assembly compatriots, and really some of them weren't all that bad. Moreover, Tom Green had been plucked from his position as B&A launch team leader—his new position not announced—and replaced by the kinder, gentler Bob Damron, who would be going with them to Atlanta. Damron had worked for body engineering for fourteen years before coming to body and assembly. He had been an *engineer*. He believed in teams. He was firm, but he would listen before he ruled, and he didn't get personal.

Back in the basement, the Christmas holidays had generated a momentary surge of good feeling. Many people were amazed to find cards from Dick Landgraff in their mailboxes at home. They thought Wendy Dendel had put him up to it, but she reassured everybody that was not the case. She wondered if it had been Connie Landgraff's idea.

But now it was January, a cold hard month in Detroit. Come May, some people would have been in the basement three years. A number of them had come to believe they were slowly being poisoned. They attributed chronic colds, sore throats, headaches, and coughs to something in the air or water. Dendel recruited company experts to test the air for carbon monoxide, carbon dioxide, bacteria, and humidity. It was all normal. It was, in fact, the same air that was piped throughout the Design Center. But people still refused to believe it was okay. Then the coffee club said the water must be bad, because when they came in on Mondays it ran brown. The Design Center health and safety team periodically inspected all the water fountains and tagged them as safe, but engineers wanted numbers, so Dendel had the water checked and posted the results. Lead was less than 1 part per billion, the chlorine level was normal, and there were no bacteria. She put the information in a memo and posted it. "Our water is *very safe to drink*" her memo said. Shortly afterward, another memo, unsigned, appeared on the same bulletin board. "Particulates found in the water have never been shown to be of a toxic nature," the guerrilla memo said in part. "The occasional signs of animal life should be viewed as further proof that the water is good for living organisms." In case people wondered why members of the water safety committee drank bottled water, the memo said, "Let us assure you it is merely to benchmark the competition." Given its cleverness, Dendel supposed the finance people had written it. Their little corner of the basement was generally where plots were hatched.

Living like moles, cut off from sunlight and their extended engineering families, it was easy for team members to believe that not only their health was in jeopardy, but also their careers. The team was what was known on organization charts as a matrix, because each person belonged not only to the team but to a home office. What that meant to most people was that they had two bosses. One was their boss on the team, to which they were in a sense on loan, and the other was their boss in the home office that had loaned them and retained their records, the Form 60s. In some cases, this gave rise to a situation where they spent all their working hours with DN101, but a supervisor in another building gave them their performance reviews. Andy Benedict, the DN101 body engineering manager, successfully fought to get the Form 60s for his engineers, the largest contingent on the team. But that didn't solve all the problems. Guys like Steve Kozak had been gone from body for so long that they were convinced people were forgetting them when promotions came up. Either that, or they were told that their work on Ford's most important car program had a higher priority just now than a promotion. A grade ten, Kozak had watched a choice grade-twelve opening go to someone with no sheet-metal experience, a thirty-year-old woman.

At Ford, when one assignment ended, it was up to the individual to beat the bushes, call up old friends, and otherwise network to find another; otherwise, you risked being shoved into any old job. People worried that when their time came to leave the team, no one would remember who they were. In some cases their old bosses had moved on. Would anyone take them back? Kozak, at least, had been told to be patient. But meantime he still had to come to work for the next two years at his current grade.

Sometimes the matrix tugged people in two directions, trying to please two bosses. No one was more loyal to the team than Andy Benedict, Landgraff knew that, but he had watched with interest Benedict's reaction to a recent cost overrun. At a review in October, Landgraff announced that body engineering was $40 over on the variable cost. "What are we doing to get that back?" a body engineering superior asked Benedict. Benedict, who had not shown a great deal of interest in the overrun until that moment, or so it seemed to Landgraff, was suddenly *very* interested. Landgraff had the feeling he might unilaterally attempt to rectify the situation with a cost reduction. Landgraff sent him a note reiterating that the team had to make those decisions. "Just a little reminder not to sneak off and make side deals."

NOTHING DID MORE that spring to lower the spirits of the team than the death of Hank Buick, the well-liked marketing delegate to the team, who had been there since the D–FC55 days. And no one felt the loss more keenly than Tom Gorman, who considered Buick his best friend, despite an age difference of more than twenty years. When they first met, Gorman confessed, he had decided almost immediately that Buick was a burnt-out case. "I yelled at him. I didn't think he was doing his job." As he came to know Buick, Gorman realized that what he had interpreted as indolence or worse was in fact a determination to resist stress and pressure. Some years earlier, Buick told Gorman, he had removed himself from the marketing fast track to spend more time with his son. Gorman himself had just become a father. "Hank always wanted to make sure things in my life were in balance. He would say, 'Go home.' I'd say, 'I can't go home.' He'd say, 'Go home. You got a kid.' " Buick was a devout nature lover. Dick Landgraff often spoke of problems as this or that "worry bead." But Buick carried the genuine thing in his pocket, a pebble from the lakefront where he had a cottage, whose presence he found soothing.

Buick's idea for improving morale was to start every meeting with a joke. He liked to tell how he had once worked with young Edsel Ford. Ford would shake his head and say, "The first name's okay, but I don't know about the last name." One day Buick turned to him and said, "The last name's okay, but I don't know about the first name."

On March 19, a number of team members attended a memorial service crowded with people of all ages. The front of the room had been turned into a nature scene, landscaped with trees, shrubs, stuffed birds and squirrels, Hank's fishing poles, his old, worn hat, and his tackle bag. Sounds of lapping water and birds played over a sound system. In eulogies, several speakers recalled Buick's passion for the outdoors.

In a letter, Karin Dean wrote of the effect the service had on her and others from the team. "Many of us learned that we'd like to be remembered for important things, like what kind of friend we are, what kind of a spouse, what kind of a parent, what kind of a person. Suddenly what kind of a workhorse we were was pretty unimportant."

For a time, those kinds of thoughts circulated throughout the team. Even Landgraff caught the mood. He found himself worrying about the health of some of his people, and even to a degree about his own. Not that he thought Buick's death was related to the job. "A lot of this stuff seems to be hereditary." But he was willing to concede that there might, in fact, be such a thing as working too hard. If there were, then George Bell was doing it. "I'm a little concerned," said Landgraff. "I mean, he's working twelve hours a day. . . . He gets tied up in knots about all these kinds of things. . . .

"For all I know *I'm* building up some stress and strain that's going to come popping out some day. I don't think so, I don't know for sure. As I look around at the guys I work with and so on, I sort of think, are we working too much here? Is this too much of a strain, are we trying to do too much here?

"Our processes are not very robust. They don't work on their own. Unless you take personal interest they don't get solved. For example, I've got a $200 cost problem I gotta go worry about now. We won't make any progress unless I spend a lot of personal time and energy.

"Ten years ago it never even occurred to me. But when you see friends of yours having problems. . . . Nobody I know works as hard as we do. Nobody."

SIXTEEN

A Sit-Down Strike
and the Princess
of Seats

SLENDER, FIVE-FOOT-NINE,
with shoulder-length brown hair, large brown eyes, fine features, and perfect skin, Heather Morrissett looked as if she had stepped off the pages of *Seventeen*, rather than the grease-soaked floor of the experimental or X garage. Even the casual slacks and blazers she wore had a look of studied informality. A fourth- or fifth-generation automotive princess—depending on whether you began the count with her great-great grandfather, who graded the site for a General Motors plant with a rig and a team of horses, or started with his son who worked there—she was a graduate of the University of Michigan and an MBA student at Wayne State. In meetings, amid the bland males in white and pastel shirts, whose ties hung round their necks like nooses, Morrissett stood out, a graceful birch among scrub pines.

Morrissett had been raised by supportive, churchgoing parents who liked to emphasize the positive side of life's travails. She had been coached in team-building, where people were to accomplish much by working together. Long before the flimsy, misshapen seats in the protoypes caught Dick Landgraff's eye, she had been having problems with the supplier, Lear Seating Company, which was missing deadlines left and right. "All I do basically is complain," Morrissett complained. Lear was so disorganized, Morrissett didn't know how to help. She got so tired of listening to her own criticisms that she sometimes longed to say something nice. She also had responsibility for the power seat tracks, made by a different supplier, and they were another horror story.

As the build of the confirmation prototypes approached, Morrissett's boss, development manager Tom Moran, had sounded an alarm. "I'm becoming quite concerned about what level seats we're going to see on the CP," Moran reported to George Bell at a weekly prototype readiness meeting in September 1993. "The seat evaluations are scheduled, the promise date comes. And Lear says, 'We don't have seats for you.'"

Bell thought perhaps Moran meant seats for the SHO, the subject of recent controversy. Last month Bob Bondurant, a former race car driver and owner of a driving school, halted an SHO drive in mid-track because the seats he was hired to evaluate were so bad. At a subsequent review in the Design Center courtyard, Brad Nalon called them "flat as a park bench . . . moosh city." "Is this a La-Z-Boy or a Lear?" Doug Gaffka asked after his turn behind the wheel. Production delays affecting the limited-edition SHO, whose introduction trailed the Taurus and Sable sedans by four months, wouldn't be as big a deal as a holdup in the sedans. "Seats for the SHO?" George Bell inquired hopefully of Moran.

"The SHO is more on time that the rest," Moran answered. "It's high and low series." Rats! It *was* the sedans, both Taurus and Sable, base and luxury models. In other words, every car in the starting lineup. Lear seemed to have its priorities reversed. "Like the toothpaste that's slowly going into the tube," Bell said, as unflappable as always.

Seats were the first thing the customer saw on opening the car door, and the biggest. They had to first look good and be pleasant to touch, and then to feel good when either a big man or a small woman, or vice versa, slipped into the car for a test drive, and they had to continue to be comfortable hours into a long drive. Seats were important and they were also complex to design and manufacture, even more so if ordered with the power option—standard on the high series—so they not only slid backward and forward, but ascended, descended, and tilted up in front and down in back. You could also get an inflatable lumbar cushion that puffed up like a football in the small of your back. The seat belts and head restraints were subject to safety tests, the fabric to wear-and-tear analysis.

In the past, Ford engineers had designed the seats, Ford purchasing had contracted out frames, cushions, tracks, motors, and other parts to various suppliers, and Ford workers had put them all together at the assembly plants and then installed the finished seat in the car. In the case of the new Taurus and Sable, however, circumstances had dovetailed to put the entire program, with the exception of the power seat tracks, in the hands of a single supplier, Lear Seating, on whom the company was now dependent for some 600,000 units a year. Ford had no fallback position, having disbanded its internal seat-making capacity, indeed, having *sold* a chunk of it to Lear. You could hear the nervousness in the voice of Shabbir Kathiria, the head of the interior trim chunk team whose turf for a time included seats. "First time we have to trust the supplier; give him the responsibility and just trust him."

There were people at *Lear* who couldn't believe Ford had gotten itself in this position. One Lear executive, a friend of Wendy Dendel, told her that Ford was crazy—Lear had them by the short hairs. "They can keep saying they need more money and more money, and Ford has nowhere to go," Dendel reported. And indeed, Landgraff was already gearing up to do battle over Lear's request for an additional $4 million to cover unexpected engineering costs, plus an additional $70 per seat for content and labor.

Iᴛ ᴡᴀꜱɴ'ᴛ ꜱᴜᴘᴘᴏꜱᴇᴅ to be this way. Having single suppliers who developed and manufactured complex components was the direction in which not only Ford but the entire automotive industry was headed, having been persuaded by the Japanese that it was better to establish long-term, familial relationships with a few suppliers rather than play them off against each other with constant rounds of bidding. The result was supposed to be a harmonious give-and-take between supplier and supplied, not the acrimonious haggling that so far characterized the Lear-Ford union. In the Japanese model, the supplier became almost an extension of the customer's company, working closely to solve problems and reduce costs. Having a single supplier also reduced variation in the product, improved quality, and cut inventories. It was Mom and apple pie.

Not only was Ford shrinking its supply base, but it was giving more responsibility to those suppliers that remained. Ford wanted to concentrate its resources on "core businesses," ones in which it had a proprietary stake or that were critical to the success of the company. Metal stamping was a core business, and so were engines. (Some people worried that purchasing the SHO engine from Yamaha was a dangerous departure.) But it didn't pay to be an expert in everything. Certain other systems—seats, for example—could be farmed out. Where once Ford handed a supplier the drawings for a part and said "Make this," now suppliers were to do the up-front design and engineering. So it was that Ford had disbanded its seating unit in body engineering and hired Lear Seating to do everything. In addition, Ford sold Lear three large Mexican plants that made seat covers, armrests, and headrests. Part of the deal was that these plants, which absorbed Ford management, would continue to make products for Ford cars.

Around the same time, body and assembly operations decided it would like to parachute out of the seat business as well. Up to now, seat suppliers made the parts; the plants assembled them. But as cars grew ever more complex, factory space was at a premium. And the people who worked on seats were prone to crippling carpal tunnel syndrome, owing to constant tugging, stretching, and stapling motions that took a terrible toll on the wrists. The fingers of the afflicted went numb and pains that felt like electrical shocks shot up their arms. The condition could require surgery and lengthy rehabilitation. As long as there was no net decrease in jobs, and Lear pledged not to contest a union election, the United Auto Workers agreed to relinquish the seat jobs in Atlanta and Chicago.

The initial plan for the 1996 Taurus had called for carryover seats, but that changed with Dick Landgraff's Camry campaign. It was not that the Toyota seats were better, although they did have one nifty feature: a rear seat that folded down, so long items could extend from the truck into the car's interior. But for comfort, Taurus seats were hard to beat, thanks to Lew Veraldi's quality crusade way back when. Complaints about seats ranked thirteen on the list of TGW issues, a good indication people liked them. "If you notice a seat, there's a reason you're noticing," pointed out Andy Benedict, the DN101 body engineering manager. "And it's probably a bad reason rather than a good reason."

Still, with all-new seats, the DN101 team could remedy some long-standing irritants. The seat belt rattled and the seat itself had a tendency to slip forward when the car stopped abruptly, a condition known as "chucking." The fabric and trim looked cheap. And, of course, they could restore the back-seat armrest that Landgraff had whacked in 1992. With new seats, DN101 could have the same fold-down feature in the rear as Camry. Ford could upgrade the fabric and employ more tie-downs, a construction technique that made the covers fit more smoothly, even if it did seem to trigger carpal tunnel syndrome. And all-new seats could have a snug, sporty, more contemporary feel.

Lear was willing to design and engineer the seats, as long as they could manufacture them as well, because that was where the profits were. The company had been in the seat business since 1917 under various names. Since 1966, it had been part of Lear Siegler, Inc., a conglomerate. In 1988, following a corporate takeover, three principals bought out the seating unit, changed the name to Lear Seating, and aggressively went after more business, promoting just-in-time deliveries of fully assembled seats. To service the DN101 program, Lear planned to open manufacturing facilities near the two Taurus assembly plants that would sequence the seats according to style, color, and options in the same order as cars on the line. As a high-series Willow Green Taurus scheduled for a saddle interior traveled down the chassis line, an electronic message would flash to the nearby Lear plant. A pair of tan, power-operated bucket seats would arrive two hours later on an overhead conveyor just as the green Taurus approached the installation point. It was Factory of the Future–type stuff.

But first, there were a few snags to work out.

L OOKING BACK ON IT, you couldn't blame Lear for all that went wrong, just most of it. In committing to design and manufacture seats for two sedans, a station wagon, and the SHO, the young company had plunged in way over its head. Even a cursory investigation by Ford would have revealed that Lear had a shortage of engineering talent. Where body engineering would have assigned five specialized engineers to develop a set of front seats, a guy on the frame, another on the pad, a third on plastic, and so forth, Lear had just one. Lear could have refused the job, of course. But a company would have to be nuts to turn down a megamillion-dollar Ford contract.

Nor did it help matters that Ford had awarded the power seat tracks to Lear's arch rival in the seating business, Johnson Controls Inc. (JCI). Their parts had to work together, but engineers from the two companies could barely bring themselves to talk to each other, lest they inadvertently divulge proprietary information. The rivalry also played out in competition for the contract employees known as "jobbies" who did computer-aided design. To acquire twenty-five new jobbies for the DN101 contract, Lear manager Mike DiMatteo had raided GM and Chrysler. "I had to. Ford wouldn't allow me to take Ford designers." Then JCI raided Lear, and DiMatteo lost nine experienced designers. Fortunately he had anticipated the raid, stashing backup designers on other seat programs that could be pulled for DN101. He was convinced JCI would strike again. "You know what? I'm ready for them. I've got the resources on call, ready to roll." Jobbies jumped around like kangaroos. They would work for whoever paid the highest hourly wage, which was currently approaching $30. One applicant submitted a seven-page résumé, listing jobs with thirty-three companies. DiMatteo thought he must be forty years old, and then he met him. "The guy was twenty-five." There was so much intrigue in this business, DiMatteo said, that it had inspired him to write a book: *As the Compass Turns*.

Through no fault of its own, Lear had gotten a late start on the DN101 program. By the time Ford okayed the plan for all-new seats, most of the other DN101 engineering work had been under way for a year. One thing planner Brad Nalon had learned about the car business, "If you start late, you never catch up. You might say you'll work harder, but there's too much you can't foresee." Although the equipment to make seats was a lot simpler and faster to build than the complex tooling fixtures for body and chassis components, the seats themselves took a lot of time to design; agreeing on shape and firmness was largely a matter of trial and error.

In a sense, every seat was born anew. "No one does it very well and it's so basic," lamented Michelle Krebs, a seasoned automotive writer, who critiqued cars for the *New York Times*. The best pair she could remember, she said, had turned up in an obscure Land Rover. Among the worst were those in the new Ford Windstar minivan. "The front bucket seats must have been tested by thin-hipped 20-year-old women and wide-bottomed men," Krebs wrote. "The cushions are contoured up the sides, squeezing the hips and thighs of small-to-average-size men and women with a touch of baby spread. A booster-style child seat would not sit securely."

One of engineer Heather Morrissett's assignments was to periodically scoop up a dozen or so Ford volunteers and take them on seat evaluation trips through the Michigan countryside. The participants rotated through the cars in two-hour shifts, filling out questionnaires after each ride. These groups tended to be composed largely of white male engineers, with an occasional stylist or planner. Among the missing: old people, fat people, smokers, children, and a statistically significant representation of females. It was kind of incredible that a company as reliant as Ford on state-of-the-art data collection and analysis had not discovered a better way to test seats than to pile a bunch of white male engineers into cars and ask them what they thought. But no one, not even the Japanese, had come up with a scientific way to design a seat for the all-American rear end. An electronic technique called pressure-point mapping was sometimes used: a person or mannequin sat in a seat covered with a sensor-laden mat; a computer recorded readings at strategic points. Pressure-point mapping was handy in the early design phases. But because Ford lacked a substantial data base that correlated pressure-point patterns with human comfort levels, its value was limited.

Comments from riding around tended to be wildly diverse. One rear-seat evaluation produced the following remarks about a seat back: "Back was overall much more comfortable in this car compared to the carryover vehicle." "This seat had no lumbar support." "Very uncomfortable." "Outside bolster on seat back makes me feel like I'm turned toward center of car." "I can feel the structure in the center of the seat back."

"Tail burn" was certainly a complaint worth noting. The tailbone or coccyx hurt or fell asleep when there was too much pressure from the cushion. But people griped if the center armrest dipped forward, or if their jeans stuck as they slid across the fabric, or this: "When in a slouch, the hard spot feels like a football under your butt."

If people drove well-appointed luxury cars, they tended to think more highly of the seats. The electronics division had a similar difficulty to overcome with audio systems. They called it the "Lexus syndrome." Some vice-president who had taken home a Japanese car over the weekend always wanted to know why Ford's premium sound system wasn't as good, when actually it might even be better according to objective criteria. The amateur listener did not know what to listen for, or how to describe it. To that end, electronics was training seventy-five or so employees to be a standing jury. However, Ford did not have a similar cadre of trained sitters. The poor seat guys had to sort through the comments and ratings, hoping to find a consensus that would give them some direction: an additional ten millimeters of foam here, or fifteen fewer there.

Even after two years, people were still arguing over the DN101 seats. The current version was modeled after a carryover Taurus bottom and the back from the Toyota Lexus 300. It was a compromise with the studio, which had wanted a more cupped bottom, curved back, and firmer foundation, in line with what Europeans had. Even the Taurus/Lexus combo had detractors. In blind tests, drivers and passengers kept saying they liked the old Taurus seats best of all. But there was no going back. They no longer fit the car.

In October, Landgraff recruited Len Landis, a seasoned seat supervisor from body engineering, to ride herd on the DN101 program. He arrived not a moment too soon. In November, as workers started bolting seats into prototypes, it didn't take an expert to see that they left a lot to be desired. It wasn't just that the fabric was so peculiar. The fabric wasn't even Lear's responsibility. It was the 180 other things. The plastic seat-back panels were falling off in shipment from Lear's plant in Lorain, Ohio. The side shields—workers couldn't assemble them, or the parts broke; there were major gaps between inner and outer portions. And they didn't look the way the stylists had designed them. You could bend the recliner handle in any direction; the recliner mechanisms were ratcheting and had to be replaced. When they tested the first armrest, it broke too. In tests that simulated heavy sun, some of the plastic parts shriveled, unable to take the heat. Making his rounds of the pilot plant, Rand Bitter eased into a car and felt something hard. It turned out to be a pair of pliers sewn into the seat.

THE ATTACKS ON LEAR were getting vicious. Landis tried to stop the bloodshed. "I said, 'Hey, our job is to make this happen. If they fail, we fail.' " He could see that Lear desperately needed technical help. The first year Landis had worked on seats as a young engineer, the supervisor entrusted him with only a plastic part and a couple of screws. It took him three years to get a front seat. But Lear was hiring green college graduates who barely knew a bolster from a bezel. They couldn't even do an engineering drawing, so changes weren't documented. They were evasive when asked about stress tests. Landis dispatched two Ford veterans to train Lear's engineers; he himself was there three days a week. Other Ford experts held Friday classes on various aspects of seat engineering.

Even with all the pressure, the Lear guys didn't seem to have the same sense of urgency as Ford. Landis and his people were in at 7 A.M. Why wasn't Lear? Rand Bitter, the finance guy on seats, had the same complaint. "They don't start till eight-thirty or nine. How hard are they working to optimize my tooling cost if they're not even in at eight o'clock over there?"

Meetings at Lear had a relaxed quality, owing in part to a conference room with lighting that didn't hum and comfy swivel chairs around a big seamless table. A small table in the corner featured a fresh pot of coffee, soft drinks, big fat chocolate chip and peanut butter cookies, nut-filled muffins, sometimes brownies. Nobody from Ford objected in public to this expenditure of seat funds, they wolfed down the food, and yet it sent a certain message, and that message was that Lear had money to spare.

Meanwhile, Heather Morrissett felt she was getting nowhere with JCI on improving the power seat track. It was promised to be five decibels quieter than the carryover Taurus, but it was distinctly noisier. If anything, the track performance was getting worse. These days she was practically begging JCI, "Just *give* us carryover. Get us back to where we were." It seemed to her they had given up. The day Dick Landgraff drove the first prototype, she waited in the X garage with her supervisor Subhash Sethi, to see what the program manager would say.

"The seats are noisier than shit," Dick Landgraff said when Sethi asked what he thought.

Sethi giggled at Landgraff's candor. "I'm glad you said something about that, Dick. We have been saying the same thing for about two months."

Tom Moran had listened as well. "It sounds like it's just not going to make it in one direction. And it's too loud in the other direction."

Since October, Landgraff had been attending weekly seat meetings at Lear to review progress on the troubled seat program. Every time the guys from JCI turned up, there was bad news. One key guy spoke with an accent, he was German or something. Once Landgraff sorted out what he was saying, he could understand why things seemed to be getting worse. JCI had headed off in the wrong direction. "They benchmarked against Lexus, against Camry, against the old Continental and the new Continental, and now they've discovered Camry is no good. . . . Bunch of dumb shits, why isn't the carryover Taurus in there?" Also on his list of peeves: JCI seemed always to send different people to the meetings; he seldom saw the same faces. And another thing: their engineers weren't showing up at the pilot plant as they were supposed to, to assist with the prototype build. Landgraff shared that gripe at a Monday staff meeting. "JCI said they couldn't get in. I said, 'What do you mean you can't get in?' Suppliers . . . we have to take away all the excuses."

At the seat meeting at Lear on December 1, Landgraff read the riot act to two representatives from JCI. "I want to hear a track and Tom Moran wants to hear a track that meets the objective of the outgoing car and hopefully better. Up, down, forward, backward. You guys have got to show us a track that works." And while they were at it, "We see you guys every week, right? I want to see the same faces."

The two JCI guys nodded numbly. "We'll be there." They promised "no excuses" seats by the end of January. From another meeting next door came the sound of repeated bursts of loud laughter. "Pretty soon we'll get to the point where we have as much fun as they have next door," Landgraff said. His little quip was met with grim expressions.

The Maximum Leader was just revving up. Lear's request for more money really irritated him. On December 17 he fired off a memo to Carlos Mazzorin, the head of NAAO product purchasing, saying he was "shocked to discover that Lear Corporation has submitted a variable cost for the control model seat assembly that is about a $70/unit increase." It was, he said, an "unjustified and unacceptable cost increase that is flatly rejected by the DN101 team." The cost request, Landgraff wrote, was just one of several major issues. Lear had missed deadlines, failed to meet weight objectives, and furnished parts that didn't work. In sum, Landgraff said, Lear is "the biggest problem supplier we have." Landgraff sent a copy of the letter to Lear's president, Robert Rossiter. "You've got to get a guy with real responsibility for the success of the business, you've got to make it clear you're unhappy and then you've got to follow up."

WHEN THE TROOPS gathered at Lear after the Christmas holidays, there was a new face at the table: Bob Rossiter, Lear's number-two guy. He announced he was taking charge of what constituted "the biggest crisis in Lear-Ford history."

Rossiter managed to sound both deeply concerned and highly optimistic. "I'm not going to let you down . . . I feel that we have not done the job for you. . . . [Our people] have done a lot of good things, but some not so good. . . . [This] needs my personal attention and you're going to see a lot of me."

Already he had reorganized Lear's DN101 unit. There was a new program manager, five more engineers, five new designers, five people to check drawings, and five engineering aides. Lear was placing an experienced plant manager at its Atlanta property. This team would set priorities daily, and meet Ford's sign-off dates. "What I want to try to do is regain your confidence."

"Thank you, Bob," Landgraff said quietly. "That's quite a commitment."

At his January 31 staff meeting, Landgraff announced victory in the financial dispute. "Lear's agreed to meet our cost objective. The entire goddamned overrun is coming out. End of story."

BUT THAT WAS NOT the end of the story. Indeed, sometimes it seemed as if the seat saga would go on forever.

When the seat fabric ripped at the seams, Lear proposed to fix it with a bonded scrim backing that would cost $15 to $20 a car. No way could Ford pay that much, Landgraff said. "Pick another fabric," he told Brad Nalon. The DN101 planner went up to color and trim, but the pickings were slim. On an impulse, he looked up Lear's paperwork. "Scrim required," said the spec. Scrim was included in the price! Nalon sprinted to Landgraff's office with the good news. "Going to tell Landgraff. . . . That was one of my favorites." He knew the boss would be thrilled. "Life doesn't get much better than that."

On the face of it, Lear looked bad, as if it had made crummy seats, and then claimed it would cost extra to fix them. Nalon thought Lear had made an honest mistake. And cost analyst Rand Bitter was inclined to agree. "They're not venal, just incompetent." But for a time Landgraff continued to regard the company's performance with mistrust. Everybody knew Lear was going public any day now. "We're down here struggling"—he was in the basement at the time, talking after hours—"and those guys are zillionaires."

At a staff meeting in March, Fred Jorgensen told Landgraff that Lear's failure to deliver seats was holding up the prototype build. "Crash cars can't ship because we're waiting for seats."

"The problem is," Landgraff said, "I can call Rossiter, pull fifty-two chains, but I don't know if they can get them any faster. . . . Unfortunately, we've hammered on Lear so much, they've grown an asbestos ass."

Some problems, such as a rear-seat latch that didn't stay latched, wouldn't go away. "I'm gonna ask for a professor from MIT to come in and design a goddamned latch that works," Landgraff said in exasperation.

But the pressure on Lear was paying off. The body and assembly change count had begun to dive as soon as Rossiter took over. It went from 180 in November to below 20 in February. Then, in May, when Rossiter was attending fewer meetings, it bounced back up again to 50. Only now they were just two months away from a design freeze prior to sign-off. Landgraff went into the attack mode again. "For whatever reason you got to keep the pressure on; people slack off. And Lear's slacking off."

At a meeting in May, Rossiter was back at the table. "We will definitely have good seats," the Lear president promised. "We're going to have great seats. We have the finest plants." Rossiter promised to give a party when the last concern was closed out, if anyone from Lear was still standing. His people, he said, "are under emotional stress. They could crack in the next month." The Ford engineers on the Lear rescue squad were not impressed. Two of them had just worked twenty-four hours straight trying to solve Lear's problems. But they did concede that the supplier was putting forth more effort. "We were here Mother's Day. . . . They were here Mother's Day," Len Landis reported.

Once again the concern count dropped. By summer, Landgraff had begun to hold up Lear to other suppliers as a model of cooperation. Even the seat tracks were better. JCI had come up with a "Quiet Motor System" that seemed to soften sound levels, although they posed other problems. On a development trip out west in July, the seat track twanged, it was bumpy, its coating flaked. Back in Dearborn, Subhash Sethi passed around snapshots showing light-colored flakes on the carpet. Landgraff took off his glasses and peered intently. The outgoing Taurus used grease on the track; so did Camry. "Go back and grease it," Landgraff said. JCI was reluctant; assembly workers who handled a greased track were likely to soil the car. "Can you put on a little flake catcher?" Len Landis asked. He was joking of course, but the idea had powered up George Bell's mental CAD screen. Such a device, the chief engineer said, "would have to move with the movable part of the track."

JCI said they couldn't fix the twanging noise before Job One. Sounding annoyed, the head Lear engineer said that was news to him. "We can't have this situation," Landgraff protested. "This is insane. Lear and JCI have to get together so Lear knows what's happening." Privately he thought JCI was too secretive. Even in the beginning he'd had to pry cost figures out of them.

Also out west, Sethi's guys discovered that the map pocket on the back of the front seat stretched. They had put a fire extinguisher in it. . . .

This was too much for Landgraff. "Wait a minute. You put a fire extinguisher in it?"

"We put a Coke can and it still stretched out."

"What's the design requirement? A Coke can? A fire extinguisher?" He sputtered out his own answer. "A map . . . map."

"Put a map in the map pocket," chimed in George Bell.

"Why is it so hard to do?" Landgraff asked.

T HESE DAYS THE MEETINGS at Lear took place without Heather Morrissett. In her place was the former brake guy in development, who had a paunch, chewed a toothpick, and seldom spoke up. In March the Princess of Seats had transferred to a different program. "We miss her," said Len Landis. "She was a great team person. You could count on her to do a lot of things."

Her defection was one event that could not be blamed on either Lear or JCI. For months Morrissett had chafed at minor irritations in vehicle development. When she went on a trip, her supervisor wanted to know, did she have this? did she have that? She felt like a kid. "I was ready to ask for spending money." One of the bosses told her she could be ripe for advancement, if she were more like . . . and here he mentioned a woman who Heather thought hewed strictly to the party line, whatever it was at the moment. She felt as if no one took her seriously. She was actually beginning to feel incompetent. But these feelings paled beside the revulsion she felt when a manager in another section of vehicle development starting dropping by her desk, making suggestive comments and rubbing her shoulders in a non-therapeutic way. On a trip, he arranged a room close to hers. She canceled out. Then another female engineer who became the focus of similar advances filed a complaint and cited Heather Morrissett as a victim as well. The manager had threatened to ruin Morrissett's career if she ever told of his advances, but when asked about him, she chose to do so. Ford warned the man to stay away from the two women. That's it? the women asked. Case closed, they were told. If there were penalties, Heather Morrissett was not informed. A Ford spokesman later insisted Ford had taken "appropriate" action.

Morrissett was contemplating leaving the company altogether when an opening came up in the Lincoln Continental program. She turned down offers from Nissan, which had a research and development center in nearby Farmington Hills, and TRW Inc., a company that made restraints and steering systems, and stayed with Ford. But when she learned that the manager who harassed her had received a big promotion in a company reorganization, she began to wonder if Nissan might be a better place after all.

When she sought the advice of her father, Dick Morrissett thought back to a similar scene some thirty years ago, when he broke the news to his parents that he was leaving General Motors for Ford, the enemy. A different generation, a different chapter in automotive history.

I T   S E E M E D   T O   D I C K   M O R R I S S E T T   that he had grown up knowing "cars were my destiny." His maternal great-grandfather, Adam Minto, a livery operator from the little town of Hemlock, Michigan, used his rig and horses to grade a site for a factory in nearby Flint that would build cars called Chevrolets that would eventually put men like him out of business. Morrissett's grandfather, Thomas Minto, worked with his father preparing the site, then donned a carpenter's apron and helped construct the plant. When it was up and running, he worked in the trim department at Fisher Body, on seats for GM cars. Stuffing his mouth with tacks, and a wad of chewing tobacco to shield the points, he'd deftly tongue them onto a magnetic hammer and pound them into the seat frames.

Morrissett's mother, Helen Minto, sewed seat covers, alongside two of her aunts. In 1937, Thomas Minto and his daughter stood outside the plant; inside there was a sit-down organizing strike. The UAW got them a nickel an hour raise, but the victory that meant the most to Helen Minto was ten-minute morning and afternoon bathroom breaks. A half century later she could still remember the relief. "It was like heaven."

Morrissett's father, Richard Sr., was a tool-and-die maker for Buick. He had come to Flint as a child, when his father abandoned a railroad job in Jonesboro, Arkansas, to work for high wages in the burgeoning auto industry. Dick Morrissett, Jr., went to the General Motors Institute in Flint, a technical college that provided professionals to many industries, and went to work for Buick as a process engineer. He married Judy Keene, a Buick secretary and the daughter of Orville "Guy" Keene, who proudly drove finished Buicks off the line. Morrissett had worked at GM for eight years when a GMI classmate at Ford told him the company needed engineers and urged him to apply. Ford offered Morrissett 50 percent more than he was making, and laid out a lucrative ten-year career path.

"You're going to give up all your seniority and all your benefits?" Richard Morrissett, Sr., asked his son, who was twenty-six. A depression youth, he had worn shoes that were lined with cardboard and repaired with pasted-on rubber soles. He had grubbed fire trails by hand on the Upper Peninsula for the Civilian Conservation Corps, sending home $23 of his $30 monthly pay. But that was his father's only objection. "You only get a few great opportunities in your life," his father said. His mother worried only that he was moving so far away. Dick was astonished. All the anguish over betraying General Motors had been in his own head. His parents were on his side.

Relocated at Ford's body and assembly operations, Morrissett was branded "high-pot"—high potential; he went from a grade seven to a twelve in five years. The company rounded off his training with tours of duty in design engineering, marketing, and then product planning, where he stayed. Those were golden years for planners.

Growing up in Dearborn Heights, attending Crestwood High, Heather Morrissett and her older sister, Michele, enjoyed the status accorded kids with Ford dads and Ford transportation. During the week, the Ford brats drove their moms' lease cars to school, modest little Escorts or Tempos. On weekends, they got Dad's fancier car, washed and waxed it, donned cool clothes, and went cruising on Telegraph Road, a north-south slice through Dearborn. "Car driving was how you met people," said Michele Morrissett, who had brown eyes and brown hair like her sister, and also, like her sister, turned heads when she entered a room. "You knew them by their cars. If you saw a cute guy in a red Mustang, you'd go look for the red Mustang." Sometimes they offered advice to their father for future products, such as, "The stereo isn't loud enough."

It was the good life . . . *the Ford life* . . . and it inspired loyalty in both girls. Michele, armed with a marketing degree from Michigan Technological University, turned down an offer from Steelcase to work for Ford's customer service division. Sent to Omaha, she met her future husband, Mike Sowers, also with Ford. In 1991, not only Heather, her sister, brother-in-law, and father were at Ford, but also her mother, a Kelly Girl, was a secretary in the Ford powertrain division. Then Dick Morrissett was asked to take early retirement.

For planners such as himself, the end was already beginning. "We had seven good friends over fifty be asked to take early retirement," said Judy Morrissett. "Some were told on a Friday night not to come back on Monday." But it was still a painful conclusion to a career that had begun with such promise; he imagined it might be even more painful than a divorce. He had loved the industry and loved his job, and had not planned to retire until his late sixties.

When Heather came to her father for advice, the Ford oval had lost its luster, but Dick Morrissett still had a sick feeling at the thought of his daughter working for the Japanese. "I spent the majority of my career doing everything I could do to try to beat the Japanese." He remembered when Japanese businessmen toured Ford plants in the early sixties. As he and others shared ideas—things they had done or wished they could do—the Japanese went around taking photos of everything in the plant: from automation to ashcans. "We used to laugh at them. This is the absolute truth. We used to think that they were not all there." A decade later, Americans were going to Japan, cameras in hand. In the photos they brought back, said Morrissett, "there would be your ideas. The Japanese took the best of everything."

"Let's do a matrix," he suggested to his daughter. The benefits of staying at Ford on one side of the chart, of going to Nissan on the other. Sitting at the computer, they listed the pluses for Ford: lease cars, great health benefits, seniority. For its part, Nissan would give Heather more money, new opportunities, trips to Japan, more diversity, more learning. Throw in Nissan's cars—there was certainly nothing wrong with an Altima or Maxima—and Nissan's health plan, and it was hardly a contest.

Heather accepted the Nissan offer. She knew the Japanese were not known for enlightened attitudes toward women. But how much better was Ford? The *Wall Street Journal* had just published a survey based on government statistics that ranked Ford number 198 on a list of 200 companies in the number of managers who were women, with a mere 4.4 percent. "The fact is that the system is still prejudiced against women," Dick Morrissett said. "It's still an old boy's game out there, and when you get to be fifty years old, you're dead. They take you out there and they shoot you."

SEVENTEEN

Heat Wave

DARREL WANDLESS, A
vehicle development engineer assigned to climate control, pulled his camouflaged Taurus into the nearly empty parking lot of the Searchlight Nugget, a
down-at-the heels roadhouse casino in the sere Nevada countryside thirty
miles south of Las Vegas. He had expected to see a crew from engine cooling waiting in their camouflaged DN101s, with three 1,000-pound U-Haul
trailers. Both development teams performed tests with trailers, hauling them
up hills in hot weather to place maximum stress on the cooling systems. The
engine guys had finished their runs; climate control needed the trailers to do
theirs. The trailer exchange was scheduled for 5:00 P.M. and it was 6:30 P.M.
So where could the engine guys be? Had they come and gone? Wandless
parked and waited for Wayne Williams and the rest of the climate control
team to arrive.

Climate control and engine cooling had started out two years ago on the
same side, united against the stylists in a quest for a big mouth in the front
end of the new Taurus that would suck in enough fresh air to meet their
needs and those of others under the hood. The stylists seemed to think the
only good grille was no grille at all. They could barely bring themselves to

design a little thin-lipped opening front and center, with two modest intake holes under the bumper. Just to protect those openings, the stakeholders in cooling had to be vigilant; people kept trying to stick a lamp or a sensor in the grille. In the end the engineers were forced to compete with each other for what little air there was. The engine system required airflow not only for combustion but to cool its various bodily fluids, the oil and transmission fluid, and most of all the coolant circulating through the radiator. Chassis wanted air to draw heat from the power steering fluid. The fuel-handling guys had to worry about overheating and the possibility of vapor lock. When too hot, the alternator produced less current. And of course the climate control system wouldn't function without air. With each transaction, the air got hotter and less useful for cooling. The more that the condenser sucked in, for example, the hotter it was when it reached the radiator.

Every Monday as 1993 drew to a close, the warring parties had convened with Dick Landgraff and George Bell at a meeting refereed by Tom Breault and his band of packagers. Landgraff got so upset at the internecine squabbles that the engine cooling guys started having meetings before the meeting—"pre-meetings"—to prepare. First they huddled with their management to decide what they were going to tell climate control; then they had a meeting with climate control to tell them what they were going to tell them; then both groups had a bull session with Tom Breault to screen what they were going to tell Landgraff and Bell.

"It's hopeless," Dick Landgraff had fulminated, emerging from one of these meetings last October. "It's the blind leading the blind." He had just been told that the engine was sucking in used, overheated air from inside the fender. Camry didn't do that. The Camry engine got fresh outside air, the way a car was supposed to. "They designed themselves into a box and they don't seem to know how to get out of it."

The engine cooling guys were young and cocky; they held all the cards. The engine was the car's big muscular heart, the air conditioning was more like its fingers and toes. But Mary Anne Wheeler was formidable; she had gotten in early and staked out her turf before the magnitude of the air shortage became apparent. Then she dug in. Her climate control division was headed by W. C. "Billy" Ford Junior. And in a crunch was Landgraff really going to call *him* up and threaten him like he did everybody else? Although, come to think of it, she said at one point, maybe there had been such a call. . . .

Once everybody recognized that the problems could be solved with some creative and cooperative engineering, things started to sort themselves out. And really, climate control hadn't fared too badly. One of their critical measurements—the pressure of the Freon inside the compressor—was targeted at 300 pounds per square inch at idle, and they had come in close to it, at 312. The lower the figure, the less wear and tear on the compressor and the longer its life span. Most of the testing by both teams in the nation's hot spots during the summer of 1994 was to confirm that everything worked and to fine-tune what didn't. Just ahead, in November, were the two events that signaled the end to design and development: the executive sign-off drive and the final engineering sign-off.

But the battles had left a residue of ill will between the veterans of climate control and the young hotdogs from engine cooling.

As WANDLESS WAITED for his colleagues, the sun dropped behind a ridge; streaks of iridescent pink illuminated the sky above the shadowy peaks. Wandless reached for the mobile phone and dialed the Marriott Residence Inn in Vegas, hoping to locate Peter Charlick, the engine cooling trip mother. His room didn't answer.

A young man came out of the casino. He had shaggy black hair and a beard, and he was wearing black pants and a T-shirt that said "Golden Nugget—Searchlight." He looked like he belonged on the streets of New York, but out of his mouth came a western twang. He looked the camouflaged auto over. "What's this car?" he asked. "Is this an Acura?"

"Why?" asked Wandless, stalling.

"My girlfriend saw three others just like it, sitting there with trailers."

Wandless snapped to attention. "Which way did they go?"

"Now what model car is it?" the guy in black asked, cagey.

"American," Wandless said.

The young man went back into the casino and returned with a slender, long-haired young woman in shorts, who said she saw the cars headed north, toward Vegas. Wandless got back on the mobile phone. Finally he reached Charlick.

"Peter, have you got our trailers?"

"They're our trailers now," Charlick said.

When Wayne Williams arrived a few minutes later, Wandless recounted the conversation. "I said, 'I suppose we're going to have to come and get them. Can you drive down and meet us?'

"He said, 'You're only a half hour away. Come in and get them.' "

THE LAST THING the climate control guys felt like doing was driving to Vegas, then turning around and driving for another hour back to Laughlin, at the foot of Davis Dam, where they were spending the night. The next day they would rise early to drive the dam road with the trailers, then return them to Ford's proving grounds. The engine cooling guys were heading for Death Valley, where temperatures were even higher than in Arizona, and the highways in and out offered long steady grades of seven to nine degrees.

Len Flack had lucked out, staying behind in Laughlin to work the data from the "pull-downs" they had been doing in Lake Havasu City for the past two days. Pull-downs were to air conditioning what the Bemidji warm-ups were to the heating system. Cars "soaked" in full afternoon sun until the inside temperature hit 160 degrees. Then four people jumped in—one at a time, so the hot air didn't rush out through an open door—and drove around for half an hour with the system on maximum cool, recording the time that elapsed as everyone in the car cooled off from "hot" to "comfort." Until a few years ago they had done these tests in Phoenix, but the city's humidity had increased as a growing populace planted yards, gardens, and trees; now clouds often blocked the sun's rays. Lake Havasu City, in western Arizona, was convenient to Kingman, where Ford had a proving ground. They stayed at the Xanadu Condo Resort, which each year commissioned T-shirts for the Ford visitors. More pleasant in winter than summer, the town aspired to be a major tourist destination. In addition to its location on a large reservoir, Lake Havasu was the home of London Bridge, which was bought in 1968 for $2.5 million by Havasu founder Robert P. McCulloch, a power tool magnate. Amid much British breastbeating, the bridge was dismantled stone by stone in London, shipped to Arizona, and rebuilt over a channel in the lake.

As the neon Vegas skyline lit up the sky ahead, Williams was still stewing over Darrel Wandless's exchange with Pete Charlick. His voice sputtering over the two-way radio, Williams managed to work in a dig at Charlick, "a University of Michigan graduate." UM was to Ford engineering what Harvard was to its finance division. Engineers from lesser schools regarded UM grads as elitists. "If he says they're *his* trailers, we're out of here," Williams declared as they turned into the Marriott drive. He would skip the towing test, and the engine guys would have to return the trailers to King-man and screw up *their* schedule. They spotted the three U-Hauls in a corner of the motel parking lot.

Charlick, tanned with light brown hair, and his colleague, Andy Van Damme, another young engineer, came loping out in shorts and T-shirts, looking as if they were taking a break in a fraternity volleyball game. Why hadn't Williams left a message that they were late? Charlick asked. He and the other engine cooling guys waited in Searchlight for an hour, watching two cops run a speed trap.

Williams decided not to make a stand. Mechanic Gary Kraus hooked up the trailers. Watching the climate control entourage depart, trailers jiggling behind them, Charlick said they didn't have to do their own tests; they could use the data his team had collected. In his opinion, the climate control old-timers just wanted to demonstrate their disdain for the engine cooling team.

LIKE BEMIDJI, DEATH VALLEY was a mecca for test teams from various carmakers. Temperatures typically climbed to 120 degrees, hot enough to singe the feet of people standing in a parking lot who didn't know to wear rubber-soled shoes. In the spring, according to the guidebooks, the Death Valley desert was carpeted with brightly colored flowers. In the summer, however, it was a monochromatic brown, the colors of sand, boulders, gravel, dead wood, dried shrubs, parched earth. Hence some of the names: Funeral Mountains, Chloride Cliff, Mud Canyon, Salt Creek, Furnace Creek. "They don't call it Furnace Creek for nothing," said one engineer. "When it's windy and 120 degrees, you feel like you're standing in front of a furnace."

In 1849, emigrants heading for the California gold fields left their guide in search of a shortcut. They stumbled into the valley, and some never stumbled out. They burned wagons to cook their oxen; as the provisions gave out, they eyed one another hungrily. The heat could make people do crazy things, even today. George Bell had once shelled out $30 for a cap to ward off the Death Valley sun.

Because it was a national monument, the U.S. government required visitors to secure a permit. When the engine guys got to the visitors center the morning after the run-in with climate contol, Isuzu, Hyundai, Mercedes, and BMW had already signed in. Among tourists, the center was doing a brisk business on Death Valley history books.

The team of ten had three confirmation prototypes, wired with fifty data collectors; the most critical measurements were the temperatures of the engine oil, the power steering fluid, the transmission fluid, and the coolant going into the radiator. A computer lodged in the trunk logged readings at preset intervals. Back at the motel that night they would analyze the data. While driving, they could tune in a channel on a monitor up front. But for the most part they just drove, taking in the sights and trading observations over the two-way radios, as the computer did its job.

The day before, they had run an eighteen-mile stretch of Interstate 15 known as Baker Hill, southwest of Las Vegas, loaded to the gills with equipment and pulling the trailers, to test the system at high temperatures, high speed, and high loads. They could simulate the same conditions back home on computers and in the wind tunnel, but doing real-world tests provided an extra level of comfort. On hills, the Duratec engine, with more power than the base model Vulcan, could stay in a higher gear with a correspondingly lower temperature; in one instance the modular was at 280 degrees, the Vulcan at 312. Lower temperatures translated to less wear.

Baker Hill reminded Andy Van Damme of the breakdown scenes in *The Grapes of Wrath*. They had passed a Corvette in flames and dozens of cars with their hoods up. The highway was stained with coolant. Driving back and forth several times, the Ford team had counted seventy-five singed spots left by burning cars. Buses were going up the hill with their engines uncovered to maximize air intake. But for the hill, the town of Baker, California, population 650, appeared to have little reason to exist. The business district featured several garages with tow trucks, augmented by a couple of fast food restaurants, motels, and not much else. Baker claimed to have the "world's largest thermometer." It stood in a parking lot, towering over the one-story town.

D EATH VALLEY NOT ONLY drew prototypes but also paparazzi. Parked for lunch at a restaurant oasis, the Ford group caught several people with cameras peering at the camouflaged cars. The prototypes were especially vulnerable on the open road. Because the vinyl camouflage cover on the front of the car partially obstructed the front openings, they had permission to remove it during testing. That afternoon two guys in a white Mustang bird-dogged them, one guy hanging out the window with a camera as the other drove. Headed back to Vegas late in the afternoon, the Ford group pulled into a Shell station in the small town of Beatty to replace the camouflage. Two long-haired guys in a rusty Volkswagen bus from the sixties, en route to a Grateful Dead concert in Vegas that weekend, came over to ask what the prototypes were. "I could tell you but then I'd have to shoot you," said one of the engineers. It was a stock answer.

Just then a gray Chevy Cavalier pulled in and some aging tourist type in a baseball cap and dark glasses jumped out and started snapping photos of one of the prototypes. Three Ford guys ran to the car, waving their arms and yelling at him to stop. "Hold your hands up," he called back. "I want to take a picture." He snapped away with a big black Nikon as they stood in front to block his view.

A S HE DROVE AWAY from the Shell station, the man in the cap, Jim Dunne, allowed himself his customary moment of triumph. "Yes! No man alive is this good!" Dunne was the country's most notorious spy photographer. Even after three decades in the business, he still got a thrill when he nailed a target. Those poor engineers hadn't known *what* to do. He didn't mind having them in his picture, trying to block the view. It added drama.

Dunne had flown into Vegas that morning and rented an inconspicuous car: nothing red, four doors, please. The doors on a sedan were smaller and lighter, making it easier to pop in and out of than two-door coupes. He took Route 90 into the southern half of Death Valley, slowing down at the Furnace Creek country store where test teams sometimes made a pit stop. He registered at the visitors center and turned east on Mud Canyon Road. He was driving into the dusty little town of Beatty, where Mercedes rented the high school for its summer headquarters, when he saw the DN101 crew.

By now, he was quite familiar with the Taurus, and so were a growing number of Americans, thanks to his photos. Back in the fall of 1993, his shot of a structural prototype, its lowered snout in plain view, was published in a number of magazines and papers. A few months later, he'd been driving past the Ford pilot plant after a storm when he spotted two new DN101 confirmation prototypes in dishabille. He shot through the fence. What else could he do? "God sent a big windstorm down and blew the covers off the front end of the Taurus and the back end of the Sable."

In May 1994 several publications ran a Dunne photo of the DN101 station wagon, shot without camouflage. During a staff meeting, Landgraff asked how it happened. Tom Moran, who had investigated the incident, said the uncamouflaged wagon had been shipped in a covered truck from Romeo back to the Dearborn Proving Ground. Then someone from an electronics section drove it to the electronics Tech Center. "How long was the camouflage off?" one of the engineers asked.

"At least five-hundredths of a second," George Bell said.

For once Landgraff seemed stumped. "I have personally signed at least three letters on camouflage," he said. In Henry Ford's day there would have been an all-out witch hunt to find the culprit. Some engineers said the smartest response was to get out of the way when you saw a spy photographer. The worst thing that could happen was to be in the photo with the car.

Dunne would deliver his Nevada photos first to *Popular Mechanics;* he was its Detroit editor and author of a monthly column. But he was free to sell them elsewhere as well. At a minimum, a shot of a minor facelift of a minor model brought $150; a cover photo could bring $3,000. His work was in demand not only by the car 'zines but also by newspapers and business magazines, when they wanted photos to illustrate stories on a company's plans for the future. *USA Today* was a frequent customer.

Dunne did not claim to be an expert photographer. He operated with the finest point-and-shoot electronic equipment: a Nikon 8008, with two lenses, a 35- to 105-millimeter zoom, augmented by a doubler, and a 500-millimeter telephoto. If a photo were fuzzy or out of focus, so much the better. "It adds to the mystique." His computer artist could switch backgrounds, change color, graft a partial shot onto another, or simulate an entire model from some strategic details.

His greatest coup had been right here in Death Valley, when he nabbed the 1986 Corvette for *Car and Driver.* "We'd kill for that photo," an editor at the magazine had told him. Dunne chased it for two days, but the car was too fast. Finally he hired a helicopter. They flew over the Corvette, and landed two miles ahead, kicking up a cloud of dust. The Corvette stopped, and two guys got out to see what was going on. "I hop out," said Dunne. "Click, click, click."

On vacation in northern Michigan, Dunne once happened across an advertising shoot of the 1977 Monte Carlo. As company people tried to shoo him away, a model tore off a wraparound skirt to shield the car. In telling this story, Dunne delivered his punchline with an impish smile. "She gave her all." Another time he snuck into a General Motors market research clinic in Dallas, where six different models were on display, and snapped photos right under the nose of security. At another GM clinic in a convention center near Chicago, he was not so lucky. Walking in to case the building, he was stopped by a guard who recognized him from his picture. "We've been waiting all week for you," the guard said. GM called the local police chief. Although he had committed no crime—he wasn't even carrying his camera—the chief told him to get out of town, as if this were the Old West, and he were a gunslinger. It was *too* choice.

One might say that snapping prototypes in Death Valley was like shooting fish in a barrel. But Dunne had his standards when it came to wordplay. "I would never use a cliché like that." Often he flew into Phoenix and followed a fertile route past the proving grounds of Ford, Chrysler, General Motors, Nissan, and Toyota. It was not this easy back in Detroit, where General Motors had planted evergreens at its proving ground in Milford to block the view of a straightaway and Chrysler had put up a wall at another prime location. When another photographer appeared on his favorite hill overlooking GM's test track, Dunne decided to take action. He drove over to the GM guard shack. "I don't know if you're interested," Dunne told the guard, "but there's some guy on the hill up there taking photos." He waited five minutes. Sure enough, here came the GM guards. "As soon as they chase him off, I go park my car and go up there."

His stakeout locations were secret, his company sources "deep throats." Off the job, however, Dunne was anything but furtive. In Detroit, he had a radio show and a wide circle of friends. He was an institution among automotive scribes, many of whom had written about him for their publications. His annual Christmas lunch at an atmospheric Hamtramck restaurant called the Ivanhoe was a much-sought-after invitation.

Dunne was very serious about his work, but he didn't take himself too seriously. When a writer proposed to do a piece for *The New Yorker*, Dunne protested, "I don't want to come off as a character." The writer asked what he meant. "Someone who's silly," Dunne said. And then he thought about it. After all, this *was The New Yorker.* "Oh, I don't care," he said.

WHILE THE COOLING TEAMS were out west, driving uphill, Jackie Stewart turned up once again at the Dearborn track to critique the new 1995 Lincoln Continental, the new 1995 Contour/Mystique, and, yes, the new 1996 Taurus/Sable. The Conscience was back! He was in rare form, leaping from car to car, thumping trunks with his fist, inviting people to watch them quiver. He sounded resigned as he unscrewed the Ford gas cap. "If you're going to keep this, put a hook on it or a magnet or clamps so when the tether does break, the customer has a place to put it."

Stewart was as close as Ford guys could come to an impartial review of their cars in the early stages. Everybody else who drove the car worked for Ford. "You're having Ford Motor Company people evaluate Ford Motor Company products," Landgraff said. "I don't know how you get at it objectively, but I think there's built-in bias. I probably have that too. Subconsciously, I can't get rid of it. So it's good to have a guy come in who's got no ax to grind like Stewart." But sometimes Jackie Stewart rubbed Landgraff the wrong way. At the moment Stewart was on a campaign to stamp out Ford's use of the word "craftsmanship."

"It's an error of judgment of our company to be talking about craftsmanship, because we don't have craftsmanship," Stewart declared to the troops who had gathered at the track to hear his critique. "If we improve to a level where we are really turning out superlative cars, what are you going to call it?" To see true craftsmanship, Jackie Stewart said, one had to look no farther than Jackie Stewart's feet, encased in soft handmade leather shoes, cut and sewn by some elf back in the Old Country. "Twenty-four years old and resoled once," said Jackie Stewart. "They take eight to ten months to make . . . on a last, individually by hand." Now *that* was craftsmanship, that and his handmade guns. He was wearing a white golf shirt with a small gold logo that said "Jackie Stewart Shooting School."

When it came time to discuss DN101, Tom Moran reported, "We're very close to Camry in the shift quality." *Very close.* Stewart pounced. "So you're saying 'almost as good as best in class'? We've got to get out of that. . . . I would not be here to be listened to if I had been almost as good as best in class. . . . You've got to win every time. Nobody remembers who's second." Stewart could go on like this forever. Landgraff shut him down. "Okay, let's not get too carried away with this, guys."

You had to listen carefully, but in fact the little Scotsman thought DN101 was dynamite. After driving a base model powered by a Vulcan, he said, "The engine performance was sweet. You've done a great job steering-wise. The integrity is superb." The modular four-valve: "The power felt good. The steering just as good." The station wagon. . . .

Okay, he didn't like the station wagon. There was too much "road noise from the back and it lacked steering precision. It was unacceptable." Noise and vibration were "poor throughout." But two out of three wasn't bad. And they were still working on the wagon.

As the summer wore on, Landgraff was having trouble keeping people out of the DN101 cars. One Monday he got a memo that "Newman" had driven a prototype: "Newman" liked this, and "Newman" said that. "Newman, who's Newman?" he asked Tom Moran. "Newman" turned out to be actor Paul Newman, who was a friend of vice-president Neil Ressler. Landgraff threw up his hands. "Who's running this program? An actor's driving our cars and making recommendations." Next, an influential group of dealers finagled their way in without Landgraff's knowledge. He believed that exposing dealers to cars during development was a mistake. If they didn't like something, it would dampen their spirits, but they would have to sell it regardless. Sure enough, at a management review the company vice-president Bob Rewey said dealers were complaining about rear-seat headroom. It was true that there was an inch less than in the old Taurus because the roof of the new car had been lowered for the fast, bullet-shaped rear end. Landgraff refrained from reminding Rewey that he had sat in a mock-up two years ago and approved the dimensions. He did try to reassure him: in the prototype driven by dealers, the Lear-built seat was an inch too high, and the headliner was sagging. Still, Rewey wanted to check out the headroom himself; so they had to get a protoype and smash the rear seat down to the right dimensions. It was a pointless exercise. "If someone says they don't like the headroom, it's too late." But it was typical of what happened every time outsiders drove the car. Afterward Landgraff got a list of questions that took up his time and that of his engineers, who were still scrambling to meet deadlines.

The team's mission that summer was to wrap up its testing. Told at a briefing that the durability cars were behind schedule, owing in part to transmission foul-ups, Landgraff went into his attack mode, elbows on the table, gesturing with both hands, pointing rapidly with his index finger, and blinking rapidly at a group of nervous engineers.

"I don't give a shit what it takes. I want to talk to the test track guys. I want a plan to get this thing done by July 22. . . . We're gonna make the dates if I have to drive the goddamned car myself. I don't believe we're running seven days a week, twenty-four hours a day. I want engineers standing there so when this car fails like it always seems to do, they get it running again in twenty-four hours."

Tom Breault, who had just finished taking a Teleometrics course in management styles, watched his boss's display with newfound interest. Sometimes he was a 9,1 taskmaster. *"If it's somebody's fault I want to get that guy on the team so I can fire him."* Other times, he was a good guy 9,9 team manager. *"If you want my help I'll be glad to give it to you."* A shortage of fuel tanks. *"We can't run a car without tanks. . . ."* He would take care of it. *"I'm gonna call goddamned Dearborn [Stamping Plant]. . . . crapass tooling . . . now they've delayed the program."* Landgraff rehearsed what he would say. *"Bob, you totally screwed up. We need sixty tanks by Friday."*

And sometimes he didn't fit a category. Teleometrics didn't provide for a philosopher. *"I've made this speech a hundred times. If this was our own operation [heh-heh-heh], our own little company, we would have collapsed in a heap of rubble. To the extent we sit around this table, or a hundred other tables missing dates, it communicates that these dates don't really matter."*

THERE WAS NO SINGLE MOMENT when they finished. But on September 28, at the weekly meeting of the program steering team, Landgraff scanned the durability reports. "It's kind of done," he said, sounding surprised. Steve Kozak pointed out they hadn't found the usual sheet-metal cracks. "Except on the station wagon," said Tom Moran. "And you have to look very closely." Mark Jarvis reported the testing on electronics was 96 percent complete, with "no new failures." Mary Anne Wheeler's climate control tests were complete on the base car, with just one left on the cooling module. Chassis would be 93 percent done by the end of September, 100 percent by November 24. George Evalt said there was one more test on the Duratec engine.

"That's the last test to run on the four-valve?" Landgraff asked.

"Yes," said Evalt.

"The transmission's not experiencing any failures with the various forms of testing that are going on?"

"No," Evalt said.

Larry DeFever from metal stamping reported that the assembly tools were on schedule, and tool tryouts were starting. "And the tryouts are on schedule."

About all Landgraff could find to worry about were how the fenders and deck lids fit . . . and, oh yes, the gimps. "The sun has not set on this one."

Sayonara

F ORD MOTOR COMPANY
was crashing down around him. Whole divisions were disappearing. Management pyramids were collapsing. In its biggest reorganization ever, tagged
Ford 2000, the company was fusing its European and United States automotive operations into a single empire, and simultaneously reconstituting product development as a 30,000-man technocracy. When the millennium
arrived, Ford would be nimble, Ford would be global. Whatever, the turmoil
was consuming too much of Dick Landgraff's time. He vowed not to go to
any more management thumbsuckers on the future of Ford. "I've already
been to two of those meetings," he said at his May 2 staff session, muttering
about the one in "Toronto . . . three break-out rooms. . . ."

But when Landgraff was summoned that June to London with other E-
Roll executives, he went after all. Everybody knew the Reorg, as they were
calling it at the moment, was another way to do more work with fewer people. So the big question was, who would get the jobs? They heard they might
find out in London, but when they piled into the London Hilton, Ed Hagenlocker, who was now the president of the bicontinental merger, Ford Automotive Operations, said there hadn't been time to work it all out. And maybe

that was just as well, thought Landgraff. He didn't think *he* was in danger, but he sure wouldn't want to fly back sitting next to an old colleague who'd just been canned.

The two-day London session was jammed with optimistic speeches from the moment it started to the moment it ended. When Landgraff walked into the cocktail hour the first night, Jacques Nasser, the new head of product development, was holding forth. "Nobody was drinking. It was nonstop business." The next day began with breakfast at 5:30 A.M. Landgraff was turned on, in spite of himself. "Some of the things we say we're going to try to do are kind of amazing, like make money on small cars, achieve a much higher return on assets than we ever have in the past."

Alex Trotman, who had started the whole thing, grabbed Landgraff during a break to inquire about DN101. "Is this car going to be pretty decent?" the new CEO asked.

"Fantastic," Landgraff assured him. He passed along Jackie Stewart's compliments.

"On time?"

"Yup. It's on time."

TROTMAN HAD ARTICULATED his idea for the reorganization on October 28, 1993, a scant three weeks after taking over as CEO, at a meeting of vice-presidents in Ford's London office. They had been instructed to come without backup books, the infamous black, three-ring binders chock full of information on every subject, which were a symbol of Ford's statistical mindset. Trotman wanted to know what was in their heads. He himself did little of the talking, owing to a horrible cold, instead channeling his questions through vice-chairman Lou Ross. The Ford managers were asked to rate the Big Three automakers and a fourth company, Toyota, from one to ten in such categories as development, investment efficiency, and engineering costs. For most of its history Ford had been content to follow the lead of General Motors. Nancy Badore, a Ford management coach in the 1980s, remembered asking a group of executives to articulate a corporate goal. The answer came back: "To be a better number two." No one these days thought General Motors was number one in anything but production. At the London meeting, by far the most tens were in the Toyota column. The experience was something like the drive Dick Landgraff took in the Camry. Did Ford always want to be second best?

Ford had been quietly churning out reports on Toyota since 1990, compiling statistics, sifting through books and studies, and interviewing academics, Mazda brethren, and past and present Toyota employees, including

Konen Suzuki, the president of Ford of Japan, who had been Toyota's general manager of corporate planning. Japanese culture was so different that some people questioned the value of studying a Japanese corporation. "The squeaky wheel gets the grease," people said in the West. In Japan, they said: *"But for the cry of the pheasant it would not get shot."* Toyota ran on precepts that sounded like Zen koans. *"Walk to where the problem is 100 times and you will find the solution."* Or this one from its "Ten Commandments of Management": *"Be just one personality. Scold yourself when you want to scold someone."* There was one plank in the company's operating philosophy, however, that Ford had no trouble comprehending. "If there is a road there, Toyota should be there."

From 1960 to 1990, Toyota had increased its production from 155,000 vehicles to 4.9 million; it was the world's third largest carmaker, after GM and Ford. The most compelling argument for using Toyota as a role model was financial; in years when Ford bled billions, Toyota made billions. Ford earnings seesawed; Toyota's crept steadily upward. The Japanese company was sitting on an estimated $20 billion to $30 billion in cash reserves.

So it was not much of a surprise to those in the know that the new global Ford bore a more than passing resemblance to the already global Toyota. Toyota did not track its profits by geographical regions. Ford would no longer force Ford of Europe and North American Automotive Operations to operate as profit centers, funding their own programs out of revenues. The two would become one: Ford Automotive Operations, under Ed Hagenlocker as president. Toyota organized product development around platforms that could be tailored to different markets. Ford product development henceforth would be carried out by five permanent teams called vehicle centers, organized around platforms: one in Europe for small cars like the Escort, and four in Dearborn for large front-wheel-drive cars like Taurus, large rear-wheel-drive cars like the Crown Victoria, light trucks, including the F-series and Explorer, and commercial trucks. The creaky old PEOs—body engineering, chassis, electronics, plastics—were shrinking to core groups of experts; their engineers were being divided among the five vehicle centers.

In April 1994, after briefing E-Roll executives in Toronto, Trotman announced the changes to the world. Neither Landgraff nor his colleagues had imagined the reorganization would be so extensive. Stunned executives didn't know what to say, except: "This is quite a challenge." It became a refrain.

People down in the basement understood what was happening better than most. The five platform teams were going to look a lot like DN101, only bigger—mini–Ford Motor Companies, peopled by designers, engineers, planners, financial analysts, marketing representatives. Like the team,

Ford 2000 was a matrix organization, with people in the vehicle centers reporting to two bosses: one in the vehicle center, the other in their functional area, such as chassis or body engineering.

While the actual reorganization wouldn't take place until January 1, 1995, the bosses were already changing. DN101's old vice-president, Ken Kohrs, was taking charge of the rear-wheel-drive vehicle center. The DN101's new boss was Jim Donaldson, a Scot who had been vice-president for truck operations. A "great guy," Landgraff said. He had worked for Donaldson before. As soon as Donaldson was appointed, the talking drums began to beat, carrying messages from office to office. Donaldson was said to dislike the big meetings that were popular at NAAO, where Ed Hagenlocker, the outgoing vice-president, had filled the executive conference room, telling his people to bring their people. According to one report, Donaldson walked into one of his first meetings and asked, "Who are all these people?" That's what Donaldson wanted to know. "Who are all these people and what are they doing in my meeting?" Henceforth meetings would be in his office around a table that sat maybe ten people. Also, he closed the door at the appointed hour. Anybody who was late had to knock and the vice-president would open the door personally. And teams. The tom-toms suggested Donaldson didn't really trust them. Someone once had started to tell Donaldson, "The team believes . . ." And Donaldson had been heard to say, "Team? What do they know?" He called engineers "plumbers," joking no doubt. But they didn't think it was funny.

Donaldson's boss was another stranger, Jacques Nasser, a Lebanon-born Australian, who went by "Jac." Most recently chairman of Ford of Europe, he was now the product development group vice-president, presiding over all five vehicle centers. Nasser was telling people to think of him as a product guy, not a finance guy, but everybody knew better. He had a reputation as a cost-cutter and head-chopper, "Jac the Knife." Within months Nasser was being mentioned as second in line for the chairman's spot when Trotman retired, right behind Hagenlocker, or maybe even first, if Hagenlocker slipped. The net result of these appointments was that three of the four people in the chain of command above Landgraff—Trotman, Nasser, and Donaldson—were short men who spoke with accents.

During the spring and summer of 1994, a Ford 2000 transition team composed of vice-presidents and staff holed up in tiny cubicles on the seventh floor of World Headquarters, planning the details of the reorganization. "Heaven on Seven," they called it. Astonishing stories drifted back to the basement of the Design Center. The veeps, clad only in casual clothes, had been seen answering their own one-button phones, while seated at computers, tapping out their own memos. Ken Kohrs was glimpsed emptying a wastebasket. This was roughly equivalent to the vice-president of the United States coming over to mow the White House lawn.

When the E-Roll positions were announced in August, Landgraff was on the list with a promotion to one of eighteen new positions called "vehicle line director." In addition to the Taurus/Sable, he was now in charge of the Lincoln Continental. Three other line directors were women; of 150 appointments, 9 percent went to females.

Three hundred people, 15 percent of those at grade thirteen and above, were asked to retire, sometimes in rather brutal fashion. Fred Simon, who had been the program manager of the Continental, was one of them. "I was called in by Ken Kohrs and offered early retirement. I was told it was purely voluntary. If I chose not to retire, I would be given a position at the PSR [Private Salary Roll], 'but you have no career path in Ford 2000 and can't ever have any hope of recovering E-Roll.'" Just fifty-three, Simon had joined Ford in 1964, to the dismay of his Jewish family. In those days, Jews didn't buy Fords, let alone work for the company that made them. They had not forgotten that Henry the First had published anti-Semitic articles in his newspaper, the Dearborn *Independent*, based on *The Protocols of the Elders of Zion*, a forged document that attributed the world's ills to a conspiracy of Jewish bankers.

But the setbacks Simon had suffered during his career had been prompted not by bigotry but efficiency. He had lost two grades during the infamous Blue Ribbon period in the early 1980s, which took its name from slash-and-burn committees that sought to thin management ranks. A decade later people still talked about having been "blue-ribboned." "It was like a scarlet letter," said planner Brad Nalon. One organization had a dozen grade thirteen to fifteen managers; overnight all but two were gone. In another organization, the grade-nine parking places were suddenly empty. Everybody had been bumped back to eight. People fled overseas, where grade levels were protected. In those days an overseas assignment was bad for careers, but not as bad as Blue Ribbon. Dick Landgraff, a grade sixteen, was bumped down two levels, and his boss was demoted. The boss's reaction was a class act, according to Landgraff. "He dropped his keys to his E-Roll car on his desk, got in a Chrysler, and left." Later he became a Chrysler vice-president.

Having recovered from Blue Ribbon, Simon in recent years had become a disciple of Peter Senge, an MIT management philosopher and author of *The Fifth Discipline*, which laid out the architecture of an enlightened "learning organization." As the Lincoln Continental program manager, Simon brought in Senge consultants to work with his team. Informed of Simon's career crisis, Senge telephoned Kohrs on his behalf. Simon was invited to a second meeting; there was coffee on the table, kind words, but no new job.

As more new positions were announced that summer and fall, DN101 managers scanned the lists for their names. Among those who came up short was Tom Breault, a large, good-humored, bespectacled engineer, respected for his competence and concern; he made time for his people, the packagers, whether their problems were professional or personal. Wendy Dendel looked to him as a management ally on team projects. Moreover, Breault had just been assigned to Atlanta for a year as the DN101 team's point man on the launch. It seemed particularly unfair to ask him to spend a year away from home and simultaneously hand him a demotion. His people tried to make sense of what had happened. Breault didn't politic enough; he didn't speak out enough. Tom Gallery, one of Breault's engineers, thought the demotion might be a payback by the planning community. In the early days of DN101, some planners had sought supervisory engineering positions to bulk up their résumés. Breault had turned them down. Some blamed Landgraff for not protecting team members; it was well known that the Maximum Leader had not attended sessions where personnel decisions were made. Tom Moran, another popular DN101 manager, had also slipped a grade and so had the business planner Brent Egleston.

Breault, too, had suffered during Blue Ribbon. A grade-nine weight specialist on the first Taurus, he was bumped to a grade eight and sent to an NVH lab in Allen Park, to do vibration analysis, which was highly mathematical and the very thing he disliked most in engineering school. In the next decade he recovered his grade and moved up to a twelve. Breault took this latest demotion stoically. He said he would worry about his future when he got back from the year in Atlanta.

I N T OYOTA PRODUCT DEVELOPMENT, the equivalent of a program manager was a heavyweight engineer called a *shusa*. Under Ford 2000 the *shusa* spot would likewise be reserved for engineers. On DN101, the position, now called chief program engineer, was going to George Bell; essentially, he got Landgraff's old job. He still reported to Landgraff, who had ratcheted up a notch, but showed no signs of letting go of day-to-day Taurus activities. Steve Kozak's promised promotion had come through, and then some. He was taking the place of Andy Benedict, head of DN101 body engineering, who had been promoted off the team. Kozak lept from a grade ten to a grade thirteen.

Engineers now had a lockhold on product development. In addition to chief program engineers, there were executive engineers, chief engineers, chief vehicle engineers, engineering managers, and engineering directors. If engineers had solidified their gains, confusion now surrounded the role of planners. Ford 2000 was largely silent on their responsibilities. Even engineers felt sorry for them. "The planners got chopped off at the knees," said Rick Schifter, the bodyside engineer who was taking over for Kozak. "They got drilled. In my personal opinion as an engineer, it needed to be done in some way, but it was awfully extreme." Planners with engineering degrees were scrambling for technical positions, among them Brad Nalon's two junior planners, Ron Heiser and Pete Sharpe. Heiser went to the DN101 sheet-metal team, Sharpe to chassis.

Ford management staged a final mega-meeting that year in Orlando for its top 1,800 managers. It was as much a pep rally as a training session. Ed Hagenlocker kicked it off with an invitation to sign a "Wall of Commitment," maybe thirty feet long and twenty feet high, pledging allegiance to the goals of Ford 2000. "My father was instrumental in creating Ford of Europe," said Edsel Ford, in an impromptu speech from the floor. "And I'd like to tell you all that I'm sure if he was here today, he would be happy to sign 'the Wall.' " Three days later Trotman closed the meeting with a quote from Shakespeare. "All things are ready if our minds be so." Then he asked the assembly, "Are you ready?"

"Yes," they roared back, with loud applause.

George Bell was moved. The new CEO seemed to be "really connected with the company. He's not just an intellectual leader, he's an emotional leader as well."

To be sure, there was at least one manager (not Landgraff) who thought it was merely a "media event without the media," and who wondered irreverently how much it had cost to fetch, fete, and feed so many hundreds there in Orlando, at the Dolphin and Swan Hotels. Five million dollars? Ten? "Why not take it all and give it to the 2,000 people who went?"

In some of the smaller meetings at Orlando, people worried about the potential for chaos on January 1, when Ford 2000 officially began. It had taken seven months to assign the E-Roll positions, two months for second-tier managers. And now just two months remained to post 12,000 engineers. People were really nervous. Andy Benedict went to one meeting where there was a review of matrix organizations that had failed in the past. "People wanted to know," he said, " 'if this is so difficult to make work and it's failed so many times, why do it?' " The answer seemed to be that it was a way to give people two jobs. In the vehicle centers, for example, engineers would report to both their program engineer and a manager in their specialty. "More for less," Landgraff said crisply. "It's the story of world capitalism in the last half of the twentieth century."

The Ford finance community, for so long a center of power and prestige, saw little to applaud in the reorganization. Like everybody else, financial analysts were being split up among the vehicle centers. At Orlando, Trotman had made some joking remark about the finance group—the beanies having to give up power, now it was the engineers' time. The remark was widely circulated back in Dearborn, absent his humorous tone.

With two car lines to supervise, and a deep reluctance to delegate, Landgraff's own workload had approximately doubled. Although the design engineers had finished their work on DN101, the always frantic manufacturing launch was about to begin, triggering a new wave of changes for ease of assembly. He had no intention of abandoning the car now, even though it would mean frequent trips to Atlanta. Meanwhile, the Continental was in the styling phase of a redesign, and Landgraff was leading daily walkarounds in the studio, just as he had once done with the Taurus.

He could hardly find time to shave, let alone buy shaving cream. Quick stops at a market on the way home to pick up something for dinner were out of the question. One night he told Connie Landgraff they had to have a serious talk. For several years, since their three children had grown and gone, she had been working part time as a medical case manager. He didn't tell her she *had* to quit. He said, "One of us has to quit our job, and it's not going to be me."

W HEN DICK LANDGRAFF MET a young pediatric nurse named Connie at a party in 1964, he decided she was just what he was looking for in a wife, he could stop right now. "She had her head screwed on right, not a dizzy sort of person who didn't seem to know what she wanted to do. She came from a good family; she had a job. She was interested in family life. . . . Some people don't seem to have roots or stability. She was never that way." He warned her how their life together would be. "I told her at one time, you're going to have to conform to the life I lead. I've got to go do my thing and work. If it takes ten hours a day, it takes ten hours a day." Ten hours, as it turned out, was a short day. Often it was twelve or longer.

Even before they married, his work interfered. Her mother had booked the church and the country club on Grosse Ile, a narrow island in the Detroit River, where Connie's father was a doctor. Then Landgraff realized his work schedule conflicted. "I'm not going to be there, Connie," he said. Some men might have found it easier to negotiate a schedule change. But they moved the wedding date. Connie could laugh about it now. "I should have known the rest of my life would be like that." Connie's mother had told her daughter never to marry a doctor, as she had done. After she got to know her son-in-law, she thought his schedule was worse than that of her husband.

By any measure, Ford was a good company to work for. In 1993, mid-level secretaries earned over $40,000 a year. Grade nines and grade tens were raking in $70,000 to $90,000 a year. And grade sixteens like Landgraff were in the $200,000 range. In good years, there was profit sharing in the lower echelons; at grade eleven, bonuses kicked in; at Landgraff's level, they could amount to more than a year's pay. Grades thirteen to fifteen, private salary roll, and those above were eligible for stock options and life insurance. Regardless of grade, there were generous medical benefits, dental benefits, education benefits, and disability benefits. Every year there were twenty-one days available for illness and "personal business," although it was not necessarily politic to take them all. Nor did most people have time. The shutdown during Christmas week was a recreational dividend above whatever amount of vacation people had coming to them. And then there were the cars. At a minimum people could get up to four a year at just above dealer cost. They bought them for themselves and their families. But grades nine and up got cars on cut-rate leases, serviced at a company garage, with cheap insurance that was the chief benefit for a family with teenagers. For the executive roll people like Landgraff, the car and insurance were free, and so were the service, gas, and a daily wash. All they had to do was periodically fill out a questionnaire about the car's performance.

Those who climbed the rungs paid the price in their private lives. "The grade nines and tens are the workhorses of the company," George Bell said once, "the guys putting in seventy-hour weeks. You have very little time for anything." Marriages suffered, as he knew from personal experience. "When you get married as a kid, that's not the deal you made. . . ." He met the woman who would become his second wife when he was on assignment to Mazda, spending a third of the time overseas. He told her early on: this was how it was going to be.

For a time the Landgraffs had lived in Grosse Pointe, an old-money Detroit suburb where other husbands on the block got home at 5 or 6 P.M. "What's wrong with them?" Connie thought. Her husband never got home before 7 P.M. She gave up her job and raised their three children. She went to the school conferences alone. When Landgraff was assigned to Mexico, he deposited Connie and the three children in a house with six bathrooms and an army of Spanish-speaking underlings. The next day he left on a trip. Connie didn't even know her phone number.

"We love the perks," said Bev Ogren, wife of Dick Ogren, Ford friends of the Landgraffs. The couple had four children. "We love the way we live. It would be nice to have it all." Once Ogren was asked to accept a six-month assignment in Brazil. The family took a vote on whether he should go. "There were five no votes and one yes. He went."

Business planner Rich Pettit's wife, Sharon, once gave him an anniversary gift with a barbed message: a gold heart with their telephone number on one side, and on the other, "Please phone home." One Ford wife with breast cancer asked a friend to take her for the first round of chemotherapy. She thought about asking her husband, but he had just started a new assignment. "I would have felt guilty."

Something Dick had once said was so firmly implanted Connie could summon it up to her memory screen as if it were on a save-get key. "This guy's wife wanted him home at 5 o'clock everyday, and he decided he would do it. He's stuck in the same job he had thirty years ago." There was one family surely that was not enjoying Ford's full bounty. *The good life.* And all because the wife screwed it up.

Looking back on her own thirty-year marriage, Connie was neither bitter nor regretful. She had long since made her peace with her husband's priorities. "I feel that Ford has come first in his life. . . . I was in it by myself raising my kids. I accepted that was my life and that was what I was going to do."

"She says she raised our kids entirely on her own," Landgraff said in a separate discussion. Each knew how the other told the story. "It wasn't that bad. . . . My memory is, she did 80 percent, but she didn't do 100 percent."

Time had not diminished Landgraff's devotion to his job. "Dick, you *have* to be there," Connie protested, when her husband told her over dinner he'd have to miss an important wedding to be in Florida for a DN101 event. Her voice carried a note of resignation.

Connie Landgraff was by no means the only car widow to whom it occurred from time to time that they were not alone so much because their husband was making the world a healthier place, or a safer place, or a place where justice ruled. They were not married to a doctor or a cop. No lives hung in the balance. They were being jilted by a car! "I tell him, what's the big deal about the car?" Connie said. "It's going to be there tomorrow."

In return for Landgraff's devotion to Ford, they had reaped the benefits. Although the Landgraffs did not live ostentatiously—their buff-colored French colonial home on a leafy street in Bloomfield Hills was comfortable but by no means a palace—they had no financial worries. They had been able to put three kids through college, buy a second home in a Colorado ski resort, and go on yearly trips and cruises.

And when her husband said he needed her help, Connie gave notice to her employer. Truth to tell, she didn't mind all that much. What was supposed to have been a part-time job had swelled to almost full time. She had a new granddaughter, her younger son was getting married, the house in Colorado needed attention. And stuff wasn't getting done at home. She knew her husband loved to smell dinner in the kitchen when he walked in. He liked fresh flowers in the house. Any lingering regrets she may have had were put to rest after a few weeks. She was so busy she found it hard to imagine how she had ever found time to work.

O N N O V E M B E R 6 , A S U N D A Y , Tom Moran was lounging around the Shilo Hilltop, a hotel in Pomona, California, with little to do but ponder the arrival that evening of seventeen executives and executive stand-ins for the two-day sign-off drive that began the next day. This drive, to win final approval from top management, was a ritual of little utility, because it was far too late for major changes, but great significance, because these were impor-tant people. In a sense, it was a performance review for the DN101 team. Said Moran, the vehicle development manager, "The guys that run the com-pany are coming in and telling us whether or not we've done what they paid us to do for the last three years." Moran had the weathered face and casual authority of a battleship commander who had faced many crises, and the gravelly voice of a lifelong smoker. In twenty-six years, he said, this was the first car for which he had to make no excuses. "The car is right and it's a wonderful automobile that will kick Camry right in the butt." He wasn't one to get carried away, but this was "*almost* an emotional event." Once approved, DN101 could proceed to the final engineering sign-off on November 15, and thence to launch. "At this point, we're really done with the car," George Bell said, "except for preparing for mass production."

Tom Moran's development guys had been planning the drive for three months. They had to ensure that the prototypes—two sedans and two wag-ons—looked and performed at Job One level, and they had to invent a route that would incorporate a variety of road conditions with a pleasant restau-rant for lunch. Each executive got an elaborate sign-off binder that detailed DN101 test results on every system. They had chosen a route in the L.A. area over one farther north, where the 1994 Lincoln Continental had done poor-ly in its final market research. Why jinx DN101? After driving the Conti-nental, customers had rated it lower in performance and several other critical categories than the Cadillac Seville and the Lexus. Jackie Stewart had also panned the car. To counter the criticism, the Continental guys changed the final drive ratio of RPM to wheel revolutions. In so doing they threw the program into upheaval and a lot of development work was incomplete at sign-off. The Continental hadn't yet gone on sale, and already Landgraff, the new boss, had a morale problem on his hands. He felt sorry for the Conti-nental guys, who "thought they had delivered a pretty damned good prod-uct." To his way of thinking, the problems were the fault of Ford management, which had established the Lexus as a target without giving the Continental program sufficient resources.

Rarely was a car program in such good shape that someone in Moran's position would find himself on the afternoon before the drive with time to spare, his engineers scattered. Usually they all worked until midnight, updating the sign-off books, fine-tuning the cars, maybe substituting one pair of tires for another. The only person down in the garage at the moment was Dennis Morgan, who was programming in some L.A. radio stations and loading the compact disc player. The execs could listen to the soundtrack from *The Big Chill, The Best of Mozart,* or *The Best of Van Morrison.* George Bell was heading to the hotel dining room where a Ford crew was eating a big Sunday lunch. The chief program engineer had not received a last-minute flurry of assignments from Landgraff, a good sign. "Dick is like a canary in the mine. If he starts getting agitated, you better start looking around at what's agitating him. It's probably going to be coming after you next."

Tom Moran had been to enough of these events to have a pretty good idea what the next two days would bring. It was highly unlikely that people would endorse the cars 100 percent. They didn't earn big bucks to keep their mouths shut. They would feel compelled to offer criticism, which Moran predicted "will fall into two categories: Things you *must* do before you can build the car—these would be major risks. Others are 'personal quirks' if you will . . . things they would like to see a little different. These will be running changes on '97 or '98."

With Ford 2000 on the horizon, this drive had additional significance. Even before the reorganization, the 1996 Taurus carried a lot of baggage that had nothing to do with trunk space. The happy-faced family sedan with the all-American pedigree embodied Ford's ambitions to wrest both sales and self-respect from Japan. Now, the Taurus would be a report card on the dedicated, collocated teams that were the cornerstone of Ford 2000. The sign-off drive would send a signal to the rest of the company. "If it were to come off badly," George Bell said, "it would cast doubt on the Ford 2000 effort."

Owing to the reorganization, some of the managers in the large front-wheel-drive vehicle center who were coming to California were new in their positions; they had not been involved with DN101 and were, in a sense, not bound by the agreements. That was especially true of two of the three vice-presidents, Jim Donaldson and Jacques Nasser. When Landgraff rolled the dice for Camry, Nasser had been in Europe, Donaldson in trucks. Nasser, in particular, was a question mark. Nobody knew much about his tastes, except what they had read in the papers: fast cars, Italian motorcycles, and antique watches. In fact, Nasser was a last-minute addition to the roster; he had not planned to come on the drive. As if to acknowledge the Taurus's symbolic value, he had changed his mind in Orlando. Both Nasser and Donaldson had skipped a meeting with the vice-premier of China to be at the DN101 sign-off. Donaldson revealed this tidbit at a late-night buffet after he and the other managers had checked in. "That's got to tell you something about how this company is changing," he said. Landgraff took the opportunity to remind the group of the DN101 mission. The next day, as they drove the California roads, he said, "Just look at how many Japanese cars there are out there. Forty, fifty, sixty percent of the market. DN101 is designed to get part of that back."

T HE GROUP OF TWENTY set out the next morning in pairs, driving five sedans and five station wagons, half of them green, on a route designed to expose the cars to stop-and-go in-town traffic, freeway travel, and twisting two-lane mountain roads. Besides the 1996 Taurus and Sable prototypes, there were two outgoing 1995 models, three Camrys, and an Accord wagon. They were linked by two-way radios, the electronic umbilical cords.

"Nice to drive," said Neil Ressler, vice-president for advanced vehicle technology, a Ford 2000 title, a few minutes into his drive rotation. He was piloting the base-model GL sedan into the mountains, taking curves at 55 miles per hour.

"I like the ride," said Glen Lyall, trying out the back seat; he had been Tom Moran's boss until the reorganization. "Basically, it's hardly moving around back here at all."

"You feel like you could drive a lot faster and be pretty safe at it."

Was it all going to be this easy?

"This car doesn't have any dual sunvisors," complained Bob Widmer, an engineering director in Ressler's division, when his turn came to drive the GL sedan. "I thought that was a standard Taurus feature forever and ever."

"I think it was part of the $50 cost reduction," said David Ford, no relation to the founder, who was Moran's new boss.

Widmer found fault with the transmission shifts, "not so slick." But he liked the handling. "It's very confident going around corners. . . . You like to have a car make you feel like you're a better driver than you are."

When Lou Camp got into the GL sedan, he commented on the Orient design right away. "The fabric has an antiquey feel," said Camp, the chief engineer for chassis. Not to his taste, but what did a chassis guy know? He guessed customers were clamoring for this kind of thing. "Ford fabrics have a reputation for being boring."

"The car sets up nicely to turn," said his driving partner Burt McNeal, the vehicle center's top engineer, during his turn at the wheel.

At the end of the day, everybody gathered back at the hotel for a debriefing. Tom Moran stood at a flip chart, prepared to write down comments. On the wall was a banner: "The DN101 Team has a passion for PRODUCT, People and Profits."

Moran started down the list of prototypes, beginning with the base model. "Is there anybody who believes we should not proceed to sign-off in a week?"

The criticisms, such as they were, sounded forced, and no one answered yes to Moran's question. David Ford noted that the car had missed some of its powertrain objectives; he thought the rear door was somewhat recalcitrant.

Nasser and Landgraff had felt a bump in shifting from first to second gear. Bob Widmer didn't bring up the sunvisors.

"Okay to proceed," Moran wrote.

He moved to the high-series car. "Any reason not to proceed?"

"No," said Nasser. "Superb car."

The only strong objection to the station wagon came from Paul Morel, representing Ford Divison sales, who thought the Vulcan engine did a poor job moving the car off the mark, a characteristic known as "performance feel." He realized, he said, that the high altitude at which they had been driving was a factor, but he still thought it was "mediocre." Landgraff said there was no way they were going to change the final drive ratio as the Continental had done.

"Our history is that we're still trying to make changes," interjected Neil Ressler. "If tomorrow were Job One, we'd be trying to make changes."

"We're going to have some press guys driving the car who will call it anemic," Morel warned.

"I don't think so, Paul," Landgraff said. "Because we're not going to let them drive in high altitudes." Everybody laughed, the tension defused.

"Okay to proceed," Moran wrote.

Engineers were always suspicious of marketing. Perhaps Morel was laying the groundwork for a future defense if wagons sold poorly. But anyway, only Landgraff, Donaldson, or Nasser could decide to hold up the program at this late stage. And there didn't seem much danger of that. At a dinner later than evening, Nasser was effusive in his praise. "This car deserves every single accolade it can get."

O N   T H E   M O R N I N G of the second day, the people who had driven sedans the day before switched with those who had driven station wagons. They would drive for just half a day, and more than a few were grateful. The awful truth was now apparent: there was so little to criticize that the drive was boring. "This sign-off has less emotion than normal," said Dick Ronzi, the chief engineer for transmissions, sounding almost wistful. "In others, the issues are strong. There's more animation, more questions, more car-to-car talk."

"In the past we would hear, 'We haven't done that yet,'" said Bob Damron, the body and assembly DN101 launch captain, during his turn at the wheel of the base model sedan. "'We haven't calibrated it.' 'That'll be ready for the FEU car.'" The Field Evaluation Unit was a pre-production car, to be built during the launch period and used to pinpoint potential Things Gone Wrong. "This is the first time the car's been really ready."

On a break Moran had to lecture two of his guys who had been joking back and forth over the radios. He didn't want the execs to think they were getting complacent.

THE SECOND DEBRIEFING produced another round of "okay to proceed" conclusions. Donaldson, the new DN101 vice-president, had the only major reservation. "I know you're all going to giggle," he began. His objection was to the way the flip-fold console, which housed the cup holders, opened out, blocking the ashtray. As he spoke, Donaldson was holding aloft a cigarette. And his boss Jacques Nasser smoked cigars. There were smiles but nobody giggled. "It's going to hurt us on fleet," Donaldson predicted. "People do sometimes drink and smoke at the same time. If ever there were people who liked to smoke and have their coffee . . ." Those people would be the salesmen and other heavy users of fleet cars. And maybe Jim Donaldson. The Ford vice-president was also displeased that the grab handles had been removed from the station wagon to save weight. Landgraff made no promises about the ashtray. But he did say he would put the grab handles back.

NINETEEN

DN101 Goes Public

SINCE 1988, WHEN the city
of Detroit expanded the floor space in Cobo Hall, its riverside convention
center, the Detroit Auto Show had grown from a respectable regional event
into the biggest and flashiest of the nation's seventy-odd auto expositions, a
two-week extravaganza of parties, press conferences, speeches, forums, con-
ventions, new vehicle debuts, futuristic concept car displays, industry awards,
and TV and radio broadcasts. Reborn as the North American International
Auto Show, Detroit had eclipsed the other major domestic shows in Chicago, Los Angeles, and New York and now ranked with Paris, Geneva, Frank-
furt, and Tokyo as a must-see. The night before it opened, a black-tie charity
preview, dubbed "prom night in Detroit," drew upwards of 10,000 guests for
the first look at each year's car crop: some 700 gleaming cars and trucks, displayed in carpeted architectonic pavilions, their prized bodies tended by
scores of workers wielding feather dusters, rags, and spray bottles.

The media and the manufacturers played off each other. The more new
car introductions, the more media representatives, the more media, the more
new car introductions. In 1995, some 4,500 international and national journalists would pour into Detroit, of whom perhaps half to two-thirds were

bona-fide reporters, photographers, and camera crews, the remainder having only tangential connections—a friend or a neighbor willing to fabricate a credential, perhaps—to actual media outlets but an irresistible urge to run with the pack. For three days these people would flock from press conference to press conference, scheduled back-to-back in thirty- to sixty-minute segments, trolling for news, features, and interviews.

For most of the year car company executives dwelt in remote towers, their schedules or proclivities rarely permitting a return phone call, especially to lesser publications. Here they not only were available for hours on end, but occasionally could be found wandering around the displays unprotected by the usual phalanx of secretaries and public relations people. A hardworking scribe could harvest enough quotes for two or three months of stories. And even someone from *Tirekicking Today* or *Fleet Management Journal* who was usually not on any company's A-list could grab some quotes. *Business-Week* sent three reporters and an editor. The *Wall Street Journal* turned out its bureau of six and then some. For journalists looking for handouts, the show was a bountiful cornucopia of breakfasts, lunches, and dinners, with refreshments at every briefing. A press room was stocked with drinks and snacks.

So, really, it was a foregone conclusion that Ford would unveil the Taurus and Sable at the 1995 Detroit Auto Show, even though it took place the first week of January, ten months before the cars would go on sale. In February, Ford would take the wraps off the station wagon at the Chicago Auto Show, and in April the SHO would debut in New York. The marketing guys wanted everyone to understand the difficulty these early introductions posed for them: they would have to sell almost a full year's production of 1995 Tauruses and Sables to a public that might prefer to wait for the new and improved version they had seen in the press. But to pass up Detroit would be to sacrifice unparalleled publicity, heightened by the suspense and expectation that were, the company hoped, building to a fever pitch. And if the Taurus didn't make its move, Chrysler's new minivan, also slated for introduction, would get all the attention.

CHRYSLER CORPORATION WAS to Ford Public Affairs what Toyota was to product development: The Enemy. Thanks to adroit maneuvering over the past few years, Chrysler had acquired an image as a hot, lean, nimble performer in the showroom and the boardroom. Graduates in transportation design lusted to work for the company that had minted the *cab-forward* Intrepid, the muscular Ram pickup, the clever little Neon.

This was quite a transformation. In 1989, with cars like the clunky Dodge Spirit and Plymouth Acclaim, Chrysler sales were in the sewer, the company's very survival in question. Seeking to persuade the world that Chrysler had a future, its public affairs department decided to invite the press into the studio for an early peek at the LH cars. Early? The cars wouldn't go on sale for three years. In automotive terms, this preview was the ice age. Next, Chrysler put reporters *in* prototypes and let them drive, eighteen months before production.

In 1991, still with little to show in the way of new product, Chrysler took reporters through an assembly plant under construction on Jefferson Avenue in Detroit, and touted the 1993 Jeep Grand Cherokee, to be built there. Reporters also toured the $1 billion Chrysler Technology Center going up in suburban Auburn Hills to house the new Japanese-style platform teams that would surely make the company a more efficient competitor. Company executives were made accessible. A reporter on a Chrysler "ride-and-drive," the standard product review, might find a vice-president in the back seat, chatting him or her up about new products. At the auto shows, where futuristic concept cars were displayed as novelties, Chrysler rewrote the rules by going ahead and building the ones that people liked. Its much-admired $50,000 Viper roadster, star of a short-lived NBC television show by the same name, had started life in 1989 as a Chrysler concept; in production, it came to symbolize the born-again, hard-charging company. The LH cars had resembled a concept car called the Millennium. To reporters, the possibility that the one-of-a-kind vehicles could evolve beyond techie toys made them more worthy of attention.

But it was at the Detroit Auto Show, where car companies went head-to-head for headlines, that Chrysler public affairs had distinguished itself with outrageous stunts to introduce new models.

In the typical time-honored new car "reveal," a middle-aged executive in a suit stood next to a sheet-covered model and read a speech stuffed with statistics; then the music came up, the lights came on, and—*voila!*—he pulled the sheet off. In 1992 Chrysler broke glass and broke tradition. Its new Jeep Grand Cherokee boldly slammed through a window into Cobo Hall, with Chrysler president Robert A. Lutz at the wheel, and Detroit mayor Coleman Young riding shotgun in a cowboy hat. That same year the Dodge Intrepid stole the show from the plain-jane 1992 Taurus, and the Viper went on sale. The following year, as 500 reporters surrounded a veiled Dodge Ram pickup, the glass-breaking stunt still fresh in their minds, Lutz assured them there would be "no monkey business." Then the real Ram dropped from the rafters. In 1994, to introduce the Chrysler Cirrus and Dodge Stratus, Chrysler had staged a skit with *Mission Impossible* star Peter Graves that included a modest explosion.

Chrysler was making not only headlines but money. In 1990, the stock was priced at $9 a share. By 1993 it was up to $42.50 a share. The day after the Cirrus and Stratus debuted it shot up to $56 a share. In 1994, earnings rose 246 percent and its sales were up 20 percent. Employee profit sharing averaged $7,500, an industry record. So what if quality was only average, or worse? *Consumer Reports* took the Intrepid off its recommended list after a couple of years on the market. It didn't seem to matter. A writer for the *Detroit News* gave a favorable review to a Dodge Ram pickup even though the brakes failed on the prototype he was driving. "Can this company do no wrong?" queried automotive columnist Paul Lienert.

A DECADE EARLIER, Ford had been the hot company with the savvy hype. The lavish introduction of Taurus I on January 29, 1985, took place in an MGM studio where scenes from *Ben-Hur* and *Gone with the Wind* had been filmed. Such was the anticipation that acceptances to the dinner gala far exceeded expectations. Limos, cars, and buses carrying 1,200 guests turned the MGM lot into an enormous traffic jam. Inside, in a bar area with a spaceship decor, R2D2-type robots milled about, carrying trays in their little robot paws.

The cars were onstage, shrouded by gauzy car-scale cones. A miniature satellite hovered over each table. At the appointed hour, scenes from space films flitted over the walls. The music, "Thus Spake Zarathustra," the theme from *2001*, built to a crescendo. Colored lights swept the room, the satellites descended, and the cones lifted to reveal two sedans and two station wagons. After a moment of silence that seemed to last forever, a kind of collective hysteria broke out. Caught up in the frenzy, CEO Philip Caldwell threw away his prepared notes like so much confetti and delivered a few extemporaneous remarks. In the audience, Caldwell's speechwriter Judith Mühlberg watched transfixed as the index cards sailed over one of the prototypes. She had labored on the speech much of the night before. Years later she would remember two things about the event: a flaming dessert and her speech floating through the air. The Taurus event had doubled as a retirement bash for Caldwell. Very early the next morning his successor, Don Petersen, called a meeting. The Taurus premiere had cost $1.6 million, he said. Never, never, never again, he told the public affairs staff, were they to spend that kind of money on a product debut.

Now Mühlberg was in charge of introducing the 1996 Taurus, Sable, and all other North American cars and trucks. A lifelong Republican from Wyoming, she had started her career in politics as a researcher for Pat Buchanan when he was President Nixon's speechwriter, then gone on to work for Republican honchos Donald Rumsfeld, Richard Cheney, and

David Gergen. When the Republicans fell from power, she took a job at Ford in government affairs and went to law school. Smart, well educated and conservative, Mühlberg had good credentials for corporate America. She also had the right stuff for public relations: energy, a sense of humor, and the personality of a cheerleader. With the Ford 2000 reorganization, Mühlberg had been boosted from her post as manager of corporate affairs to the top position in North American Communications. Ford was kicking off 1995 with America's best-selling car and winding up with the launch of the F-150 pickup, America's best-selling truck. In the next thirty-seven months, Ford would unveil twenty-seven new or redesigned products, including several Jaguars. If ever Ford were to snatch the limelight from Chrysler, the first auto show of 1995 was the time to begin.

But what an awkward time it was turning out to be. The year-end holiday calendar and some weird extended playoff arrangements involving both the NFL and NCAA had created a set of circumstances, Mühlberg said, that made Tuesday, January 4, 1995, "the absolute worst time to open an auto show." Someone said it couldn't happen again for seven years. But it was happening this year, on Ford's clock. For the Taurus and Sable intro, the company had the very first time slot on the first press day, an 8:30 A.M. breakfast. Here was the problem: to be there, reporters would have to cut short the New Year's holiday and travel on Monday. For European reporters the situation was more demanding: given flight limitations, they would have to travel on Sunday. Another drawback was the likely loss of televison crews to the sporting events. Still, you had to play the hand you were dealt. So Ford had plunged ahead gamely and reserved a large arena for the breakfast press conference, swearing the auto show organizers to secrecy so that Chrysler wouldn't have a clue that something extraordinary was in the works. Bids went out for a boffo stage event. But what if nobody came?

Thus was hatched a fail-safe plan to bring the media to Dearborn on December 6 and 7, brief them on the Taurus and Sable, allow them to interview Landgraff, Bell, Gaffka, and other team principals, provide photos, and then embargo the stories until the eve of the auto show. Talk about getting the jump on Chrysler! Reporters not only would have plenty of time to write, but their stories would appear even *before* the auto show began. It was, if not brilliant, quite clever. Then Ford would stage the breakfast introduction and snag even more publicity.

The press release announcing the events in early December could not mention Taurus or Sable. "FORD TO UNVEIL NEW TAURUS": That would be a story in itself. And if every news outlet in the world knew you were introducing the two cars, it would make the embargo extremely difficult to enforce. Secrecy was vital to the scheme. If Chrysler found out that a

Taurus debut was on the December agenda, there was no telling what they would do. When Ford's new front-wheel-drive Windstar minivan was on its way to dealers, Chrysler had the foresight to invite reporters to a sneak preview of *their* forthcoming minivan. Now every Windstar story mentioned the soon-to-appear Chrysler. "It's a brilliant tactic," Mühlberg said generously. "I admire it."

To lure the press to Dearborn without telling them the real reason, Mühlberg's group mapped out a two-day media menu that would begin with the introduction of a $3 million twelve-cylinder concept sports car called the GT90, loosely styled after the historic GT40 race car, "the Ford that beat Ferrari." For this event, the Design Center showroom would be decorated with flags and bleachers to evoke a mini Le Mans, where GT40s had won four consecutive races in the late 1960s. As the show began, the GT90 would rumble onstage, and out would step Ford vice-president Jacques Nasser and old-time racer A. J. Foyt, who had driven an original GT40 to victory in 1967. The GT90 event would be followed that night by Ford's annual Christmas bash, which was on the record and well attended by company dignitaries. Following lunch on the second day, there would be a year-end executive briefing, where reporters could ask about Ford 2000.

The agenda would also allude to an embargoed presentation at 10 A.M. on the second day, which would, of course, be a full-blown Taurus/Sable reveal. Ford PR felt they had a winning formula. If the GT90 and the executive briefing weren't bait enough, the promise of free food, booze, and insider talk at the Christmas bash ought to do it.

So much to do, so little time. It was never the other way around. One order of business was media training for the more prominent members of the DN101 team, who would debut along with the car. No way was Ford going to throw such lambs to a pack of wily wolverines from the media without some coaching on how to fend off unwelcome questions, deliver sound bites, "bridge" from a sticky topic to another that was more congenial, and other tricks of the trade.

One morning in mid-November, Doug Gaffka and his DN101 colleague, business manager Brent Egleston, reported to a small studio on the first floor of World Headquarters, where two men from a company called MediaPromptInc. positioned them onstage before a camera. One of the men looked awfully familiar, and for good reason. He was Richard Valeriani, a former NBC Washington news correspondent, right here in Ford's little studio with his partner, David Horwitz, a former CBS producer.

Where once Valeriani had been a tough newsman who pinned down people in authority and demanded answers, now he taught these same people to evade the kinds of questions he might once have asked. "Reporters get into the business because they have missionary zeal,"Valeriani told the pair of Ford neophytes, who wore looks of apprehension. "They want to tell where and why society is not functioning. . . . A reporter looks for conflict, controversy, contradiction. Your job is to deflect conflict, controversy, contradiction." One could conclude, from the sound of it, that Valeriani had *switched sides,* that for whatever reasons he had given up honest journalism and joined with another turncoat to thwart former colleagues in pursuit of truth and justice.

There was nothing unusual in side switching, of course. It was the American way. Just as government prosecutors often became defense attorneys after learning the ropes, and losing politicians became lobbyists, public relations departments everywhere were filled with former print and television reporters screening information for their former colleagues. But reporters didn't like to use quotes from company flaks. Reporters wanted to talk directly to decision-makers. That was where media training came in. Unschooled, Gaffka and Egleston didn't have a chance against a practiced reporter. Media training evened the odds. "You wouldn't go into a courtroom without a defense attorney," Valeriani said. "This training is the equivalent of a defense attorney."

Valeriani and Horwitz had their work cut out for them, turning car company middle managers like these into silver-tongued, confident, on-screen personalities. They started with simple stuff: Wear suits in dark solids, no white shirts, and stay away from ties with tiny patterns. Socks should be generous enough to cover the ankle in a sitting position. "If the skin is showing between your pants and your socks, you're dead," Valeriani said. "It's a sign of terminal nerdiness and you will not recover from it." Horwitz called attention to Egleston's failure to maintain eye contact during a practice Q&A. "The percentage of time you looked away from Richard's eyes was about 75 percent. . . . It's got to be 80–20 the other way. People make decisions based on eye contact more than any other single feature." He told him to sit up straight. "You take off twenty pounds," Horwitz said, demonstrating. His paunch disappeared.

Egleston's pen, twirling nervously in his hand, had to go. If he were on TV, all eyes would be on the pen, and no one would be listening to what he had to say. "People are trying to decide whether it's a Papermate or Mont Blanc," Horwitz said.

Valeriani and Horwitz took turns quizzing Gaffka and Egleston, then they played back the tapes. Most of the time, the trainees could pick out their own shortcomings. "What is your name?" Valeriani asked Gaffka. "Doug Gaffka?" the designer answered uncertainly. He winced when he watched the exchange.

"You don't *have* to answer a question," Valeriani told them. "But you can't ignore it." He suggested they say instead: "'I'm not sure that it's the right question. A better question would be . . .' Then you ask your own question and you answer it." This sly maneuver worked particularly well on camera. "You're on live. This is your interview. There is no way I can cut you off."

Egleston, an engineer as well as a planner, seemed to have learned jargon as a second language. Every time he spoke, Valeriani or Horwitz interrupted, weeding out stilted expressions. When Egleston mentioned "product requirements," Valeriani asked, "What are those?" Egleston referred to "more customer-oriented features." "Tell us the best feature," Valeriani prompted.

And the word "vehicle"—"That's a word cops use and carmakers use," Valeriani said. "I never said, 'I'm going to go out and buy a new vehicle' in my life."

"You've got to give us a sense that, 'Hey, I can't wait to tell you about this stuff,' " Horwitz said. "Billions of dollars, a lot of years, and it's exciting. I bet you're all damn proud of the product. Let us see it." At the end of the day, they did a final round of taping. "What will knock my socks off?" Horwitz asked Egleston.

"It looks different from anything else developed by Ford. You drive it, you'll be surprised at the way the controls are laid out . . . the way it feels on the road."

Valeriani praised him. "That's the real you."

"What about Mom and Pop who *want* a boxy little car?" Horwitz asked Gaffka.

"I'm not sure that Mom and Pop want a boxy little car," Gaffka replied deftly, leaning slightly forward and looking Horwitz in the eyes. "They want a car that's easy to get in and out of, but nobody's ever against a little flair and excitement in their lives."

There was one last thing. "A reporter's always working," Valeriani warned them. "If you do not want to see it in print, if you don't want to hear it on the air, don't say it."

THE SUGGESTION TO MAKE a movie of the DN101 team came from Ford's ad agency, J. Walter Thompson, after Ross Roberts, vice-president of Ford sales division, said he didn't want to introduce the Taurus in the usual fashion, mouthing a bunch of statistics as slides flipped on a screen. With a five-minute film, JWT promised to capture the dedication and excitement of the team as it carried out the redesign.

Brad Nalon got the assignment to help with the filming. When he fell ill with the flu, he turned it over to Alan Jacobson, the most recent intern from the Ford College Graduate Program assigned to the planners. "Make it happen," were Nalon's parting words as he went home to recuperate. Jacobson's first job was to find a bright, airy space that was consistent with an image of Ford as a progressive company and the Taurus as advanced in both design and technology. The basement clearly conveyed the wrong message.

Jacobson located a bright, airy truck studio under construction in a wing of the Design Center. The agency's next request was for 100 desks. "That's when I knew I was in trouble." He found some in storage, and borrowed others from an office no one had yet occupied. Computers and phones came from J. Walter Thompson; Jacobson re-created a wall of charts from the basement conference room, scene of so many dreary meetings. A computer engineer, the young man found himself negotiating with unions, security, and food services. Four nights running he slept with the equipment in the Design Center because no Ford guard was available overnight. But Jacobson did his job well. The video habitat was clean, airy, and light. Actors hired to play engineers and designers were intense and animated. Ford's dedicated, collocated team came across as a fresh, contemporary approach to car design.

Among the team members who gave taped interviews, Landgraff proved surprisingly telegenic, his intensity coming through as he talked about safety, security, and craftsmanship. Nevenka Schumaker and Mark Jarvis landed cameo roles describing the ICP. When Schumaker couldn't find her knob collection for the show-and-tell, Jacobson sent an urgent e-mail message to his friends around the company asking to borrow some.

The movie closed on Steve Kozak. Encapsulated in his moment on camera was all the energy, all the enthusiasm, all the excitement that the ad guys hoped to convey. His boyish face, interrupted by a mustache that looked as if it belonged to someone else, filled the entire screen. "I wake up in the morning," he said. "It's not like I get up and *have* to go to work. It's 'I gotta go to work.' The car waits."

When the video was finished, it played round the clock on the VCR in the basement conference room. People watched it over and over, marveling at how the animated Kozak had stolen center stage once again. *The car waits.* He became famous for the line. "Oh, you're 'the car waits' guy,'" some marketing people said when they met him. "That was so *powerful.*"

The team wished they could work in a big sun-flooded office like the team members played by actors in the movie. If anything, conditions in the basement had deteriorated over the course of the year. There had been mice and cockroach sightings; one day the toilets wouldn't flush. And black rain was falling from the ceiling onto desks. Several people agitated until environmental services did an analysis. They said it was just dirt, but no one believed them. At a staff meeting in October, Wendy Dendel's replacement, Nancy Hall, reported that the Design Center janitors wouldn't clean because of all the crap on the desks. Even Landgraff took offense. "I wouldn't call my stuff crap. It's important information that I have to have on top of my desk. I'm not going to take it off." Landgraff swore he'd have them out of there by March. "One more winter and we'll be out of here."

As the year drew to a close, the team's rank and file were anxiously waiting to find out what they would be doing in the new Ford 2000 reorganization; so far, it had meant only a new set of acronyms and a new dress code. Ford was going casual five days a week; department stores around the area were opening boutiques for men offering "business casual." Meanwhile some of the Ford 2000 vice-presidents had evicted the color and trim department from the second floor of the Design Center and would soon be moving into offices as splendid as those in World Headquarters. The moles in the basement heard the renovation was costing $6 million.

ALTHOUGH FORD PRESSED several dozen public affairs people into service on the December plan, those directly responsible were Judith Mühlberg and two guys on her staff: John Jelinek, who was in charge of DN101 press coverage, beginning with the auto show introduction and continuing through spring and summer with a series of media drives, and Ed Miller, a former Associated Press reporter who was handling the Detroit Auto Show.

No sooner had this trio started making arrangements for December 6 and 7 than U.S. Transportation Secretary Federico Peña dealt them a major setback with the announcement of a December 6 hearing in Washington on the safety of General Motors pickups built between 1973 and 1987. Newspapers were certain to send their automotive reporters to Washington rather than to some vague affair in Detroit. Even the AP reporter from Detroit was going. And there were other problems.

At Thanksgiving, with less than two weeks until its introduction, hardly a bolt or nut in the GT90 had been screwed together. All through the holiday, Ed Miller was getting minute-to-minute updates on the build. On November 30 the *Detroit News* ran a spy photo with a caption identifying the subject as the GT90. If the photo had been accurate, it would have blown half the Ford program. But there *were* no photos of the GT90. The car didn't exist. Miller actually had to cancel a planned shoot for that reason. The subject of the photo was a ten-year-old test mule somebody had taken on a joyride.

While Miller was out running errands the next Saturday, Detroit's public radio station announced a bluegrass concert in Lovett Hall over in Greenfield Village, the same night and location as Ford's media party. Miller nearly ran off the road. Had there been a double booking? He didn't rest until he confirmed that the announcement was a mistake.

And could they even trust reporters to honor the embargo? The release date for stories on the Sable was December 27, and for the Taurus, January 3. "Embargoed" would be printed in red on the press kit containing photos and plastered over every press release. "We want to make it very clear what the embargo is so nobody dumbs their way into breaking it," John Jelinek said at one of the many planning sessions.

"If one person breaks an embargo, that's it," said Miller. "It's out there. They all go."

O N F R I D A Y , D E C E M B E R 2 , with four days remaining until the first reporters arrived, everybody trooped over to World Headquarters to brief David Scott, the vice-president for public affairs. "You've heard of Plan, Do, Check, Act?" Scott asked cheerfully, repeating a mantra from the quality movement. "This is the plan, this is the check part. Next week we act."

But things had broken down in the plan part. Just last night Jim Donaldson, the vice-president for the new front-wheel-drive vehicle center, telephoned Judith Mühlberg to say he was unhappy with the projected Taurus presentation, it wasn't technical enough, he wanted to call the whole thing off. She explained as gently as possible that it was too late. "What would we do with the media? Give them a nice lunch and wish them Merry Christmas?"

The GT90 had been completed in time, but then a terrible thing happened. The sleek, low-slung automotive confection wasn't properly anchored during delivery to the Design Center. After banging around a trailer for half an hour, the front end was cracked, so was the windshield, and the wheels, said a guy who was there when they opened the doors to the truck, "were square." Now it was going to take a couple hundred thousand dollars to fix the car, with no guarantees it would run. "They just literally put this car together yesterday and broke it," Mühlberg reported to Scott.

Either Scott had already heard this news, or he had magnificent control, for he scarcely flinched. What appeared to worry him most was the poor response from the press. So far only fifty reporters were coming on day one. They had 192 seats. "Who's going to sit in the other 140 seats?" Scott asked. He hated it when company people had to fill in the spaces. More press were confirmed for the Christmas party—125 so far. You could always rely on reporters where there was free food and booze.

In one piece of good fortune, GM had opted to shell out $51 million in a settlement with the government to avoid a confrontational hearing over the gas tanks on its pickups. That freed automotive writers to be in Dearborn rather than Washington.

With so much beyond its control, the group focused on more manageable details such as chairs for the executive briefing, which was to follow an informal format popularly referred to as "Orlando style" after its widespread use at the October management meeting. Rather than a formal speech by the CEO, followed by other speakers in descending rank, the five top guys would sit in a semicircle onstage as if on a talk show. Down in Florida, Ed Hagenlocker had even walked into the audience with a mike, taken questions, and directed them back to his colleagues onstage. No one saw any problem whatsoever in finding comfy talk-show-style chairs for the company's top managers. "They don't have to swivel," Scott said.

The thing that worried Scott least was the embargo. What was the worst that could happen if someone broke it? "A few photos. . . ." Would that be so bad?

ON MONDAY, THE public affairs group gathered around a table in the same truck studio used for the DN101 movie, where thirty guys were hanging lights, constructing a small stage, installing a sound system, laying carpet, and draping a set for the Taurus and Sable debut in two days. A delivery bay was open; it was very noisy, and it was very, very cold. Another fifteen people were in the showroom building the Le Mans set for tomorrow's GT90 gig. In the script, the GT90 was to burst onstage as if coming over the finish line, while an announcer declared its victory in a mock race. But in case the 6.0-liter, V-12, 720-horsepower quad-turbo engine wouldn't start, the announcer would say something like, "The GT90's coming into the pit. Will there be a change of drivers?" and some guys standing by in mechanics' uniforms would push it onstage.

Tom Rhoades, a manager in public relations and veteran of many introductions and launches, suggested they have three sets of name tags, for the two press conferences and the party. You couldn't expect reporters to hold on to their name tags from one event to another. Speaking of the party, which began at 5:30 P.M., Ed Miller said there ought to be some provision to drive drunk reporters back to their hotels. Rhoades decided to close the bar at 8:30 as a precaution. Three hours of drinking was enough. "Some would stay till 1:00 A.M. if you let them." Also, no one had thought of phones for the press. They didn't need phones, Jelinek said. The only news was embargoed, remember? Reporters had to have phones, Rhoades said. A reporter without a phone was like a cop without a gun.

AT REHEARSALS TUESDAY MORNING Doug Gaffka traded scripted remarks with design czar Jack Telnack, as they stood at twin Plexiglas podiums on a small stage flanked by a red Sable and a green Taurus, positioned on turntables. Where once he held that "form follows function," Telnack now had a new philosophy: "Form *contains* function. . . . We aimed for a tension and tautness in the surface to express the energy beneath the surface." Gaffka elaborated on the elliptical theme. "We're especially proud of the elliptical headlights, which we've made the focus of front-end design. But they're not just pretty. They illuminate the road with almost twice the candlepower of some competitors." The designer did not sound proud, however. He sounded wooden, despite his media training. Watching, Judith Mühlberg wished she could give him a pep talk. "This is your best chance to tell the media how great this car is," she said to herself as if talking to Gaffka. "And tomorrow you take over for Jack Telnack. Let me hear it!"

What Gaffka was suffering was not so much a case of nerves as acute guilt. It was beginning to dawn on him that it was going to sound as if he had single-handedly designed the new Taurus and Sable. He, and not John Doughty, was giving the big-time speeches with Jack Telnack and doing interviews with *Automobile*. And shortly he, not Doughty, would be quoted in the articles, which Doughty would certainly see. Gaffka wanted to acknowledge Doughty, whose job kept him in Europe, but "the PR people said it would just confuse things." Reporters weren't interested in someone they couldn't interview.

Gaffka felt as if public affairs was pushing him around. The reference to "pretty" headlights, for example. He would never call headlights "pretty." But every time he took the word out, someone put it back in. "Bio-kinetic" was another word he couldn't seem to excise from the script. Even his clothing was under review: he was told to wear something flashy because he was a designer.

Gaffka and Telnack left. Others arrived to run through their parts. Ed Miller stopped by. The GT90 program was just hours away. "The GT90 is in transit," he told Jelinek.

"That's better than yesterday," Jelinek said. "It was in pieces."

Looking over the stage area, David Scott wanted more lights beamed on the prototypes. "When they see it for the first time, it's gotta go 'pow.'. . . It's really got to pop." Landgraff turned up, walked around, and kicked the speakers. He had similar concerns about the lighting. The producer told him there was only 50 amps of power, enough for eighteen lights, and he had hung twenty-eight.

"This is not good," Landgraff said privately, distressed by the lack of planning. "It's not bad, but it's not good. The problem with these PR guys is, it's amateur night at the movies. Their time horizon's about thirty minutes."

Landgraff returned that evening, when most people were at the media party, to rehearse his eleven-page speech. The lecterns were equipped with prompters that reflected the written words off eye-level plastic panes; the words were visible only to the speaker, who appeared to be looking at the audience, and talking rather than reading. Landgraff had never used a prompter at a major event, and he did not plan to begin now. He read his printed speech, looking up only occasionally; the words poured forth in a steady stream, with none of the pauses and inflections recommended in public speaking courses.

Landgraff's talk was packed with lists and descriptions of all they had done, for quality, integrity, for *craftsmanship*: the leather-like finishes on the instrument panel and interior surfaces, the hidden fasteners, the snugly upholstered seats ("24 tie-downs compared with eight in the present Taurus"). Molded-on rubber gimps, the one-piece bodyside, the damped glove box door, the finger grips in the inside door-pull handles, the increase in body rigidity, "Body torsion or resistance to twisting is increased over 60 percent." The upgraded air conditioning and heater, the solar-tinted glass, the heated outside rearview mirrors. He had really wanted those heated mirrors. Behind every part, every statistic, were nearly four years of meetings, debates, striving, straining, headaches and backaches, heartaches even.

"Do you think this comes off as too much?" he asked Larry Weis, a public affairs guy newly assigned to his vehicle center.

"It's a lot of detail," Weis said diplomatically.

Landgraff contemplated a phrase, "141 feet braking," as if considering whether to chop it out. "That's a pretty good number," he said. "They should relate to that." It stayed.

At the Christmas party that same night, reporters who had just come from the GT90 debut wondered why Ford had bothered. "If they're not going to build it, what's the point?" said Jim Treece, who was in *Business Week*'s Detroit bureau, summing up their reaction. "It's just another concept car." Treece was working on a major Taurus story to run later in the spring that would explore the inner workings of the team. Privy to inside information, he had known the GT90 was merely bait for DN101; both he and the public affairs guys were surprised at how well the secret had held. And continued to hold. Noticing that their schedules said tomorrow's mystery program was in a truck studio, some reporters were guessing that Ford planned to show them a four-door Bronco or a new truck.

The best food gave out early—the fresh shrimp were the first to go, then the roasts at a carving station. And then the bar closed at 8:30 P.M., per Tom Rhoades's orders. Moments later David Scott was refused a drink. The public affairs vice-president went looking for Tom Rhoades; the bar reopened shortly thereafter with orders to stay open until the last journalist left.

N ATURE DEALT FORD one last blow: five inches of snow. But reporters had a way of getting to where there was news. David Scott counted 140 at the Taurus preview the next morning, half local, half out-of-town. The *New York Times,* the *Wall Street Journal,* and *USA Today* were all represented by their first-string guys.

Nobody from Ford was disappointed when the press didn't applaud the new cars. Reporters didn't applaud. But afterward they mobbed Landgraff, and peppered him with questions. Although John Jelinek had practically begged the program manager to go to media training, he had protested he had no time. But thanks to the DN101 planners, he was prepared with answers for some two dozen prickly questions. *Is the new car safer?* "Yes." *Will the car be exported to Europe?* "It would be premature to say." *Was the Taurus/Sable a $6 billion program like the Mondeo?* After the Mondeo investment figure got out, Ford was heavily criticized by the financial press. No longer would the company release program costs. Landgraff would reply, "We now consider that information to be proprietary."

If asked about benchmarking, under no circumstances was Landgraff or anyone else to mention Camry. His vice-president, Jim Donaldson, was a bear on the subject. "We're not making a commercial for the Japanese," Donaldson had said just two days ago at a sales rally. This was what Landgraff should say: "Although we looked at every vehicle in the segment, we took a hard look at the Japanese imports."

Sure enough, the question came up. "What were some of the benchmark cars?" asked Jim Healey from *USA Today.*

"The Camry set a new standard," Landgraff answered. "It's one of the best cars in the world."

A FTER HALF AN HOUR, there was a lull. Landgraff took the opportunity to ask the reporters surrounding him a question of his own. "What do *you* guys think?" For a moment, no one spoke. By and large, these were business reporters, not gung-ho buff book writers. They weren't supposed to have opinions. *"What do you guys think?"* Could they hear the eagerness in his voice?

Then Jan Zverina from *Bloomberg Business News* said something about the "aero look." With as much snow as there had been that morning, there would have been "a lot of windshield to clean." Someone asked when Job One was. And the moment passed.

TWENTY

Anti-Chrysler

CROSS AMERICA, IN
the waning days of 1994, Ford's people were getting ready for the Detroit
Auto Show.

In Salt Lake City, a company was preparing to ship Sarcos, a $600,000
joke-cracking anthropomorphic robot who was the centerpiece of the Ford
exhibit. In Beverly Hills, above a shop a block off swanky Rodeo Drive,
workers were stitching the snug little dress suits the female narrators (product specialists) would wear as they introduced that year's car and truck crop
to the public. Closer to home, near the Detroit airport, a specialty automotive house was turning beat-up DN101 test cars into show cars, perfect in
every way.

And in Suite 202 West of Park Lane Towers, the Dearborn command
post of North American Public Affairs, Judith Mülhberg and John Jelinek
were debating how to respond to an offbeat request from Alan Adler, the
Detroit Free Press reporter who covered Ford. He wanted to follow their own
Ed Miller around for a day as he directed behind-the-scenes preparations for
the January 3 breakfast spectacular. A sort of "Anatomy of a Launch"
Mülhberg told Jelinek.

In-house, they were calling the breakfast event "Eggs with Ed" because it opened with some introductory remarks by Ed Hagenlocker, president of Ford Automotive Operations. Then, an illuminated planet Earth would appear to rise at stage rear, a ribbon of flames would sizzle across its surface and onto the stage with popping explosions, and the red Sable would burst over an artificial hill to thunderous music, followed by the Taurus and a half-dozen concept cars, including the GT90. "It says Ford 2000, it says globalization, it says everything we want to say," Mühlberg had said in approving the plan. "I think it's tasteful."

But Mühlberg suspected that the *Free Press* reporter was less interested in writing about the logistics of the show than in describing Ford's counteroffensive against the mighty Chrysler media machine. She didn't need to read about that in print, however true. And what *was* Chrysler up to? She wished she knew. The announcement of the Chrysler minivan intro, faxed to her by friendly reporters, alluded to fairy tales and reprised the high points of past years' performances. Most recently, she had heard a rumor that they were bringing in the big-time magician David Copperfield, at a cost of $3 million. "We're spending a tenth of that and using Ed Hagenlocker," she said. Hagenlocker, a tall, toothy, square-shouldered engineer, was not the most riveting speaker. "Well . . ." Best not to share these qualms with the *Free Press*. They should tell Adler no.

Jelinek agreed. "We just don't want him looking under our curtains."

"If he gets diverted to doing that, he doesn't write about product."

Jelinek and Mühlberg got on the phone with Adler.

"We want to talk to you about your request," Jelinek said.

"Why do you want to do it, Alan?" Mühlberg asked, an edge in her voice. Wearing a colorful sweater embroidered with big stitches, she perched on the desk in Jelinek's cubicle like a teenager talking to her best friend.

"It's a fascinating way to tell the story," Adler said.

"*Why* do you want to tell the story?" Mühlberg asked.

"It's a pretty darned important story, don't you think?" By January 3, Adler argued, the embargo would have been lifted on both the Taurus and Sable. The *Free Press* and every other paper in the country would have published stories and photos. The only way to get the Taurus on page one during the auto show was with a new angle.

Mühlberg was intrigued, but cautious. "What I don't want is a comparison to last year's auto show. I wasn't in charge then. . . . Nothing that says, 'In the past year, Ford got real smart . . .' or any comparison to our competitors."

Adler rejected her conditions. "Straight up, if we don't provide perspective. . . . You can't write this in a vacuum."

Mühlberg pitched some other ideas. Sarcos, the robot, was manipulated by a hidden operator wearing a control apparatus. When the operator gestured, Sarcos gestured. When the operator talked, Sarcos talked. Would Adler like to put on the Sarcos control suit and play robot?

Or he could have first crack at writing about another high-sci installation at the Ford exhibit: talking heads with facial expressions projected from within—the "blob heads," Mühlberg called them. She had an admirable way of cutting through jargon.

Or Adler could have an exclusive on the newfangled ICP, and the flip-fold console . . . anything. Why not do a nostalgia piece about the introduction of the original Taurus? Public affairs vice-president David Scott had some colorful stories to tell.

If he absolutely *insisted* on the launch story, Mühlberg said, maybe he could focus on Ed Hagenlocker rather than Ed Miller. Public relations people shouldn't be in the news.

"Hagenlocker does what you tell him to do," Adler said. "He doesn't fit. It doesn't work. He has sixteen other things he has to do that day." But Ed Miller's only job was to make the show happen. "This is his life for the next few days." Finally, Adler called in his chits. "I think I've done sensitive work with you guys in the past. I'm not your basic schmo."

They had been on the phone for half an hour. Mühlberg caved. "All right, we'll do *something*. Stop selling."

Ed Miller had just come into the office. Mühlberg put him on with Adler. Not only had both once worked for the Associated Press, but they had both attended Ohio University and worked as interns at the *Springfield Daily News*, though not at the same time. Miller was older by a few years. "You mean following me around?" Miller asked.

"Yeah," Adler said. "I can't do this by phone."

"You know how journalists don't like to be part of the story?" Miller asked. "PR people don't like to be part of the story either. . . ." He wanted to know to what extent Adler planned to invade his life. "If I pray at Paul Lienert's folk mass on Saturday . . . will you put that in the story?" Lienert was a well-known Detroit auto columnist and, apparently, a religious one.

"Does he still do that?" Mühlberg asked. "I want to go."

"Ed," Adler said, "that would be a wonderful part of the story. I think prayer is very important."

Mühlberg closed the deal. "Are you going to do a Sarcos and a blob story?"

"If it means spending a little time with my friend Ed," Adler said, "I'll do it."

In ATTENDANCE, THE Detroit show, which drew 650,000, was not as large as those in New York, Chicago, and Los Angeles. As the first show of the year, however, as well as the one with the most media, Detroit was especially important to manufacturers. "Everybody wants to look good here," said John Love, president of Event Management Corporation, the show's public relations agency. "Someone who looks weak, comes in flat, creates an image to hurdle." Every year the exhibitions got bigger and splashier. Some European companies were spending up to $8 million on elaborate two-story displays.

For 1995 the Ford sales division had decided to dazzle showgoers in Detroit and subsequent shows with a display of technical virtuosity that not only would entertain, but would also suggest that Ford was a leader in innovation. "Utilizing technology to present technology," said Ernie Beckman, the Ford display and exhibits manager. This year Ford would offer more to see and do, not only in Detroit but in other cities. Even small shows in out-of-the-way places sold cars and trucks. With so many popular vehicles under one roof, people could narrow choices in a hurry, without pressure from salespeople. Ford had discovered that one in four people who asked for product information bought a Ford afterward.

The quest for the right displays had led Beckman months earlier to an office building in lower Manhattan. There, in an anteroom as dark as a cave, where inanimate figures hid in the shadows, strange objects glowed blue and green, and disembodied helmet-headed creatures looked down from wall perches, Robert Doornick, founder of International Robotics, Inc., held forth on the virtues of "techno-marketing," or why robots were better salesmen than people.

By its very nature, an amalgam of man and machine, a robot fascinated people. Even techno-phobes were won over in conversation with a humanoid who was gentle, non-threatening and eager to please. There were evil robots, of course, but not in Doornick's stable. His were "caring." Said Doornick, "Eventually, you cannot help but fall madly in love with this machine which is trying so hard to communicate with you. And you say, 'God, it's so cute.' " As proof, he showed a video of people hugging and kissing robots, amid other silly behavior. The last thing people suspected was that the robot was trying to sell them something. Their defense mechanisms were down. And the next thing you know, said Doornick, who spoke with just a trace of accent from his native France, "you bond with this machine. You want what he's selling because you love him."

Schooled in behavioral psychology, Doornick had discovered the lure of robots while working with disturbed children, who interacted more freely with machines than with people. Machines could be controlled; machines were nonjudgmental. But he was a showman at heart—his father had been Maurice Chevalier's first stage partner before opening a night club; his mother was a singer and actress—and he had found in private industry an audience for the playful side of technology. When Ernie Beckman was chief of Lincoln-Mercury exhibits, he hired Doornick's robot Sico, who resembled a six-foot-tall praying mantis. Sico was manipulated by an operator with a remote control keypad, who spoke for the robot through a mike hidden under his shirt.

Now Beckman wanted Doornick's newest salesman, Sarcos, the brainchild of University of Utah engineering professor Stephen C. Jacobsen, who had also designed artificial limbs and remote control arms for hazardous activities. Constructed with fifty-two joints, his movements powered by hydraulic fluid, Sarcos had a wide range of lifelike motions, although he could not walk like the earlier robot. The more mobile Sico traveled by air, first class. Sarcos arrived by freight, accompanied by a crew of technicians in blue lab coats to get him up and running.

Besides Sarcos, Ford had ordered the four blob heads, called "Peoplevision Video Heads," who overlooked the exhibit and delivered fact-laden spiels. Also, there were computerized light pulses that displayed fleeting words in midair; a display case where the Ford logo formed and reformed from a few million dancing electromagnetic particles; and a kiosk of headphones with in-your-ear audio that accompanied a video of an Explorer test drive.

Ford also had a full complement of beauteous showgirls in gorgeous outfits, so traditional at auto shows the world over, who delivered memorized spiels as they spun on turntables with the cars. Men liked them, and women liked their clothes. For the 1995 show, they would wear short, sexy suits in bold colors, made by Susanna Chung, a Korean designer in Beverly Hills. Chung liked to tell how her brightly colored apparel had flopped in Manhattan, when she was a newcomer just out of school. New Yorkers would wear only blacks and browns. On the West Coast she had found a more congenial clientele.

The Ford narrators were represented by talent agent Cynthia Guenther, who had started on the auto show circuit in the mid-1970s, her ticket to a job being a title as "Miss Michigan World." In those days, the car companies wanted "contest girls." Women in floor-length off-the-shoulder evening gowns and four-inch heels stood by the cars and waved airily to features on the car, while men did all the talking. Gradually women got speaking roles. When the first Taurus came out, Guenther encountered the word "aerodynamic" for the first time. She called her boss to ask what it meant. Today's representatives were briefed on answers to frequently asked questions and they also were armed with a laptop computer packed with information. Ford was promoting a new label, "product specialist," befitting their upgraded status. But the two questions posed most frequently by the great wits who went to auto shows really had nothing to do with cars: "Do you come with the car?" And, "Don't you get dizzy up there?"

Downtown Detroit was even emptier than usual on Monday, January 2. But within the Joe Louis Arena, drills whined, hammers banged, cherry pickers rose up and down. Workers were clambering up rope ladders to adjust equipment in the rafters and people swarmed over the stage. A half-dozen women were setting places at big round tables that seated ten.

At 4:00 p.m. the crew did a technical run-through of the opening moments for tomorrow's show. A $140,000 Aeromax 120, a truck with a cab twenty feet high, eased into the rear of the room and tooted its horn. Ed Hagenlocker would climb out with some joke about his wife wanting to keep it, and walk to the stage.

"We're getting there," Ed Miller told the show's producer, an amiable New Yorker named Doug Pope, who was coming off introductions of a Xerox machine and a French perfume and who also produced shows for Neil Diamond. "But I don't think the truck thing is spontaneous enough."

The GT90 had been up and running since the December 6 show in Dearborn, but it smoked like crazy whenever it started. Judith Mühlberg had visions of Alex Trotman enveloped in noxious clouds. And how would the people closest to the stage—the biggest executives and the best reporters—feel about eating breakfast amid carbon monoxide fumes? "What are we going to do?" Judith Mühlberg asked Miller. "We can't put a catalytic converter on it." Rex Greenslade, vice-president Jacques Nasser's public affairs guy, said it would smoke less when warmed up.

"Who's David Scott on the phone to?" Mühlberg wondered edgily. The public affairs boss was sitting at one of the tables with a cellular phone to his ear. Without waiting to find out, she went on to the next question.

"Where's Alan?"

Where *was* Alan Adler? The *Free Press* photographer had been there all afternoon. But the reporter had not appeared to follow Miller around for his behind-the-scenes story.

Miller said he had talked to him on Friday. "Maybe he's waiting for the 6 P.M. rehearsal."

Looking aggrieved, the women who were setting the tables suddenly began to remove the silverware and china, and then to pull off all the white cloths. The public affairs consensus was that the cloths had looked "kind of dull," explained John Jelinek. They began to spread mauve cloths, topped by others that were gaily striped.

Adler arrived. He was short and heavy, but solid, a bench presser. The 1996 Taurus was Ford's biggest story of the year, he said, and he planned to be all over it. As the reporter for Motown's largest daily, a member of the giant Knight-Ridder newspaper chain, "nobody should be doing more than me." The embargoes lifted, his story on the Sable had run a week earlier; tomorrow's paper would carry one on the Taurus. He expected the breakfast intro to make page one the day after, barring any real news to claim the space. He set off to look for his friend Ed Miller.

Chrysler's plans were still a mystery. No more had been heard about David Copperfield. But a wall of gray curtains surrounded the company's floor space in Cobo's main hall, and the sound of croaking frogs and jungle birds came from within. Guards patrolled the perimeter. Across the aisle at the Ford exhibit, where he was monitoring the finishing touches, Ernie Beckman waited for the coast to clear. He edged over and slipped between the curtains. Before Chrysler chased him away, he managed to glimpse a lift mechanism. He pieced that information together with other intelligence. "They're going to jump over the competition," he predicted.

ED MILLER HAD "empowered" the engineers to rule on how to handle the noxious GT90. It was their call, and they made it at dawn on Tuesday, two hours before the breakfast. They would push the car onstage. The official story was that the wind chill factor was minus twenty. If they ran the car outside for the time it took the engine to stop smoking, the mighty quad-turbo aluminum V-12 might break. The real story, which the engineers were too embarrassed to tell Miller until several weeks later, was that they had run the car so much that by showtime it was out of gas.

As it happened, that was the right decision for more than one reason. The other cars in the show produced so much smoke, along with the flames streaking across the stage, that a chorus of coughs mixed with the applause. In another glitch, Ed Hagenlocker's bum knee was acting up so badly he said he couldn't do the truck thing, and could he also please have a podium onstage to lean on? So it was Trotman who made an entrance in the Aeromax. But no one expected perfection from companies whose essential activity was the manufacture of cars and trucks. Even Chrysler's presentations had an antic, slapdash quality. And all the essentials had worked.

"The house lights darken," Adler began his story. "A backlighted globe 75 feet across rises eerily behind a custom-built hill. Higher it rises, then halts. Strobe light. Fire. Two circles of fast-moving flames score the hand-painted globe."

"Ed Miller sighs, relieved. The gimmick works."

In some ways the piece confirmed Mühlberg's worst fear. "FORD FIGHTS HYPE WITH HYPE," said the headline. After duly noting Ed Miller's role, Adler wrote, "This is Ford's answer to Chrysler's dominance of the North American International Auto Show publicity sweepstakes." On the other hand, there was a splendid photo of a red car on page one. "The 1996 Ford Taurus emerges from special-effects smoke," said the caption. Only, the caption was wrong. The car was the Sable, not the Taurus.

Now it was Chrysler's turn. When the curtains were removed Wednesday, there was an enormous swamp scene, ninety feet wide, dominated by a massive banyan tree painted on a backdrop, and a real pool of water. A crowd of 1,500 gathered for the show, and a country singer tried with little success to lead a sing-along. Reporters didn't sing. Then Chrysler chairman Bob Eaton and president Bob Lutz came onstage in cardigan sweaters, perched on make-believe rocks, and read doggerel from storybooks. "All-wheel drive is very pleasing/for those who drive through many seasons." A nonsensical frog much like Kermit held forth from a video screen. At one point the frog said he had seen the minivan, and a fuzzy minivan photo flashed on-screen. Where did he get the photo, the frog was asked. "Jim Dunne," said the frog. "It wasn't cheap and it wasn't in focus either."

In the audience, Dunne smiled at the joke along with everyone else. He was playing his own games with Chrysler, having just purchased a 4.5-acre spit of desert surrounded on three sides by Chrysler's 3,800-acre Arizona proving ground. He told his buddy Jack Keebler, who reported the purchase in *Automotive News,* that he might build an observation tower.

As Ernie Beckman had predicted, the new minivan vaulted through the air and landed with a splash, "leap-frogging the competition." Jim Healey from *USA Today,* reviewing the show's hits and misses, labeled Chrysler's the "wackiest skit" and Ford's "the most dramatic." Keebler roundly panned the Ford event in *Automotive News.* "Ford, with a sulphurously smoky stage, dull speeches, a blinding light show and a deafening sound system, did not impress the media." Ford really didn't care much what the pencil-pushers said. TV was the name of the game, and a video clip of the Taurus bursting onstage was played over and over by Detroit stations.

Members of the DN101 team had been waiting eagerly to see their baby on display like a fine piece of jewelry. After the press departed, the show was open for two days to industry people before the official opening. On Thursday, Steve Kozak and Andy Benedict boarded one of Ford's chartered buses for the trip into Detroit. In Cobo, Kozak saw the people before he saw the car. "Look at the crowd around it," he said excitedly.

"The striker bracket," Benedict said with dismay. The bracket for the door latch was supposed to be red like the rest of the car. But the people who prepped the car had left it black. It wouldn't show with the doors closed. And Landgraff had given strict orders to keep the doors closed because the interior of the car had not been finished to production level. But both doors were open on the driver's side, and you could plainly see the black bracket.

Kozak was eavesdropping. "I heard, 'It looks like a Contour.' I heard, 'I don't like the back end.'"

Judith Mühlberg cornered them. "We want to do something with you guys." In half an hour Ross Roberts, Ford Division vice-president for sales, was scheduled to announce that the 1994 Taurus was number one again. Afterward, public affairs wanted to take pictures of Taurus team members with the 1996 prototype. Mühlberg told them to round up everyone they saw from the team.

Kozak spotted Zyg Gregory, the engineer in charge of headlamps and gimp. "Hey, Zyg. Even the aeroshields look good."

"I looked at all the other cars before I looked at ours," Gregory said. "Ours is the best."

Kozak and Benedict left the Ford area and wandered over to Mercedes-Benz, where a stage was occupied by a sporty coupe. A blond saxophone player in a slinky black dress was trading riffs with a percussionist in an African dashiki and a black female scat vocalist. As she played, the saxophonist vamped the car.

"I don't care for the front end," Kozak said. And he thought the Mercedes taillamps looked as if they came off a Mustang. "If I didn't know better, I would say that's a Mustang concept car. This is a company that's hurting for leadership."

On the way back to the Ford exhibit, Kozak paused to pinch the gimp on a Lexus. "Closed-cell foam," he said admiringly.

As he waited for the press conference, Kozak saw two release analysts deep in conversation. He remembered how these same two had bottled up a part for three months. Not until the analysts signed off with the correct codes could the part be authorized for production. The part in question was a piece of sealer with an adhesive backing. Kozak considered it a single unit, but they had said the adhesive backing made it an assembly, requiring a different code. "It's the principle of the thing," they told him. "There is no principle to the thing," he insisted. "The principle of the thing is that it's three months late and you're holding up the part. What are you going to do about it?"

The woman analyst got her back up. "We're not going to do anything about it," she said. Kozak went ballistic. She remained cool. "You probably cheat on your income tax," she told him. Then he really lost it. "No one ever questions my integrity." That battle might be over, along with countless others that had plagued the Taurus redesign, but that didn't mean it was forgotten. These were people without passion for the car.

The boom of a bass drum announced the entrance of the Wayne State University marching band in green uniforms. Ross Roberts lept to the podium in a hockey helmet and jersey emblazoned with a big number one and began exchanging jibes with Sarcos. His outfit was tied into the notion of three consecutive goals, known in hockey as a "hat trick." After Roberts announced that Ford had five of the top ten best-selling vehicles in America, some guys placed an oversized cowboy hat on the *numero uno* F-series pickup truck, and a big top hat on the Ford Ranger, its third biggest seller, and then a huge red velvet crown atop the hood of the outgoing 1995 Taurus, once again the first-place car. Then Kozak, Benedict, Gregory, and maybe thirty other team members, including Doug Gaffka, clambered onto the turntable to pose with the 1996 car. Cameras flashed a dozen times, and then another dozen, and another dozen. "Can you clap?" called the Ford photographer.

The very next night, Kozak and Benedict were headed back to the car show with their wives for the black-tie charity preview. Rank-and-file engineers did not normally turn out for this event, which was not a comfortable scene for introverts, and besides, it cost $125 a head.

The subject of the preview had come up during a discussion in Landgraff's office. Kozak said he was planning to go. Then they all started talking about it. In three years of working together they had never gotten together outside of Ford. There were days and weeks when they saw more of each other than they did their families. "You know," Kozak told Benedict, "my wife's never met your wife. There's another whole side to this."

Landgraff chimed in. "We should get together. Just make a party of it." Landgraff was the last person you'd expect to say something like that. But even he had been carried away with the emotion of the moment. When he ordered the tickets, Kozak asked if you really had to wear a tux. The woman told him a black suit would be fine.

The minute he entered Cobo Hall, Kozak knew he had made a dreadful mistake. His wife Jean was wearing a long, sexy black dress that set off her creamy skin and long blond hair. All he saw were guys in tuxes. And he was wearing . . . his Tuesday–Thursday black pinstriped suit. Kozak silently reamed out the woman from whom he'd ordered the tickets. Thank God Andy Benedict was there in an almost identical suit, on Kozak's say-so. As long as he stuck to Andy he felt okay.

"Don't worry about it," Jean told her husband. "You're different."

A LIGHT SNOW WAS FALLING as Connie and Dick Landgraff set out for the preview shortly after 5 P.M. Connie was excited. Usually they ducked into the auto show on a weekend like everybody else, but this was a night to celebrate. It was partly her reward, too. Landgraff piloted his 1995 silver Taurus SHO over the backstreets of Bloomfield Township. He took Big Beaver Road to the I-75 South on-ramp, merging into the southbound stop-and-go traffic.

"At this time of day, I would have taken Woodward to Royal Oak," his wife said in a conversational tone. "Then Fourth Street to Twelve Mile, and *then* got on 75."

"Really?" her husband said, sounding mildly interested.

"But I know better than to tell you which way to go." No, you didn't tell Dick Landgraff which way to go, even when he was halfway to Timbuktu and still refusing to ask for directions.

Landgraff exited I-75 onto Jefferson Avenue and found himself bumper-to-bumper with other cars headed for the show in Cobo Hall, a number of them stretch limos. The glare of streetlights turned the falling snow into a gauzy white curtain. "I didn't know there were going to be 11,000 people," he said. "I've never seen this much traffic in Detroit. There haven't been this many people here since the riots." In fact, the official count would be 13,527. Overhead, Detroit's people-mover, its municipal rail system, was ferrying people who'd parked blocks away. "I've never taken that thing in my life," Landgraff said. Car guys did not take public transportation.

The snow was coming down hard now. They found a parking lot and walked briskly to Cobo Hall three blocks away. After checking snow-dusted coats, they picked up a couple of glasses of champagne and headed through the well-dressed crowd into the hall. As far as the eye could see, Cobo was filled with gleaming cars, vans, and trucks positioned on thick carpet beneath a skyline of automotive logos. It looked like a gigantic automobile show-room. Earlier that week, *Washington Post* reporter Warren Brown had thrown open his arms and offered a declaration as he entered the hall. "I love this stuff! All this money!"

Spotting Ford's venerable blue oval in the distance, Landgraff took off at a sprint. When Connie caught up, she found her husband standing with other onlookers before a spinning red 1996 Taurus, a happy smile on his face. He seemed not to notice Sarcos, who moments earlier had suddenly twitched, slumped, and fallen silent. In the control tower, technicians were frantically splicing and shunting wires to get their robot up and moving. It was a terrible moment for Sarcos to collapse—in front of the very people who were paying the bills.

Landgraff introduced his wife to Doug Gaffka. "Your husband's just great," Gaffka said. Connie felt a surge of pride. As they moved on to the Lincoln-Mercury pavilion, where the Taurus's sister car, the 1996 Mercury Sable, was making its debut, Landgraff greeted two guys in black suits with their wives. "I would do anything for Dick," Steve Kozak told Connie. "If he told me to jump off a bridge, I'd ask, which one?"

Connie smiled, loving every minute of this. "I wouldn't," she said.

A s s o o n a s t h e Detroit press days were over, public affairs moved on to their next venue, Chicago, for the February 9 station wagon debut. Mike Moran was the majordomo in Chicago, as Ed Miller had been in Detroit. "Wagons ho!" he yelled gamely, gathering up reporters in the hallways of McCormick Place, the Chicago convention center, and herding them into the theater Ford had reserved. If it took this kind of silliness to add pizzazz, Moran would do it.

A lighthearted video traced the history of station wagons, from Conestogas on. Wagons had peaked in popularity in the early 1960s, with 15 percent of the market. Now, they claimed just 5 percent, and half of those were Fords: Escorts, Tracers, Tauruses, and Sables. A cute little boy and a cute little girl entered, pulling cute little red wagons. Trotman made his entrance in a dark red "Woodie," a vintage wagon mass-produced between 1929 and 1948. The DN101 wagons debuted through a shimmering curtain of silver strands to the sound track of a waterfall.

Chrysler's uninspired introduction the day before of its Sebring coupe had been no competition. But Chrysler made news anyway. The *Chicago Tribune*'s auto writer, Jim Mateja, snagged president Bob Lutz, who was at the show for a speech, and queried him about a U.S. Commerce Department report that said the average price of a new car in 1994 topped $20,000 for the first time, half the median family income in America. "We simply build what the market wants," Lutz said. "If they want a Rolex, we don't give them a Timex." The *Chicago Tribune* bannered the story in its business section.

It was old news, and Ford had already had its say on the subject. The *New*

York Times in January quoted Alex Trotman's remark that the report was "rubbish." The government failed to take rebates into account. Moreover, customers were choosing expensive cars of their own volition. "We're not forcing them to buy Explorers," Trotman said.

The wisdom of such statements by Trotman, who collected more than $8 million in salary, bonuses, and stock awards in 1994, was questionable. Ford was getting a reputation for arrogance on the price issue. A rise in sales of used cars clearly demonstrated that many people couldn't afford new ones. And Ford's new cars *were* more expensive. The Ford Contour and Mercury Mystique, which went on sale the previous October, were roughly $3,000 more than the cars they replaced. The new 1995 Lincoln Continental was up $14,000 over the 1994 model, to $40,000.

The morning after the Chicago story featuring Chrysler, David Scott and Judith Mühlberg huddled at breakfast in Ford's convention center hideaway, wondering if they could get some mileage out of the Ford Division's average price—$16,900, including taxes and transfer, according to their figures. "That wouldn't be bad to say," Mühlberg said.

The price tag on the new Taurus was a big question mark. "I observe lots of interest in pricing," said Dick Landgraff, who had popped in for breakfast before the wagon show. Pricing powwows were going on at that very moment, but he wasn't allowed to say anything. "Everybody's anticipating a big price increase, which of course is not going to happen. We're going to surprise the hell out of them."

Landgraff's firsthand experience with the media so far had left him disillusioned. Few of the details he had fielded at the December press conference on the Taurus and Sable had made it into the first round of articles. Writers devoted more space to the car's showy ellipses and Ford's desire to reach a younger market. Landgraff was especially unhappy about a January 9 article in *Business Week*. The lead was fine: "There's no denying that the new Ford Taurus and Mercury Sable are stunners." But farther down reporter James Treece wrote that "the sheer number of features Ford has added—everything from gimmicky multi-purpose center consoles to an optional filter to winnow dust and pollen out of the air—means they take longer to build. That's a major reversal of the industry's trend toward cars that are easier, quicker—and cheaper to make."

Anybody who knew anything about manufacturing knew that plants were always less efficient at the beginning of a model cycle than at the end. And though it was true that assembly labor on DN101 had risen from ten to twelve hours, it would likely shrink as the plants became more adept. It was one of the reasons a model became more profitable over time. "Some of these press people are awfully naive," Landgraff said. "They're looking for a fight."

But it was the word "gimmicky" to describe the flip-fold console that really stung. Up until then Landgraff and Treece had been on good terms. In the fall, Landgraff had granted the *BusinessWeek* reporter entree to the DN101 team for in-depth research on the Taurus redesign. Treece had talked at length to Bell and Landgraff, sat in on a meeting or two, and made plans to visit Atlanta during the launch, before doing a major story in the spring. After "gimmicky," Landgraff declared him *persona non grata*.

Alan Adler had also stepped on Ford's toes, though not with his Taurus coverage. The Contour/Mystique, Ford's vaunted $6 billion world car, had hit the market with a resounding thud. Adler detailed all that had gone wrong, from a recall that coincided with the beginning of a $100 million ad campaign, to a hailstorm that damaged 300 new cars. A recall was the kiss of death, particularly as in this case, when it involved the fuel system. Also, a seat supplier strike shut down the plant for a week; and car reviewers were critical of rear-seat head and leg room. Perhaps Ford's biggest miscalculation was to put big end-of-the-year rebates on the Taurus at the same time it put a big price tag on the Contour. Ford was advertising Contours for $14,655. But the average sale after buyers loaded up on options, according to a marketing source, was $17,900. People could buy a larger, more powerful Taurus for very little additional money, if any. Given that, Ross Roberts told Adler, it was "a miracle" they had sold as many Contours as they had. "Ford's first true world car is selling well in a lot of countries," Adler wrote. "But the United States isn't one of them."

Judith Mühlberg called first, to protest the *Free Press* headline: "Ford Contour Hasn't Caught On." Listening to her feelings of betrayal, Adler had the impression that public affairs would have liked to have bought and destroyed every copy of that day's paper. Then he heard from Bob Rewey, group vice-president for sales. According to Adler, Rewey said, "I thought we had a good relationship."

Said Adler, afterward, "I thought, 'What relationship?'"

Rewey said the story had as much as accused Ford of bait-and-switch advertising.

"Where did you read that?" Adler asked. Rewey cited a section that said customers ended up paying more than they had intended.

"Well, that's true," Adler said.

Then Rewey told him he had never interviewed Ross Roberts.

"Would you like to hear the tape?" Adler asked.

When Adler hung up, his newsroom colleagues applauded. "If Rewey doesn't want to talk to me, it's no great loss," the reporter said philosophically. "He never talked to me anyway."

AT THE NEW YORK Auto Show in April, where Ford was introducing the Taurus SHO, Chrysler had the opening event, a breakfast address by chairman Robert Eaton. Ford's press conference was scheduled three hours later, and they had hired a sizzling off-Broadway dance troupe called Stomp to draw attention to the performance sedan. Dressed like street kids in baggy paint-spattered jeans and T-shirts, the dancers beat out intricate rhythms on galvanized trashcans and used lids as cymbals. The act was a departure for staid Ford—Ross Roberts had blanched on seeing their video—but he knew it would be a hard act to follow.

And anyway, Chrysler was going first. Tom Lankard, who wrote a syndicated column called Road Warriors, decided to pass up Eaton's speech. "What's Eaton going to say that I haven't already heard?" Michelle Krebs, who wrote for the *New York Times* among other publications, almost skipped the whole show. Nothing sounded very newsworthy.

That morning, as the moment for Eaton's speech approached, something seemed to have gone horribly awry. Appearing shaken, Chrysler's public affairs vice-president Budd Liebler announced that Eaton was on his way to Las Vegas. At first people thought it was another Chrysler stunt. Then Liebler proceeded to read a statement he had just been handed. Financier and casino owner Kirk Kerkorian had launched a campaign to buy Chrysler.

Reporters raced for phones, Krebs among them. She had jumped on a plane without packing her phone or her tape recorder. When Lankard arrived two hours later, the exhibition hall was like a tomb. He went down to the press room, where people were listening to the disembodied voice of Kerkorian's spokesman, Alex Yemenidjian, coming over speakers in a telephone press conference. "Everybody called him by his first name, because they couldn't pronounce his last name," Lankard said. "Nobody knew who he was or where he was." A Chrysler PR guy was taking more notes than anybody else.

Ford's rousing reveal of the SHO played to a thin crowd. Chrysler had upstaged them again.

TWENTY-ONE

Rebel Yells

N 1972, TOM BRAND, the manager of the Chicago assembly plant, called a scrappy young general foreman named Wheeler Stanley to the front office. Stanley arrived, apprehensive. In those days, a summons from the front office was like a trip to the principal. But no, the famous Studs Terkel was there to interview an auto plant foreman for his new book, *Working*. And Brand thought Stanley was just the man. The plant manager left them alone.

Then thirty, Stanley had gone to work at the plant ten years earlier, as an hourly worker on the seat cushion line. He grew up near the plant on the south side of Chicago in the shadow of steel mills, in a blue-collar neighborhood called Slag Valley, and joined the 101st Army Airborne, for one reason: "to jump out of planes." But while on leave one Christmas, he fell in love with a small, blond timekeeper named Pat, who worked at a box factory. They met through her sister, who had been a waitress at the bowling alley where Stanley had been a pinboy. He decided to leave the army, marry her, and raise a family.

The army, he told Terkel, had helped his career; it had taught him respect and self-control. In those days at Ford, you didn't need a college degree to become foreman, and Stanley had been promoted off the line. Terkel asked him how far he hoped to rise. "Who knows?" said Stanley. "Superintendent, first. That's my next step." When the plant manager returned to his office, he told the author in Stanley's presence, "In traveling around plants, we're fortunate if we have two or three like him, that are real comers."

In the years afterward, Stanley moved from plant to plant, working his way up the Ford chain of command, from foreman to chassis superintendent, pre-delivery manager, production manager, quality control manager and final area manager, and then to assistant plant manager. And in 1993 he had risen to the most exalted post of all, plant manager, with the toughest assignment he would ever have, to launch Ford's most celebrated car at Atlanta assembly. *He* had the corner office. *He* owned the customized Ford Bronco in the choicest parking spot in the executive garage. "I got all the stripes," Stanley said. "It's the first time I can make all the decisions."

Age had brought a slightly receding hairline and the need for reading glasses, but it had not softened Stanley's style. "I've been known to be hard-headed and hard-nosed and real stubborn if I have to be," Stanley had told Terkel more than two decades ago. The description still fit.

Launching a new model was more complicated than it had been as recently as five years ago, when Ford plants routinely shut down to move in new equipment. The drawback was months of lost production and lost revenues. In another lesson learned from the Japanese, the company now found it not only more profitable to continue operations as a new model came on line, but less disruptive. When a model was introduced gradually on the same lines that were turning out the car to be replaced, workers learned their jobs more quickly and quality levels stayed high. This was called an integrated build. Even before Stanley arrived, his predecessor had been working on a master plan to carry it out.

But sometimes Stanley wondered how he was going to do it all: reinvent the body shop with almost all new fixtures, start them up, debug them, reprogram the robots in the plant to work on both the old and new models, find space for two inventories and orchestrate dual deliveries to the line, as well as train some 3,300 workers, supervisors, and managers in new jobs, all without missing a beat of 1995 Taurus production. In addition, in the year before launch, close to a thousand Atlanta workers would be eligible to retire. The plant would have to hire and train replacements unfamiliar with the work or the culture.

During the summer of 1993, following Stanley's arrival earlier that year, the retooling began. The plant equipped two lines of robot welders with a modern conveyor system that could handle both the 1995 and 1996 Tauruses. Over the Christmas shutdown, the plant prepared a site for the wheelhouse assembly equipment; the following spring people installed it. In the summer of 1994, they dug a pit 10 feet deep, 80 feet long, and 20 feet wide for a giant fixture called a framing buck, a massive chunk of steel, hydraulic hoses and cylinders, weld tips and electrical connections, which applied dozens of basic welds to a loosely attached car body. That fall the framing buck itself arrived, along with the biggest machine of all, a two-story body-side assembly unit that rose from the plant floor in two sections, each 220 feet long.

In the third week of September 1994, four 1996 prototypes, their rounded steel bodies glistening with fresh paint, started down the assembly line in Atlanta, a car per shift. A swarm of product specialists, who had trained at the pilot plant near Dearborn back in the winter of 1993–94, accompanied the cars like a medical crew hovering over a Code Blue patient en route to the emergency room. They pounded and pressed, riveted and twisted, adding fenders, bumpers, moldings, and interior trim, seats and hardware. As each car neared the end of the line, workers came from around the plant for a glimpse of the future.

Only two serious problems turned up in these, the first 1996 Tauruses to travel the line. The transmission wouldn't slide properly into the engine, which arrived at the assembly point suspended on chains. Engineers designed a cradle to set the two big chunks of steel in place and slide one into the other. The second issue involved the parking brake assembly; it was in the way of two wiring harnesses that needed to connect. The solution was to divide the brake assembly into two sections, then install one, connect the harnesses, and install the other.

A MANUFACTURING LAUNCH could be good or bad, depending on whether parts arrived on time, how easily they fit together, and how well they worked afterward; the same was true for new tooling. Veterans still spoke of the first Taurus launch in 1985 as one of the most horrible experiences of their lives.

After millwrights had gutted the plant to make room for new machinery, plant manager Pete George, who had started at the Atlanta plant in 1947, the year it opened, fought feelings of panic. Years later the emotion was still fresh. "It was frightening. When you see and you live with something as many years as I did, you thought you knew everything, and then everything you lived with, worked with was all of a sudden gone, and you wonder what the hell's coming in and how's it going to work."

Well he might have wondered.

Enamored of automation, Ford had ordered large numbers of bright orange bobbing and throbbing, wheeling and sealing, fire-spitting robots. In the body shop there were five different kinds: German robots, American robots, Japanese robots, a veritable Ellis Island of robots, and no matter whose they were, they broke down constantly. George hired a bunch of college kids that summer as "loggers." Their sole job was to hover over the line and take notes on equipment failures.

The plant had done away with the old "gull-wing" system of installing trim and hardware on doors as they traveled down the line attached to the car. It was a bad system; the doors were forever banging into something or being banged. Now, after the car was painted, the doors were removed and sent down a separate line. If all went well, they mated with their car body on the final line. But too often it didn't, and the doors and bodies got out of sequence indefinitely. Before they devised a way to hang them securely, the doors moved along the line like washrags, forcing workers to steady them with one hand while trying to attach parts with the other. Once completed, the doors attached with difficulty.

The launch team from Dearborn worked out of rented trailers beside the plant, which was so close to the Atlanta airport that landing lights twinkled atop the plant's high metal roof. Every minute and a half, all conversation would be obliterated for fifteen seconds by a jet blasting off, and the trailers would quiver. Looking up, you could just about count every rivet on the belly of the passing plane. The summer of 1985 was particularly hot, even by Atlanta standards. In late afternoon, as air conditioning use peaked, the city would ask the plant to suspend unnecessary power. The plant would cut voltage to the trailers that housed the launch team and the air conditioners would quit. The mobile homes were like saunas on wheels.

Every morning the launch team came in earlier and earlier to deal with problems. One morning they scheduled a meeting to examine little dents and dings in the trunk lids. When they gathered at the appointed hour, it was still too dark to see.

Scheduled to be in Atlanta just four months, the Taurus launch team ended up blowing the July Job One date, and staying until October. Ford clamped a lid of secrecy on the operation, lest word leak out that the launch was in trouble. There were no weekend trips home, no visitors from Dearborn. Back in Michigan, reporters who had been to the California blastoff were pressing to drive the new car. Lew Veraldi came up with a cover story: Ford would not put the Taurus on sale until it was perfect. The company managed to get it to dealers just before the end of the year, to qualify for the *Motor Trend* Car of the Year award. The public never knew how much had gone wrong.

Ten years later, some things had not changed: the trailers were back, the jets roared overhead, many of the same robots were still there, only now they were old and cranky, and come June Atlanta was going to be plenty hot. But everyone was confident that DN101 was in far better shape than its predecessor.

T HE LAUNCH TEAM from Dearborn reported for duty in January, filled with a sense of mission. Working with plant management, they would have six months to perfect the assembly of a fast, quiet, untroubled, unblemished, harmonious machine from 1,775 disparate pieces—the vast majority of them being parts that contained parts that contained more parts, plus multiples of 453 standard items, such as screws, bolts, straps, plug buttons, washers, rivets, clips, studs, spacers, and rubber bumpers, and 87 varieties of bulk material that could be measured in pounds or gallons, such as paint, grease, power steering fluid, epoxy, windshield washer, and adhesive. In the end, all anybody could do was guess that there were between 15,000 and 30,000 parts in the new Taurus, depending, of course, on the model and the options.

Ford Motor Company had manufactured cars in Atlanta since 1909, when a small shop on Ivy Street turned out Model T's. In 1947 the Atlanta assembly plant opened eight miles south of downtown in the town of Hapeville, on a two-lane road dissected by multiple sets of railroad tracks and lined with low-rent businesses. The road's name seemed too grand: Henry Ford II Avenue. Henry II himself had come down for the dedication. At the time, it was thought to be the only thing in the company named for him and not his grandfather. The town's most famous native was redneck comic Jeff Foxworthy. It was also the birthplace of Chick-Fil-A.

Ford's far-flung plants were like self-contained city-states, run by the manager and his chieftains. As the highest-ranking Ford representative in Georgia, the plant manager had clout with congressmen and the governor; he put on a tux and went to black-tie dinners to benefit the zoo, a Ford charity. Within the Atlanta plant's 128-acre confines, Stanley's word was law.

Even more so than at the pilot plant, the princes and princesses from Dearborn found themselves on foreign turf. Some 50 of the 240-member launch team worked for body and assembly, the manufacturing division that ran the plants. But even they were outsiders here. "It's their house," said Art Cairo, a B&A supervisor. "We're like visiting cousins." The South's vaunted hospitality was little in evidence. The front offices for the team managers were crowded and dirty. The computers didn't work, the phones were overloaded, and they had to set their trashcans in the hall for collection.

At a January briefing, Stanley made it clear that he didn't want the Dearborn troops getting in the way. Workers were on ten-hour shifts, six days a week, cranking out 1,200 Tauruses a day, so that Ford could milk every last penny from that great cash cow and finish ahead of the Accord in the annual cattle drive. Everybody knew the figures. Each unit represented $5,000 to Ford Motor Company, a sum that covered their salaries among other overhead costs. A lost hour of production cost the company $335,000. Production would plummet to twelve cars an hour when they started making the new Taurus on June 19, 1995; not until fall would the plant again see sixty-seven jobs an hour.

Jody Butler, Stanley's chief launch coordinator, weighed in to the effect that he cared a lot more about the workers in the plant than he did the people on the launch team. Butler was a formidable figure as he walked the creeping, clanging line, something like a sheriff patrolling Main Street in a John Wayne movie, his radio on one hip, his pager on the other, and his back straight as a Georgia pine.

There were lots of rules. Anyone caught without safety glasses would be banished from the plant floor. Engineers weren't allowed to torque a nut or turn a screw—that was union labor and violations were subject to grievance. In other words, engineers couldn't tinker with parts on a car. And woe to the newcomer who parked in an off-limits area. The plant police slapped "no parking" stickers on both windows with the same crash-proof adhesive used to fuse the windshield to the car, or so it seemed to anyone who tried to chip the stickers off with a razor blade.

Even launch leader Tom Breault's effort to foster goodwill between the team and the plant with a get-acquainted party ran afoul on the shoals of suspicion. He convened the Dearborn people a half hour early for a pep talk on the need to mix with their Atlanta brethren. The plant people thought it was a secret meeting to complain about *them*.

Removed from family and friends, the Dearborn contingent found themselves in a world of hard men doing hard time, where each day brought a new skirmish between plant people and engineers, or engineers and suppliers, over a part that wouldn't fit, didn't work, didn't match, looked bad or rattled, squeaked or leaked. Out on the plant floor, over the thunder of metal and the clamor of bells, buzzers, and whistles, people yelled, cursed, fumed, and threatened. In follow-up meetings, they sniped and snarled.

To the footloose young princes and princesses from Dearborn, launch was awful and it was . . . wonderful. It was *intense*. They passed around bootlegged copies of *How to Speak Southern,* by Steve Mitchell. "*Bawl:* What water does at 212 degrees Fahrenheit. 'That gal can't even bawl water without burnin' it.' *Far:* A state of combustion that produces heat and light. 'Ah reckon it's about time to put out the far and call in the dawgs.' " It was all in good fun, but the truth was, the southerners did talk funny. As in, "We're having trouble in pint." Pint? Oh, right, the *paint* department.

Ford installed the team members north of Atlanta in $1,700-a-month terrace apartments, with twice-weekly maid and linen service, and furnishings that included a VCR and a blender. It was like being in college again, only better. There was always someone to hang out with. They played soccer, softball, hockey, went bowling, took weekend trips to Lake Lanier, and went whitewater rafting in the north Georgia hills, all the while building up bank accounts and joining investment clubs with the money they saved on rent and the $31-a-day meal allowance. They had parties. "Hi, I'm in sealing." "I'm in restraints." Every other weekend they could hop a company plane back home. And thanks to Ford 2000, the first six months of 1995 had turned out to be a good time to be somewhere other than Dearborn. So many jobs had been abolished or reformulated, and filled with new people, that no one was sure who was responsible for what. Mercifully, the DN101 team was more or less intact, though March had come and gone and they were still in the basement.

Some of the Atlanta launch team members who were married without children, or whose children were grown, had brought their spouses along. But for the guys and gals who had left behind families, it was harder. At least one of Art Cairo's four kids cried every night when he called home. There was scarcely a dry eye, including his, when he had to return to Atlanta after the weekend he watched his son start Little League baseball and took his daughter to a father-daughter Brownie dance. Back home in Detroit, Tom Breault's wife was in charge of two houses—a new one he had barely finished building and their former home that was now for sale; he missed her and he missed his weekly Healey night, restoring a 1968 roadster with his buddy. He was a car guy without his car.

For nine days in February, every 200th car on the line was a DN101, for a total of thirty. On March 10, George Bell, Dick Landgraff, and a management contingent from body and assembly flew in for a formal review of how that build had gone. The visitors took seats at a long table across the front of the conference room, facing rows of engineers, who were neatly seated at tables with name plates and their oversized Franklin planners. A select few with status also had little white cards that invited them to stay for lunch with the guys at the head table; they would break cornbread together. George Bell always looked forward to the fried okra prepared by the plant cafeteria, Grease City.

The engineers gave their reports. The aluminum trunk lid suffered from a major case of the dreaded springback, whereby a piece of bent metal strived to return to its former state. On three-dimensional diagrams that looked like topographical maps, the front corners were marked 3.7 millimeters low, the side margins were out of spec, and there were splits in the rear corners. In another sheet-metal problem, the upper rear corner of the station wagon body was so warped they had been forced to postpone the first wagon build.

The squeak-and-rattle team reported a regrettably high average of 12.8 squeaks and rattles per unit. Water leaks, detected as the car sat in a 20-minute downpour inside a water booth, were 4.4 per unit. The Nova-C auditors from body and assembly had gone through the cars as well; they were critical of front-door wind noise and the fit of the rear-door windows. The dome light stayed on when the door was closed, and the sunvisor was difficult to pull down. They also noted, once again, that the "seat console in open position interferes with IP [instrument panel] ashtray." Just in case anybody cared.

Dave Gorman, manager of front-wheel-drive vehicle operations, couldn't believe no more than this was wrong. Compared to some builds, this was rinky-dink stuff. "That's it? There's no underlying issues that you guys have been fighting about like cats and dogs?" His suspicions were understandable. Wary of repercussions, body and assembly guys believed in telling higher-ups only about problems that were either under control or belonged to someone else. This operating philosophy was perfectly expressed by a B&A operative, who said: "Why should we explain to someone what we're doing to achieve an end, when all they care about is the end?" And really what was the point of telling Gorman and the other B&A bosses that the so-called integrated build had bogged down in the body shop, where the underbody fixture could not handle both the 1995 and 1996 Taurus models as planned? Workers were being paid overtime to come in on the weekends to cobble together DN101 underbodies by hand, and it looked like it was going to stay that way through all the pre-production builds.

Gorman continued to probe. "There's not going to be some car driving around Dearborn, parts falling off, blaming Atlanta? . . . Everybody knows what we're doing and agrees on it? Of all the 800 or 900 new tooled parts, these are the only major issues we have?"

"The launch team has done a tremendous job," Jody Butler said with a smirk. It was his little joke. The launch team basically believed that Butler couldn't wait till they were gone and he could run the car through the plant the way he wanted. He said "fuck" to them so often—a word you could go all day in Dearborn without hearing—that one of the Dearborn princelings was threatening privately to buy him the self-improvement reading and writing course widely advertised on TV, "Hooked on Phonics." Maybe it would help his vocabulary.

But wait, there *was* some bad news about the instrument panel sound absorber. Rather than the requisite heavy piece of cardboard shaped to sit inside the dash, the supplier had delivered a flimsy substitute. "You put it in and it falls off like a pancake," reported one team member. The supplier's engineer owned up to the mistake. While he was still standing after his report, one of the B&A managers lit into him. Why, it was Tom Green, who had terrorized the DN101 team back in the pilot plant days when they were hammering out changes to the engineering design. Green had been promoted, but he had not mellowed. "You engineered it, you PSW'd it, you made it, you screwed it up, and you have a problem, you're going to handle it," he told the supplier. "Is that right?" PSW stood for "part submission warrant," a certification that the part met all the production requirements.

"Yes sir," said the supplier. He explained that the tooling people "took liberties" with the design. "They flattened it out."

"Just cut the bullshit," Green said, "and get back to design intent."

T WELVE SQUEAKS AND RATTLES per car was twelve squeaks and rattles too many. Absolute silence was the goal of the squeak-and-rattle team of two engineers, two Ford College Graduate Program trainees, and two assembly plant workers. They tested every DN101 that came off the line.

The squeak-and-rattle team. The name sounded like a joke, until you considered the consequences. One tiny noise on a test drive could send a potential buyer scurrying to the nearest Toyota lot. One tiny noise, repeated many times, could result in a high TGW count and millions of dollars in warranty costs. In the world of squeaks and rattles, there was "no such thing as a onesy," said engineer Jeff Sholtz. If it happened once, it would happen again. They sought to find the cause, not fix the car.

The squeak-and-rattle team had at its disposal a $3.5 million mobile test station called the Transportable Environmental Four Poster, housed in a tractor-trailer. The TEFP or "Four Poster" had attracted 17,000 visitors when it was on display at a University of Wisconsin technology fair. And now this exotic piece of technology was parked on the east side of the Atlanta assembly plant. Their wheels positioned on four hydraulic computer-controlled pads, DN101s bounced and rocked within the trailer on a simulated drive as taxing as a durability run. Sometimes irreverently referred to as the "freezer truck," its temperature could plummet to -20 and soar to +140 for climate testing. In this truck on the Explorer launch, they had discovered that exterior moldings fell off at high temperatures.

But for routine daily testing, the squeak-and-rattle team worked out of a garage area off the plant floor. As a freshly minted DN101 pulled into their service bay, Larry Crawford, a tall plant worker with a mellow southern voice and a relaxed manner, opened and closed all four doors several times, rocking them back and forth over the hinges. He rolled the windows up and down, up and down, on the right and the left, back and front.

Hearing a metallic sound from the rear when the front door slammed, Crawford released the seat backs and ran a practiced hand around the opening, probing the torsion bars that controlled the trunk door hinges. The clip that separated the bars was out of place and they were rubbing together. He drove the car onto rollers built into the plant floor that simulated a 40-mile-per-hour ride on a rutted dirt road; there he heard another noise from in back. Opening the trunk, he thumped the spare tire and tugged at the fasteners. "Spare tire's loose," he told Meg Grundstrom, one of the Ford College Graduate Program trainees, who was taking notes.

"Wasn't it the torsion bar?" Grundstrom asked.

"It was the torsion bar, too."

In addition to squeaking or rattling, parts could *tick* or *click, hum* or *whine, snap* or *slap, chirp* or *creak, buzz* or *bang,* or, if words failed, "contact" something. It was Grundstrom's job at the moment to pick the right descriptive word for a vibrating piece of door trim. "It's more of a feeling than a noise," she said, stumped. Crawford called it a "flutter." She wrote that down. Looking for the source, he removed the panel and found that the pins that held it in place had been loose. There was also a rattle in the driver's-side airbag cover. Workers were refusing to use a new fixture to hold the steering wheel as they bolted the airbag cover because it took too much time. Instead, they were holding the airbag in place with one hand and shooting bolts with the other, and the fit wasn't tight.

Next, Crawford and another worker, Ed Moore, took the car on an improvised test route around the plant that included some railroad tracks and a section of gravel. As Moore drove, Crawford heard a creaking sound and eased his long body, head first, through the rear-seat opening into the trunk. "We got a weld missing," he called back. On their return they radioed weld engineer Ed Stackpole, who arrived a few minutes later on a bike loaded down with gear. Stackpole found damaged metal where a robot had to reach through a speaker hole for a weld. "It's only got one-sixteenth of an inch clearance. It looks like the robot caught it and beat it up."

Usually the squeak-and-rattle guys could locate the source of a noise within minutes, sometimes using a stethoscope armed with a long needle for out-of-the-way locations. But Crawford once spent two days trying to track down what sounded like a loose screw in the instrument panel every time he pressed the gas pedal. He pulled the panel out of the car, turned it upside down, and shook it. Nothing. Then, by chance, he put his hand on the engine computer, and a piece of it moved. It was a five-minute job to tighten the loose material. Another time, he gutted the instrument panel, only to find that the culprit was a dipstick hitting an air conditioning line. Now that was one of the first places he looked. Once there was a rattle that sounded like a loose washer in the steering column. Two guys took turns driving around; one lay on his back under the column as the other drove. When the first guy's back got sore, they swapped positions. It was the steering wheel lock pawl.

After a tour in squeak-and-rattle, a guy was like the princess who felt a pea beneath a stack of mattresses. When Jeff Sholtz drove a DN101 from Atlanta back to Detroit, he said hello to his wife and spent the rest of the afternoon tracking down sounds he had heard on the way up. When they headed out to see his brother-in-law, he heard yet another noise from the rear. He pulled into a parking lot, crawled into the trunk, and asked his wife to drive around.

J UST AS R ICK S CHIFTER had predicted back in the studio days when he fought with the stylists over curves and corners, the sheet metal was arriving daily in Atlanta with A-margins, V-margins, and just plain too-big margins. The sheet metal of a car was like the foundation of a house; if it wasn't right, nothing else fit right either. Build after build there were leaks in the roof ditch—the joint between the roof and the one-piece bodyside. Three different sealants had failed, and now workers were laying down a strip of weld tape between the two metal slabs and 3-M tape on top. If the roof ditch was too narrow, owing to variation in the sheet metal, the molding stuck out; if it was too wide, the molding rode too low and the seal might not hold. Factor in variation in the way the guys in the plant slapped it together, and you had . . . more leaks. The roof ditch was simply too goddamned shallow, the result of a concession the team had made years earlier to the metal stamping people. Schifter got angry every time he looked at the goddamned candyassed thing.

Schifter's job frequently took him to Ford's Chicago stamping plant, located south of the city in a semi-rural area across the road from a truck farm. On June 5, he and the other men of steel gathered around the latest, greatest sheet-metal parts from all the different suppliers, assembled on a fixture that instantly disclosed their accuracy. Schifter was particularly distressed by the doors that were coming in from Ford's Buffalo stamping plant—they wandered in and out of spec, some over flush and others under. "On April 11, they told me they'd have a new door," he said. And now it was June 5, he was looking at the same old door, or at least one that wasn't any better. If the source were an outside supplier, they'd issue a QR or "Quality Reject" and the supplier would get the message pronto. But Ford plants could get away with murder, knowing they wouldn't lose business or go out of business. Buffalo was represented at the meeting by a quality underling. "They didn't even send a player," Schifter complained. The Buffalo guy promised new doors by June 9, four days hence. Schifter didn't believe him. "They'll be the same doors they got now." Schifter was a wrestling referee, and he was missing the season back home in Detroit. But on the job, out of town, he would call them as he saw them.

Schifter never came to Chicago without thinking of the worker who had been crushed in January while modifying a DN101 bodyside die. The worker realized he'd left a tool behind in the press and motioned his co-worker that he was going back in. Thinking it was a signal to start the press, his buddy hit the button. Schifter was in Atlanta when he found out about it. He had never met the worker, never knew his name, but it bothered him nevertheless. Shaken, he sat in the sheet-metal trailer after everybody else had left, visualizing the press and the die. He called his wife and friends. "Some place I've been, some part I designed, and it killed somebody," he told them. "It left him about four inches thick." He didn't like to think about it, but that same die was now in the magnificent new Schuler press, stamping out DN101 bodysides.

In the last year, a lot had happened to the seat fabric going into the base model Taurus—none of it good. Landgraff had never much cared for the stylish, swirly design chosen by design executive John Doughty before he left for Europe in 1993. On one occasion, when Landgraff happened to refer to it not as "China," its proper name at the time, but as "that icky thing," planner Brad Nalon decided to set him straight. "It's not icky, Dick," Nalon said. "It's our most expensive cloth." Landgraff's eyes went wide, as if someone had waved a thousand-dollar bill in front of him. "What do you mean? What's the Sable?" Amazingly, Landgraff hadn't realized they were spending $1 a yard more for the China fabric that was going into the low-series Taurus than for "Autumn," a bland design earmarked for the higher-priced Sable. It not only made no sense financially, it was very nearly immoral. The more expensive car should have the costlier fabric. Landgraff immediately proposed to switch the two, saving $21 on every base model Taurus. Autumn for the low-series GL; China for the high-series LX. He could scarcely contain his glee. "It doesn't require added engineering, saves the company money, and it doesn't add any cost. . . . We're never going to get another opportunity like this." But Ford Division nixed the switch. They had been promised China, they *liked* China, and they would keep China.

After that, every time Landgraff looked at China, he felt a double pang, owing to its cost and appearance. So when Lear said they could save $8 a car by simply changing the manufacturing process from a knit to a print with no change to appearance or quality, Landgraff didn't hesitate. But the printed version, called "Orient," had turned out to be nothing but trouble. It looked like China, all right, only not as good. On the armrest and the bolsters, Orient had a brownish hue that made it appear worn and faded. Nothing either Lear or the fabric supplier had done seemed to help.

Examining a gray Taurus GL with a Willow Green interior one afternoon under a hot Georgia sun, Landgraff listened to Lear's program manager, Ray Bomya, propose as a fix to change the direction of the nap or to use a dye with deeper root penetration. "We learn this over and over," Landgraff said, as much to himself as anyone else. "Don't program an invention." Someone told him that it wasn't an invention. Toyota used prints on 20 percent of their cars.

"Let me talk for a second about the unthinkable," Landgraff said. "If none of these works, can we go back to the China fabric?" In the silence that greeted his question, a jet screamed overhead.

In January, Ford had begun to divert some DN101 prototypes into a growing fleet that was cumulatively to log a million miles by Job One in the hopes that any problem, particularly any problem that might lead to a recall, would surface before the cars went on sale. Now close to the million-mile target, drivers reported that the Taurus, which was supposed to be as free of wind noise as an idle fan, in fact had two problems. At high speeds, air coming from the fender forced its way through a hollow cavity and exited at the A-pillar with a hooting noise around the windshield; the other came from a front-door seal. When Steve Kozak brought up the windshield noise at a plant review, Jody Butler complained he didn't know about it. "You ain't talked to me, Steve."

"We been talking about it all week," Kozak shot back.

Kozak felt bad enough about the wind noise. These prototypes were earmarked for upcoming media drives; for sure, speed-addicted scribes would notice the high-velocity whine. And now he was getting into scraps with people. He tried to make light of it. "I guess we've got two hooters," Kozak joked. It got a snicker from the group, but one of his female buddies took mock umbrage.

"And *he's* a manager?" she said.

It was the third dig that day. Something was clearly wrong with his management style, but he didn't know what. He had been to every charm school course Ford gave. Kozak thought about his predecessor in this position.

"What would Andy Benedict do?" he asked his friend, Zyg Gregory, who was now one of his chunk team leaders. "Andy wouldn't have been here," Gregory told him. Kozak got the message. He was still acting like a chunk team leader himself, with his finger on every inch of sheet metal.

In the last week of April, Dick Landgraff paid a quick visit to the plant, then drove back to Detroit in a DN101 fresh off the night shift. The first Wheeler Stanley heard about it was a memo from Landgraff demanding action on sheet-metal shortcomings. "Deck lid corners are low; deck lid margin is high in side view; front doors are outboard at sail mirror; front door B-pillar proud to rear door B-pillar. . . ." Thirteen ticks in all. Landgraff had also sent copies to three B&A managers. Now *they* wanted to know what was going on.

Stanley was steamed. Here he was in the middle of what was probably the most complicated vehicle launch in history, and Landgraff hadn't had the common decency to tell him he was in the Atlanta plant . . . *his* plant. And then he gets this memo, which said, in part: "It may well be that these issues are well understood and plans are in place. . . . I am unable, however, to get a comfortable feeling that this is the case from talking with Team members here or in Atlanta." It made Stanley look bad, as if he had lost control. "A guy of his caliber," Stanley fumed, "doesn't stop in and say hello to the plant manager. We could have resolved half these issues."

The incident was preying on Stanley's mind the following Monday, May 1, as he sought to get the plant running smoothly again after the usual weekend crises. A well-water pump had self-destructed, one of three on which the plant depended. And a white DN101 station wagon had almost been shipped with its luggage rack missing, a leaky gas cap, and off-color parts.

It was 6:30 A.M., far too early to try to reach Landgraff. "Status, Charlie, status," Stanley barked into the radio, calling for a report from Charlie Harper, the body shop manager, on the 6 A.M. start-up. "You bucked the fifty you had in overbuild? How many 101's you got to go through two and five right now?" "Two" and "five" were two banks of robots that applied spot welds on what was called the "respot line."

At 7 A.M. Stanley was standing on a bridge with his jacket pushed above his elbows, watching the robots below zap unpainted steel bodies, cued by a light sensor that announced whether a 1995 or 1996 model was approaching and whether it was a Taurus or a Sable, a sedan or a station wagon. The robots were programmed to apply different welds to each of the six bodies. If the car didn't move on after forty-five seconds, a buzzer went off, signaling trouble. And indeed, one of the robots was down.

Before and after each DN101 going down the respot line was an empty space, "air" Stanley called it, rather than a 1995 Taurus, a sign that the integrated build wasn't as integrated as it was supposed to be. "If I lose two cars every time I run one, I lose 105 cars a day," Stanley shouted over a harsh symphony of buzzers, bells, hissing robots, and the crash of metal on metal. "I can't afford it." He wanted to see the cars march past the robots in an unbroken line, he said, "just like Grant went through Richmond."

With fifteen miles of moving line, 250 robots, and so much aged body shop tooling that it would fill 168 rail cars when they finally yanked it all out, there was never a day when nothing broke. The plant was still trying to make up production from last week, when a major electrical ground fire had cost seven hours of 1995 Tauruses.

The plant's solution to the inevitable breakdowns in the body shop was to run the line through it at eighty jobs an hour, twelve and a half more than the speed of the final line. The surplus bodies were squirreled away in storage areas, fifty cars here, twenty there, to feed the rest of the plant when the body shop went down. "With sixty in storage, I got an hour," Stanley said. That was usually enough time to make a repair. Everybody knew this was the wrong way to do things. The right way was to do enough preventive maintenance that things didn't break. But there was never enough time or enough people, and some sections of the old machinery were almost totally inaccessible.

At 7:50 A.M. Stanley punched the keys of a nearby computer. The screen filled with figures. The plant had built sixty-five cars in the first hour, and forty-seven so far in the second. With ten minutes to go, he calculated they'd hit sixty-three. The forty-five-second buzzer went off. "Overtime," Stanley cried.

At 8:20 A.M. he was on the final line for a half-hour "tire kick" with other managers, looking for blemishes in the paint, uneven margins, doors out of flush. Maybe these were the last of the '95s. "But we can't let it slip. If they don't like this one they ain't gonna like the new one." At 9 A.M. he was in the pre-delivery area, inspecting the DN101 wagon that had almost been shipped with major flaws. "Before they go to pre-delivery they better have the designated sign-off or somebody's ass is mine, understand that?" Stanley snapped at G. T. Stewart, the final line area manager, a plant veteran who had chassis and trim operations. "Are there *any* DN101s we haven't beat the shit out of?

"Tell me about the off color. Ain't nothin' on this car that matches. . . . Don't run another car in the next build unless we run a color match. You're area manager. You make it happen."

He drew a breath and calmly introduced a new paint superintendent. "He's part of the family and I'm glad to have him."

Stanley's temper was legendary. "I've heard he's a yeller and a screamer," said his son, Wheeler Stanley, Jr., who had followed his father's footsteps right into the Chicago plant, where he was a general foreman like his dad when Studs Terkel had done his interview. The father he knew didn't lash out; he always made time to toss a ball around, no matter how tired. A romantic, he served his wife Pat breakfast in bed, bought her flowers, and left mash notes on her car windshield, thanking her for all that she did for him. When his daughter Melanie needed a date for the prom, he donned a tux and took her. Unlike her brother, however, Melanie had seen her father transformed by anger during a visit to the plant when she was young. Afterward she told her mother, "Mom, I never want to be on the other side of that finger."

RETURNING TO HIS OFFICE Stanley placed a call to Landgraff, and waited for a call back. His polished wood desk occupied one end of an office the size of a spacious living room, with an inviting gray leather couch, a conference table, and prints of antique autos. A few minutes later Landgraff was on the line.

"I understand you were here last week," Stanley said. He listened to a long response. "Everybody's all panicky over this letter," he said, picking up Landgraff's memo and beginning to read. " '. . . unable to get a comfortable feeling.' A little time with me, you might have been a little bit better." Better sheet metal was on the way, Stanley said, but not until the end of May. In the meantime, he would appreciate it if Landgraff let him know when he was coming. "Honestly, you create a problem and nobody likes problems."

Stanley hung up the phone, satisfied with the way the conversation had gone. "Maybe next time he'll spend some time with the plant manager."

And then he was back on the radio to Charlie Harper, checking on the troubled respot line. "Two and five. . . . Son of a bitch didn't run last week and it's not running this week. So what's giving me the warm feeling it's going to run for DN101?"

TWENTY-TWO

★

The Goodbye Car
and Job One

THE UNPAINTED sheet-metal car skeleton emerged from the octopus embrace of the big steel framing buck, journeyed by overhead conveyor across the railroad tracks that split the body shop, and descended to ground level, then clattered toward the two banks of waiting robots. Scrawled in large blue chalk letters on the right rear fender was a single word: "Goodbye."

Ten years ago the Atlanta plant had built the very first Ford Taurus, Lew Veraldi's crusade car, the home run that Ford Motor Company needed to stay and play in the big leagues. The last Taurus of that generation would be built in Chicago on June 26, two weeks hence. But this 1995 Taurus with "good-bye" scrawled across its flank was the end for Atlanta assembly, number 1,853,553 in the ten-year run. In its wake was space. The robots wheeled and turned, scraped and bowed, applying big flaming farewell smacks to the car whose shape had so enchanted America. One by one, they slumped and fell silent. A worker gave the rear end a pat before stripping off his heavy white gloves and stepping back. Out of nowhere, Wheeler Stanley appeared in a white golf cart. "That's the very last one," he yelled over the din. He gave a worker a thumbs-up sign. "Adios."

But the plant manager was preoccupied with the future, not the past. This weekend, demolition crews would rip out the last of the old tooling and load it by the ton into waiting rail cars. "Tomorrow when I see the bodyside getting crushed, I'll be happy," Stanley said. "I spent a lot of sleepless nights over that shit." His eyes glistened in the gloom of the plant's interior. "We have a new generation of cars coming in, new processes, a new workforce." Then he gunned the cart, hurtling down the paved alleys between the moving lines of men and machinery. "How 'bout it, Leon?" he called to Leon Garner, a dent-and-ding man. "Ready for the new one?"

That night, workers in a far corner of the plant put together just enough great, comfy Taurus seats to finish the run. Their area would be emptied for conveyors to receive seats arriving by truck from Lear's plant a mile away. "You come in here, all you see by Thursday is a concrete floor," said supervisor George Brown, as he and his people celebrated "Farewell to Cushion" with a spread of salads, nachos, fried chicken, chicken wings, green beans, and cakes. Turning up here too, Stanley accepted an offering of sweet potato soufflé.

When the plant shut down for the weekend, the Goodbye Car was marooned in the paint department. On the move again Monday, the scrawled farewell on its flank covered with bright red enamel, it traveled the six trim lines, and by afternoon sported a gray interior. "The end . . . The end . . . The end . . . The end . . . The end," said a computer printout taped to the front bumper. Sidelined through a shift change, the car began to creep forward again at 4 P.M. as four bells sounded and Henry Ford's assembly line jerked into motion. Giant yellow pincers slid down from the ceiling and gripped the roof of the last old-model Taurus, carrying it aloft for its trip through the chassis department. A supervisor in a crisp blue-and-white-striped shirt reached up with a green felt marker and signed the underside. A worker took the marker and added his name. Soon the car had a dozen signatures. Mark Winter, an electrician with long hair and an unruly beard, pulled over on his bike and watched. "I hate to see it go," he said. He added his name to the others. At the engine stuffer, Cheryl Melton, an electrician in a New York Yankees baseball shirt, was waiting with a Sony compact video cam. "The last one," she said. "The last one." Pat Wright, a chassis engineer on the DN101 team, ducked under its body and looked up. The parking brake grommet on DN101 was loose; she wanted to see what made it stay put on its predecessor.

As the Goodbye Car crept along the final line, collecting wheels, doors, and a rocker panel, and the usual hearty whacks from fitters aligning the doors, hood, and trunk lid, it also attracted a growing knot of people, who walked alongside. At the end, where he did his morning tire kick, Wheeler Stanley waited to drive it off. On Friday, back in the body shop, Stanley had struggled to express what Lew Veraldi's Taurus had meant to Ford Motor Company. "It was the most aerodynamic. . . . The plants that produced it were the most productive. . . ." But words failed him and he took the easy way out. "Adjectives on top of adjectives."

Now he made another stab at it. "A great, great car," he said.

F OR TEN YEARS, the ever-popular Taurus and its sister Sable had financed homes, cars, trucks, and boats, put thousands of kids through school, and bought their books, braces, and bicycles. Fat Taurus paychecks swollen with overtime had underwritten countless births, weddings, funerals, and other rites of passage. There were years when other Ford models sold poorly, and other Ford plants cut back shifts, but the Taurus had kept right on selling, and 6,000 people in Atlanta and Chicago kept right on working, assembling a total of 4,564,275 cars.

But the old Taurus was history. On June 19, 1995, Job One of the curvilinear new model would roll off the line. To people in Atlanta and Chicago, it was not merely a car; it was their paycheck into the twenty-first century. And a decade of stability had not erased the memory of the plant's vulnerability to market forces.

Like other Ford plants, Atlanta assembly in its early years had suffered the cyclical ups and downs of the auto industry. But not until Ford laid off the entire second shift in 1979 had these Georgians known really hard times. To be sure, Ford had not shut Atlanta down, as it had other assembly plants whose distance from the automotive heartland made them expensive to operate. And for a time, workers thought the layoffs would be short-lived. J. C. Phillips, a member of the union bargaining committee then and local chairman now, watched with a sinking feeling as people streamed from the plant. "They were yelling and screaming like they were really happy. 'We'll be back next week.' 'We'll be back in six weeks.' " But the weeks stretched into months, then years. "It took us five years. They lost homes, they lost families, because they kept thinking they'd be back."

Ed Moore, a diminutive man who worked in squeak-and-rattle, liked to tell new hires the cautionary tale of Deano, his buddy from those days. They had worked opposite each other on the line. "I walked in here one day. They said " 'The night shift is gone.' " Moore had seniority, but Deano was out on the street. Deano lost his home, his car, his truck, his family; he was a regular one-man country-music tragedy. One day Moore and his wife were headed for Harold's Barbecue in Lakewood Heights, when they saw Deano at a red light. Disheveled and disoriented, Deano didn't recognize them. First thing Deano said as he approached the car was: "Got a quarter so I can get something good?"

The ease with which Ford had disposed of an entire shift had convinced workers of the need to outperform other plants to keep Atlanta up and running. "That's when they woke our ass up," said Paul "Crazy Horse" Harris, a repair man on the chassis line. No more the freewheeling days when he would perform a crazy stunt and the plant would tolerate it, like the time in Paint when he stripped buck naked because it was just too damned hot. Or the time he sent a supervisor to the hospital with a bite on his shoulder. "They said it looked like a horse bit him. I said, 'Well, they call me Crazy Horse.'" (Later, said Crazy Horse, this supervisor had the plant build a car for him to his specifications, then he drove it off the line and never came back. "Shows you the caliber of the man he was," Crazy said. "He didn't treat Ford right. He could have finished the shift.") Crazy became a new man, and then he became a product specialist, assigned to mother the new car into production. "My attitude has changed, not just *my* attitude, everybody. They don't mind doing good work. Now since we got more quality oriented, seems like people likes their jobs better." But people still called him "Crazy Horse," or even—ever since he had a little fender bender with one of the DN101 prototypes—"Crash Horse."

An outsider could scarcely get ten feet onto the plant floor without being cornered by someone spouting off about quality. "It's nothing in the water," Stanley's predecessor, Bob Anderson, used to joke. Had not a nearby GM plant closed even though its workers were native to the same red clay Georgia soil? Researching an article in 1990, *Forbes* reporter Jerry Flint grew so suspicious of what sounded like a party line that he asked public affairs chaperone Tom Boyle to turn him loose. Afterward, Flint wrote, "This writer has tromped through car plants around the world, in eight countries from the Trabant plant in old East Germany to Nissan's Infiniti works in Japan, from Zaragoza, Spain, where the three-shift assembly was invented, to Buick in Flint, Mustang in Dearborn, Chrysler in Detroit, yes, even Studebaker in South Bend. But this writer has never seen such common purpose among union and workers and management."

"There used to be a lot of bickering over work allocations," said Jody Butler, who had feared for his own job during the second-shift layoff. "People complaining they had too much. I can remember fifty or sixty grievances in the system." There were still plenty of grievances, but rarely over work allocations, always the stickiest. When Wheeler Stanley arrived in 1993, he pushed cooperation a step further, asking the UAW chairman to join his operating committee. Phillips worried that members would think he had been co-opted, but he joined anyway. He was amazed to discover how much it cost to run an assembly plant. Now the union campaigned to hoard stock and energy. "It's money in the profit-sharing check."

By 1992, Atlanta was one of the country's most efficient plants. It could move a Taurus through the lines in 17.6 hours, a reduction from 25.8 hours in 1986. But now, three years later, on the eve of the most important and complicated model change in a decade, a 30 percent turnover in the workforce had Ford worried. Every month Wheeler Stanley officiated at a mass retirement ceremony. Some 900 retirees had so far put on jackets and ties and brought their families to watch them accept their plaques and a farewell handshake from the plant manager. Their stiff smiles were frozen in rows of Polaroid snapshots mounted in glass cases along the entrance corridor. And the question at hand was this: Could a workforce with close to a thousand inexperienced employees, who had not suffered the sobering consequences of slapdash assembly and customer abuse, launch the new car without a setback in quality levels that would give it a bad name? Ford would find out shortly.

In 1992, when Ford had twenty temporary openings, traffic en route to the county employment office so snarled the interstate that TV stations dispatched camera crews. Ford got bigger crowds and more press than George Bush, who was in town campaigning. This time, the state knew enough to hire a hall and spread applications over three days. Seven thousand hopeful people showed up. At $18 an hour plus overtime, bonuses, and profit sharing, Ford's hourly workers were making as much as $70,000 a year. People in skilled trades were breaking $100,000. Health, dental, and vision benefits were fully paid. The applicants came from every dead-end corner of the economy; they were cashiers, custodians, truck drivers, sales clerks, security guards, yard workers, fast food employees, gas station attendants. They all yearned for one of the last great jobs in America.

And then they found out the bad news. "You see them coming in so excited," said Anne Kilcrease, the plant's seasoned training coordinator, sounding genuinely sympathetic. "They only see $18 an hour. They don't realize that what they've been hired for is the assembly line."

The line. In 1913 Henry Ford had introduced the assembly line at Highland Park to make Model T's, and it had been running ever since. "It don't stop," a twenty-seven-year-old spot welder named Phil Stallings had told Studs Terkel twenty-three years ago in the author's Ford interviews. "It just goes and goes and goes. I bet there's men who have lived and died out there, never seen the end of the line. And they never will—because it's endless. It's like a serpent. It's just all body, no tail. It can do things to you. . . ."

Fifteen miles long, the Atlanta line demanded a rapid but mindless sequence of motions sixty-eight times an hour, eight or ten hours a day, five or six days a week, forty-eight weeks a year, for thirty years. Some workers would eventually escape its monotony as inspectors, repairmen, torque monitors, truck drivers, maintenance and cleanup people, perhaps as a utility man, who worked different jobs around the plant, or a relief man, who worked on a single section of line, filling in for people on breaks. But many were lifers.

Back in 1965, when J. C. Phillips hired in, he waited his turn to see personnel manager C. C. Martin. Martin asked him to hold out his hands. "If you had calluses or rough hands, he would hire you on the spot," said Phillips. Having cobbled soles for $1 an hour at a shoe factory in Tennessee, he qualified to hoist 100-pound hoods for $2.85 an hour. Jobs today were better orchestrated and less physically taxing. The workforce was different as well. One in eight was a woman. And there were almost as many blacks as whites. The presence of females and blacks had toned down language and pranks. Today's workers had high school diplomas, and 23 percent had some schooling beyond that. By the time Ford hired them, they had survived a four-hour battery of tests for aptitude and dexterity. But they had soft hands and soft bodies. Sometimes today's managers spoke longingly of a previous generation of country boys who had baled cotton or cut timber, who knew, as one put it, that physical labor was "more than carrying garbage out to the curb."

The people on the line had changed. But the line went on. One night Ernest Bennett, a relief man in the trim department, watched a new employee trying to learn a job on the relentless procession of cars. "If this person were to fall out, pass out in that car, we'd just pull her out, put her to the side, keep on going. We do not stop for nothing." The line was tough, but the line was powerful. Bennett respected it. "In Body, somebody with a hammer slams the pieces together, you get a shell. In less than a day you got a car you can drive to California."

"I hurt all the time," said Hugh Capes, clutching his thirty-year retirement plaque, about to leave the plant forever. And now his son, a new hire in Chassis, hurt also. Capes said he had to laugh the other day when he helped his son out of the car because his leg had cramped up so bad. "That's life around here." But the mental anguish could be worse. "I've seen some jocks . . . weight lifters, and the assembly line eats them up," said Anne Kilcrease. "They leave crying." Or they left angry, just walked out saying nothing to nobody.

So high was the dropout rate among new people—25 percent quit or were fired in their first ninety days—that the plant held small group sessions on Saturdays to warn prospects what they were in for. "You're going to give up a lot of things," Phillips told a group of forty fresh-faced recruits. "The assembly line takes away your freedom." The union chairman was wearing a blue, yellow, and white windbreaker that said "Taurus" on the right arm and "Sable" on the left. Gold links encircled a fleshy neck, and a diamond glinted on his hand. His message was downbeat, but his jewelry flashed money.

Down on the plant floor, at a simulated workstation, the trainees tried their hand at representative tasks. They pressed a weather seal firmly around a door, tightened nuts on bolts using a ten-pound motor, and turned other tiny nuts with gloved hands. Back in the conference room again A. W. McCord, who represented the UAW local on production standards, handed out squeezable chunks of rubber to strengthen their fingers. "It's fast, very fast work," he warned. "You're going to suffer out there. You're gonna be tired the first night and you got four more, and you can't lay out. . . ." McCord held up a fist. "Your hand will be like this." Not only would they hurt, they would have to do their hurting on the night shift, where they could expect to spend years before gaining the seniority to move to days. He gave them one final piece of advice. "If you got a pretty good job and it pays close to what you get here, I suggest you stay with it."

"Are you sure you really want to work here?" queried the title of a five-minute video that Kilcrease and McCord had helped put together for these sessions. Said an announcer, over an upbeat musical background, "You'll be completing sixty-eight jobs an hour, one every fifty-two seconds, every hour of every workday. The pressure can get pretty intense, and you can't just walk off the line to get a cup of coffee or a Coke . . . without *the bell*." The video cut to a shot from *The Hunchback of Notre Dame.* In the belltower, the hunchback cackled "the bell . . ." and scuttled over to pull its chain.

The bell. "It's kinda like high school," said a black woman, with a rueful expression. "It's a bell to start, a bell to eat, and a bell to . . ." She mugged into the camera. "You get the picture." The next shot was of an old-timer with a deadpan expression. "I hear those darn bells in my sleep."

The video was funny, it was even *inspired*, and it was also true.

In Atlanta, the line began at the southern end of the body shop, where sections of sheet metal that surrounded the rear wheels arrived on hooks like slabs of beef. Joined with two smaller pieces, they formed a section called the wheelhouse assembly, the cornerstone of each Taurus. This assembly connected to a rear section called the quarter inner, consisting of an additional fifteen pieces, which married up in turn with graduates of the new bodyside unit, nicknamed the "batwing," for big arms that swung up and out twenty feet, moving sections from station to station, welding roof rails, a rocker panel, the outer A-post, the inner A-post, and other reinforcements in seventeen automated operations.

At the north end of the plant, protesting with loud, hydraulic groans, the aging underbody fixture welded a front structure to the center floorpan and rear floorpan. The underbody section joined the built-up bodysides in the middle of the bodyshop, where five workers fit metal tabs through slots and hammered them down, an operation called "toy tabbing" which held the parts together for welding.

Now a loosely joined "body in white" traveling on a skid, the car disappeared into the octopus arms of the framing buck and reappeared with a roof, its seams anchored by basic welds. Like the Goodbye Car, the 1996 Taurus crossed the railroad tracks into the east side of the body shop, where the robots waited to add more welds by the hundreds. The body shop was noisy, dirty, and dangerous, but some men preferred to work there because the line went down so often, thanks to equipment failures.

On its way out of the body shop, the Taurus passed down a line of workers called metal finishers, who sanded and ground out tiny imperfections, then it disappeared into the paint department, to spend the next seven hours being dunked, sanded, sprayed, and baked in an automated operation that employed just over a hundred people on each shift. The paint job was critical; it was the first thing the customer saw; a single speck or discoloration could ruin a sale.

During the first hour, rinsed of body shop grime, its surface etched with phosphate to better hold paint, the car plunged into a tub of muddy, bubbling, electrically charged water known as "E-coat" and then through a series of rinses with purified water, purged of minerals that could mar the surface or bacteria that could multiply and form slimeballs. Once oven-toasted and cooled by fans, the body looked as if it were made of dried-out chocolate. A line of workers smeared gobs of sealer into the floorpan, the doors, and the roof ditch to keep out water and wind noise. Another oven toughened the sealer. More workers sanded out blemishes.

Descending an elevator, the chocolate Taurus glided toward the paint line, where spinning bouquets of ostrich feathers, suspended like brushes in a car wash, flicked away dust. Ostrich feathers, collected and shaped to fit its curvy profile, were far superior for dust removal to the prior method—four guys with sticky tack cloths. A vacuum system sucked the dust from the feathers. No one in the department knew how many ostriches sacrificed their lives every year to assure perfect coats of paint, probably plenty. And no one made a big deal out of it, because who needed animal rights people picketing the plant on behalf of ostriches.

After a robot applied a layer of urethane stone repellant to a vulnerable area of the hood, saucer-shaped disks sprayed overlapping coats of primer on the moving car and two workers with spray guns coated the engine compartment. As it exited from a prime coat oven, other workers masked the black door frames and prepped interior and exterior surfaces; a machine blew off the fine particles. Another caress from ostrich feathers, and the car was ready for its enamel. Guys with spray guns hit the trunk and interior, then automated disks coated the body with the first coat and nozzles sprayed a second. A clear coat was next, then the Taurus disappeared into an oven for a final toasting. Cars whose glistening bodies passed inspection could proceed directly to the plant for the six-hour trip through trim and chassis.

The six trim lines, and four of the five chassis lines, each about the length of a city block, ran from east to west across the width of the plant. Eighty percent of the plant's workers manned positions in the two departments. And 90 percent of them used air guns that dangled from cords each step of the way. The buzzing mingled with the clatter of heavy iron skids carrying cars between lines along moving tracks embedded in the plant floor, creating a din that was more even but only slightly less noisy than the crunching and crashing of metal over in the body shop. Dozens of forklifts and carts scooted up and down the aisles bearing supplies for the always-hungry lines.

N EARLY EVERY F RIDAY in the spring of 1995, A. W. McCord had led a new crop of workers with forty hours of orientation behind them out onto the plant floor, and deposited them one by one on the line. As beginners, they would earn $13 an hour to start, with 5 percent pay raises every twenty-six weeks until they hit the top union wage. Most found themselves in either trim or chassis.

"To run this job, you got to come in here hungry," Ernest Sloan said, as he showed Sid Austin, a sandy-haired former truck driver in his mid-thirties, how to reach into the engine compartment, position the windshield wiper motor and an airbag sensor, shoot two screws in each, then snap on the wiper blade. Jobs like these, where you had to stretch and bend, were among the toughest. In his first weeks, Sloan said he had dropped twenty pounds and sought out a chiropractor. He pointed to Austin, whose legs were straight as he bent over the car. "They're going to hurt. When he gets home, he bends 'em, he gonna feel like they popped." Sloan predicted Austin's wrists would throb as well. "He's supposed to hold them straight but it's hard." Sloan did the job easily with time left over to pull six motors and six sensors from boxes, and throw them into a staging box where he could pull out one of each as a car approached. After a few cars, Austin took stock. "It's unique," he said. Later in the shift, his body had begun to ache. "I see now the reason they want you to exercise hands and arms before you come in. I did some of it. I didn't do it enough." The next night, his lunch bucket was packed with ibuprofen, Band-Aids, and vitamins.

Three months later, Austin was doing the same job on DN101. Where once he had aches and pains, "All I have now is calluses." Now he had time to do all that Sloan had done, and move a wire out of the way for the worker at the next station. "People fuss, but when you get down to it, it's really not that bad of a job."

Austin's buddy from training, Tony Bishop, had started next to him, but now he was working on the instrument panel. His biggest regret, he said, as he tightened two screws to attach the "multipurpose handle" that operated the headlights, was in not having come to Ford ten years earlier. "When I get thirty years in I'll be sixty-one. Am I going to feel like working here?" His hands, he said, "sleep more than I do." He had to get out of bed several times a night to run cold water on them.

Over on the door line, Gregory Henderson had spent the first week on the job constantly behind, "in the hole" it was called, his supervisor badgering him to get with it. Now he easily popped two plastic rollers onto the window, set the window into the door, shot two rivets to hold it, and pressed in a weatherstrip. Henderson had been a well-paid electrician in a nuclear power plant in New Jersey before coming south for personal reasons. Thanks to Ford, he had quit a job as a school custodian, but he wanted badly to make his way into the plant's elite contingent of skilled tradesmen.

THE DN101 LINE was replicated in the plants all over the country, where an army of workers turned out carpet, trim, headlamps, taillamps, motors, electronics, handles, pumps, cases, windows, windshields, wheels, and wheelcovers. From those plants the line reached to others, in this country and overseas. For the seats alone, the line stretched from Atlanta assembly to Lear Seating's assembly plant down the road, and from there to Mexico, where Dora Ramirez Alarcon, thirty-two, a small cheerful woman who lived with her mother, sewed seat covers in Ciudad Juárez, across the border from El Paso.

Like their American counterparts, Lear's Mexican employees worked fast, they worked hard, and their bodies ached. Once a minute Dora Ramirez reached for a seat-back cover with the distinctive swirly pattern, positioned it on her heavy-duty industrial machine, sewed one line of stitches up, turned it and sewed the next line down, removed it, and reached for the next. When she sewed standing up, manipulating pedals with her feet, her ankles and the calves of her legs hurt. Sitting down was worse. The pain spread across her shoulders. She wasn't used to it, even after more than four years. Like workers at Ford's Atlanta plant, she frequently worked overtime, but hers came on top of a day that was already ten hours long. New Lear workers started at 28 pesos or $4.65 a day, at the going exchange rate of 6 pesos to the dollar; those like Ramirez with seniority had a base rate of 38 pesos or $6.30. One week she worked 61.4 hours and earned 351.30 pesos, about $58. The next she worked 55.4 hours and earned 280.90 pesos, about $47. A kilo of tortillas or a kilo of pinto beans could be had for less than 2 pesos, but cooking oil was 8 pesos a kilo and chicken sold by the pound at 7 pesos.

When Ramirez finished her shift, she joined a river of workers headed for buses once-yellow and used to transport American schoolchildren, and now painted blue and green and white. Not to put too fine a point on it, but never in a million years would the Dora Ramirezes of this world buy the car which bore their fingerprints, or likely any other. The seats she sewed were for wealthy American bottoms.

She boarded a bus headed for downtown Juárez. "No standees" was printed above the windshield in big black letters. Every one of the worn and torn vinyl seats was full, and so was the aisle. Just five feet tall, Ramirez stood on tiptoe to reach the bar over her head. From a speaker buried in the ceiling burst the voice of a male singer. *"Baile, baile, baile,"* he sang in a happy voice filled with static. "Dance, dance, dance."

The bus stopped across the street from Juárez's twin-spired stone cathedral, flanked by a smaller whitewashed chapel. Ramirez strode briskly across the dull red bricks of the plaza, her feet clad in stout, ankle-high black lace-up shoes, past scattered derelicts who she said made her nervous. "Plaza of the Bums," she called it. Her route took her along a pocked sidewalk lined with newsstands, boot stores smelling of leather, shops selling *tortas*, scruffy Mexican dogs. Her second bus was waiting in front of a juvenile furniture store with a window full of colorful enamel babywalkers. Sometimes, she said, she had to wait half an hour. Sometimes she was so tired she fell asleep on the way home and missed her stop, then had to walk back. Although Juárez had several hundred foreign-owned plants, some closer to her home, Dora Ramirez preferred Lear, even though the journey took as long as an hour and a half, because the company had hired and trained her five years ago when she couldn't get work elsewhere.

Formerly owned by Ford, many of whose managers had stayed on, the three Lear plants in Juárez were clean, airy, and well lit. The company took pride in a low 5 percent turnover rate, compared to a high of 20 percent at other *maquilas*. Jobs were so plentiful in Juárez, and the wages so uniform, that workers frequently returned to distant pueblos at Christmas and didn't drift back until February. Companies were forced to stockpile inventory in November to meet their orders. Lear provided two hot meals a day, a company park with a swimming pool, and periodic celebrations: a Christmas party for children, corsages and a steak dinner for mothers on Mother's Day, an important holiday in Mexico, and an annual beauty contest. But most important to Dora Ramirez, everybody got along.

Leaving the bus, Ramirez trudged two blocks down a dusty dirt road lined with a jumble of houses in assorted shapes and colors. In the mornings, she said, boys came down from the hills and threw stones at the people heading for the *maquilas*, just for the sport of it. This morning, the bus had lurched, thrusting her into the lap of a stranger. Was he handsome? She laughed. It was too dark to tell.

In this *colonia*, carved from the desert, there were no yards planted with grass and flowers, or shaded by trees. Where the road ended, there was a large stucco home on the left, but it stood out more for its surprising bright pink color than its size. Ramirez and her widowed mother had painted it on her last vacation. The living room contained old but comfortable heavy wood frame furniture with cushions. On the imitation wood-paneled walls were color photographs of her brothers and sisters in formal wedding dress. An older black-and-white photo was of her parents' wedding. There was a phone, a sign of prosperity. Living in a fine home left by her father, an electrician, and with no children to support, Ramirez was better off than many workers.

How many foreigners like Dora Ramirez labored on the network of sub-assembly lines that snaked back to Atlanta? It was a matter of some national interest, but no one really knew. Car companies were required to report the domestic content of each model to the federal government under the 1992 American Automobile Labeling Act. Eighty-five percent of the 1996 Taurus met the criteria, a figure that included the Georgia-assembled Lear seats. But regulations did not require disclosure of how many subcomponents were made offshore.

D AY BY DAY, in Atlanta the line was gaining speed. Twelve cars an hour, soon it would be twenty then fifty. . . . One after another, the creatures were popping off the end with Doug Gaffka's headlamps, Tony Paladino's steering wheel, Rick Schifter's one-piece bodyside, Lichia Bucklin's front-end package, Nevenka Schumaker's ICP, Len Flack's heating and cooling system. Theirs but so many others', too numerous to mention. Larry Moliassa, just for example, the princeling who presided over the electrical systems, and Dave Hall, the program manager from United Technologies who harnessed Moliassa's wishes to wires. You could thank them for the myriad of electrical signals that started the engine, heated the outside mirrors, and filled the cabin with sound and light. And down in Juárez, a skinny youth named Eleuterio

Lares Martinez, age seventeen, from Durango some 800 miles to the south, inserted the fuses.

Tim Mangan, who . . . but enough! The car was done. Or nearly so.

Three days before Job One, at a daily meeting with launch team engineers, supervisors from trim and chassis reported that brake lines were loose . . . a left front door turned up with a cracked hinge . . . every time the worker pushed down a certain wiring harness, it popped up . . . a clip wouldn't hold. They were having to punch taillight holes so the taillight would go in. The holes in the floorpan did not line up with the holes on the seat.

"I'll get you the repair procedure," chassis engineer Pat Wright told a supervisor with a misbehaving weld nut. "We've got a concern in the system."

"A concern in the system?" At the head table, area manager G. T. Stewart allowed himself a note of incredulity. After all this time, engineers *still* didn't understand the urgency. "What do I do immediately? Before Monday morning? . . . I got a car coming down the line right now, the pin don't sit. What do I do?"

"At the moment the repair procedure is a hammer," said a female supervisor with a sense of humor.

Stewart dismissed the engineers. What he was going to tell his twenty-five supervisors was not their concern.

"This is the best car in my twenty-eight years that I've seen at Job One," he said. Their assignment now was to crack down on workers who weren't doing their jobs. "If you will make each instance a major event when somebody misses something, it'll be a long time before it happens again." He sounded one note of caution. "We'll get some flak from the UAW. The UAW can't stand pressure. They like to give it out. They'll come down and tell you you're not doing things right. So make sure you do it right, make sure you do it politely, and then you do it."

In the launch team front office they were calling Stewart a "statesman" for the way he had handled the model change in his area. Now he was putting his leadership to a new test. He wanted workers to *stop the line* when something was wrong, even if it meant that the whole plant ground to a halt. In the past, unless a safety issue was involved, workers merely flagged a problem; repair guys down the line fixed it. But there was always the danger it would slip by. "In the past we would jump on them for holding the line," Stewart said. Only if they did so now, he said, could the new Taurus hope to avoid the usual spike in defects that accompanied a start-up.

That afternoon, Wheeler Stanley and his quality director, Phil Spann, visited the final line to select a Taurus to star in the Job One festivities. Cars paraded by like Miss America contestants. The winner wore a coat of rust-red Iris Frost, one of the new colors marketing wanted to feature; it had chrome wheels and a moon roof.

On the big day, this car would be positioned at the end of the final line as it came to a deliberate mid-shift stop at 12:50 P.M.; employees would gather in a roped-off area by 1:15, and then the Job One Taurus, followed by a Toreador Red Sable and a Moonlight Blue Taurus wagon, would drive off past a platform of cameras into a makeshift tunnel of curtains before bursting through a screen of fog, kicking off a half hour of speeches.

Beforehand, at noon, there would be the first of two press conferences. After the Job One show, the press was invited to return for a panel discussion, which would feature three of the product specialists who had been to Dearborn to test-assemble DN101 back in 1993, including Paul "Crazy Horse" Harris.

O N   T H E   M O R N I N G of the Job One festivities, Bob Damron, who shared the launch team command with Tom Breault, was in his office huddled over an outerwear catalogue with Dawn Denton, the team's representative from purchasing. All the workers and the managers in the plant had been given $53 red, white, and blue nylon Atlanta assembly plant windbreakers with a DN101 emblem on the left breast. Launch team members from Dearborn had been calling Damron and asking wistfully if they could have jackets too. He could hardly stand it. When the plant offered him one, he was so angry he turned it down. He didn't want a jacket if his team couldn't have them. One report had it that Wheeler Stanley had, in fact, planned to buy jackets for the launch team, until the UAW protested that the money was from a special fund to be spent on union members.

Tom Breault felt partly responsible. Landgraff had okayed the purchase months earlier, as long as the team stayed within budget, and he should have bought jackets right then and there, but now their new Ford 2000 vehicle center back in Dearborn was millions over budget, and suddenly it wasn't okay anymore.

Elsewhere that morning, seated beside the final line on tall, square-topped stools, Wheeler Stanley and Jody Butler waited for J. C. Phillips to join them for an interview with the Ford Communications Network, which broadcast a daily diet of company news and features. As it happened Phillips was late because he was handing out the last of the 3,100 jackets to workers so they could wear them to the Job One ceremony.

Dick Landgraff was examining some sheet metal with Bell, Kozak, and Schifter. Perhaps Stanley knew he had arrived, perhaps he didn't. Contrary to the plant manager's expectations, Landgraff had not repented of his controversial visit. To him B&A acted as if the plant was "eighteenth-century France. A big castle with a moat around it. . . . I don't pay attention to that stuff."

Landgraff looked at the car approvingly. "I must say the ditch molding looks fantastic." George Bell felt certain Landgraff's satisfaction wouldn't last. Whenever he returned from Atlanta, the boss inevitably issued a flurry of assignments. "He comes back with a good feeling; the half-life of that good feeling is three days."

In another area of the plant, G. T. Stewart was sounding off at a supervisor over scratched paint on a Sable fender. "The people don't have the message. You don't have the message. If you did, this junk wouldn't be out there."

THE OPENING PRESS CONFERENCE took place in a windowed room that had been a cafeteria for salaried workers until a wave of egalitarianism engulfed Ford. Now it was used for meetings. The walls were hung with the flags of countries to which Ford would export 1996 Tauruses. The one for South Korea had posed a problem; no one knew which end was up. Then someone remembered there was a South Korean on the launch team. He looked at it both ways, but even he couldn't decide.

Jim Donaldson, the ranking Ford official, told reporters that the Taurus provided 100,000 supplier jobs, benefited 700,000 shareholders, generated sales revenue of "many billions," and its 40,000 export units would "help the balance of trade" and "showcase American automotive engineering ingenuity." All but unnoticed among the superlatives was his announcement that it represented the "culmination of thirty-eight months of work." Shrinking the product development time had, of course, been the whole point of World Class Timing. And this glorious reduction from four years and sometimes longer was impressive indeed, but it was not the total picture. Using the original guidelines, DN101 development had consumed forty-four months, a lesser improvement over past programs. How could Donaldson claim they did it in only thirty-eight months? Simple. Ford had recalibrated the clock to start later, at Theme Decision in April 1992, the historic moment when the exterior design was approved, rather than with the initial engineering phase, as before. Toyota timed programs that way, which partly accounted for why the Japanese company turned out new cars in as little as twenty-four months. Buyers could care less about this figure, but it was important to the financial community.

Wheeler Stanley stepped to the podium, looking proud. "Today's the longest day of my life," he said. Was it a slip of the tongue? You could never be sure with Wheeler. He turned to prepared remarks on how they had renovated the plant and trained workers for the new model.

A T 1:00 P.M. EVERYBODY headed out to the final line for the big moment. Jim Donaldson jumped into the waiting Iris Frost Job One Taurus with Georgia governor Zell Miller; Wheeler Stanley and UAW vice-president Ernie Lofton were next in the Toreador Red Sable, then Landgraff and Phillips in the Moonlight Blue wagon. The entourage drove the cars off the line past flashing cameras and video snouts, and disappeared into the tunnel of drapes. At the other end was a stage, and hundreds of workers seated on folding chairs. With a burst of fanfare, a curtain was to slide open and bright lights would silhouette the cars as they made their entrance through artificial fog.

Inside the tunnel, seated in the Sable, Wheeler Stanley heard the unmistakable sound of a dead battery as Donaldson turned the key in the Iris Frost Taurus: *click . . . click . . . click.* It couldn't be happening . . . but it was. Job One had a dead battery. It had been in preparations all morning long, with lights blazing, air conditioning on max, and the doors open. And now, after sitting idle for a few minutes, it was pooped out. "That's not the first time it's happened," Donaldson said calmly, a gracious reaction for which Stanley would always be grateful.

Seated out front, Anne Kilcrease couldn't figure out what had happened. The Sable came out with Stanley and Lofton, the station wagon came out with Landgraff and Phillips . . . and also Miller and Donaldson, who had jumped in the back seat. Where was Job One? The Iris Frost Taurus never came out.

A FTERWARD, IN THE OLD CAFETERIA, J. C. Phillips paved the way for the product specialists. "Nothing wrong with engineers by the hundreds that come down here," said the UAW local chairman. "But we felt like there was a better way. . . . Our people are more adept to take care of the problems." In the back of the room, engineers from the Dearborn launch team exchanged looks that said, "What are we, chopped meat?"

"'When we come up with an idea, management listens," said John Collins, the first of the product specialists to speak. "Ten years ago this would never have happened. This is one of the greatest advancements I've been connected with."

Crazy Horse was second. He barely got out the words, "This is one of the smoothest model changes that I've seen yet," when he started to choke up. " . . . credit to others. . . . caught me at a standstill. . . ." Too overcome, he couldn't go on.

But reporters weren't writing any of this great stuff down. Tom Boyle, Ford's public affairs guy in Atlanta, tried to coax the product specialists into giving some concrete examples of how they had improved the car. But Crazy Horse was in no shape to talk about the torsion strut bushing he had carved in two with his penknife back in the pilot plant days. There was some talk about a radiator, but it fizzled out. Some reporter asked Landgraff a question. "I'm delighted to be a part of the management team that did all the listening," the Maximum Leader said deftly.

THE PRINCES AND PRINCESSES from Dearborn gathered that night at the Three Dollar Cafe on Peachtree Road in suburban, well-to-do Buckhead, which offered 300 kinds of beer in which to drown their disappointment at the day's events. For six months they had given up homes, husbands, wives, children, boyfriends, girlfriends, friends, families, pets, and plants. On call at all hours, they had worked nights and weekends, while the old plant hands, their cheeks swollen with Red Man chewing tobacco, abused and ridiculed them. Where were *their* kudos? Where were their *jackets?* "It was like it was our birthday and nobody gave a party," said Kellee Condra, a blond engineering princess assigned to sealing. She had spent entire days flopping around the car on her back and belly with water dripping on her as she tried to track down leaks in the water booth. And the only recognition from the plant for her work were three grievances alleging she had done union labor.

There were more Job Ones ahead, for the export model, for the SHO. But the ceremony today marked the beginning of the end of the launch team involvement. By summer's end they would be packing up to go home. And DN101, on which Condra had worked for three years, would belong entirely to the plant. The team had known it would happen, but not this way. "We were handing off the car," she said. "And they just took it."

TWENTY-THREE

Meet the Press

TO POWER-LOVING, torque-tracking, tire-squealing, car-tuned journalists, the opportunity in December 1994 to see but not drive the curvilinear 1996 Taurus had been a cruel tease, like serving a hungry person a sizzling steak with orders not to eat it. Car writers had been itching to get their hands on the wheel ever since, to give the new Duratec engine and the vaunted DN101 suspension system a full court press, and to trot out some of those wonderful writerly words: *unabashed sheet-metal flair . . . Swiss-watch smoothness . . . muted, silky-sounding engine.*

Most writers were resigned to waiting until May or July, when Ford's public affairs department planned two "ride-and-drives" for the media. Scheduled for Dearborn, the first was primarily for magazine writers, who had lead times of two to three months; the newspaper scribes with daily and weekly deadlines would attend the second, in Charlotte, North Carolina. If all went according to plan, news of the Taurus's second coming would blanket America in the weeks before the car went on sale, followed by a predictably hyperbolic TV advertising blitz, so that one in every two people old enough to answer the phone and talk to a market researcher would know there was a new Taurus in dealer showrooms. This achievement would represent 50 percent "awareness," the target for both public affairs and advertising. Presumably the double-barreled publicity would awake a craving to own the car so powerful that showrooms would overflow with eager buyers.

In holding reporters at bay, however, Ford had made an exception for the fab four car 'zines, *Car and Driver, Road & Track, Motor Trend,* and *Automobile.* Each was offered a sneak preview at the Dearborn track and interviews with DN101 executives and engineers. Sure it looked like favoritism, but such was the power of these fuel-injected monthlies to influence less astute writers, or so Ford believed, that the company would be nuts to do otherwise. Besides, the other car companies did the same thing. And now that the auto show publicity had played out, Ford could use a little boost to keep Taurus in the spotlight. The official sale date for the new car was September 28. That was a long time off.

The February *Automobile* hit the stands with the Taurus on the cover and an article that said the handling was significantly improved over the old Taurus, but the engines were "no great departure." The June issue of *Motor Trend* was out in May with a "driving impression" that also commended the stiffer body. *Motor Trend* had kind words for the seats, "comfortable" and "supportive," and an overall positive view of the car. "Ford has clearly redefined the midsize American sedan and raised the class standards to new heights." But like *Automobile,* its writer lamented the engine performance: "May not be much quicker than the 9.2-second 0–60-mph run we recorded with the previous generation."

"The automotive press just talks to each other," said Dick Landgraff, unfazed by the criticism. It seemed to him that the only publication that could really help sales was *Consumer Reports,* consulted by an estimated 30 percent of new car buyers. When its April new car issue went on sale, the magazine's regular readership more than doubled, to half a million. Landgraff was a big believer in the value of *Consumer Reports.* When the *Consumer Reports* bumper-basher did over $700 worth of damage to the 1990 Taurus, Landgraff made sure the bumper on the 1992 model could take the hit. The Taurus was the best of the domestics, in the magazine's opinion, but an also-ran after Honda and Toyota. DN101 targets had been set way back in 1991 with the intent of reordering that lineup. And last July, Landgraff had driven a prototype over the magazine's thirty-mile test route in rural Connecticut with dealer Bob Tasca and a bunch of development guys in other cars to see how well DN101 measured up. They picked up some unfamiliar wind noise around the rear windshield, but nothing else they didn't know about.

Consumer Reports aside, automotive writers divided into two distinct camps. There were product people, True Believers who cared passionately about cars and their attributes, and there were business reporters, who might not know torque from torsion, but had a handle on the yen–dollar relationship and studiously tracked the plays and players in the corporate games.

True Believers were the guys and occasional gal who wrote for what were known in the trade as buff books, *Car and Driver* et al., plus the car writers from what were commonly called "screwdriver books"—*Popular Science* and *Popular Mechanics*—and dozens of specialty publications, and also automotive writers for daily and weekly newspapers. To True Believers, being paid to test and tout new cars, often in exotic surroundings, was the best job in the world. "We don't have people who are putting in time waiting to go to the *New York Times,*" said the editor-in-chief of *Car and Driver,* Csaba Csere. "For them, it would be a step down." Sometimes True Believers worried about the future of their profession. Given the complexity of cars and the popularity of computers, technically gifted young people were more likely to be computer jocks than gearheads.

Even among True Believers, there were stratifications. The truest of all were the guys from the buff books—and, by the way, they hated that name—who looked down on newspaper reviewers with their bland family readership and piddling fifteen inches of copy. What did they have in common? "We exist on the same planet," said Patrick Bedard, a columnist for *Car and Driver.*

Among publications that assigned business reporters to the auto industry were the *Wall Street Journal,* the *New York Times, Reuters, Bloomberg Business News, USA Today,* and magazines like *Fortune, Forbes,* and *BusinessWeek.* To them, the remake of America's most popular car was a hot story. These writers were less interested in how well the Taurus performed than in how well it would sell. Already there were questions about whether Ford was pricing itself out of the market. "Our readers want us to hold auto executives even more accountable than politicians," Jim Healey, the senior automotive writer for *USA Today,* had explained at the Chicago Auto Show, when the affordability issue surfaced. "There's no tax increase that's going to cost $20,000. You can't vote a CEO out of office." He and others in the business press were continually on the lookout for opportunities to pry clues and quotes from executives who turned up at media events. His job, Healey said, was "to make these people explain themselves."

At communal meals, True Believers would sit down with engineers, whereas business writers crowded around the table with the vice-president for sales. True Believers seldom used proper names for cars. They talked about the time they strapped themselves into a DRM 600 ZR-1 or the 850 T-5R. They drove the 200SX SE-R, the C280, the E300, the Q45 or the MX5. Why say Lexus when there was only one LS400, or Jaguar when everyone knew who made the XJ6?

The hometown newspapers, the *Detroit Free Press* and *Detroit News,* had writers in both categories who paid close attention to every move the auto companies made. In March, Alan Adler was the only newspaper reporter to slip into a Ford sales division meeting for dealers in Naples, Florida, and thus the only one to hear a loose-lipped speaker say that Ford planned to be 20 percent better in quality than Camry. Adler's story announcing the claim put Ford in a terrible quandary. To deny it would sound terrible. But the 20 percent goal was an internal objective, and an uncertain one at that. Dick Landgraff was bombarded with worried calls from vice-presidents. "There's nothing I can do about it," he told his secretary Nancy Donaldson philosophically, and asked her to look into getting tickets for a bird-hunting event.

After Detroit, Cleveland was Ford's next most important manufacturing and supply base, its "second city," and Chris Jensen, the automotive writer for the *Cleveland Plain Dealer,* was on Ford's short list of important media connections. Among writers, those who were syndicated were more important to the car companies than those who were not. The *Plain Dealer* fed the Newhouse News Service. Jim Mateja covered cars for the *Chicago Tribune* but his stories went out over a news wire to six million readers. Freelancers were at the bottom of the heap, just a cut above freeloaders who took the free auto company trips and didn't produce. That said, several freelancers had risen above the pack. Paul Eisenstein had a varied list of clients, from *Investors Daily* to Northwest Airlines' magazine, and by his account earned over $100,000 a year. A hard worker like Eisenstein need not limit his subject matter to cars and their features. He could also peddle stories on sales trends, profits and volumes, manufacturing processes, technological advances, government regulations, management fads, and politics within and between corporations. More and more auto industry articles now bannered China, Thailand, India, and Vietnam in headlines. While other news beats such as sports, politics, and medicine might attract more mainstream press coverage than cars, none had a larger number of specialized publications hungry for material. Even *Automotive News,* the weekly newspaper owned by Crain Communications Inc., with its own staff and a circulation of 76,000, bought freelance pieces. "It's a very different business," Eisenstein said, "and the volume of copy it eats is incredible."

As a woman and a freelancer, Michelle Krebs, who had worked for *Automotive News* before becoming self-employed, started with two strikes against her. In the beginning, people called her "that girl writer." None of the True Believers would sit with her at meals, or share a car on media drives. Not until her work appeared regularly in the *New York Times,* she said, did people take her seriously.

In recent years, Ford had cultivated a group of writers, including Krebs, who had banded together to give annual awards for the best car and the best truck, as had been done in Europe for many years. For the first two years, minivans had been considered trucks because that was the way the government did it. But for the 1995 awards, the Car and Truck of the Year jury placed minivans in the same category as cars. They did, after all, carry people more often than cargo. This change was of great significance to Ford, for it meant that the 1996 Taurus would be competing with the 1996 Chrysler minivan for Car of the Year, with the winner to be announced in January 1996 at the Detroit Auto Show.

BECAUSE PROTOTYPES were in short supply, every division at Ford competed for them, and press drives traditionally suffered the handicap of having too few. With just seven DN101 prototypes available for the first media drive, Ford scheduled reporters in four waves of a dozen each. John Jelinek, the public affairs point man for the Taurus/Sable launch, was not happy to learn that all the cars would be either silver or blue, because that's what the plant was painting the week their order was filled. That was better than black or white, but not as good as red. "*I* don't care what color it is," a magazine editor once told public relations, "but the vice-president for sales says if there's a red car on the cover, he gets 20,000 more sales."

Ford's decision to stage a media drive in the Detroit area for a model as important as the new Taurus was something of a departure. Detroit lacked sizzle. The weather was temperamental. And the roads were flat, crowded, and usually under construction. Public affairs preferred California, with its good roads, benign climate, and photogenic locations. But reporters had been to California so often they were getting jaded. At the recent Lincoln Continental drive in Monterey, one told Tom Rhoades that it was his sixth time there that year, and his third overnight stay at the Carmel Valley Ranch. East Coast writers were complaining about having to make the cross-country trek so often.

But Detroit did have an abundant supply of engineers and executives. Reporters, said David Scott, the public affairs vice-president, always wanted to "talk to anybody who had anything to do with the car." And Ford could use its Michigan Proving Ground at Romeo, as long as they juggled the media schedule to accommodate durability drivers. Romeo was an excellent course, and DN101 had been groomed on its hills and dales. The car would shine.

In a different era, Ford had chosen Detroit to usher in the 1958 Edsel, the most famous flop in automotive history, with a three-day blast for 219 reporters and their wives, flown in first class and lodged at the old Sheraton-

Cadillac Hotel. A dinner-dance featured the Glenn Miller Orchestra, a dancing fountain, a chorus line, a comedian, a stunt violinist, and the singing McGuire Sisters. The *Detroit Times* society editor called it "a coming out party for a debutante on wheels." After the festivities concluded, 71 reporters were given Edsels to test-drive back to their newspapers.

That was when the trouble began.

While still at the track, one guy started in gear and ran into a post. En route to Dodge City, Kansas, another lost an oil plug and his engine froze in a town called Paradise. The Ford PR manager, who borrowed an Edsel to visit his parents, was exiting the Pennsylvania Turnpike when his brakes failed at the Fort Washington exit. He rolled through the tollbooth lane with the collector in pursuit. Overall, representatives of the media were not impressed with the Edsel, which offered little new technology and more than a few glitches. Customers agreed. Pretty soon all the good feelings generated by the splendid party had dissipated, and the press was making fun of the car's horse collar grille. Reporters could turn, just that quick.

For whatever reasons the car failed, the launch wasn't one. "There was nothing wrong with the launch," said Judith Mühlberg, who was entering her first season as head of North American Communications.

The media send-off was a time-honored tradition, no matter how pallid the offerings. There had been years, said Tom Rhoades, a public affairs veteran, "when the only thing you had to talk about was new paint. You'd trot out some tired old cars, give some sales figures, and that was it." In the late 1960s and early 1970s, launches had a wild and wacky flavor. Playing on a Wild West theme for the Maverick, Ford had rented a movie-set town for a pretend shootout. As they waited for the action to begin, reporters quaffed real drinks in an old-timey saloon. They were supposed to watch robbers steal a Conestoga wagon, a band of cowboys recapture it, and its sides clamshell down to reveal the new car. Only, some of the reporters for whose benefit the hijinks were staged never left the saloon.

The debut of the Mustang II in San Diego featured a fireworks extravaganza, with the car's numerals spelled out in the night sky. Below, cars circled a pool at the Hotel Del Coronado, where Sea World swimmers in a water ballet pushed around a plywood Mustang logo. The press had covered the rehearsal, and on the night of the show 10,000 rabid Mustang fans were waiting on the beach to see the sky light up. So was Henry Ford II. Also waiting were six Phantom jets, scheduled to land at a nearby naval base. The base, in radio contact with Tom Boyle of Ford public affairs, warned that one of the planes was running out of fuel. Boyle radioed his boss, David Scott, who was timing the fireworks. "You've got to let them go," Boyle screamed. Scott gave the order to set off the fireworks. Through the lights and the smoke screamed the six Phantom jets. Henry Ford turned to Scott, impressed. "Who the hell thought of this?"

To launch the 1992 Taurus, Ford had invited 250 press to Atlanta, piled them into new Tauruses and Sables, and given them directions to Lake Lanier where they spent the night at the Stouffer Pine Isle Resort. The next day they drove a handling course at Road Atlanta, an all-purpose track.

Reporters loved these drives and the get-togethers afterward—the cars and the car talk, driving and schmoozing, schmoozing and boozing. And automakers typically bestowed a gift to show their appreciation. Veterans of many launches had closets full of jackets, luggage, cameras, radios, binoculars. At the Edsel debut, Ford presented three well-known scriveners with gold-plated typewriters. For the upcoming Taurus and Sable drive, public affairs launch leader John Jelinek had amassed fifty briefcases made from the same soft leather available on DN101 seats. For the all-media drive in August, Ford would give away luggage carts.

Few in the automotive press questioned whether to accept this bounty from the people whose products they wrote about. The gifts were the least of it. The car companies paid for the lavish trips and provided year-round access to loaner cars. When a writer from *Town and Country* overslept and got left behind in Morocco, BMW sent a plane to retrieve him. When another took a cab 120 miles to the wrong hotel, Chrysler shouldered the blame for giving bad directions and picked up the tab. Some publications even allowed their writers to do "crossover" work—to moonlight for the very people whose cars they were supposed to criticize, and who were their major advertisers.

In 1990, the *Wall Street Journal,* which had a ban against freebies whatever the industry, broke a gentlemanly silence on the subject in a page-one story. "Welcome to the world of automotive enthusiast journalism, where the barriers that separate advertisers from journalists are porous enough for paychecks to pass through—as well as airline tickets to Japan, free rooms at fancy resorts, gift certificates, clocks, briefcases, and, of course, free use of some of the hottest new cars on the market." All the buff books were on the dole, along with most of the trade press, including *Automotive News,* as well as many newspapers. By and large, newspapers owned by large national chains and national magazines paid their way and turned down gifts, though many of their writers drove a new "test" car every week.

The *Journal* article had done nothing to put an end to the extravagance. Introducing the Infiniti Q45 $50,000 luxury sedan in 1993, Nissan hosted writers and their spouses at the Ritz Carlton Rancho Mirage, a tennis spa near Palm Springs, where they could have facials and massages at company expense. For dinner, they supped in a house once occupied by Elizabeth Taylor, on food prepared by Wolfgang Puck, a prominent Los Angeles chef and restauranteur. During the first day, Nissan turned the couples loose in a Q45 with a map and a picnic lunch. The wicker picnic basket equipped with tableware was theirs to keep. The next day the company took them for hot air balloon rides.

For its 1996 minivan ride-and-drive, Chrysler also invited spouses; the company flew everybody in four successive groups of thirty each to San Francisco, gave them a sporty Dodge Stratus sedan to drive to Napa Valley, and put them up in the Auberge du Soleil, a collection of mini-villas smack in the middle of a hillside olive grove overlooking the California wine country. The next morning the gang tested the cars at a nearby racetrack, then drove back to San Francisico, swapped the cars for minivans, and headed south to Big Sur country on U.S. Highway 1, selected to demonstrate that the minivan handled as well as a car on the narrow, twisty coastal highway. They spent the night at a small, secluded hotel called the Post Ranch Inn, in either cliffside cabins or treehouses, both with ocean views. On day three of this odyssey, Chrysler gave these very special reporters picnic lunches and maps, along with video cameras to shoot marketing messages for a make-believe competition judged by their hosts. They had to turn the cameras back in, but they got to keep their tapes. Many headed south for the William Randolph Hearst castle, San Simeon, a monument to yellow journalism. On the fourth and last day, they returned to San Francisco for flights home.

For a time in the 1970s, when the *Washington Post* uncovered the Watergate scandal, many mainstream newspapers and magazines banned corporate trips in an effort to eliminate their own internal sources of corruption. The *Journal* article had raised the issue anew at a time when only a handful of reporters, perhaps 10 percent, still paid their way; it made some publications squeamish once again about accepting subsidized stories.

Freelancers like Paul Eisenstein were in a bind. If he financed his travel, he'd go broke in the first ten minutes. "I like to think nobody can buy my copy," Eisenstein said. Warren Brown, the automotive writer for the *Washington Post,* which had a squeaky-clean policy against freebies, was sympathetic to freelancers like Eisenstein, his buddy. "We're self-righteous and clean because we can afford to be. We make a lot of money."

Since the *Journal* article, *Car and Driver* no longer allowed employees to take a paycheck from car companies, although they were still expected to go on free trips and they could accept gifts. As editor-in-chief, William Jeanes had initiated the policy against crossover work, and he extended it to *Road & Track* when he became publisher of both. He also thought accepting car company trinkets unworthy of writers like his who earned upwards—often more than twice upwards—of $45,000 a year. "They're not Bolivian tin miners." He had seen people—always freelancers, of course—fighting over gifts. It was, in a word, "repugnant." Given his druthers, said Jeanes, he'd prefer to do away with the trips as well. "All we need are the cars. We don't need Beef Wellington."

SPANNING JUST A DAY and a half, the Taurus/Sable preview for the long-lead press began with an afternoon of speeches and technical displays and continued the next day with a drive. The group that arrived on May 22 was filled with heavy hitters: Patrick Bedard and Dan Ross, True Believers from *Car and Driver,* one writer each from *Fortune, Forbes,* and *BusinessWeek,* and Paul and Anita Lienert, a couple who reviewed cars for the *Detroit News* and other newspapers in a duet format called "He Drove, She Drove." The Lienerts were a dynastic family in media circles. Paul's father, Bob, had been the executive editor of *Automotive News* for many years. His sister, Jean Lindamood, was one of *Automobile's* rough-writer columnists.

In a departure from custom, *Consumer Reports* had also sent a writer and a test driver. In times past, the magazine worried that these events might jeopardize the objectivity of staffers. The writer, Gordon Hard, said that the idea to come to media launches was his, to increase his exposure to cars on the market. Staffers assigned to other industries often attended trade shows; he said he had argued that drives fulfilled the same purpose for people like him. Hard was neither a True Believer nor a business reporter. Until two years ago, in fact, he had been the magazine's food editor. "I wrote about popcorn, olive oil." He promptly dubbed the rounded Taurus styling "the melted cheese look."

As the writers checked into the Dearborn Inn, a vintage hotel built by Henry Ford across from his airport and now managed by Marriott, media-trained DN101 engineers wearing bright green Taurus golf shirts reported to their posts at technical displays set up for the press in the Scientific Laboratories, a new building with an auditorium where the speeches would take place. This was the third press wave and DN101 team members felt like pros. The week before, *USA Today's* Jim Healey had cornered engineer Mark Jarvis and designer Nevenka Schumaker at the display for the football-shaped radio and climate control unit. Somehow plans to come up with a new name had never materialized, and it was still the Integrated Control Panel. Healey wanted to know why there was no separate on/off air conditioning button like the Japanese had. And had they equalized the speakers "so the sound doesn't jump out at you?" And why weren't the stove-type climate control knobs big and round instead, like the volume knob?

"People love these knobs," Jarvis told him. "They really do."

"That's what people say?" said Healey, a fair-skinned man with shrewd eyes. "People love this? Am I not people?"

"You're very special people," Jarvis replied smoothly.

Dick Landgraff kicked off the speeches. "Why do you want a design that looks smaller?" queried the *Forbes* reporter, Jerry Flint, during the question period. Flint was a garrulous, white-haired veteran of many launches, and several publications. "Most people want a car to look bigger."

"That's not true of women," Landgraff answered.

"How do you know?"

"We asked them."

Flint refused to believe him. "Just on the surface, bigger is better. If you're charging more for cereal, do you want the box to look smaller? That's why we're into the Wonder Bra. Bigger is better."

One of the few women present, Anita Lienert, didn't know which was more offensive: Landgraff's contention that women didn't like big cars—as if to say, blacks liked Cadillacs—or Flint's allusion to big breasts. In fact, by day's end, she had gotten a lot of negative vibes. As a woman, she said, "I felt, like, hostility." She thought Ford was defensive about the design. "Where's that insecurity coming from?" And then she strolled through a corridor of technical displays: laser welding, NVH, the exhaust system. The mystique of cars was lost on Anita Lienert. "I see being a car enthusiast as being a blender enthusiast," she said. "They're just tools."

DURING DINNER THAT NIGHT at the Dearborn Inn, the talk drifted to radar detectors. Patrick Bedard of *Car and Driver* said he owned one, designed by a friend, that had four-way directional signals. "It's brilliant," Bedard said, "just to see such an elegant piece of machinery." You could hardly put a dollar value on it, he said. "A hundred dollars? A thousand?"

"Sure," said Landgraff enthusiastically. He was always on the ragged edge of losing his license. "I've calculated what it would cost to have my wife drive me to work." Even the guys from *Consumer Reports,* who were not very talkative, were drawn in by the topic. Radar detectors, Hard said, were in the same category as guns—one of those products *Consumer Reports* would never rate.

"THIS CAR IS VERY GOOD," Patrick Bedard said the next day as he guided a new Taurus around Romeo roads and slalomed through a stretch of cones. Compared to competitive cars on hand to drive—the Camry, Accord, and Lumina—he predicted the Taurus would be "more controllable . . . under very adverse circumstances." An adverse circumstance might be running a wheel off the road. "Most driving is very mundane, so when something unexpected comes up you're not ready for, this car will cover for you." Bedard had a flair for pronouncements that left listeners wondering if they had just heard something profound. "Part of the fun of cars is parts that move," he said, "but some of the fun is the parts that don't move because they're not supposed to."

He was a thin man with a wide mustache, who was pictured in his column with a clenched-teeth grin and a dangling toothpick. The toothpick was pure *Car and Driver,* a saucy, bad boy touch, the kind of thing that gave the magazine a reputation for irreverence. In its December 1994 issue *Car and Driver* featured a mock dustup between the Taurus SHO and a Taurus rocket made by Orbital Sciences Corporation. "Ford's power-assisted steering rack keeps its Taurus straight and true, but OSC's three-axis inertial attitude control has the kind of feel and response that usually only comes from European-bred, race-ready missiles developed and sold to garrulous [*sic*] Third World nations." That, too, was *Car and Driver.*

B Y   T H E   S E C O N D   N I G H T Ford had lost all but a handful of reporters. This was always the danger when events were at headquarters. After a day of driving cars in Romeo, the people who lived in Detroit just went home.

The press who were left assembled for dinner in Greenfield Village, Henry Ford's re-creation of a nineteenth-century town. A horse-drawn cart ferried diners from the gate along a narrow road past Henry Ford's childhood home, to a replica of the factory where he had built the first Model T. The meal was served by candlelight at big round tables in an upstairs room. John Jelinek took a seat at a table with Landgraff and the writers from *Forbes, Fortune,* and *Business Week.* The launch leader was thirty-nine, but he looked younger with lustrous black hair and matching mustache, and people had a tendency he found annoying to call him "Jay-Jay."

This was the third time in ten days Jelinek had been to dinner here with reporters, and the third time he had been served a big plate of sliced roast beef, pork, and veal, with a heap of steamed vegetables and two kinds of wine. The food didn't change, only the cast of characters. One more time, and this long-lead media event would be over, then on to the all-media drive in Charlotte. Overseeing the complicated Taurus media rollout was his biggest assignment in his six years at Ford. So far so good.

Landgraff sat between Jerry Flint, the *Forbes* reporter, and Kathleen Kerwin, *Business Week's* Detroit bureau chief, known to friends as "Katie," who was small with dark hair and a soft voice. Her colleague Jim Treece had left the magazine, and she had taken over the in-depth story he had begun on

DN101, currently slated for a cover sometime that summer. Under the ground rules, everything said during these events was on the record. Across the table sat Alex Taylor of *Fortune,* an urbane New Yorker who was making his first such media drive in three years. He was always amused at the fuss the car companies made at these events. "They treat these cars like they're one-of-a-kind masterpieces," he said. "In fact, they come out every week."

At the other table, Patrick Bedard and George Bell were deep in a True Believer conversation. Bedard was impressed that Ford had shelled out $5 per car for gas-assisted hood struts, when the competition didn't have them. "It was the right thing to do," Bell said.

Jelinek listened with half an ear as Flint, on his left, engaged Landgraff on the subject of CAFE, the government's fuel economy mandates. Flint argued that CAFE had accomplished precisely what the government had intended, forcing automakers to make affordable, fuel-efficient cars that reduced pollution. As it happened, Dick Landgraff hated CAFE. To sell the requisite numbers of fuel-efficient cars, Ford had to set prices so low it made no profit. He thought it was no way to do business.

"I'm not concerned about affordability," Landgraff said. "If Joe Blow can't afford a new car, tough shit. Let him go buy a used car."

Jelinek was normally as expressionless as a blackjack dealer. Suddenly he looked as if he had swallowed an ice cube. Landgraff was a PR man's nightmare. The guy just said whatever was on his mind, and Jelinek couldn't even nudge him to shut up because Flint was in the way. Unaware of Jelinek's distress, Landgraff kept on going. "I'm concerned about making money for Ford Motor Company," he said. "I'm worried about making profits and returns for our company and ourselves. I don't think anyone would argue that if CAFE were not in effect, we'd have much higher profits. Why would we charge $10,000 for a car, when the cost is $9,000?" Jelinek looked around. At least none of the business writers were taking notes.

His relief was short-lived. A few weeks later he got a call from Katie Kerwin, who said she wanted to check some quotes for her Taurus story. Jelinek arranged a three-way telephone conversation between himself, Landgraff, and Kerwin. "I am going to say that you said this," Kerwin said, reading the Joe Blow quote twice, which she had cleaned up slightly so that instead of "tough shit," Landgraff was saying, "I don't give a damn." She said she wanted to check the quote because it had arisen during a discussion of small-car prices in connection with CAFE, but she was using it to make a point about the more expensive Taurus. "Do you have any problem with it?"

"Say 'Yes,' " Jelinek thought to himself. " 'That will cause a huge problem for me. . . . I would rather you did not use it. . . . It was the wine talking.' "

"No problem," Landgraff said.

T HE J ULY 2 4 ISSUE of *Business Week*, with a green Taurus on the cover and the headline "TAURUS—Remaking America's Best-Selling Car," came out after Ford had announced the prices of 1996 models. The Taurus GL sedan base price was $19,150; the LX, $21,530. The Sable low-series GS was $19,545; the LS was $21,845. The article's inside headline posed a question: "It's jazzy, but is it too pricey?"

Landgraff picked up a copy of the magazine in the Detroit airport, en route to Charlotte for the second media launch. Both he and George Bell were concerned that the test course show DN101 to its best advantage, given that Alex Trotman was planning to be there. In addition, public affairs had invited sixty Wall Street automotive analysts, to impress them with Ford's new product, and to give them a briefing on earnings and plans. "By the time journalists writing stories call the analysts for comment," Judith Mühlberg said, explaining the strategy, an experiment, "they'll have something positive to say." Landgraff was looking forward to meeting a few. This was his chance to ask a question that had long puzzled him: why Ford's price-to-earnings ratio was so low.

His flight delayed by a huge thunderstorm, Landgraff had plenty of time to study Kerwin's *Business Week* article. The 1996 Taurus styling was "a bold design departure." The base engine offered "a smoother, quieter ride." The car was "stuffed with little extras." Concluded Kerwin, "The new Taurus should bring Ford nearer to winning import buyers." Nothing wrong with that. But he was dismayed by an extensive discussion of pricing and market strategy. He had hoped the magazine would analyze what the DN101 team had set out to do and render a judgment about how well they had succeeded. He barely noticed his quote, which appeared on the last page.

Bad news awaited Landgraff when he got to the Charlotte Motor Speedway the next day. He had expressly ruled out a gymkhana, the kind of twisting cone-marked routes used in autocross courses. These media hotheads would drive the Taurus like a sports car if they had the chance. He had even seen dealers peeling rubber at a gymkhana at a Lincoln-Mercury sales show.

So what had they laid out? "A goddamned gymkhana, all those little tight turns. It was all wrong." Moreover, Bob Bondurant, the driving ace, was there with helpers from his school to coach the media and give them hot laps on the high-speed track. Helmets waited on a table. Landgraff didn't like that either. Helmets sent a certain signal. "You're going to be driving at such a speed you could roll over." Then he heard one of Bondurant's guys say, "Don't drive beyond your abilities." The whole thing was just crazy for the launch of a family car.

The first day of the drive was set aside for the analysts. Landgraff couldn't believe how young they looked. None of the ones he talked to could answer his question about the price-to-earnings ratio to his satisfaction. These were the people whose prognostications could make or break Ford Motor Company? One of the more prominent complained to Landgraff that he had heard the hooting noise around the windshield at 90 miles per hour. "I said, 'What are you doing going 90 miles per hour?'"

Given the course, Landgraff wasn't really surprised later to hear that one of the reporters had cracked up a Taurus. The reporter wasn't hurt, but the car was a goner. They cannibalized it for parts.

As the day wore on, Landgraff learned his quote in *Business Week* had become the talk of Ford. Trotman, who had flown in to Charlotte after attending Chicago's Job One ceremony, told him not to worry. "You're going to get all kinds of letters calling you an elitist pig," the Ford CEO warned. "I get letters like that all the time." Indeed, back in Dearborn, protests were starting to arrive, from inside the company as well as outside. One Ford secretary faxed Landgraff a message. "You probably don't realize it, but we poor people read *Business Week*." Landgraff decided not to worry. "Nobody's going to shoot you. This isn't Bosnia. What's the next worse thing? They fire you. That's not the end of the world."

TWENTY-FOUR

The American Dream

WHAT LATER CAME to be known among the folks at J. Walter Thompson, Ford's advertising agency, as "the Saint Patrick's Day Massacre" had begun auspiciously enough in Naples, Florida, at the Registry Resort, where some 500 major Ford dealers from east of the Mississippi were driving the 1996 Taurus for the first time, an important milestone in what Ford Division, the marketing arm for the Ford badge, was calling "the launch of the century."

The dealer meeting per se was not what had drawn a delegation from JWT on March 17 to the lavish coastal compound, where rooms cost $350 a night. Rather, it was the opportunity to sit down in one place at one time with the peripatetic Ford Division hierarchy—vice-president Ross Roberts and his second-in-command, Steve Lyons, along with national advertising manager Gerry Donnelly. So important was this meeting that Peter Schweitzer, the head of JWT's Detroit office, and the second most powerful man in the whole agency, was also here. The hour had arrived to nominate ideas for a TV campaign that would absolutely overwhelm the American buying public with the magnificence and desirability of the new Ford Taurus. The winning campaign would fill TV screens on every network prime time show for the first five days in October, and some other programs besides. Only the most adept channel switcher could escape. Readers turning to any one of a dozen national magazines would find the Taurus there as well, in glorious, glossy color.

Once Roberts gave his go-ahead, J. Walter Thompson would test the proposed campaigns in shopping malls around the country. In what were called "mall intercepts," a pollster would invite shoppers into a small screening room to watch a "clutter reel" of seven commercials that included Taurus, then answer questions designed to measure how well they remembered it. In addition, a group of dealers would vote on a favorite campaign. The high scorer in these competitions would go into production in July.

For each of three proposed campaigns, writers and art directors working in pairs had created four spots, emphasizing design, performance, safety, and the station wagon. And for each design spot, the agency had put together what was known as an "animatic," a filmed sequence of hand-drawn scenes with an audio accompaniment that imitated a finished commercial. The remainder were on storyboards, frame-by-frame cartoon-like depictions of proposed commercials.

When they got to Naples, someone from the agency had the idea to demonstrate that the commercials would be even more powerful with music, so writer Lauren Crane had made a last-minute dash to Wal-Mart to buy a $170 Sony boom box, and then to a music store for some big movie themes—*Star Wars* and *Jurassic Park,* played by the Boston Pops. As a finishing touch, they had hung a banner that said "Design, Design, Design" on the wall of the elegant hotel conference room, which had a crystal chandelier and an aqua carpet splashed with big pink flowers. "Design, Design, Design" was a quote from Ross Roberts stating the top three qualities offered by the 1996 Taurus. The three words were also embroidered on the black extra-large golf shirts that JWT had purchased, hoping to put Roberts and the others in a receptive mood. But, alas, the shirts had not arrived from Detroit. A new employee, thinking to save money, had sent them by UPS rather than Fed Ex.

As the meeting got under way, Mike Priebe, JWT's creative director for cars—his counterpart handled trucks—rose to introduce the first campaign, titled "Once Again There's Nothing Like It." One by one, big bold capital letters jumped onto the screen, spelling out T-A-U-R-U-S. In between each letter was a shot of a new feature—the headlamps, the ICP, the flip-fold console—described in an assertive voice-over narrative. First Priebe showed the animatic, then the storyboards. When he finished, all eyes turned to Roberts, a genial Texan with steel gray hair, wary eyes, and a broad accent. The sales vice-president wore a deep frown. "I don't like it," he said abruptly. Where were the people? he wanted to know. Where was a Taurus threading its way through scenic vistas? "You've lost the emotion. You've become a goddamn engineer. . . . Emotionally it doesn't do the car justice." Grumpily, he asked to see the others.

The next, titled "What the Future Looks Like," opened with free-floating elliptical line drawings that solidified into assorted oval features found on the Taurus. Again, there were studio shots of the car and a noticeable absence of people. Roberts shook his head. "Show me your third one." The meeting had grown very still, the JWT people were, like, frozen, their high spirits dissipated. No one made a move toward the boom box. The third, called "Design Rules," pictured people eagerly awaiting the arrival of the new Taurus. "I'm glad you finally got a person," Roberts said, with an edge to his voice. But like the others, these commercials were cool and clinical. In one, an X-ray revealed a steel safety shell; another talked about horsepower and precision steering. "You never said it's America's best-selling car," complained Steve Lyons, Ford's marketing manager. "You never talk about mainstream value. . . . You also missed spaciousness. People want to know if there's enough headroom . . . enough trunk room."

Roberts started to rise. "It's more than the best-selling car. . . . This is America. This is a new revolution." He told the agency to think of the people who bought the first Taurus in 1985, to imagine them as today's buyers. "You don't have to sell the facts. We've got 3.2 million people out there who like the car." He suggested they "go look at Aurora." This was not the first mention of the current commerical for the Oldsmobile Aurora, which opened on a woman gazing into an abstract painting. An Aurora appeared on a brushstroke shaped like a road. Now the woman was in the painting, at the wheel, driving into a sunset, to the rousing strains of "Appalachian Spring." Roberts really liked the Aurora ad.

"Go get emotional. Get high. This son of a bitch is big. We've got to get people into the stinking showrooms." And one last thing, Roberts said before he left, "Don't talk to any more engineers."

The JWT guys were in a state of shock. What did Roberts have in mind? People going gaga over the car, rolling their eyes and pointing, singing and dancing? "I'm used to rejection," said Lauren Crane. "But I really thought we got this one right."

As they quietly began to pack up their gear, the golf shirts arrived. The opened box sat on the table, beneath the chandelier. "We can't give them to them," said Dick Howting, the executive creative director. "They don't want anything we've got."

Y OU COULD HARDLY blame the agency for being confused. Every Ford marketing paper since the DN101 program got under way in 1991 had identified the target customer as a discriminating import buyer, personified by Dick the Varsity Captain and Jane his cheerleader wife. With approval back in 1992 of a budget increase to match Camry, top management had endorsed the same strategy. In December 1994, the advertising agency reviewed its target buyer with Ford for the umpteenth time. "While imported cars may have seduced them in the past, now they question their intrinsic value," said a strategy summary. "They are inclined to buy American this time, but Saturns are too small, the Lumina and its GM clones too boring, and the LH of dubious quality." That left, *ipso facto,* the 1996 Taurus.

The creative teams had based their campaigns on research that showed import buyers wanted facts, not hype. They were interested in features and performance, safety and security, the engine and the driving dynamics. "A hundred thousand miles without a tune-up" was always a high scorer on a list of verbal hot buttons. Mentions of the trademarked MicronAir filter and dual airbags also rated high. Probably no Ford was ever subjected to more marketing research than the 1996 Taurus. In focus groups around the country in late 1994, Ford floated themes to reach import buyers as well as current Taurus owners. One suggestion was to push "craftsmanship," but the word confused some buyers, who weren't sure what it meant in connection with cars. The idea of cars designed by "empowered teams" also did poorly. One respondent called it "corporate bullshit." Mere quality had lost its novelty as a selling point; people now expected it. But the phrase "Quality you can see, hear, and feel" yielded a strong response.

In still other research, "family car" had proved a dubious virtue. People with families thought it sounded apologetic; people without families found it offputting. Besides, sedans weren't as likely to be family cars since the advent of minivans. They carried an average of just 2.1 occupants per trip, while minivans averaged 3.2. Some marketing people had thought references to the vaunted "Taurus heritage" might motivate buyers, but it seemed to be of no value whatsoever, at least not to import owners, who actually snickered when they heard it. The best news was that Americans were still passionate about design. Both Ford and JWT agreed that the new Taurus offered the opportunity to recapture leadership in that arena. Armed with such insights, and long lists of Taurus attributes, JWT's creative people had come up with five campaigns that they believed were sophisticated enough to attract import buyers and appeal as well to discriminating owners.

Ford's advertising manager, Gerry Donnelly, had narrowed the number to the three they showed Roberts. The Naples meeting was as disappointing to Donnelly as it was to JWT. An earlier review of truck advertising had been a big success. Roberts had loved the truck ads. The Taurus meeting "could have gone better," Donnelly said wistfully. "It could have gone more like the truck meeting."

F ROM R OBERTS'S POINT OF VIEW, it was madness to ignore 3.2 million Taurus loyalists to chase after finicky import drivers. "Ford Division is not going to go after the import owner," he said repeatedly that spring. "We think the import owner will come in."

If there was one thing Ross Roberts knew how to do, it was sell cars. His first exposure to the car business had been his stepfather's used car lot in Norman, Oklahoma, where he worked as a teenager on weekends; he had been selling cars for Ford Motor Company since 1963. In 1991 he had taken over the most powerful division in the company. Body and assembly operations might claim to make the cars that made the money for Ford Motor Company, but without orders the plants came to a standstill. And since 1992 Ford Division had delivered the top-selling truck and the top-selling car in America, plus three others in the top ten. Ross Roberts himself had led the charge that elevated the Taurus to the number-one spot in 1992. When it came to Taurus advertising, Roberts called the shots. His division paid the bills.

Roberts blamed himself for the false start he had witnessed in Naples. He should have intervened earlier, he said, to put J. Walter Thompson on the right track. He felt bad about it. But he also felt optimistic. "They'll get it. They're the best in the industry."

N AMED FOR ITS nineteenth-century founder, J. Walter Thompson was one of the world's largest advertising agencies, with 204 offices in 69 countries. Ford was the company's largest account, with an estimated $700 million in billings, and because of that Detroit was JWT's largest office. The agency occupied six floors in a handsome new Detroit high-rise, just a fifteen-minute sprint through glass-enclosed skyways to Ford advertising on the thirty-sixth floor of the Renaissance Center tower, a trip JWT people made frequently. For fifty years, the agency's fortunes had been intertwined with Ford. "There's a Ford in your future!"—that had been the agency's first slogan for Ford, in 1944. The 1960s began with "You're ahead in a Ford" and ended with "Ford has a better idea," with a clicking lightbulb logo. "Have you driven a Ford . . . lately?" came about in the 1980s. In the 1990s they dropped the dots. Such was the magnitude of the Detroit operation that the agency president, Peter A. Schweitzer, was in charge there. In 1994 Schweitzer had turned down a promotion to CEO rather than return to the company's New York headquarters. He had grown attached to Detroit, and fond of Ford, he said.

While JWT handled the national or "tier-one" advertising, other agencies were involved in tier-two regional and tier-three dealer campaigns. "Tier one," Ford's Gerry Donnelly once explained, is "'Buy a Ford, the Taurus.' Tier two is 'Buy a Taurus today, 2.9 percent financing for the next seven days,' and Tier three is 'Buy a Taurus from me.'"

For JWT employees, working on the national Ford account meant big budgets, first-line production crews and casts, and a lot of visibility, all without having to take up residence in New York or Los Angeles. The Ford account also offered variety, from big trucks and pickups to sport utilities and sports cars to minivans and sedans. Said Mike Priebe, "Some people think working on cars is too stifling . . . totally uncreative. But always, automatically, every year you have all new products. . . . And I like cars. There are a lot of different ways to talk about them."

And in the case of the dramatically styled, heavily equipped 1996 Taurus, that had been one of the problems. So much to say, so little time. If nothing else, the job was simpler now. Roberts had not necessarily backed away from design, design, design. But he also wanted commercials with people, people, people . . . and emotion, emotion, emotion. But not too many facts.

The switch in strategy put Priebe in mind of the old joke: In the hold of a Viking ship, where slaves man the oars, the guy holding the whip makes an announcement. "Rations of bread and water are being doubled. That's the good news. The bad news is that the captain wants to water-ski."

So what if the captain changed the orders? The Taurus was Ford's most important car, and it was Ford's money. Priebe was the guy with the whip.

Ten years earlier, when the original Taurus debuted, the creative people at J. Walter Thompson had found themselves with a major model to launch that had no name recognition. "Everybody was scared to death," said Kinder Essington, the creative director at the time. "We didn't know what to do." At one meeting, they ran through thirty-five ideas. Essington knew they had hit a low with a commercial that opened up on a valley out west, filled with a milling herd of nondescript brownish sedans. On the rim of the canyon appeared a silver Taurus. It charged down the mountain and began to herd the other cars into a circle.

There is an old saw in advertising: "Let's sing our way out of it." In 1985, JWT had decided finally to commission a big piece of music, something that went *ta-da!* Essington recognized the winner the minute he heard it. "It felt

big. It said this was a car for America." To be sure, it took a slight mispro-
nunciation to get the rhyme to work. And they only used it for three months.
But that was long enough to penetrate the American psyche.

"TaurUS—for US!"

RETURNING FROM NAPLES, writer Lauren Crane and her colleagues in the creative group had work to do on other car lines, including a
batch of new commercials for the Contour, which Ford was launching once
again after its troubled debut. In their spare time, they watched the Aurora
commercial over and over, looking for clues to what had so appealed to
Roberts. They were also mindful that he had singled out the first Taurus campaign for inspiration. And what the two commercials had in common was a
big piece of music. *Let's sing our way out of it.*

Crane retreated to the old, settled suburb of Ferndale, where she lived in
a cozy Tudor furnished with antiques and fringed with a garden. Like her
house, Crane was calm and unassuming. But it was well known among her
friends that she harbored the passions of a country-music lover. Not only was
she taking guitar lessons, but she had once written a song for a dealer show
that country-music singer Joe Diffie recorded. Country lyricists often
employed word play and so did Crane. The Taurus, she had written in the
"Design Rules" campaign, "doesn't have a sharp edge anywhere, except over
the competition."

Although she did not watch much TV—she found it awfully noisy—
Crane was devoted to *Ellen*. And when she finished her song, she did something Ellen DeGeneres might have done. She called her mother and read her
the lyrics. "Is it silly?" she asked. "Oh, Lauren," her mother answered. "That
is *very* professional."

Her mother's response amused her. Not "wonderful," not "catchy." But
professional. . . . "Like maybe I'll go do this for a living," Crane said dryly.

IN APRIL, THE CAST of characters from Ford and JWT reassembled
in a different luxury hotel in a different southern city. Once again the agency
people were in high spirits. The last conclave with Roberts had been as good
as the first one was bad. They had caught him on the fly at 6 A.M. one morning in Dallas, and he had endorsed four new campaigns. The purpose of this
meeting, at the Ritz-Carlton in Atlanta, was to bounce them off Ford's dealer council, to choose two for testing.

The ellipse-filled commercial, "What the Future Looks Like," had been
held over from the first round, because it focused so imaginatively on design.

Per Roberts's instructions for new commercials with emotion, the "Future" team of writer Linda Teegarden and art director Scott DuChene had come up with a people-packed alternative titled "A Portrait of America at Its Best." It framed the Taurus with Boy Scouts, the Taurus with a female jogger, the Taurus with a briefcase-toting businessman in a hurry, and the words "This is what America's about. The will to become something more, the desire to build something better, the courage to go beyond that which has always been. It is the new Ford Taurus, *a portrait of America at its best*." Back in Detroit, Teegarden and DuChene eagerly awaited news of the meeting, to see how their submissions had fared. Not only was it important from a career standpoint to win from time to time, but a campaign's creators got to assist with the production and go on location.

A third option, "Once Again, There's Nothing Like It," was set to contemporary music, with Taurus and people filling the screen between clicking sounds, as if they were snapshots brought to life.

For the fourth, Lauren Crane's lyrics, set to music by an L.A. composer and sung by a chorus, filled the room.

> *It's the American Dream,*
> *You can hold in your hands.*
> *Taurus stole your heart once.*
> *It'll steal it again.*
> *It's promises made. It's promises kept.*
> *It's a dream within reach,*
> *And it's you at your best.*
> *Taurus, the American Dream come true for you.*
> *The American Dream come true.*

Among the dozen dealers present, there was considerable sentiment for the ellipse-filled "Future." "People are looking for change," said Jack MacKenzie, who owned Hopkins Ford in Philadelphia. "We've got to tell them what's new." But the dealer next to him preferred "Dream." "Taurus deserves the pomp and circumstance that goes with it."

"This is what we're going to do," Roberts said. He told the agency to combine the free-floating ellipses with the snapshots into a single campaign centered on "Design," and similarly to combine "American Portrait" with the song-filled "Dream" for a second campaign, and then to test them. All the agency people knew that Roberts, a patriotic Boy Scout fundraiser, preferred "Dream." To Roberts, the Taurus truly was a symbol of America's can-do spirit. He believed in the Taurus, and he believed in the American Dream. Born poor in a dust-bowl Texas town, to a mother who was part Indian, he had worked his way through the University of Oklahoma pumping gas at an all-night station. From humble beginnings he had risen to become wealthy and powerful. Like the song said: *"It's a dream within reach/And it's you at your best."*

Already the words had caught on. "The American Dream come true...," joked Steve Lyons as he left the meeting room. "Now with $500 cash back."

Both "Design" and "Dream" scored well in the mall research, but neither was the clear winner. At a May vote of 75 dealers in Orlando, however, "Dream" averaged 4.66, out of a possible 5, while "Design" scored 3.86. In verbatim remarks on "Dream," dealers praised the "excellent music." They said, "Go with this campaign," "a great concept," and "best Taurus campaign in years."

But for one teeny-weeny little problem, everything would have been fine. And that problem was this: The Taurus song contained two of the same words as the commercial for the Oldsmobile Aurora, which had so enchanted Roberts, and which the JWT team had watched repeatedly to divine his wishes. Never spoken, the words appeared in small print in the final frame of the Aurora spot, and at the bottom of the print ads. Without realizing it, they had incorporated the words into the song, and not until after it was approved, had anyone spotted the duplication. And those words were "American Dream."

Gerry Donnelly didn't think Ford would have a legal problem. "How can you copyright an American Dream?" he asked rhetorically. In fact, since the duplication had surfaced, people had noticed the phrase in other ads, for motorcycles, for motor homes. The American Dream was everywhere. And what *was* the American Dream anyway? Many people thought it was a job, not a car. But Ford didn't want to risk a controversy. Best merely to replace a word, the "[blank] dream" or the "American [blank]." "Ideal" perhaps. "The American Ideal"?

In the end, Ford and JWT decided that "dream" was the more essential word. They could show America with pictures. Rather than *"The American Dream come true for you,"* the lyric would be *"Making the dream come true for you."* And so forth.

Lauren Crane had always imagined they would go east rather than west when the time came to film. The East Coast looked so much more American, more settled, and much greener. "It gets a little brown in L.A.," she said. And now the time had come. JWT producer Carl Spresser lined up a production company in New York, where most of the scenes for four thirty-second commercials and one sixty would take place, with some scenic outdoor American-style footage in Maine and Wyoming. Actors were hired, locations rented. And on Wednesday, July 12, Lauren Crane and several colleagues set out in a van at 6:30 A.M. from Manhattan's U.N Plaza Hotel to capture a dream.

Their first stop was a shuttered redbrick college in East Orange, New Jersey, for a scene where a middle-aged mom and dad delivered their son for his freshman year. Youthful actor Jonathan Hershfield, who in real life would start New York University in the fall, assumed a stoic expression while his actress mom, standing next to a green Taurus wagon and wearing a sweater set in a lighter green, gave a tiny wave and exchanged a sad look with her actor husband standing on the other side. It was so realistic that JWT's account executive Matt Stoll, though ten years out of college, felt a pang. The place reminded him of his own alma mater, a small Michigan school.

At the next location, a camera crew shot down on the Taurus wagon wheeling through a wooded hillside park. "This is a heavy tick area," one of the technical crew warned people sitting on the ground. Lauren Crane happened to have clipped a story that very morning from the *New York Times* on Lyme disease. Everyone gathered round to look at the life-sized sketch of a deer tick.

At 11:30 A.M., the Taurus production crew, now swollen with actors and actresses playing assorted Taurus moms, dads, kids, and a grandfather, descended on a rambling three-story house in the New York suburb of Montclair, New Jersey, on a quiet street shaded by old trees. Painted pale yellow, with white trim and green shutters, the house chosen as that of a typical Taurus owner, whose median income was less than $50,000, had a big green lawn and the kind of wraparound front porch where people used to sit in swings and wooden Adirondack chairs before there was television. The Stars and Stripes fluttered from a flagpole in the front yard. Listed with location scouts, this site in recent years had starred in commercials for a chain of home centers, a wallpaper company, and Vick's Vaporub. No question, this house was a dream. It had a tennis court, a basketball court, a swimming pool, and a greenhouse. And it had cost its owner of two years $970,000, according to the woman he had recently wed, a slender barefoot blond artist in a sleeveless black sheath, who popped out from time to time to watch the action. As it happened, her husband, an investment banker, had also just bought a new car, although the Taurus had not been among the candidates. Indeed, the closest he came to a domestic purchase was rejecting a Cadillac. He had dismissed the Lexus as "too common"—everybody seemed to be buying them. It took him three months to decide, she said, but he finally bought a $50,000 BMW.

The day had started with a drizzle, and for a time the weather remained overcast, bathing the car in soft, even light as the camera crew set up shots. The production schedule called for five scenes at the Montclair house. But before they could film a single one, the sun came out, making the sheet metal look hard, hot, and ugly. Three hours went by as they waited for the light to fade.

With time on their hands, people explored the house and grounds. A Montclair cop, hanging out with everybody else, volunteered that some homes in this neighborhood paid $53,000 a year in taxes. This drew a whistle from Jim Williams, a truck driver for the big van that transported the cars. He thought he had been doing well, he said, to earn $68,000 last year. But those taxes were more than his take-home pay.

At 4 P.M. they shot an interior scene of an eleven-year-old field hockey star fingering a medal around her neck in a room filled with pennants and stuffed animals. The actress was Faraday B. Rosenberg—she was very insistent about the "B"—and this was her second commercial.

By 5 P.M., the light was soft enough to shoot outdoors. Playing a Taurus dad, Dan Pinto, an actor with wavy blond hair and laugh crinkles, tossed a ball to a little kid wielding a big red bat. In another scene, leaving for work, Pinto hoisted aloft a red-headed tyke who had sneaked into his dad's shoes, only the shoes kept falling off, which was not part of the script.

At 7:15 P.M., their performances concluded, Rosenberg and Pinto boarded a van to Manhattan with Frank O'Donnell, who had played a grandfather in a scene on the front porch. As they left, the crew was still at work, setting up a twilight shot on the basketball court.

"What does it mean to be an extra?" Rosenberg asked.

"It means you don't get paid very well," said Pinto, who had appeared in 100 commercials over the last ten or so years. "I used to be cool," he continued, reflecting on his career as the van bounced over potholed streets. " . . . do all the cool stuff." Beer was one of the cool things he did. "I'm not cool anymore. You get older, you do all the body problems. Dandruff, deodorant." O'Donnell, the grandfather actor, laughed. He had just done an ad for Polident.

Rosenberg, a bundle of questions in a ponytail, wondered how much money she would make from her role. Pinto and O'Donnell cautioned her not to count on anything beyond her $470 one-day fee. There was no guarantee she wouldn't end up on the cutting room floor, destined never to collect the residuals that came with repeated showings. O'Donnell did not expect to earn them either; they were paid when actors were recognizable, and in this commercial the camera had caught only his profile.

Taurus filming concluded later that month with trips to Maine and

Wyoming. The deadline for the finished commercials was mid-August, so that Ford Division could show them along with upcoming campaigns for other car and truck models at the annual dealer meeting in San Antonio. Before he gave his approval, Roberts asked the agency to make a few changes. JWT had gone overboard, he said. There were *too* many people, especially kids; it looked like a damned Windstar minivan campaign. He wanted "more product."

The pros' advice to Rosenberg had been prescient. The engaging young actress didn't make the final cut.

——— ✦ ———

Deals on Wheels

THE FIRST CROP of 1996 Tauruses began to trickle into dealerships in late August, a month before the official introduction date. Winner Ford, a large dealership in southern New Jersey, across the Delaware River from Philadelphia, sold its first one on September 2 to a thirty-four-year-old benefits coordinator from an Atlantic City casino corporation. It was a Pacific Green LX with a Duratec engine, green leather interior, remote keyless entry, and anti-lock brakes that listed for $24,120. She paid $22,000. In the story of the 1996 Ford Taurus, the final chapter had begun.

IF THE TAURUS were to hold on to its customers, the test would be at dealerships such as Winner, located in a populous market area that spanned both sides of the Delaware River and included the city of Philadelphia and its suburbs. Like other Ford dealerships across the country, this area was under siege by the Japanese. Of the top ten cars retailed here in 1994, six were made by the Japanese. The Accord had ranked number one in new car registrations at 12,827, followed by the Escort at 12,598, Taurus at 12,237, Saturn at

11,719 and Camry at 11,059. The Nissan Altima was a distant ninth at 5,908, although considering that the Nissan Maxima was next with 5,488, Nissan was a major force in the Philadelphia–South Jersey area.

Winner was on the outskirts of Haddonfield, New Jersey, a wealthy, set- tled community with Quaker origins and historic landmarks. As a stand- alone dealership, it was a rare species. More and more, Ford's big blue oval signs presided over lots that sat side by side with domestic and Japanese com- petitors in auto malls or highway strips. Often several franchises were owned by a single mega-dealer.

As much as the name sounded fabricated, Winner Ford was named for a person, Charles S. Winner, who incorporated the company in 1946. In 1981, Tom Hatzis, a Greek immigrant who had accumulated considerable money in the wholesale flower business in Delaware, became its fourth owner. Day- to-day authority over sales, service, and a fleet rental business rested with general manager Don Slipp, an outgoing, confident man of fifty who presided over his 140 employees with the informality of a small-town mayor. His brown hair was cut short and brushed back from a face that was seldom without an expression of interest, perplexity, or amusement. Slipp was an inveterate storyteller, and one of the stories he liked to tell was how he got into the car business in 1978. A native of Levittown, Pennsylvania, the grand- daddy of the postwar suburbs, he was living in San Antonio at the time, debating whether to sell cars or insurance next, having thus far eliminated tires and wholesale produce. Deciding cars were the better bet, he appealed to three dealers, who turned him away. He invited the third to lunch anyway, and bought him drink after drink. The dealer called him "Rocky," because Slipp's Philadelphia-flavored accent reminded him of Sylvester Stallone. The next day, Slipp reported to work before the dealer arrived. "What are you doing here?" the dealer said when he got in. "I didn't hire you."

"Yes, you did," Slipp told him, hoping the man would be confused about precisely what had transpired at their liquid lunch. Then Slipp delivered the coup de grâce. "I sold a car already." He was a salesman only briefly. Return- ing to Pennsylvania in 1978, Slipp got a job as a manager at a Ford dealer- ship; and he had been in management since.

Despite their popularity in his market area, Slipp did not consider imports his fiercest competition. Customers who pulled up to Winner's blue- and-white canopy had usually decided to buy a Ford. His job was to get them to buy a Ford from him. "My competition," Slipp said, "is with other Ford dealers." Within a twenty-mile radius of Winner there were nine, and one of them, Rice & Holman, was formidable indeed; it was Ford Divison's ninth largest outlet. The Ford stores challenged each other in big, flashy type on the weekend pages of the *Philadelphia Inquirer* and South Jersey's *Courier-*

Post. Slipp liked to think Winner's ads were more readable than others, with plenty of white space and no abbreviations. A man of taste, his home was filled with original paintings by promising American artists; more paintings and art show posters hung in the dealership.

As with other major model introductions, Ford Motor Company kicked the Taurus campaign off with seminars around the country to coach salesmen on the car's finer points. That the 1996 Taurus was, for example, longer than the old one. It now appeared that the studio had delivered so well on its pledge four years ago to stretch the Taurus without making it appear longer that people actually thought the car had shrunk.

On September 6, Jim DiBella, Fred Ostroff, and Milt Alson made the hour-long trip from Winner in Alson's 1994 Taurus to their designated training site, the privately owned Valley Forge Convention Center. None of the three had started out as a car salesman. DiBella had been in the restaurant business; Ostroff had been a stockbroker, then switched to selling optical frames; and Alson had been in real estate for many years.

Slipp had insisted the guys attend the training. But he didn't say they had to stay for the ride-and-drive. Salesmen did not like to expend time on non-revenue-producing activity. "There's a high correlation between working and making money," said DiBella, who had a wife, four children, and a grand-mother-in-law in his household. On the way back to Winner, they talked about buyers, a favorite topic. Everybody thought car salesmen were scum of the earth. But what about buyers? "Buyers are liars," DiBella said, voicing the universal plaint of the car salesman. Buyers lied about having been offered better deals elsewhere; they whitewashed their finances and exaggerated the well-being of their trade-in. Salesmen had a joke: "How do you know when a buyer is lying?" Answer: "His lips are moving." "The average person is not a liar, but in a dealership, all's fair," Don Slipp said on one occasion. "I have had the priest and the rabbi lie to me."

Fred Ostroff mimicked a comparison shopper, haggling for a lower price. "'I got a quote, same car, $200 a month.'"

"The average car on the road is seven years old," DiBella said. "People come in, they're in sticker shock." "'My first house didn't cost that much.'"

"I tell them, 'Go sleep in the car for a week,'" Ostroff said. In front of them at that moment was a Mitsubishi Galant. Ostroff decided the rounded rear end looked much like that on the 1996 Taurus. "They're all the same. I don't care what they say. They're all the same."

"He probably got it for $200 a month," DiBella said.

B UYING A CAR was like having an operation: a painful, expensive, imprecise, humbling experience. Rather than a straightforward exchange of funds with goodwill on both sides, the purchase was characterized by haggling of the grossest nature that was almost guaranteed to leave both parties unsettled if not dissatisfied. Fixed prices, a vogue in the early 1990s, had seemed to offer a way out of the madness. But as much as they claimed to dislike yelling, begging, and whining, buyers disliked fixed prices more. They could not bear the idea that there might be a better deal around the corner. Often there was. Other dealers willingly undercut their fixed-price brethren.

The $19,150 price that Ford had announced for the base-model Taurus would be only a starting point. It was the rare buyer who was dumb enough to pay the list price. Many went from dealer to dealer until they found one who would sell at the invoice price, which was widely available in magazine rack publications. In a new wrinkle, Internet users were coming into dealerships armed with specifics on deals. And some educated buyers knew that the invoice price incorporated a 3 percent charge known as the "holdback" that the company returned to dealers on a quarterly basis. The Taurus base-model invoice price was $17,019; the true price to the dealer was more like $16,500. Of that, roughly two-thirds represented the variable cost of the car that Dick Landgraff struggled so to keep under control, its bits and pieces and the labor it took to assemble them. The remaining third covered fixed costs—the salaries of the DN101 team, plant operations, the amortization of what had grown to a $2.7 billion investment—plus a portion of the company's overhead, and the profit, which like the other figures was so closely held that even dealers didn't know it.

Dealers, independent businessmen who owned their own property and purchased their inventory, complained that they were barely scraping by under their low margins. The National Automobile Dealers Association estimated the average net profit in 1994 on a new car was just $150. Indeed, every year a few more dealerships went out of business. In 1995 there were 22,417 dealerships, 34 fewer than in 1994, down from 47,000 in 1950. Many now sold as many used cars and trucks as new ones, at a bigger profit. Thank God for used car sales, and cars that broke down. They paid for the golf club memberships.

D ON SLIPP DIDN'T TRACK how many of the thirty-two Tauruses he sold in September were 1996 models mixed in with the '95s. He'd only started with three '96s, and the public didn't even know they were for sale. And frankly, he'd as soon put September behind him. Usually it was a good month, with people streaming back from vacation, ready to put the kids in school and their lives in order, which often meant buying a car. But this September had been lousy; the guys had moved just 59 new cars, against 105 in September of 1994. On Taurus Introduction Day, no one bought a Taurus, new or old. So far in 1995, new car sales were off 60 percent against 1994, although he reminded himself that 1994 had been a banner year. And business was bad at other dealerships as well.

Slipp knew his salesmen were as unhappy as he was at the slow pace. Their pay was composed entirely of commissions and bonuses, so when cars weren't selling, salesmen weren't making money. Winner paid them a commission of 35 percent of the sale price minus the invoice cost and a $300 charge for overhead, called the dealer's "pack." Thus, on a car where the invoice price was $17,700, and the salesman negotiated an $18,400 sale, the commission was 35 percent of $400, or $140. If the buyer extracted the invoice price, the salesman got just $50. This was known as a "mini-deal." Mini-deals, while they didn't yield much commission, counted toward a bonus based on volume.

Unlike commissions, bonuses were a tool to focus a salesman's attention on a particular goal, such as selling lots of cars. If a Winner salesman sold eleven cars or more in a given month, he got a bonus. If his buyers for the month also purchased at least seven dealer's options, such as extended warranties, alarms, or the loan of a car during service, he got a bonus. Special September bonuses were hanging from the showroom ceiling in the form of silvery blue balloons. Any salesman who sold one of the 300 1995 cars and trucks still on the lot got to pop one and pull out a chit worth $20 to $100 in cash. In October, at the sales breakfast that began each month, Slipp announced an additional bonus to get the month off to a fast start. Anyone who made seven deliveries in the next six days would get an extra $350. "Are the balloons still up?" asked one salesman. Not only were they still up, Slipp said, but also the values had doubled.

When it came to their bonuses, salesmen did not trust dealers. Pat Broomell had worked at one place where the dealer dealt you a hand of blackjack. If you won, you got the bonus; if you lost, he kept it. "The biggest thing salemen have to worry about in this business is the dealer robbing you," Broomell said. "This is the straightest store I've ever seen and I've been doing this for twenty years."

Even at Winner, however, a salesman could lose half his bonus if he didn't get top grades on the surveys Ford sent out to new buyers asking about their "purchase experience." Ford used the results of these surveys to rank dealers on a customer satisfaction index, and those who did not do well received the company's unwelcome attention.

Customer satisfaction was the new frontier in the battle among automakers for the consumer dollar. And Ford wasn't doing so well. In the 1995 J. D. Power and Associates annual survey of customer satisfaction among 55,000 new car and truck buyers, Ford ranked number eighteen, several points below the industry average. Eighteenth place was "not a happy position to be in," Ross Roberts conceded to a reporter at the Taurus press conference in Charlotte. "My wife even asked me about that. How can you be that bad?" Toyota had a different problem. Its customers so seldom returned for service that dealerships had a difficult time cultivating a relationship.

At dealer powwows, the Ford hierarchy issued exhortations to be more courteous, more straightforward, more attentive, more professional. People showing visitors around town might say, "That's my church," Roberts told dealers at the 1994 annual session. "That's my kids' school." But you didn't often hear, "That's my car dealer."

Roberts and other Ford employees, however, by and large were spared the purchase experience the company so avidly inquired about. On becoming CEO, Alex Trotman told James Bennet of the *New York Times* that he neither owned a car, nor had he ever bought one from an American dealer; indeed, the last transportation he could remember buying was a Japanese motorcycle. Managers and supervisors leased their vehicles from Ford or got them free, and service was at company garages where they gave you a lift to work. All employees could buy cars at a cheap, fixed price with no haggling. Jerry Brohl, a young supervisor in vehicle development, had found himself in sticker shock when he happened into a dealership a year or two back and saw prices in the low twenties for the Ranger Splash, a small Ford pickup. "Even the Taurus is getting close to twenty. I wondered, 'Who's buying these cars?' "

Ford's surveys asked buyers to rate their reaction from one to ten on such matters as "promptness of your greeting" and "explanation of delivery paperwork." Many buyers thought they were being generous in giving sevens and eights, which signified "very satisfied," rather than nines or tens, for "completely satisfied." But Winner salesmen needed a 90 percent average for the month to hold on to their full bonuses. To get the average, they had to swallow their pride and ask customers to give them the highest rating. Pat Broomell refused to do it. "I can't ask for a ten," Broomell said. "The words won't come out of my mouth." And there was always the mooch who would ask you to throw in floor mats or a free tank of gas in return for a top rating. But however the salesmen did it, they got high marks. Winner ranked first in both service and sales satisfaction in 1994 among nineteen high-volume dealers.

If selling lots of cars brought salesmen rewards, selling too few carried a penalty. Every month Slipp calculated the average number of sales per sales-man, and subtracted one unit. Failure to sell that many resulted in a warning called a production letter. Four production letters in nine months and you were out. A good, solid performer might sell thirteen or fourteen cars a month and earn $40,000 a year. And then there was Art Talansky, month in and month out the top dog at Winner, a man with big hair, a big ego, and a big paycheck—$109,000 in 1994, he said. At 7:30 A.M., he was in the service area, handing out his card to people who might decide their old car wasn't worth fixing. He gave each of his buyers three $100 coupons. If they sent him a customer and a coupon, he sent them $100. "To make $40,000 you got to show up," Talansky said. "To make six figures, you've got to think it, drink it, eat it, sleep it. To make six figures, you've got to *be* a car."

THE DAY AFTER the sales meeting, Jim DiBella watched his friend Greg Gullo walk across the used car lot, sit down on the steps of a small empty building, and open the pint of Ben & Jerry's frozen yogurt he'd just bought at the 7-Eleven across the street. Gullo was thirty-two, twelve years younger than DiBella. His hair was a rich dark brown, and DiBella's was nearly white, with flecks of black. DiBella decided to join him, even though it meant abandoning his post at the door and any new business that might walk in. He knew Gullo felt bad. "He hasn't sold a car in two weeks," DiBel-la said.

When you weren't selling, Gullo said later that night, "it's horrible. You start talking to yourself. 'I worked fifty hours a week and didn't sell a thing.' You ask yourself, why?" The worst thing a salesman could do was give in to those feelings of despair. On average, one in every three to four people a salesman pitched would buy a car. "The minute you stop talking to people," Gullo said, "then you got no chance."

"Dial 2780" the loudspeaker announced, signaling that a caller was on hold for information. The first salesman to dial the extension got a potential customer. Gullo reached for the phone. The caller's name was Yolanda. She wanted a price on a model. "You come in here, Yolanda," Gullo said. "Just hear me out. . . . You got a lot more to think about than just the price. We've got the number-one service department. We've got a smoke-free service shuttle, drop you off at the shopping center." He asked where she lived. Any way a salesman could relate on a personal basis could break down barriers. If a customer had as much as driven through upstate New York, Gullo invoked his family origins in Batavia, near Buffalo. Yolanda lived in Marlton. Well, what do you know, *he* lived in Marlton. "What do I have to do to earn your business?" he asked her. She kept pressing for a number. Finally he gave her the invoice price. "She called four other dealers. They all gave her the same price within four dollars. If I didn't give her a number I never would have heard from her."

Everybody was happy when Gullo sold a Contour the next day to an elderly couple trading in a Mocha Frost 1992 Crown Victoria with 14,000 miles on it. Everybody was happy as well about the car they had traded in. With such low mileage, it should sell fast and make someone a nice commission.

W H E N   H E   F I R S T   S A W the radically shaped 1996 Taurus at the winter dealer meeting in Naples, Don Slipp had braced himself for buyer resistance. People would need a little time to get used to it on the road, he told himself. That was what had happened with the original Taurus. Alarm bells went off when Ford announced the price three months later. Although the base price of the new Taurus was only $500 over the outgoing car, by his calculations it was $875 more once equipped with the most popular options. But the real differential was even larger, owing to the discounts and sweetheart leases Ford had piled onto the Taurus year after year to win the sales race with the Accord. For most of 1995 the Taurus had carried a $1,000 rebate; in the fall it jumped to $2,000, meaning the sticker price on the new car was effectively $2,500 more than the old one. People who had leased Tauruses for $299 a month on a two-year agreement now were looking at payments approaching $400. In the spring, Ford had experimented unsuccessfuly with a three-year lease, with $1,500 down and monthly payments of $339, that put the customer in a 1995 model for a year, then behind the wheel of a '96. Said salesman John Grealy, "The best I can get to on a '96 is $350, and I tried it every which way. . . . And that's for three years." The price posed a mental hurdle not only for buyers but for salesmen. Grealy said he had a hard time believing people would pay that kind of money, even for a car as good as the new Taurus. "I mean . . . it *is* a Ford."

Ford's prices had been set months earlier after a protracted debate. Overruled by Ford Division, Dick Landgraff had advocated raising the price immediately on the 1995 Taurus, while it was selling well, then introducing the 1996 model with no price increase at all. At introduction, Ford could honestly say it had not raised prices. "They thought that was a really stupid idea."

Not only did the company want retail dealers to sell 12 percent more Tauruses, so as to reduce its dependence on fleets, but it also wanted them to increase sales of the expensive high-series LX from 25 to 40 percent of their mix, and station wagons from 12 to 24 percent. Slipp thought some of Ford's projections were unrealistic, to put it mildly. He figured Ford would be forced before long into incentives of one kind or another.

But what caught Slipp off guard was the negative reaction to the seat fabric in the base model GL, the wondrous cost-saving printed Orient, which he had barely noticed on the prototypes he drove in Naples. On opening the car door, customers appeared perplexed. "I don't know about the fabric," said Carol Moran, an elementary school teacher, when she and her husband Jim went for a ride in a silver Taurus GL with a dull-purple interior called Nightmist. They had planned to buy another Pontiac until they read a rave review of the Taurus in the *Philadelphia Inquirer.* "I think the Taurus/Sable is now the best popularly priced family car in the world," wrote auto columnist Al Haas. As her husband drove, Carol Moran ran her hands over the seat. "I'm not wild about the pattern. Does it come in any other one?" When they returned, Pat Broomell talked to the husband about the car's technical attributes. "The only thing I'm not sure about," the wife told Broomell, "I haven't had seat covers in patterns."

"All companies are going to patterns," Broomell said with authority. "They use materials that resist stains." As the Morans drifted down the row of Tauruses, he peered inside. He liked the Taurus so much he thought he might buy one himself, if Ford came up with a rebate. But he was mystified by the choice of fabric. "They had a design team sit down for fourteen years," Broomell said, exaggerating for effect, "to come up with this?" There was one bright spot. The LX, the Taurus high-series car with the Duratec engine, had a fabric people liked better. Two of his customers had traded up to get it.

The same thing happened later that day. "I'm just not crazy about the cloth," a young woman told Duke McCarthy, a high-energy salesman with a military haircut. Her husband didn't like it either. "It's like a marble. I'm surprised they didn't use a solid."

McCarthy was bouncing from car to car, gesturing. "How 'bout red. Is red out? How 'bout blue, is blue out? You don't like the green over there?"

"The pattern," she said, "I just don't like it."

McCarthy opened the door to a silver LX. "Want to take it for a drive?"

"No, that's all right," said the husband.

"It's going to be a lot more peppy," McCarthy told him. Not to mention, the seats looked better.

"Give me a price," the man said, his voice suddenly urgent. "I need a price."

"Any particular car?" McCarthy asked politely.

"I like a lot of them. The interior's turning me off."

"Is it even possible to get a solid color?" the woman asked.

O N O C T O B E R 1 0 , when Jeff Purcel from Ford Division paid a sales call, Winner had moved a total of only eight 1996 Tauruses since August. Concluding its five-day run on October 5, the advertising campaign had scored off the charts on awareness—64 percent of Americans knew there was a new Taurus. People all over the country were humming the song. But it didn't seem to be motivating customers, whether loyal Taurus owners or import buyers. A reviewer for *Advertising Age,* Bob Garfield, had written a biting critique. "The new Taurus TV campaign is saccharine and smarmy and too short on particulars. The jingle is positively insipid, there are too many closeups of handsome people being automotively fulfilled and not enough specifics about the improvements themselves."

Purcel was a zone manager, the entry-level position in the sales division. To the car salesmen these Ford emissaries were clones. Like Purcel, who was tall with stylish short hair and a white shirt, they were always young, clean-cut, and eager to please. Their job was to sell Ford cars and trucks to dealers.

"Has anybody knocked down the door on Taurus yet?" Slipp asked.

"I don't have anybody who's begging for more," the zone manager told Slipp. They were in Slipp's office with Gary Apel, who managed Winner's inventories, and Carl Thompson, the sales manager. "Koch seems to be sell-ing LXs."

"They seem to be or they actually did?" Slipp asked, trying to pin him down. Chris Koch Ford was one of Winner's competitors.

"Any talk on doing something on the Taurus?" Apel asked. "Something" meant a program—a rebate or a dealer incentive.

"Only two ways they'll do something," Slipp said. "If there's no orders going into the factory or Camry and Accord get close." Slipp placed his car order: seven T-Birds, thirty Escorts, zero Contours. As a rule, a dealer tried not to exceed sixty days' inventory on any single model. But Slipp decided to order forty-two Tauruses in addition to the fifty he had on hand. He could-n't risk having too few if sales picked up, which could happen if Ford sudden-ly put some money on them. "You'll see a race in December," he predicted.

Slipp held out some hope for a promotion coming up the next week-end. Employing one of Ford's marketing suggestions, he had spent $4,500 to order and mail brochures to 7,200 import owners inviting them to a recep-tion and TV/VCR drawing on October 13 and 14. But when the weekend rolled around, fewer than a hundred people turned up. Where were the Var-sity Captain and his cheerleader wife when you needed them?

The salesmen were out there, scrabbling. Anthony Perrella thought he had a sure deal on a Taurus LX with a teacher who taught high school with

Perrella's wife. With leather seats, anti-lock brakes, and some other options, the car would run around $24,000, and Perrella was looking forward to a nice commission. You could always count on making a little money on your friends, he said. They wouldn't shop you. And then the teacher shopped him.

Maybe he hadn't meant to, maybe he had just stopped in at Rice & Holman for a quick look and a salesman cornered him. But here he was at Winner one night with a quote for a 38-month lease with $383 monthly payments. Perrella's heart sank. There went his commission. The best he could do if Winner would even match the deal was $50. But at least it would count toward a bonus. For two hours Perrella ran back and forth to his manager, until they finally put together a rock-bottom counter offer of $385 a month. The teacher said okay and then he noticed the lease was for 35,000 miles. "We've got a problem." Rice & Holman had given him a figure of 48,000 miles. Then Perrella really got worried. "Smoke's coming out of my ears trying to match this," he said. "Are you sure they included tax?" To his relief, Perrella got an okay on the higher mileage from the manager. But when the teacher came back two nights later with his checkbook, the manager said there had been no agreement. Furious, the guy stormed off and leased a Camry for $407 a month.

Next, a nineteen-year-old Mexican youth tried to buy a Taurus. At first, Perrella thought the kid didn't have a chance. Skinny, with a mustache struggling to take hold and a whispy ponytail poking out the back of his baseball cap, he had come in one rainy Saturday with a girlfriend in jeans. The pair had gone from Taurus to Taurus, pressing their noses to the windows. Talk about pining for the American Dream. Perrella hadn't even asked if he wanted a demo ride, the kid's prospects were so hopeless. A Nissan dealer had sold him a 1993 Pathfinder just six months ago, but they'd hit him over the head in the deal, just bashed him, and he was $3,000 upside down. "Upside down" meant you owed more money than your car was worth. His payments were $470 a month. Still, you would think that a nineteen-year-old would be happy with a three-year-old Pathfinder, but the girlfriend wanted the Taurus bad. Perrella noticed that she kept nudging the kid, and saying what about this, what about that?

When the kid returned with his father as a co-signer, Perrella allowed himself a moment of hope. The father had a steady factory job. The kid had worked for a year as a photo equipment operator in a printing firm. As Carl Thompson, the sales manager, pointed out, a year was a long time in the life of a nineteen-year-old. He had so far made every single one of his five Pathfinder payments, and the Taurus he wanted, a GL with anti-lock brakes, would cost $100 a month less on a long-term lease. On a scale of one to ten, Perrella now rated the deal as a five. The kid, the girlfriend, and the father were closeted with Dino Rucci, one of the finance and insurance guys. "In the box," the salesmen called it.

Lenny Polistana walked by Anthony Perrella's desk. Polistana was another F&I guy. Perrella asked him if he thought a bank would accept the father as a co-signer.

"The father's gotta be gold, not have any derogatory."

"The father's not gold," Perrella said. The father's credit report listed state unemployment compensation to which he wasn't entitled and a mortgage that he had not reported to Winner.

"Then it's not going to happen."

Don Slipp watched the would-be buyers walk out. It would be several days before the bank ruled, but no matter that Winner was trying hard, the deal didn't look good. "Spanish surnames are tough," he confided. "The bank guys were all collectors. All they can remember is calling them and hearing, 'I no speak English.'"

A week later, Perrella got a solid hit. "I'm going to sell a Taurus tonight," he said, all business, emerging from the back seat of the 1996 Taurus parked on the showroom floor. "It's a non-traditional family."

Two blue-eyed, gray-haired men in jeans climbed out of the front seat. They were of similar age and build; even their paunches matched. One had a beard, and the other did not. Two hours later, they left their old Taurus behind and drove away in a new one. Standing outside, the salesmen watched them out of hearing distance, then cracked a few truly tasteless jokes. Turning serious, one of the older guys said that he read an article that gay men have too little testosterone in their brains. "This is the point of the evening," Greg Gullo said, "at which car salesmen turn into medical experts on everything."

GULLO WAS HAVING another bad week when Christine Klimeczko, a senior "solutions consultant" for Apple Computer, walked in and landed on a Pacific Green Taurus GL with a saddle interior. "Landing" was salesman's lingo for matching a customer with a car. First you greeted them, then you landed them, and then you handed them the keys for the demo drive. You *had* to get them in the car for a demo. "The key to the deal is the feel of the wheel," the saying went. They would think, "This could be my car." And when the two of you got back from the drive, you told the prospect to pull in beside the crummy old car, so he or she could not avoid seeing how the two looked side by side.

Klimeczko, who wore an Apple watch and a tailored shirt with an Apple logo, told Gullo she was from Buffalo. Gullo told her about his grandfather in Batavia, New York. He didn't have to do much more. Klimeczko said "yes" to power seats, she said "yes" to anti-lock brakes. She bought the service loaner program and she bought the Winner Appearance Package for under-coating, paint sealant, and Scotchgard. She wasn't upset that the open console blocked the power outlet for the phone. She didn't mind that there were no door pockets for her maps. It didn't bother her that the four big boxes of paraphernalia for Mary Kay Cosmetics that she sold on evenings and week-ends wouldn't make the move from the trunk of her old Taurus to her new Taurus. "I told you it was smaller," she said cheerfully as Gullo struggled to make them fit. She loved the Orient fabric. She loved the cupholders. The green was "almost a teal, my favorite color." The car could do no wrong.

After three hours of buying, Klimeczko stood with Gullo by the new car, ready to drive away. Winner Ford was lit up, a blue-and-white island in the night. "I need all tens," Gullo told her. "Anything less than that, they take me in the back room and rip my lungs out."

"No problem," she said. It was proof once again of what the salesmen always said. The customer who bargained least and bought the most was the happiest. The people who came in with *Consumer Reports* and a computer printout of prices never felt satisfied.

O N   T H E   L A S T   S A T U R D A Y of the month, it looked like the 1996 Taurus might have a future after all. Gullo sold a wagon right off the bat. And Anthony Toffoli, who was younger and brasher than Anthony Perrella, sold a silver GL to a married couple. "She was married. He was married." But, Tof-foli said, "they weren't married to each other." The woman had come in first, alone. She told the salesman that she was going "to have a very close special friend come and look. If he comes in with his wife, you don't know me. You've never heard of me. I've never been in here." But, as it happened, the guy bought the car without either woman.

Now Jim DiBella was sitting with a father and son of Indian descent, who were negotiating for a Willow Green Taurus GL with the saddle interi-or. *Dots.* "Dots" was one of those terrible ethnic slurs for Indians and Pak-istanis—it came from the little peel-off *bhindis* with which women adorned their foreheads—that were so inappropriate in polite society but widespread among people in retail who knew and feared them as tough, tough negotia-tors. Naturally it was wrong to typecast an entire culture. But case in point? The son, who was negotiating on his father's behalf, had said point-blank to Mike Bowers, a lively dark-haired manager with a British accent, "I don't trust a word you say."

"It's nothing personal," the father had the grace to add. "It's business." The father, a small, thin man, was a civil engineer. The son, who was larger and sturdier, also had an engineering degree, but he had gone on to become a doctor. His wife, also a doctor, was waiting for him in the car. She was very fair and very blond—no *bhindi* on her forehead—and she was due at the hospital. The son kept looking at his watch as DiBella assembled the final paperwork. In addition to being a dot, the son was what the salesmen called a "sea lawyer," maritime slang for an individual who complained, criticized, and pretended to a familiarity with rules and regulations. When it came to cars, sea lawyers were people recruited by friends or relatives to help with negotiations for their supposed knowledge of the business. Because they usually knew less than they claimed, they were dangerous; they got insulted if you corrected them. So manager Mike Bowers and Jim DiBella were tiptoeing around these negotiations, trying to say that the son's offer of invoice minus dealer pack plus 5 percent was not quite the same as 2 percent of invoice.

The Winner showroom that day was like a crowded fishbowl. Male and female shoppers nosed around vehicles as salesmen and managers darted back and forth from one end of the showroom to the other. It being almost Halloween, the sales force had talked Don Slipp into awarding prizes if they reported to work in costume. Bob Novey came as the Tin Man from *The Wizard of Oz;* Rich Holmes, as a French maid in black net stockings. Except for sales manager Carl Thompson, the others had long since changed back to street clothes. He was still wearing his costume, a green surgical scrub suit. But in the fray, the sea lawyer, a real doctor, appeared not to have noticed. For two hours, he said, he had yelled—that in itself was unnerving—and he still felt like he could have done better if he'd had time to log onto his computer and get more numbers. "Here there's a vagueness that's disconcerting to me." A *vagueness*. Numbers flipped back and forth. This much down did that to the payments . . . stretch them out, tighten them up. Numbers could change, changing other numbers. Pretty soon even someone with multiple degrees in engineering and medicine lost clarity, awash in so much *vagueness*—so well put—that there was nothing for it but to sign the papers and bolt, get your wife to her job.

After his son left, the father relaxed with a smile. He had known all along he would buy a Taurus and that he would buy it from Winner Ford. During a particularly icy stretch of winter two years ago, his '92 Taurus had crapped out on him. His regular garage, whose owner was like a son to him, claimed its tow truck couldn't make it through all the ice. Marooned for two days, he finally called Winner. Two hours later, the dealership's tow truck turned up and took the Taurus in and fixed it. He told Winner also to do a tune-up. Winner didn't charge for the towing. Or for the tune-up. He had never had service like that and he was profoundly moved. Also he had wanted to buy an American car. "You see me different," the father said earnestly. "But I'm an American too. Why should I pay for foreign exchange?" His son, the father said with a trace of regret, "does not feel the way I do" about American cars. The son drove an import. "I grew up with Fords all my life and I'm sick of them," the son had said, on driving away.

The son was a loose cannon. Jim DiBella could imagine what would happen if he ever got his hands on the customer satisfaction survey. DiBella's bonus for the month would go up in smoke. The salesman made his pitch to Dad: "I need all tens, no nines, tens. I treated you very professionally." The father nodded. "I give you tens."

"When the survey comes, make sure *you* fill it out," DiBella added for good measure. The father gathered up his papers. Mike Bowers came over to say thank you and goodbye. "You have a tremendous service department," the father told him. "I'm very happy with it."

After the father left, DiBella took out a thin, sanded piece of wood measuring three by eight inches. Each end was cut at an angle and a third of the way down was an elongated hole. With one hand, he held it on his desk at a sixty-degree angle. With the other, he picked up a bottle of Gallo fumé blanc that had been sitting on his desk next to the photo of his wife and children, and stuck the cork end into the hole. When he let go, the wood held the bottle aloft, parallel to the desk, in a way that appeared to defy gravity. "What do you think?" DiBella asked.

The little bugger was sensational, no doubt about it. He and another salesman, Tom McHugh, had formed a partnership to sell them to local liquor stores. They were easy to make and McHugh had found someone to do it. Already they had orders for 400 at $3 a pop. Maybe they would paint them, personalize them. "Happy Thanksgiving." "Happy Holidays." As McHugh said later, perhaps not entirely in jest, "This is my ticket out of the car business."

At the moment, though, McHugh was out on the lot. After today, there were just two working days left in October to build toward a bonus. It was a time when salesmen started calling people who had been in earlier, to ask if they'd bought a car yet. When a 2780 call was announced, they dove for the phone. Anthony Perrella had his eye on a guy to whom he had just sold a Windstar, who was now in the box. "I hope he's buying something. I need another alarm and a warranty to qualify."

Today's Taurus sale brought DiBella's monthly total to seven. He estimated that the dealership average for October would be nine or ten, meaning production letters would go out to people who had sold no more than eight or possibly nine units. "So I need two more to be safe." He stuck the wine paddle in a drawer, closed it, and stood up. It was 3:55 P.M., two hours till closing. "I've got to sell a car. I've got one more shot today."

TWENTY-SIX

Joe Blow's Revenge

AUTOMOTIVE WRITERS
were enchanted with the 1996 Taurus. Ford has "created a car that takes a
bold step style-wise and also raises the ante for all-around competence,"
wrote *Detroit Free Press* reviewer Tony Swan. In "He Drove, She Drove," Anita
Lienert gave it her highest rating, four stars to her husband's three. Although
he thought that the Taurus and the Sable were "two of the best looking cars
on the market," Paul Lienert, who was over six feet tall, had hit his head getting into the back seat, and, once seated, "felt cramped." Michelle Krebs complained in the *New York Times* that the "glove box is small, and the doors have
no storage pockets." But she raved that "the Taurus's smooth, flowing lines
make everything else look staid and boxy." Patrick Bedard of *Car and Driver*
said the newest Ford had "an expensive, quality feel never available at ordi-
nary American prices before."

Opinions varied on the way the car handled, an expression of its stiffer
body. Comparing the ride in the 1996 to the 1995 model, Paul Lienert was
surprised, he said, to find "no dramatic difference." Krebs had the same reaction to the two cars, driven back-to-back. "I was struck by how similar they
felt." But Bedard, the car 'zine expert, found the 1996 model "much more

agreeable to drive because of drastic improvements in steering and suspension." In a comparison drive with the Toyota Camry and the Chevrolet Lumina, the *Detroit Free Press* proclaimed the Taurus "the winner by a knockout" and said it offered "an exceptional blend of ride and handling" and a "rare feeling of stability and solidity."

The *New York Times,* the *Wall Street Journal,* and *USA Today* singled out the ICP in feature stories, labeling it a bold departure in radio design. "The buttons and dials are large and well spaced," wrote Krebs, "making it possible to push and turn them even when wearing gloves."

But neither the critical praise nor the advertising blitz was sufficient to jump-start sales of the new Taurus. In October, its first official month on the market, sales were 16 percent less than those of the old model in October 1994. Certainly a month or two was not a lot of time to pass judgment. The first Taurus, too, had been slow off the mark. And Ford was ready with several explanations. They had intentionally reduced low-profit sales to daily rental fleets. And the previous autumn, the numbers had been especially strong because the company had offered returning Taurus lessees, hooked with two-year sweetheart deals during the 1992 sales race, more bait to re-up. In a way, Ford had set a trap for itself. Without these special deals to pump up the volume, the October 1995 figures looked anemic.

The business press sniffed blood. The next wave of stories had a hard edge. "Faster Everywhere but the Showroom . . . Revamped, Pricier Ford Taurus Sells Slowly," proclaimed the headline on a November 4 article by Warren Brown of the *Washington Post.* He quoted an Alexandria, Virginia, dealer who blamed "styling and price" for the lukewarm reception. Older buyers were rattled by the radical design, the dealer told Brown; younger buyers were put off by a price tag that typically started at $19,390.

The press also jumped on the announcement that Ford profits had declined 68 percent in the third quarter, measured against the third quarter of 1994. Ford attributed the drop to the start-up costs of the Taurus and the redesigned F-150 pickup coming in January. But Wall Street was not persuaded that the poor showing was temporary. Even before the 1996 Taurus went on sale in the fall of '95, Mary Connelly of *Automotive News* had reported that Wall Street analysts feared Ford's generous expenditures on content, labor, and development would squeeze profits. With October's drop in sales and the third-quarter decline in profits, that complaint became a chorus.

As 1995 drew to a close, Ford took heart. By some measures the Taurus hadn't fared so badly. Even with the autumn slump, the Taurus outsold the Accord in the final quarter, if only by a hair, 82,728 to 82,590. In addition, the Sable, which normally sold about 25 percent as much as the Taurus, performed better than expected, with sales of 26,597. And Taurus claimed the title of best-selling car for the fourth consecutive year with a margin of 25,000, thanks to the comfortable lead the outgoing Taurus had built up in the first nine months of 1995.

Maybe the media had gone overboard in its negative analysis. But Ford reacted nevertheless. It could not let its bold new Taurus become road kill, even if it meant offering the discounts that buyers now seemed to expect but Ford had so hoped to avoid. In January 1996 the company grudgingly plunked down $600 rebates on the Taurus and Sable and several other stalled sellers. In the Northeast, where record-breaking snowstorms throttled showroom traffic, the company threw in an additional $500-per-vehicle to dealers, which most used to reduce car prices.

The press saw these incentives as evidence that Ford was nervous. A story by the *Wall Street Journal's* Oscar Suris led the paper on January 10 under a four-deck headline: "Dearborn Distress. . . . Ford's Rebates Spell Trouble as New Models Fail to Excite Buyers. . . . Redesigned Taurus Elicits a Yawn; Other Vehicles Overshoot Their Market. . . . Minivans With Only 3 Doors." (This latter was a reference to buyers' preference for the Chrysler minivan over the Windstar because it offered a fourth door.) Said the story, "Ford's recently redesigned Taurus sedan has been a huge disappointment. December sales of the Taurus were off 35 percent from a year earlier; sales of its archrival, the Honda Accord, were up 36 percent."

The *New York Times* followed two weeks later: "Ford Tests the Price Barrier. . . . Fancy Redesigns Illustrate a High-Cost Strategy." Skeptical in tone, the article displayed a photo of Henry Ford and his first buggy-like car, with the caption "Henry Ford . . . sought to manufacture 'a serviceable machine that would be constructed at a price within the reach of many.' The Ford Motor Company's strategy today is to charge premium prices for richly equipped vehicles."

On the defensive, in March Ford's battered decision-makers publicized a vigorous campaign to reduce costs on all their vehicles, by making some standard features optional, eliminating others, and inventing ways to reduce expenditures on parts and labor while speeding up product development. The company invited press and analysts to a day of presentations. According to *Automotive News,* Ford executives, speaking on the condition of anonymity, conceded that the higher-content, higher-cost strategy that the Taurus embodied was not working with the bargain-hungry consumers of the 1990s. If Ford needed additional motivation to cut costs, the Japanese were widely reported to have a head start, undertaken when the soaring yen in the early 1990s made their cars more expensive. The results—less expensive, more profitable Japanese vehicles—would arrive shortly. Suddenly all of Ford was engulfed in catching up by cutting back.

In business circles, the Taurus was held up as a case study of corporate bungling. "In every way it's a great car," Maryann Keller, a respected financial analyst and author, told a supplier conference in April 1996. "It is probably the finest car built by the Ford Motor Company, but it is too expensive to build. Instead of understanding what the marketplace would have paid for a Taurus, Ford designed the car that it wanted to design. . . . And it priced it to earn a reasonable return on its investment. Certainly something very logical. Now it's paying for those mistakes with rebates, content reduction. . . . increased incentives and cheap financing and lease deals. The Taurus may reach Ford's sales target, but it will not reach Ford's profit target."

As the DN101 team watched critical praise give way to negative comments, followed by pressure to shrink costs, not even the joy of moving from the basement to a handsome new brick building, with a cafeteria on the ground floor and natural light pouring through large windows, could dispel the gloom. Memories of their crusade to build Ford's finest car faded like images in a rearview mirror as words such as "thrifting" and "decontenting" permeated the corporate vocabulary. The door hinges were redesigned to save $2; plastic rather than metal moldings would surround the moon roof, saving $7.85. In the name of craftsmanship, the team once had as a motto "no exposed screws"; now a 3-cent screw cap was deemed unnecessary. Molded climate control registers would no longer receive a coat of paint to match precisely the gloss level of the instrument panel. Previously all-leather seats would get vinyl inserts. A panel to finish off the underside of the dashboard—gone. In addition, the team was asked to crash out a no-frills "G" model Taurus that would sell for $605 less than the GL. It went on sale in April 1996.

To the troops, Dick Landgraff seemed to be a changed man. These days, it was "Take this out, take that out," reported one team member. Landgraff had pushed for heated outside mirrors as a standard feature; now they were on the hit list. And so, hard to believe, was the back-seat armrest, the source of so much aggravation when he eliminated it on the 1992 model. Seldom mentioned in the glory days of DN101, GM's loss-leader Lumina, which was selling for some $2,500 less than the Taurus, had gained a certain cachet. The new team slogan, the joke went, was "Beat Lumina."

Where once engineers had deliberated for hours on end to ensure harmony under the hood, changes were approved with much less discussion. In a retrospective interview, George Bell sought to put a good face on it all. "We're making the car a little more concise than it was. Engineers like efficiency, you know. What we're doing is getting a little more efficient."

No one was more bewildered than Steve Kozak at this painful turn of events. Like others, he blamed the media. "They talked for years about how we should be competitive. We did it." Now the press was saying, after a fashion, that the car was *too* good. It contained too many features, had too much finesse. Criticized during the 1980s for failing to reinvest profits in product, the company was now being criticized for having done precisely that.

In the criticism, Kozak detected the implication that Ford had done something almost un-American by elevating "America's car" beyond the reach of the guys with blue collars, the stereotypical steelworker in Pennsylvania. "Ford has lost touch with middle America," a dealer in Spokane, Washington, told *New York Times* reporter Keith Bradsher. The tone of such criticism, it seemed to Kozak, was reproachful: Ford, shame on you.

Kozak called his brother: "Have you looked at the new Taurus?"

"Oh, no, they're too expensive."

"Are you sure?"

"Oh, yeah. They're too much."

But Ford couldn't make enough loaded $24,000 F-150 Supercabs or $30,000 Explorers. Americans were snapping them up.

It was nuts.

THE TEAM'S DISAPPOINTMENT deepened during the first week of January as the Car of the Year jury of journalists proclaimed the Chrysler minivans—the Dodge Caravan, Plymouth Voyager, and Chrysler Town and Country—the 1995 winner. The Taurus came in second. *Motor Trend* also named the Dodge Caravan the top car of 1995. And *Consumer Reports* in its January issue dealt Ford the stiffest setback of all. As in prior years, the Toyota Camry was its number-one purchase recommendation among family sedans, the Honda Accord number two, and the Taurus number three. Said the magazine, "The new Ford Taurus feels better than last year's model in many ways, but its scores in our tests haven't improved significantly. Its ride and handling are now more in line with those of its foreign-designed competitors. Its controls are better, but still cluttered. The LX version's powertrain is as sophisticated as the Camry's and Accord's. But the new Taurus still isn't as quiet inside as those two models, and its swoopy styling compromises room in the rear seat and trunk." The magazine commended the climate control system: "works very well." The seats got a mixed review. "The front seat cushions are comfortably firm, but the seatbacks lack enough side and lower-back support." The car's safety record in government crash tests drew an approving mention: "fairly good results for both driver and passenger," whereas the Camry two-door sedan's "drive-dummy sustained moderate 'injuries.' " Indeed, the new Taurus was compiling a distinguished safety record. In independent tests of mid-sized cars conducted by the Insurance Institute for Highway Safety, the Taurus topped the list of fourteen. The Camry was number five; the Accord, number seven. The Volvo 850, from the company known for safety, was number four.

The 1996 Taurus collected some design awards and also turned up on various "Best Buy" lists. But the bad news continued to outweigh the good. In the independent J. D. Power and Associates quality study, based on complaints that surfaced in the first ninety days of ownership, buyers of the 1996 Taurus reported 132 complaints per 100 cars, far more than the 77 reported by Accord owners or the 82 by Camry owners. "Taurus Misses the Mark" blared the headline in the *Free Press*.

The team had started a facelift for the year 2000. But when they weren't cutting costs, they were fixing the glitches that had surfaced since launch. The DN101 body engineers tackled the hooting noise around the door and the high-speed buzz around the windshield. The engine guys were shortening the distance the accelerator pedal traveled to counter complaints that the engines felt sluggish. The color and trim department scrambled to replace the hated seat fabric on the GL model. One irate dealer had ripped the covers off and returned them to Ford sales, suggesting they make a gym bag out of them. Searching for an inoffensive new pattern, the designers found inspiration in an unlikely source: men's sports jackets. Planner Brad Nalon came in on a Saturday and made Xerox copies of sleeves in different weaves.

Demoralized by the setbacks, the team chafed under the new corporate structure imposed by Ford 2000. Some inequities had been resolved. Respected managers Tom Moran and Tom Breault had recovered the rank they had lost during the corporate reorganization and moved on to other car programs. But to the people who remained, the reorganization seemed to have succeeded less in streamlining product development than in increasing the number of managers, and thickening the bureaucracy. Moreover, the troubled Taurus program was attracting a good deal of scrutiny from on high. DN101 veterans spoke longingly of the freewheeling days in the basement when they operated with more independence and less interference.

ON MARCH 1, 1996, Dick Landgraff completed his final report on the launch of the 1996 Taurus. He had been successful in meeting two of the most important goals for which he was accountable. He had brought the car in on time and on budget; indeed, he beat the cost target by $252 a car. Both the quality levels and measures of customer satisfaction were better than the outgoing car, although they fell short of the targets. New models almost always had more Things Gone Wrong than the cars they replaced. The 1996 Taurus was a stunning exception with 9 percent fewer TGWs in the first quarter of 1996 than the 1995 Taurus in the corresponding period in 1995.

Another manager might have been satisfied. Not Landgraff. Why wasn't the car better? By scheduling confirmation prototypes earlier in the process, World Class Timing had allotted more time than in the past to correct problems that surfaced in extensive tests and prove-out drives. Landgraff had imposed order and discipline on the process. Could he have prevented more defects by a more diligent application of his motto ("Trust no one. Verify everything.")? If he'd had more time, he said, "I could have gone through every element under the hood." Clearly that was impossible. The failures had to be rooted in the way Ford carried out product development. "What is it that we haven't done right over the years that causes this to happen?" he wondered.

Beyond numerical measures, the larger goal, to lure younger, well-heeled buyers away from imports, had proved elusive. It was easy to blame the advertising, and some did. In appealing to Taurus owners, who were older and less educated than import buyers, the commercials had targeted the very people most likely to object to the bold design. By spring, Ford Division had replaced the Dream commercials with testimonials from satisfied 1996 Taurus owners and experts who praised the car. But the advertising alone could not account for the lackluster reception, or set things right. During the four-year journey from Dearborn to dealers, the market had shifted. Americans at the ends of the economic spectrum became richer and poorer while the vast middle who bought family sedans lost ground. Pickup trucks and sport utilities gained greatly in popularity during those same years. And who was to say that the Taurus would not eventually win back the buyers of the Accord and the Camry? The Japanese had not ratcheted to the top overnight. But the quarterly profit mongers weren't cutting Ford any slack.

ONCE DICK LANDGRAFF had possessed a clear vision of the path to victory. The DN101 team would, he had declared in the mission statement, "Deliver a Product Competitive with the Japanese in Quality and Function, and Better in Styling, Features and Value." Boiled down, their mission had been to "Beat Camry."

But that vision now seemed clouded by uncertainty.

"How do you define winning?" Landgraff asked one evening in June 1996, after the cube dwellers outside his spacious office in the new building had left for the day. His windows offered a serene view of the Dearborn Proving Ground across Oakwood Boulevard, an expanse of well-watered green against a twilight blue sky. "That's really the question."

"If you define winning as meeting your [cost, time, and quality] objectives, then we can declare the battle won except for quality, and we won't know that for a while.

"If you define winning as meeting your bottom-line profit objectives, we haven't won; we've had to put so much marketing money against the car, we've lost quite a bit of profit, this year anyway.

"If you define winning as remaining number one, which I never defined as winning, then we probably will win. Ford Division's off on the assignment to become number one again.

"I guess I would define winning as having a car that satisfied the customer in terms of overall product satisfaction, and also returned an acceptable, however we define that, return to the company."

By Landgraff's definition, it was hard to avoid the awkward conclusion that he had failed in his epic thrust against the Japanese. Unless, of course, you defined winning as merely not losing. The struggle with Toyota was, after all, a war. And Ford had survived to fight another day. Said Landgraff, "You have to ask, if you had not upgraded the car, what would have happened to price, to volume, to cost and profit? It's an analytical question and it really can't be answered. Some people would say it was a mistake. We couldn't get the price for the car, we had to add marketing costs—clearly the strategy was a failure. Other people would say, me included, 'I don't agree with that logic.' We have to be competitive in this business, and we've made the Taurus into a fully competitive car. It's certainly a better car than the Lumina and it will practically equal the Camry at a lower price."

It HAD BEEN MORE THAN FIVE YEARS since the first team members had descended into the basement of the Design Center in the spring of 1991 to make a new car. Half a decade of studio skirmishes, turf wars, test trip tantrums, divisional discord, color clashes, Atlanta bashes, cost crises, supplier squabbles, power struggles, assembly line gripes and grievances, and media machinations. And so many meetings that if they were placed hour to hour around the clock, they would last a lifetime.

Many on the team now believed that such a time would not soon come again. The Taurus had been their finest moment, a sweet crusade for a righteous machine, a campaign built on inspiration, enthusiasm, dedication, sacrifice, collaboration, and a sense of adventure.

So what if it had ended on a sour note? Most people went forever without such an experience.

And anyway, it was only a car.

Postscript

———— ★ ————

IN SEPTEMBER 1996, a redesigned Camry debuted with conservative styling, fewer niceties, and lower prices than the previous model. Ever-vigilant Toyota had responded to the latest market shift.

In the annual face-off with the Honda Accord for best-selling car in America, Taurus was the winner again in 1996, but the victory cost Ford dearly. Two-thousand-dollar rebates cut deeply into projected profits. Within the company, DN101 veterans had the feeling that upper management regarded the car as a failure for its lackluster financial performance, and held them responsible. The people in charge did not necessarily go on to bigger and better things. Chief engineer George Bell accepted an early retirement offer. And Dick Landgraff was relieved of his command over the Taurus/Sable and Continental programs and given the newly created post of director for new model launch planning. His assignment was to find ways to smooth the transition from product development to manufacturing.

Index